THE NAVARRE BIBLE: STANDARD EDITION

SAINT LUKE'S GOSPEL

VOLUMES IN THIS SERIES

Standard Edition
NEW TESTAMENT
St Matthew's Gospel
St Mark's Gospel
St Luke's Gospel
St John's Gospel
Acts of the Apostles
Romans and Galatians
Corinthians
Captivity Letters
Thessalonians and Pastoral Letters
Hebrews
Catholic Letters
Revelation

OLD TESTAMENT
The Pentateuch
Joshua–Kings [Historical Books 1]
Chronicles–Maccabees [Historical Books 2]
The Psalms and the Song of Solomon
Wisdom Books
Major Prophets
Minor Prophets

Reader's (Omnibus) Edition
The Gospels and Acts
The Letters of St Paul
Revelation, Hebrews and Catholic Letters

Single-volume, large-format New Testament

THE NAVARRE BIBLE

Saint Luke's Gospel

in the Revised Standard Version and New Vulgate
with a commentary by members of the
Faculty of Theology of the University of Navarre

FOUR COURTS PRESS • DUBLIN
SCEPTER PUBLISHERS • NEW YORK

Typeset by Carrigboy Typesetting Services for
FOUR COURTS PRESS LTD
7 Malpas Street, Dublin 8, Ireland
www.fourcourtspress.ie
Distributed in North America by
SCEPTER PUBLISHERS, INC.
P.O. Box 211, New York, NY 10018–0004
www.scepterpublishers.org

Nihil obstat: Stephen J. Greene, *censor deputatus*
Imprimi potest: Desmond, Archbishop of Dublin; 12 August 1988

The translation of introductions and commentary was made by Michael Adams.

A catalogue record for this title is available from the British Library.
First edition 1988
Second edition 1991; reprinted many times
Third edition (reset and repaged) 2005
Reprinted 2008, 2014, 2017

ISBN 978–1–85182–902–6

Library of Congress Cataloging-in-Publication Data [for first volume in this series]

Bible. O.T. English. Revised Standard. 1999.
    The Navarre Bible. – North American ed.
       p.   cm
    "The Books of Genesis, Exodus, Leviticus, Numbers, Deuteronomy in the Revised
       Standard Version and New Vulgate with a commentary by members of the
       Faculty of Theology of the University of Navarre."
    Includes bibliographical references.
    Contents: [1] The Pentateuch.
    ISBN 1–889334–21–9 (hardback: alk. paper)
I. Title.
  BS891.A1 1999.P75   99–23033
  221.7'7—dc21   CIP

ACKNOWLEDGMENTS
Quotations from Vatican II documents are based on the translation in *Vatican Council II: The Conciliar and Post Conciliar Documents*, ed. A. Flannery, OP (Dublin 1981).

The New Vulgate text of the Bible can be accessed via
http://www.vatican.va.archive/bible/index.htm

Printed in Great Britain by TJ International, Padstow, Cornwall.

MIX
Paper from
responsible sources
FSC
www.fsc.org
FSC® C013056

Contents

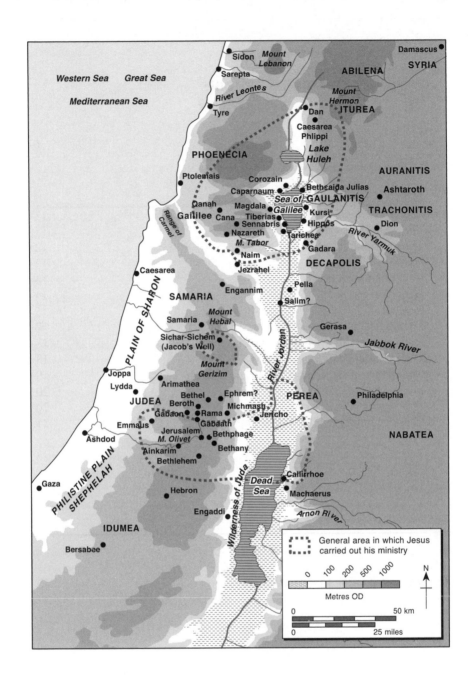

Palestine in the time of Jesus

Preface and Preliminary Notes

The Commentary
The distinguishing feature of the *Navarre Bible* is its commentary on the biblical text. Compiled by members of the Theology faculty of the University of Navarre, Pamplona, Spain, this commentary draws on writings of the Fathers, texts of the Magisterium of the Church, and works of spiritual writers, including St Josemaría Escrivá, the founder of Opus Dei; it was he who in the late 1960s entrusted the faculty at Navarre with the project of making a translation of the Bible and adding to it a commentary of the type found here.

The commentary, which is not particularly technical, is designed to explain the biblical text and to identify its main points, the message God wants to get across through the sacred writers. It also deals with doctrinal and practical matters connected with the text.

The first volume of the *Navarre Bible* (the English edition) came out in 1985—first, twelve volumes covering the New Testament; then seven volumes covering the Old Testament. Many reprints and revised editions have appeared over the past twenty years. All the various volumes are currently in print.

The Revised Standard Version
The English translation of the Bible used in the *Navarre Bible* is the Revised Standard Version (RSV) which is, as its preface states, "an authorized revision of the American Standard Version, published in 1901, which was a revision of the King James Version [the "Authorized Version"], published in 1611".

The RSV of the entire Bible was published in 1952; its Catholic edition (RSVCE) appeared in 1966. The differences between the RSV and the RSVCE New Testament texts are listed in the "Explanatory Notes" in the end-matter of this volume. Whereas the Spanish editors of what is called in English the "Navarrre Bible" made a new translation of the Bible, for the English edition the RSV has proved to be a very appropriate choice of translation. The publishers of the *Navarre Bible* wish to thank the Division of Christian Education of the National Council of the Churches of Christ in the USA for permission to use that text.

The Latin Text
This volume also carries the official Latin version of the New Testament in the *editio typica altera* of the New Vulgate (Vatican City, 1986).

Preface

PRELIMINARY NOTES

The headings within the biblical text have been provided by the editors (they are not taken from the RSV). A full list of these headings, giving an overview of the New Testament, can be found at the back of the volume.

An asterisk *inside the biblical text* signals an RSVCE "Explanatory Note" at the end of the volume.

References in the biblical text indicate parallel texts in other biblical books. All these marginal references come from the *Navarre Bible* editors, not the RSV.

Abbreviations

1. BOOKS OF HOLY SCRIPTURE

Acts	Acts of the Apostles	1 Kings	1 Kings
Amos	Amos	2 Kings	2 Kings
Bar	Baruch	Lam	Lamentations
1 Chron	1 Chronicles	Lev	Leviticus
2 Chron	2 Chronicles	Lk	Luke
Col	Colossians	1 Mac	1 Maccabees
1 Cor	1 Corinthians	2 Mac	2 Maccabees
2 Cor	2 Corinthians	Mal	Malachi
Dan	Daniel	Mic	Micah
Deut	Deuteronomy	Mk	Mark
Eccles	Ecclesiastes (Qoheleth)	Mt	Matthew
Esther	Esther	Nah	Nahum
Eph	Ephesians	Neh	Nehemiah
Ex	Exodus	Num	Numbers
Ezek	Ezekiel	Obad	Obadiah
Ezra	Ezra	1 Pet	1 Peter
Gal	Galatians	2 Pet	2 Peter
Gen	Genesis	Phil	Philippians
Hab	Habakkuk	Philem	Philemon
Hag	Haggai	Ps	Psalms
Heb	Hebrews	Prov	Proverbs
Hos	Hosea	Rev	Revelation (Apocalypse)
Is	Isaiah	Rom	Romans
Jas	James	Ruth	Ruth
Jer	Jeremiah	1 Sam	1 Samuel
Jn	John	2 Sam	2 Samuel
1 Jn	1 John	Sir	Sirach (Ecclesiasticus)
2 Jn	2 John	Song	Song of Solomon
3 Jn	3 John	1 Thess	1 Thessalonians
Job	Job	2 Thess	2 Thessalonians
Joel	Joel	1 Tim	1 Timothy
Jon	Jonah	2 Tim	2 Timothy
Josh	Joshua	Tit	Titus
Jud	Judith	Wis	Wisdom
Jude	Jude	Zech	Zechariah
Judg	Judges	Zeph	Zephaniah

2. OTHER ABBREVIATIONS

ad loc.	*ad locum*, commentary on this passage	f	and following (*pl.* ff)
AAS	*Acta Apostolicae Sedis*	ibid.	*ibidem*, in the same place
Apost.	Apostolic	in loc.	*in locum*, commentary on this passage
can.	canon	loc.	*locum*, place or passage
chap.	chapter	par.	parallel passages
cf.	*confer*, compare	Past.	Pastoral
Const.	Constitution	RSV	Revised Standard Version
Decl.	Declaration	RSVCE	Revised Standard Version, Catholic Edition
Dz-Sch	Denzinger-Schönmetzer, *Enchiridion Biblicum* (4th edition, Naples & Rome, 1961)	SCDF	Sacred Congregation for the Doctrine of the Faith
Enc.	Encyclical	sess.	session
Exhort.	Exhortation	v.	verse (*pl.* vv.)

"Sources quoted in the Commentary", which appears at the end of this book, explains other abbreviations used.

Introduction to
the Gospel according to Luke

THE AUTHOR

The Third Gospel was written by St Luke. Christian Tradition is quite clear about this, and it is borne out by scholarly study of the text. Among the more important witnesses to Tradition on this point are Origen, Clement of Alexandria, Tertullian, St Irenaeus and Eusebius; we shall cite just two sources, one chosen because it is very early, and the other, because it comes from St Jerome.

The Muratorian Fragment, a second-century Christian document written in Latin, states that "The third book of the Gospel is that according to Luke. This Luke, a physician [...], wrote down what he had heard, for [...] he had not known the Lord in the flesh, and having obtained such information as he could he began his account with the birth of John."[1]

St Jerome, around the year 400, writes in his book *On Famous Men*, 1: "Luke, a physician from Antioch, who was familiar with Greek as can be seen from his writings, a follower of St Paul, who accompanied him on his journeys, wrote a Gospel."[2] And in his *Commentariorum in Evangelium Matthaei libri quattuor* he adds: "Thirdly, Luke, a physician, a native of Antioch in Syria, a disciple of the apostle Paul, wrote his volume in Achaia and Boeotia; in this book he covered, with a broader perspective, some things contained in other books and, as he admits in his preface, he narrated things which he had heard about, not things which he had himself seen."[3]

From the early centuries onwards, the Church Magisterium, in keeping with Tradition, attributed the Third Gospel to St Luke—for example, the Council of Laodicea (*c*.360), the Decree of Pope Gelasius (492–496), the Council of Florence (1411) and the Council of Trent (1546).

Internal evidence of the Gospel itself also indicates that Luke was the author:

—the author of this Gospel writes a very elegant Greek, particularly when (as in the preface, or prologue, for example) he is writing on his own, not drawing on existing sources of information;

—in reporting cures, he shows his knowledge of medicine by the technical terms he uses and the way in which he describes particular types of illness and disease (in this respect he is generally more precise than the other evangelists);

---

1. *EB*, 1. **2.** *PL* 23, 650. **3.** *PL* 26, 17f.

—he was the same person who wrote the Acts of the Apostles, and the internal evidence of that work shows that only St Luke could have been its author;

—and, finally, the author was a disciple of St Paul, as witness the close affinity (in both language and doctrine) between this Gospel and St Paul's letters.

Aware of all these arguments, the Pontifical Biblical Commission on 26 June 1912 stated: "The clear verdict of Tradition—showing extraordinary unanimity from the beginnings of the Church and confirmed by manifold evidence, namely the explicit attestations of the holy Fathers and ecclesiastical writers, the quotations and allusions occurring in their writings, the use made by early heretics, the translations of the books of the New Testament, almost all the manuscripts including the most ancient, and also internal reasons drawn from the text of the sacred books—impose the definite affirmation that Mark, the disciple and interpreter of Peter, and Luke, the doctor, the assistant and companion of Paul, really were the authors of the Gospels that are attributed to them respectively."[4]

After confirming the general authenticity of the Third Gospel, the Pontifical Biblical Commission went on to re-affirm the authenticity of individual passages controverted by certain heretics and by some modern critics; on the same day, it replied that it was not "lawful to doubt the inspiration and canonicity of Luke's accounts of the infancy of Christ (chaps. 1 and 2); or of the apparition of the angel strengthening Jesus and the sweat of blood (Lk 22:43f); nor can it be shown by solid reasons—a view preferred by some ancient heretics and favoured also by certain modern critics—that the said accounts do not belong to the genuine Gospel of Luke."[5]

Thus, the first part of this document of the Magisterium states that these passages are inspired and are canonical; and the second, that they are authentic, that is, written by Luke.

THE APOSTOLIC FIGURE OF ST LUKE

Tradition tells us that Luke was born in Antioch in Syria—which is somewhat confirmed by the fact that the Acts of the Apostles shows him to have been very familiar with the church of Antioch. This suggests that he was of Gentile, not Jewish, origin, which is, besides, something St Paul tells us in Colossians 4:10–14 when he differentiates between Aristarchus, Mark and Jesus, who are "of the circumcision", and Epaphras of Colossae, "Luke the beloved physician" and Demas.

We do not know when he became a Christian; quite possibly it was very early on. In any event he was not a direct witness of the life of our Lord, because in the prologue to his Gospel he explicitly says he was not an eyewitness of Christ's preaching.

4. *EB*, 392. 5. *EB*, 392.

The Acts of the Apostles shows Luke to have been a disciple and companion of St Paul: certain events are reported in the first person plural, implying that he himself took part in them. For example, he goes with the apostle to Macedonia to proclaim the Gospel (Acts 16:10ff); there, in the city of Philippi, Paul and Silas are beaten, imprisoned and eventually expelled from the city. In reporting these facts Luke speaks in the third person, which shows that he himself was not expelled but had stayed behind in Philippi (Acts 16:19ff). He joins up again with St Paul on his return to Philippi (Acts 20:4ff) and goes with him to Jerusalem, where he meets St James and the elders (Acts 21:15–18). Later he goes with St Paul to Rome, when Paul appeals to Caesar (Acts 27:2ff).

In his Second Letter to Timothy, St Paul refers to Luke as being his only company during his second imprisonment in Rome (2 Tim 4:11) and in v.24 of his Letter to Philemon he mentions Luke as one of his fellow workers.

An ancient tradition says that St Luke preached the Gospel in Bithynia and Achaia after the death of St Paul. And the Roman martyrology says that "having suffered much for the name of Christ, he died filled with the Holy Spirit".

CANONICITY

From the very beginning the Church has always regarded St Luke's Gospel as a sacred book: it was used for liturgical reading and is to be found in the earliest lists of canonical books, that is, books which the Church considers to be inspired by God. Thus, in the fourth century, the Council of Laodicea laid down that only canonical books of the Old and New Testaments may be read out in church and included among these the "four Gospels according to Matthew, according to Mark, according to Luke, according to John." The same regulations were issued towards the end of the century by the Council of Hippo and the Third Council of Carthage.[6]

The *Decree of Pope St Damasus*, which contains the acts of the Council of Rome (382), also includes among the sacred books "one book of the Gospels according to Matthew, one book according to Mark, one book according to Luke, one book according to John."[7]

At the beginning of the fifth century, in reply to matters on which Exuperius, bishop of Toulouse, sought his opinion, Pope St Innocent I appended in his Letter *Consulenti tibi* a list of the books which made up the canon of Holy Scripture; this list includes the four Gospels.[8]

The Decree *Pro Jacobitis* (in the papal bull *Cantate Domino*) contains a profession of faith subscribed to by the Jacobites at the Council of Florence (in the fourteenth century) in which it is stated that "the holy men of both Testaments have spoken under the inspiration of the same Holy Spirit," and then goes on to list all the books of Holy Scripture. When it starts to give those

6. *EB*, 12. **7.** *Dz-Sch*, 180.

of the New Testament it says, "the four Gospels, according to Matthew, Mark, Luke and John; the Acts of the Apostles written by Luke the Evangelist ...".[9]

The Council of Trent in its *Decree on sacred books and apostolic tradition* (1546) solemnly defined the canon of Scripture; to avoid any doubt it gave a complete list of the books, in which it described the holy Gospels in the now traditional way—"the four Gospels according to Matthew, Mark, Luke and John." The decree ends with this solemn statement: "If anyone does not accept these books as sacred and canonical in their entirety according to the text usually read in the catholic Church [...], let him be anathema."[10]

DATE OF COMPOSITION

Christian Tradition maintains that St Luke wrote his Gospel after the Gospels of Matthew and Mark, which is why it is listed third in documents of the Magisterium.

St Luke, in the prologue to the Acts of the Apostles, expressly mentions his first book, that is, his Gospel. Therefore, the Gospel was obviously written before Acts. Now, Acts ends with a description of St Paul's situation just before he is released from his first Roman imprisonment, which suggests that St Luke finished writing Acts at that time. Since the date of St Paul's release was the year 63, St Luke's Gospel could have been written in the year 62 or at the beginning of 63. Some scholars tend to go for a date between 67 and 70.

HISTORICAL ACCURACY

We have already discussed what Tradition and the Magisterium of the Church have to say about the historicity of the Gospels. As regards the historicity of St Luke's Gospel specifically, this was confirmed by the 1912 *Reply* of the Pontifical Biblical Commission where it said that "the words and deeds which are reported by Mark accurately and almost in verbal agreement with Peter's preaching, and those which are faithfully set forth by Luke who 'followed all things closely for some time past' through the help of entirely trustworthy witnesses 'who from the beginning were eyewitnesses and ministers of the word' (Lk 1:2f), are historical and rightly deserve that full faith which the Church has always placed in them."[11] The historical accuracy of the text is vouched for by the author's declared intention to write a true account that would enlighten and confirm the faith of his readers. The prologue, which is typical of the style of Greek and Latin historians,[12] shows that St Luke is writing as a historian. He uses (Lk 1:1) the term "narrative" (*diégesis*) to make it clear from the very outset that he is writing as a historian. This can be seen also by his reference to

---

8. *EB*, 21. **9.** *EB*, 47. **10.** *EB*, 59-60. **11.** *EB*, 398. **12.** Cf. e.g., Flavius Josephus, *Against Apion*.

secular history, by the chronological information he gives at the beginning of the Gospel (Lk 1:5; 2:1; 3:1–2, 23) and by the way he plans his work (he says he intends to write an "orderly" account: Lk 1:3). He is very conscientious and diligent in seeking out his sources: they have to be eyewitnesses. True, his is a higher purpose than a secular historian's: he wants to show that the catechetical teaching which has brought Christians to the faith has a solid basis in fact. But for this very reason he goes out of his way to make sure his facts are correct.

St Luke writes history not to satisfy his readers' curiosity but to teach them the history of salvation from the incarnation of Christ to the spread of Christianity among the Gentiles. His account spans two books, his Gospel and the Acts of the Apostles; indeed, they constitute one work in two volumes. He describes "the things which have been accomplished among us" (Lk 1:1) and how God's salvific action in history has been brought to completion in the way that he ordained (cf. Lk 13:33; 17:25). A glance at the language he uses shows that salvation is the underlying theme of his work: the Blessed Virgin Mary rejoices in God her Saviour (Lk 1:47); the angels announce that "to you is born this day in the city of David a Saviour, who is Christ the Lord" (Lk 2:11); God has raised up a power of salvation (cf. Lk 1:69) "that we should be saved from our enemies" (Lk 1:71); the Baptist will preach in order to lead the people to salvation, which consists in forgiveness of sins (Lk 1:77); Simeon beholds salvation when he sees the Child Jesus (Lk 2:30); all men will see salvation, as Isaiah foretold (Lk 3:6); and Zacchaeus attains it when the Master visits his house (Lk 19:9). St Luke uses the verb "to save" thirty times in the Gospel and the Acts; he sees salvation not alone in the Cross but in all the events which came at the end—Christ's death, resurrection, ascension and the preaching of the Gospel thereafter (cf. Acts 13:47; 28:28). In arranging the teaching collected from eyewitnesses of these events, St Luke works from the standpoint of salvation history. The book of the Acts is really an extension of the Gospel, showing how salvation is brought to completion with the coming of the Holy Spirit under whose impulse the Gospel will make its way throughout the world.

CONTENT

Almost half of the content of St Luke's Gospel is not to be found in the other Gospels. Among the important items exclusive to Luke are: his account of Jesus' infancy (chaps. 1 and 2); his setting of many episodes of our Lord's public ministry within the framework of a long journey from Galilee to Jerusalem;[13] and certain parables, such as for example those of the prodigal son (Lk 15:11–32), the unjust steward (Lk 16:1–13), and Lazarus and the rich man (Lk 16:19–31); and Luke is the only one who gives us an account of the appearance of the risen Jesus to the disciples at Emmaus (Lk 24:13–35).

13. Lk 9:51—19:27. This section is usually referred to as "the great Lucan insertion".

The general scheme St Luke follows is very like that of St Mark; it is along the following lines:

• A short prologue, in which he states why he has written the book and what sources he has used (Lk 1:1–4).

• Two long chapters, usually called "the Gospel of the infancy of Jesus," or "the infancy narrative" because that is what they cover (Lk 1:5—2:52). St Matthew's and St Luke's accounts of Jesus' infancy complement one another, with each Gospel concentrating on different points and events to do with the birth and early years of the Saviour.

• Jesus' preparation for his public ministry: his baptism by John and his fast in the desert, where he is tempted by the devil (Lk 3:1—4:13).

• Extensive public ministry in Galilee, where Jesus begins his preaching, works many miracles, chooses the Twelve and prepares them for their future mission. Galilee is also where Jesus begins to be rejected by the scribes and Pharisees, whereas the people flock to him. His disciples remain faithful to him and Peter confesses that Jesus is the Messiah. This section also includes such other important episodes as the transfiguration and three predictions of his passion and resurrection (Lk 4:14—9:27).

As we have just mentioned, a feature of this Gospel is its assembly of accounts inside the framework of a long journey made by our Lord from Galilee to Jerusalem; this "journey narrative" covers ten chapters (Lk 9:51—19:27). In this section we find much of our Lord's preaching—addressed to his disciples, to crowds and even to scribes and Pharisees. Thus, he exhorts people to meekness and mercy (for example, in the parable of the lost sheep and that of the prodigal son) and to trust in God's providence. Here also we find his basic teaching on humility, sincerity, poverty (for example, in the parable about Lazarus and the rich man), repentance, acceptance of the daily cross, the need to be appreciative (the cure of the ten lepers), the importance of not causing scandal, and the duty to forgive one's neighbour. Also included in this section are other teachings of Jesus: on prayer (for example, the Our Father), on being always ready to render an account to God, on the need for faith and sincere conversion if one is to attain salvation (for example, the episode of the blind man of Jericho and that of Zacchaeus the publican), and—throughout—the living example of the Master himself, which his disciple should follow.

All this teaching is interwoven with episodes from our Lord's life (such as the mission of the seventy disciples) and accounts of miracles he worked to confirm his teaching. This long section also contains Jesus' prediction that his disciples would suffer persecution, his prophecy of the destruction of Jerusalem on account of its obstinate refusal to accept God's mercy, and the third prediction of his passion and resurrection.

• St Luke's Gospel then goes on to deal with Jesus' public ministry in Jerusalem (Lk 19:28—21:38), very much along the lines of the other two Synoptics. Jesus enters the Holy City to the acclaim of the people, ejects the dealers from the temple and defends himself against his enemies' accusations;

this gives him an opportunity to describe the real nature of the Kingdom of God (in connexion with tribute to Caesar) and to explain the resurrection of the dead. In this section comes the "eschatological discourse" on the future destruction of Jerusalem and the end of the world.

• Finally, the accounts of Christ's passion, death, resurrection and ascension (chaps. 22–24). Among the points which only St Luke gives us are: Jesus' sweating blood during his agony in Gethsemane; his promise of Paradise to the good thief; and—as we have seen—his appearance to the disciples of Emmaus.

THEOLOGICAL AND LITERARY FEATURES

In referring to the *historicity* of the Gospels, the Second Vatican Council in its Constitution *Dei Verbum* says: "The sacred authors, in writing the four Gospels, selected certain of the many elements which had been handed on, either orally or already in written form, synthesising them or explaining them with an eye to the situation of the churches, while still keeping the style of the proclamation, in such a way that they tell us the honest truth about Jesus. Whether they relied on their own memory or on the testimony of those who 'from the beginning were eyewitnesses and ministers of the word', their purpose in writing was that we might know the 'truth' concerning the things of which we have been informed (cf. Lk 1:2–4)."[14]

Each of the evangelists has given us his own portrait, as it were, of Christ; they all show us the same person, but from different perspectives. Always under the inspiration of the Holy Spirit, the sacred writers sometimes chose the very same events, the very same words (this is particularly true of the Synoptics), but occasionally they tell us things which are not to be found in any of the other Gospels. They also summarize certain items and adapt their account to their immediate readership or audience—though ultimately it is addressed to the whole Church. This explains why one evangelist stresses aspects to which another does not give such importance. When we talk of a Gospel having characteristic features we are trying to identify whom the evangelist was first addressing and what particular things he was stressing—though God is the principal author of every book in Scripture.

As regards the *literary style* of the Third Gospel, St Jerome already observed that Luke's Greek was much better and much more elegant than that of the other evangelists.[15] For example, he usually avoids bringing in Hebrew, Aramaic or Latin words or phrases, giving the Greek equivalent instead. He tends to transcribe popular jargon into more elegant language, and to omit details which might embarrass some people, or scenes which might seem a little unrefined. This sort of thing shows that he was a refined, sensitive person.

Another thing for which St Luke is noted is his concern to establish the historical framework of certain events (cf., e.g., Lk 2:1ff; 3:1; 8:3). Also he looks at

14. No. 19. **15.** Cf. *Epistola*, 20, 4.

certain things from a new angle. The most obvious example of this is the way he presents Christ's life on earth as a journey towards Jerusalem, from where, on the day of his ascension, he will go up into that heaven of which the Holy City is the earthly symbol. Other things which stand out in the Gospel are the universality, the catholicity, of the Gospel and of the Church, the divinity of Christ, Prophet and Saviour, the tender figure of the Blessed Virgin, and such aspects of the Christian life as the spirit of poverty, persevering prayer, mercy and joy.

JESUS MAKING HIS WAY TO JERUSALEM

Jerusalem occupies a very central place in St Luke's Gospel. He begins and ends his accounts of Jesus' infancy with scenes in the temple of Jerusalem—the announcement to Zechariah and the episode of the Child Jesus being lost and then found in the temple talking to the teachers. St Luke gives the temptations in the wilderness in a different order from St Matthew, with the last temptation taking place in Jerusalem. From the very outset of his public ministry Jesus begins to "make his way" towards Jerusalem, where salvation history will reach its climax. He uses this idea of his "making his way" a number of times (Lk 4:30; 9:41–53; 17:11; 19:28), to give his whole narrative the format of a long journey to the Holy City. St Luke is the only one to omit the appearances of the risen Jesus in Galilee; perhaps he does this in order to emphasize the Jerusalem appearances. Finally, the Gospel closes with a scene set exactly where it began, in the temple: "And they worshipped him, and returned to Jerusalem with great joy, and were continually in the temple blessing God" (Lk 24:52–53).

St Luke's second book, the Acts of the Apostles, begins with an account of the ascension of our Lord and the coming of the Holy Spirit in Jerusalem. It then goes on to tell of the spread of the faith and of the Church thoughout the world, under the abiding influence of the Holy Spirit. In the events which he describes in the two books, St Luke, we might say, sees the verification of the prophecy of Isaiah: "It shall come to pass in the latter days that the mountain of the house of the Lord shall be established as the highest of the mountains, and shall be raised above the hills; and all the nations shall flow to it, and many peoples shall come, and say: 'Come, let us go up to the mountain of the Lord, to the house of the God of Jacob, that he may teach us his ways and we may walk in his paths.' For out of Zion shall go forth the law, and the word of the Lord from Jerusalem" (Is 2:2–3). Jerusalem is, then, the Holy City about which God's messengers prophesied and in which Jesus, like them, is rejected (cf. Lk 4:9; 13:33).

THE IMPORTANCE OF THE ASCENSION

Only St Luke and St Mark recount the ascension of our Lord. St Mark makes the briefest of references to it (cf. Mk 16:19), but St Luke mentions it twice (Lk 24:51–53; Acts 1:1–11) and gives important details about it: in his Gospel

Jesus takes leave of his disciples, blessing them like a high priest, for the ascension marks the end of his life on earth. In the Acts of the Apostles the ascension is the point at which the risen Lord enters the glory of heaven, whence he will send the Holy Spirit to bring the Church into being.

We might say that St Luke's entire Gospel tends towards the ascension: the ascension is the final stage on Jesus' "way" to Jerusalem. The Gospel contains a number of passages which seem to refer to the ascension—the transfiguration, where Jesus speaks with Moses and Elijah (Lk 9:30–31) about his "*departure*, which he was to accomplish in Jerusalem"; the three appear "in glory"; in 9:51 it says: "When the days drew near for him to be *received up*, he [Jesus] set his face to go to Jerusalem"; in Luke 24:26 Jesus points out that it was necessary for Christ to suffer "*and enter into his glory*".

Like the other evangelists St Luke speaks of Christ's death, of its necessity, of redemption being won by the shedding of his blood (Lk 22:20; Acts 20:28), but he very definitely positions our Lord's death as a stage on the way to his glorification.

CATHOLICITY OF THE GOSPEL AND OF THE CHURCH

Throughout these two books St Luke shows the messianic largesse foretold by the prophets as coming true in Christ and in his Church, in which he lives on, and as being extended not only to Jews but to all the peoples of the world.

The Acts of the Apostles contains ample evidence of the salvation wrought by Christ spreading all over the world; but even the Gospel contains statements about this universality of salvation—particularly in prophetic passages and in the way the Gentiles are referred to. Thus, the canticle of Simeon (Lk 2:29–32) proclaims that salvation has been "prepared in the presence of all peoples" and is "a light for revelation to the Gentiles". Only St Luke applies to the mission of John the Baptist the text of Isaiah 40:5 about every man seeing the glory of the Lord (cf. Lk 3:6). And in the synagogue of Nazareth Jesus announces the forthcoming proclamation of the Gospel to the Gentiles (Lk 4:16–30). There is a parallel between this passage and Acts 13:46, where the apostles, on being rejected by the Jews, turn to the Gentiles. In Luke 24:45–47 our Lord explains to his disciples that it was prophesied that he should suffer and rise from the dead and that in his name conversion and forgiveness of sins should be preached to all nations. St Luke does not give us the text of Matthew 10:5 about the Samaritans: "Go nowhere among the Gentiles, and enter no town of the Samaritans," which seemed to limit the disciples' mission to Jewish territory. Jesus upbraids his disciples when they want the Samaritans to be punished (Lk 9:55); he sets the Good Samaritan as an example of a true neighbour (Lk 10:25–37); and of the ten lepers whom Jesus cures, the only one who comes back to thank him is a Samaritan (Lk 17:16).

All four Gospels make it clear that Christ's salvation extends to all; yet St Luke's does seem to stress this particularly. We know that our Lord preached almost exclusively to Jews; the Gentiles were to receive the Gospel later, through the apostles. Our Lord reckoned on this and said as much in his instructions to the Twelve: first the Jews, then the Gentiles (cf. Mt 10:5–6; Mk 7:27; Mt 28:18–19; Mk 16:15–16). After his resurrection Jesus made the disciples his eyewitnesses, to go out and tell the whole world (Lk 24:48).

JESUS, PROPHET AND SAVIOUR

Christ is referred to as a "prophet" in Luke 13:33; and 24:19. Because he is true God and true man Jesus Christ is the Prophet *par excellence*: like none other can he speak in God's name (cf. Lk 4:18, 43; 9:45; 19:21). In the Old Testament the prophets were moved by the Spirit of God. St Luke underlines the deep, mysterious connexion between the Holy Spirit and the prophetic ministry of our Lord: for example, at Jesus' baptism, which marks the beginning of his public ministry, the Holy Spirit descends on him in visible form (cf. Lk 3:22). After being tempted in the wilderness, Jesus returns to Galilee led by the Spirit (cf. Lk 4:14). In the synagogue of Nazareth (cf. Lk 4:16–30), when he reads the text of Isaiah 61:1, "The Spirit of the Lord is upon me, because he has anointed me to preach good news to the poor", Jesus applies the text to himself saying that in him this Scripture has been fulfilled.

Throughout this Gospel we are being told that Jesus Christ is the Saviour of men. In the infancy narrative we are constantly being shown how the prophecies of salvation find fulfilment in Christ, those promises made by God to the patriarchs and prophets of the chosen people. The Child who has been born is the long-awaited Saviour: this is the main theme of the *Benedictus*, the *Magnificat*, the announcement to the shepherds and the canticle of Simeon.

Salvation is made manifest in the healing of diseases, as in the cases of the woman with the flow of blood (Lk 8:43–48) and the blind man of Jericho (Lk 18:35–42); in the raising of Jairus' daughter (Lk 8:50–56); in freeing people from possession by the devil, as happened in the cases of the man from Gerasa (Lk 8:26–39); in forgiveness of sins, as in the cases of the sinful woman (Lk 7:36–50) and Zacchaeus, to whom Jesus announces that salvation has come (Lk 19:9–10). But in order to be saved one must believe in the power of Jesus Christ; and even though salvation is made manifest in the miracles we have just mentioned, it is not definitively obtained until the next life (cf. Lk 9:24; 13:23; 18:26). Therefore, being saved means entering the Kingdom of God, being freed by Christ from the slavery of sin, from the devil and from death.

THE BLESSED VIRGIN MARY

The Third Gospel throws special light on the Mother of Christ, a light which gently reveals the greatness and beauty of her soul. This is probably why St Luke was regarded as having actually painted our Lady in the proper sense of the word. Be that as it may, his Gospel is a basic source for doctrine of our Lady and also for devotion to the Mother of our Redeemer—and also it has inspired much Christian art in which Mary figures. With the logical exception of Jesus, no other protagonist in the Gospel story has been described with such love and admiration as Mary.

Nor has any other human creature received such sublime and singular graces as she: she is "full of grace" (*kecharitoméne*: Lk 1:28); the Lord is with her (Lk 1:28); she has found favour with God (Lk 1:30); she conceived by the work of the Holy Spirit (Lk 1:35); she is the Mother of Jesus (Lk 2:7), yet she is a Virgin (Lk 1:34); intimately involved in the redemptive mystery of the Cross (Lk 2:35); she will be blessed by all generations, for the Almighty has done great things for her (Lk 1:49). With good reason does a woman in the crowd cry out in praise of Jesus' Mother (Lk 11:27).

Our Lady responds to these gifts in a most faithful and generous way: St Elizabeth calls her blessed because she has believed (Lk 1:45); the Virgin receives with humility the archangel's announcement that she is to become the Mother of God (Lk 1:29); she asks, in all simplicity, what she has to do to obey God's will (Lk 1:34); she surrenders herself completely to God's plans (Lk 1:38; 2:50); she hastens to help others (Lk 1:39, 56); she is full of gratitude for the gifts she has received (Lk 1:46–55); she faithfully observes God's laws (Lk 2:24) and the pious customs of her people (Lk 2:41); she is very distressed when the Child is lost and makes tender complaint to him (Lk 2:48), but she meekly accepts what she does not understand (Lk 2:50–51). She has a contemplative sense of wonder towards divine mysteries, which she keeps and ponders in her heart (Lk 2:19, 51). As Paul VI said, Mary "is not only the sublime 'type' of the creature redeemed by Christ's merits, she is also the 'type' of all mankind as it makes its pilgrim way in faith."[16]

ENCOURAGEMENT OF CHRISTIAN LIVING

We said earlier that salvation in its complete form is something eschatological, that is to say, it is achieved definitively in heaven. But salvation does begin in this present life; the follower of Christ, living in this world, in the bosom of the Church, should imitate Jesus' life on earth; everything Jesus said and did constitutes both a model and a precept for the Christian. Hence eschatology and exhortation to Christian living merge into one in the Gospel; this holds good for all of the New Testament, but it is particularly noticeable in St Luke.

The phrase, "today it has been fulfilled", which is used with a certain frequency in St Luke's Gospel (cf. Lk 4:21; 19:9), shows us that the whole proclamation of the Gospel is being presented as the coming of the messianic times. The Christian must take up his cross "daily" (Lk 9:23); he must be patient (Lk 21:19). Similarly he must practise poverty if he is to respond to

---

16. General Audience, 30 May 1973.

Christ's call (Lk 4:18; 7:22) and attain blessedness (Lk 6:20) and eternal life (Lk 16:19–31). A person needs to be detached from "everything" to follow Jesus (Lk 18:22). Riches are of no value when they become an end in themselves (cf. Lk 12:13–21; 16:9, 14–15). One must deny oneself and practise renunciation as the first disciples did after the miraculous catch of fish on Lake Gennesaret, when "they left everything and followed him" (Lk 5:11), or like Levi (Matthew) the publican, who, on hearing the Master's call, "left everything, and rose and followed him" (Lk 5:28). Other things that the Third Gospel stresses are the need for persevering prayer, for merciful love and interior joy at all times. In this connexion, too, Jesus' words and actions provide the model. For example, there are a number of passages to be found only in St Luke's Gospel in which Christ's prayer is mentioned—and at particularly solemn moments: for example, at his baptism, before he chooses his apostles, at the transfiguration, and on the cross. And in Gethsemane Jesus exhorts his disciples to pray in order not to fall into temptation. Christians have to practise love, meekness and mercy: "Be merciful, even as your Father is merciful" (Lk 6:36). St Luke devotes a whole chapter (chap. 15) to three parables dealing with God's mercy, and the verses following the beatitudes are a discourse on love, including love of one's enemies (Lk 6:27–38).

The four Gospels, which contain the proclamation of salvation and which are, as the word "gospel" implies, "good news", are for this very reason impregnated with the joy of the Redemption wrought by Christ. This joyfulness is particularly obvious in St Luke's Gospel. He uses a range of words with a wealth of nuance to describe this joy and gladness. For example, an angel of the Lord announces to Zechariah that he will have a son and "many will rejoice at his birth" (Lk 1:14); the archangel Gabriel, in his annunciation to Mary, begins by greeting her with the word "hail", which literally means "rejoice" (Lk 1:28); and after telling them about the persecutions they will undergo for the sake of the Son of man, the Master tells the disciples to "rejoice in that day, and leap for joy" (Lk 6:23). The birth of the Baptist will bring "joy and gladness" to Zechariah (Lk 1:14); the angel announces news "of great joy" (Lk 2:10); in heaven there will be "joy" over one converted sinner (Lk 15:7); and Elizabeth declares that her son "leaped for joy" in her womb (Lk 1:44). Finally, the Gospel, after telling about the ascension, ends with these words: "And they worshipped him, and returned to Jerusalem with great joy, and were continually in the temple blessing God" (Lk 24:52–53).

THE GOSPEL ACCORDING TO LUKE

The Revised Standard Version, with notes

Prologue

1 ¹Inasmuch as many have undertaken to compile a narrative of the things which have been accomplished among us, ²just as they were delivered to us by those who from the beginning were eyewitnesses and ministers of the word, ³it seemed good to me also, having followed all things closelyᵃ for some time past, to write an orderly account for you, most excellent Theophilus,* ⁴that you may know the truth concerning the things of which you have been informed.

Jn 15:27

Acts 1:1

1. THE INFANCY OF JOHN THE BAPTIST AND OF JESUS

The birth of John the Baptist foretold

⁵ *In the days of Herod, king of Judea, there was a priest named Zechariah,ᵇ of the division of Abijah; and he had a wife of the

1 Chron 24:10

1:1–4. St Luke is the only evangelist to give his book a preface or prologue. What is usually described as the "prologue" to St John is really a summary of what that Gospel contains. St Luke's prologue, which is very short and very elegantly written, describes why he has written the book—to provide an orderly, documented account of the life of Christ, starting at the beginning. These verses help us realize that Jesus Christ's message of salvation, the Gospel, was preached before it came to be written down: cf. the quotation from Vatican II's *Dei Verbum*, 19 (p. 17 above). God, then, wanted us to have written Gospels as a permanent, divine testimony providing a firm basis for our faith. "He does not tell Theophilus new things, things he did not previously know; he undertakes to tell him the truth concerning the things in which he has already been instructed. This he does so that you can know everything you have been told about the Lord and his doings" (St Bede, *In Lucae Evangelium expositio*, in loc.).

1:2. The "eyewitnesses" the evangelist refers to would have been the Blessed Virgin, the apostles, the holy women and others who shared Jesus' life during his time on earth.

1:3. "It seemed good to me": "When he says 'it seemed good to me' this does not exclude God's action, because it is God who prepares men's will [...]. He dedicates his Gospel to Theophilus, that is, to one whom God loves. But if you love God, it has also been written for you; and if it has been written for you, then accept this present from the evangelist, keep this token of friendship very close to your heart" (St Ambrose, *Expositio Evangelii sec. Lucam*, in loc.).

1:5ff. St Luke and St Matthew devote the first two chapters of their Gospels to episodes in the early life of our Lord (the annunciation, his birth, childhood and hidden life in Nazareth)—material not covered by the other evangelists. These chapters are usually referred to as the

a. Or *accurately* **b.** Greek *Zacharias*

daughters of Aaron, and her name was Elizabeth. [6]And they were both righteous before God, walking in all the commandments and ordinances of the Lord blameless. [7]But they had no child, because Elizabeth was barren, and both were advanced in years. [8]Now while he was serving as priest before God when his division was

---

"infancy narrative" or "the gospel of the infancy of Jesus". The first thing one notices is that St Matthew and St Luke do not each deal with the same events.

St Luke's infancy narrative covers six episodes, structured in twos, referring to the infancy of John the Baptist and that of Jesus: two annunciations, two births, two circumcisions and two scenes in the temple; plus other episodes which have to do only with Jesus' infancy—the revelation to the shepherds and their adoration of the Child, the purification of Mary and presentation of the Child, the prophecies of Simeon and Anna, Jesus being lost and then found in the temple, and the hidden life in Nazareth.

St Luke's very poetic narrative combines simplicity and majesty, drawing us to intimate reflection on the mystery of the incarnation of our Saviour: we see the angel make the announcement to Zechariah (1:5–17); his subsequent greeting and annunciation to Mary (1:26–38); her visit to her cousin St Elizabeth (1:39–56); the birth of Jesus in Bethlehem (2:1–7); the adoration of the shepherds (2:8–20); the presentation of the Child in the temple and Simeon's blessing of Mary (2:22–38); the Child lost and found in the temple (2:41–52). St Luke also includes four prophecies in verse form, canticles, Mary's *Magnificat* (1:46 –55), Zechariah's *Benedictus* (1:67–79), the *Gloria* of the angels (2:14) and Simeon's *Nunc dimittis* (2:29–32). These canticles are interwoven with words and phrases which recall, almost word for word, different passages from the Old Testament (from Gen, Lev, Num, Judg, 1 Sam, Is, Jer, Mic and Mal). Every

educated pious Jew of the time prayed either by reading the sacred books or by repeating from memory things he had read in them, so there is nothing surprising about our Lady, Zechariah, Simeon and Anna doing this. Besides, it was the same Holy Spirit as inspired the human authors of the Old Testament who now moved to speech those good people before whose very eyes the ancient prophecies were being fulfilled in the Child Jesus. This background explains why we should take these canticles as being recorded exactly as they were spoken.

1:6. After referring to the noble ancestry of Zechariah and Elizabeth, the evangelist now speaks of a higher type of nobility, that of virtue: "Both were righteous before God." "For not everyone who is righteous in men's eyes is righteous in God's; men have one way of seeing and God another; men see externals, but God sees into the heart. It can happen that someone seems righteous because his virtue is false and is practised to win people's approval; but he is not virtuous in God's sight if his righteousness is not born of simplicity of soul but is only simulated in order to appear good.

"Perfect praise consists in being righteous before God, because only he can be called perfect who is approved by him who cannot be deceived" (St Ambrose, *Expositio Evangelii sec. Lucam*, in loc.).

In the last analysis what a Christian must be is righteous before God. St Paul is advocating this when he tells the Corinthians, "But with me it is a very small thing that I should be judged by

on duty, ⁹according to the custom of the priesthood, it fell to him   Ex 30:7
by lot to enter the temple of the Lord and burn incense. ¹⁰And the
whole multitude of the people were praying outside at the hour of
incense. ¹¹And there appeared to him an angel of the Lord stand-

---

you or by any human court. [...] It is the Lord who judges me. Therefore do not pronounce judgment before the time, before the Lord comes, who will bring to light the things now hidden in darkness and will disclose the purposes of the heart. Then every man will receive his commendation from God" (1 Cor 4:3ff). On the notion of the just or righteous man, see the note on Mt 1:19.

1:8. There were twenty-four groups or turns of priests to which functions were allocated by the drawing of lots; the eighth group was that of the family of Abijah (cf. 1 Chron 24:7–19), to which Zechariah belonged.

1:9–10. Within the sacred precincts, in a walled-off area, stood the temple proper. Rectangular in form, there was first a large area which was called "the Holy Place", in which was located the altar of incense referred to in v. 9. Behind this was the inner sanctum, called "the Holy of Holies", where the Ark of the Covenant with the tablets of the Law used to be kept; only the high priest had access to this, the most sacred part of the temple. The veil, or great curtain, of the temple separated these two areas from one another. The sacred building was surrounded by a courtyard, called the courtyard of the priests, and outside this, at the front of the temple, was what was called the courtyard of the Israelites, where the people stayed during the ceremony of incensing.

1:10. While the priest offered incense to God, the people in the courtyard joined with him in spirit: even in the Old Testament every external act of worship was meant to be accompanied by an interior disposition of self-offering to God.

With much more reason should there be this union between external and internal worship in the liturgical rites of the New Covenant (cf. *Mediator Dei*, 8), in the liturgy of the Church. Besides, this consistency befits the nature of man, comprised as he is of body and soul.

1:11. Angels are pure spirits, that is, they have no body of any kind; therefore, "they do not appear to men exactly as they are; rather, they manifest themselves in forms which God gives them so that they can be seen by those to whom he sends them" (St John Damascene, *De fide orthodoxa*, 2, 3).

In addition to adoring and serving God, angelic spirits act as God's messengers and as channels of his providence towards men; this explains why they appear so often in salvation history and why Holy Scripture refers to them in so many passages (cf., e.g., Heb 1:14).

Christ's birth was such an important event that angels were given a very prominent role in connexion with it. Here, as at the annunciation to Mary, the archangel St Gabriel is charged with delivering God's message.

"It is no accident that the angel makes his appearance in the temple, for this announces the imminent coming of the true Priest and prepares the heavenly sacrifice at which the angels will minister. Let it not be doubted, then, that the angels will be present when Christ is immolated" (St Ambrose, *Expositio Evangelii sec. Lucam*, in loc.).

ing on the right side of the altar of incense. [12]And Zechariah was troubled when he saw him, and fear fell upon him. [13]But the angel said to him, "Do not be afraid, Zechariah, for your prayer is heard, and your wife Elizabeth will bear you a son, and you shall call his name John.

[14]And you will have joy and gladness,
    and many will rejoice at his birth;

Num 6:3
Judg 13:4f
1 Sam 1:11

[15]for he will be great before the Lord,
    and he shall drink no wine nor strong drink,
    and he will be filled with the Holy Spirit,
    even from his mother's womb.
[16]And he will turn many of the sons of Israel
    to the Lord their God,

Mt 17:11–13
Mal 3:1–23,
24; 4:5–6

[17]and he will go before him in the spirit and power of Elijah,
    to turn the hearts of the fathers to the children,

1:12. "No matter how righteous a man be, he cannot look at an angel without feeling afraid; that is why Zechariah was alarmed: he could not but quake at the presence of the angel; he could not take the brightness that surrounded him" (St John Chrysostom, *De incomprehensibili Dei natura*). The reason for this is not so much the angel's superiority to man as the fact that the grandeur of God's majesty shines out through the angel: "And the angel said to me, 'Write this: Blessed are those who are invited to the marriage supper of the Lamb.' And he said to me, 'These are true words of God.' Then I fell down at his feet to worship him, but he said to me, 'You must not do that! I am a fellow servant with you and your brethren who hold the testimony of Jesus. Worship God'" (Rev 19:9–10).

1:13. Through the archangel God intervenes in an exceptional way in the married life of Zechariah and Elizabeth; but the message he brings has much wider reference; it has significance for the whole world. Elizabeth is already quite old but she is going to have a son who will be called John ("God is gracious") and he will be the forerunner of the

Messiah. This showed that "the fulness of time" (cf. Gal 4:4) was imminent, for which all righteous people of Israel had yearned (cf. Jn 8:56; Heb 11:13).

"Your prayer is heard," St Jerome comments, "that is to say, you are given more than you asked for. You prayed for the salvation of the people, and you have been given the Precursor" (*Expositio in Evangelium sec. Lucam*, in loc.). Our Lord also sometimes gives us more than we ask for: "There is a story about a beggar meeting Alexander the Great and asking him for alms. Alexander stopped and instructed that the man be given the government of five cities. The beggar, totally confused and taken aback, exclaimed, 'I didn't ask for as much as that.' And Alexander replied, 'You asked like the man you are; I give like the man I am'" (St J. Escrivá, *Christ Is Passing By*, 160). Since God responds so generously and gives us more than we ask for, we should face up to difficulties and not be cowed by them.

1:14–17. The archangel St Gabriel gives Zechariah three reasons why he should rejoice over the birth of this child: first, because God will bestow exceptional holiness on him (v.15); second, because

and the disobedient to the wisdom of the just,
to make ready for the Lord a people prepared."
¹⁸And Zechariah said to the angel, "How shall I know this? For I   Gen 18:11
am an old man, and my wife is advanced in years." ¹⁹And the   Dan 8:16; 9:21
angel answered him, "I am Gabriel, who stand in the presence of   Heb 1:14
God; and I was sent to speak to you, and to bring you this good
news. ²⁰And behold, you will be silent and unable to speak until
the day that these things come to pass, because you did not
believe my words, which will be fulfilled in their time." ²¹And the
people were waiting for Zechariah, and they wondered at his
delay in the temple. ²²And when he came out, he could not speak
to them, and they perceived that he had seen a vision in the
temple; and he made signs to them and remained dumb. ²³And
when his time of service was ended, he went to his home.

²⁴After these days his wife Elizabeth conceived, and for five
months she hid herself, saying, ²⁵"Thus the Lord has done to me   Gen 20:23

---

he will lead many to salvation (v.16); and third, because his whole life, everything he does, will prepare the way for the expected Messiah (v.17).

In St John the Baptist two prophecies of Malachi are fulfilled; in them we are told that God will send a messenger ahead of him to prepare the way for him (Mal 3:1; 4:5–6). John prepares the way for the first coming of the Messiah in the same way as Elijah will prepare the way for his second coming (cf. St Ambrose, *Expositio Evangelii sec. Lucam*, in loc.; St Thomas Aquinas, *Commentary on St Matthew*, 17, 11, in loc.). This is why Christ will say, "What did you go out to see? A prophet? Yes, I tell you, and more than a prophet. This is he of whom it is written, 'Behold, I send my messenger before thy face, who shall prepare thy way before thee'" (Lk 7:26–27).

1:18. Zechariah's incredulity and his sin lie not in his doubting that this message has come from God but in forgetting that God is almighty, and in thinking that he and Elizabeth are past having children. Later, referring to the conception of John the Baptist, the same angel explains to

Mary that "with God nothing will be impossible" (Lk 1:37). When God asks us to take part in any undertaking we should rely on his omnipotence rather than our own meagre resources. See the note on Mt 10:9–10.

1:19–20. "Gabriel" means "might of God". God commanded the archangel Gabriel to announce the events connected with the incarnation of the Word; already in the Old Testament it was Gabriel who proclaimed to the prophet Daniel the time of the Messiah's coming (Dan 8:15–26; 9:20–27). This present passage deals with the announcement of the conception and birth of Christ's Precursor, and it is the same angel who will reveal to the Blessed Virgin the mystery of the Incarnation.

1:24. Elizabeth hid herself because of the strangeness of pregnancy at her age and out of a holy modesty, which advised her not to make known God's gifts prematurely.

1:25. Married couples who want to have children, to whom God has not yet given

in the days when he looked on me, to take away my reproach among men."

The annunciation and incarnation of the Son of God

Lk 2:5
Mt 1:16–18

²⁶In the sixth month the angel Gabriel was sent from God to a city of Galilee named Nazareth, ²⁷to a virgin betrothed to a man whose

any, can learn from Zechariah and Elizabeth and have recourse to them as intercessors. To couples in this situation St Josemaría Escrivá recommended that "they should not give up hope too easily. They should ask God to give them children and, if it is his will, to bless them as he blessed the Patriarchs of the Old Testament. And then it would be advisable for both of them to see a good doctor. If in spite of everything God does not give them children, they should not feel frustrated. They should be happy, discovering in this very fact God's will for them. Often God does not give children because he is 'asking more'. God asks them to put the same effort and the same kind and gentle dedication into helping their neighbours as they would have put into raising their own children, without the human joy that comes from parenthood. There is, then, no reason for feeling they are failures or for giving way to sadness" (*Conversations*, 96).

Here is the authoritative teaching of John Paul II on this subject: "It must not be forgotten, however, that, even when procreation is not possible, conjugal life does not for this reason lose its value. Physical sterility in fact can be for spouses the occasion for other important services to the life of the human person— for example, adoption, various forms of educational work, assistance to other families and to poor or handicapped children" (*Familiaris consortio*, 14).

1:26–38. Here we contemplate our Lady who was "enriched from the first instant of her conception with the splendour of

an entirely unique holiness; [...] the virgin of Nazareth is hailed by the heralding angel, by divine command, as 'full of grace' (cf. Lk 1:28), and to the heavenly messenger she replies, 'Behold, I am the handmaid of the Lord, be it done unto me according to thy word' (Lk 1:38). Thus the daughter of Adam, Mary, consenting to the word of God, became the Mother of Jesus. Committing herself wholeheartedly to God's saving will and impeded by no sin, she devoted herself totally, as a handmaid of the Lord, to the person and work of her Son, under and with him, serving the mystery of Redemption, by the grace of Almighty God. Rightly, therefore, the Fathers see Mary not merely as passively engaged by God, but as freely cooperating in the work of man's salvation through faith and obedience" (Vatican II, *Lumen gentium*, 56).

The annunciation to Mary and incarnation of the Word constitute the deepest mystery of the relationship between God and men and the most important event in the history of mankind: God becomes man, and will remain so forever, such is the extent of his goodness and mercy and love for all of us. And yet on the day when the second person of the Blessed Trinity assumed frail human nature in the pure womb of the Blessed Virgin, it all happened quietly, without fanfare of any kind. St Luke tells the story in a very simple way. We should treasure these words of the Gospel and use them often, for example, practising the Christian custom of saying the Angelus every day and reflecting on the five joyful mysteries of the Rosary.

name was Joseph, of the house of David; and the virgin's name
was Mary. ²⁸And he came to her and said, "Hail, full of grace,ᵇ²   Judg 5:24
the Lord is with you!"ᶜ ²⁹But she was greatly troubled at the
saying, and considered in her mind what sort of greeting this

---

1:27. God chose to be born of a virgin; centuries earlier he disclosed this through the prophet Isaiah (cf. Is 7:14; Mt 1:22–23). God "before all ages made choice of, and set in her proper place, a mother for his only-begotten Son from whom he, after being made flesh, should be born in the blessed fulness of time: and he continued his persevering regard for her in preference to all other creatures, to such a degree that for her alone he had singular regard" (Pius IX, *Ineffabilis Deus*, 2). This privilege granted to our Lady of being a virgin and a mother at the same time is a unique gift of God. This was the work of the Holy Spirit "who at the conception and the birth of the Son so favoured the Virgin Mother as to impart fruitfulness to her while preserving inviolate her perpetual virginity" (St Pius V, *Catechism*, 1, 4, 8). Paul VI reminds us of this truth of faith: "We believe that the Blessed Mary, who ever enjoys the dignity of virginity, was the Mother of the incarnate Word, of our God and Saviour Jesus Christ" (*Creed of the People of God*, 14).

Although many suggestions have been made as to what the name Mary means, most of the best scholars seem to agree that Mary means "lady". However, no single meaning fully conveys the richness of the name.

1:28. "Hail, full of grace": literally the Greek reads "Rejoice!", obviously referring to a unique joy over the news which the angel is about to communicate.

"Full of grace": by this unusual form of greeting the archangel reveals Mary's special dignity and honour. The Fathers and Doctors of the Church "taught that this singular, solemn and unheard-of greeting showed that all the divine graces reposed in the Mother of God and that she was adorned with all the gifts of the Holy Spirit", which meant that she "was never subject to the curse", that is, was preserved from all sin. These words of the archangel in this text constitute one of the sources which reveal the dogma of Mary's immaculate conception (cf. Pius IX, *Ineffabilis Deus*; Paul VI, *Creed of the People of God*).

"The Lord is with you!": these words are not simply a greeting ("the Lord be with you") but an affirmation ("the Lord is with you"), and they are closely connected with the Incarnation. St Augustine comments by putting these words on the archangel's lips: "He is more with you than he is with me: he is in your heart, he takes shape within you, he fills your soul, he is in your womb" (*Sermo de Nativitate Domini*, 4).

Some important Greek manuscripts and early translations add at the end of the verse: "Blessed are you among women!", meaning that God will exalt Mary over all women. She is more excellent than Sarah, Hannah, Deborah, Rachel, Judith, etc., for only she has the supreme honour of being chosen to be the Mother of God.

1:29–30. Our Lady is troubled by the presence of the archangel and by the confusion truly humble people experience when they receive praise.

---

b2. Or *O favoured one*   **c.** Other ancient authorities add *"Blessed are you among women!"*

Judg 13:3
Is 7:14
Mt 1:21–23
Is 9:7
2 Sam 7:12–16
might be. [30]And the angel said to her,* "Do not be afraid, Mary, for you have found favour with God. [31]And behold you will conceive in your womb and bear a son, and you shall call his name Jesus. [32]He will be great, and will be called the Son of the Most High; and the Lord God will give to him the throne of his father David,

---

1:30. The Annunciation is the moment when our Lady is given to know the vocation which God planned for her from eternity. When the archangel sets her mind at ease by saying "Do not be afraid, Mary," he is helping her to overcome that initial fear which a person normally experiences when God gives him or her a special calling. The fact that Mary felt this fear does not imply the least trace of imperfection in her: hers is a perfectly natural reaction in the face of the supernatural. Imperfection would arise if one did not overcome this fear or rejected the advice of those in a position to help—as St Gabriel helped Mary.

1:31–33. The archangel Gabriel tells the Blessed Virgin that she is to be the Mother of God by reminding her of the words of Isaiah which announced that the Messiah would be born of a virgin, a prophecy which will find its fulfilment in Mary (cf. Mt 1:22–23; Is 7:14).

He reveals that the Child will be "great": his greatness comes from his being God, a greatness he does not lose when he takes on the lowliness of human nature. He also reveals that Jesus will be the king of the Davidic dynasty sent by God in keeping with his promise of salvation; that his Kingdom will last forever, for his humanity will remain forever joined to his divinity; that "he will be called Son of the Most High", that is, he really will be the Son of the Most High and will be publicly recognized as such; in other words, the Child will be the Son of God.

The archangel's announcement evokes the ancient prophecies which foretold these prerogatives. Mary, who was well-versed in Holy Scripture, clearly realized that she was to be the Mother of God.

1:34–38. Commenting on this passage John Paul II said: "*Virgo fidelis*, the faithful Virgin. What does this faithfulness of Mary's mean? What are the dimensions of this faithfulness? The first dimension is called search. Mary was faithful first of all when she began, lovingly, to seek the deep sense of God's plan in her and for the world. *Quomodo fiet?* How shall this be?, she asked the Angel of the Annunciation […].

"The second dimension of faithfulness is called reception, acceptance. The *quomodo fiet?* is changed, on Mary's lips, to a *fiat*: Let it be done, I am ready, I accept. This is the crucial moment of faithfulness, the moment in which man perceives that he will never completely understand the 'how'; that there are in God's plan more areas of mystery than of clarity; that, however he may try, he will never succeed in understanding it completely […].

"The third dimension of faithfulness is consistency to live in accordance with what one believes; to adapt one's own life to the object of one's adherence. To accept misunderstanding, persecutions, rather than a break between what one practises and what one believes: this is consistency […].

"But all faithfulness must pass the most exacting test, that of duration.

[33]and he will reign over the house of Jacob for ever;
and of his kingdom there will be no end."

Mic 4:7
Dan 7:14

[34]And Mary said to the angel, "How can this be, since I have no husband?" [35] And the angel said to her, *will* *I have no relations*

"Therefore, the fourth dimension of faithfulness is constancy. It is easy to be consistent for a day or two. It is difficult and important to be consistent for one's whole life. It is easy to be consistent in the hour of enthusiasm, it is difficult to be so in the hour of tribulation. And only a consistency that lasts throughout the whole of life can be called faithfulness. Mary's 'fiat' in the Annunciation finds its fullness in the silent 'fiat' that she repeats at the foot of the Cross" (Homily in Mexico City Cathedral, 26 January 1979).

ever, in the Old Testament there were some who, in keeping with God's plan, did remain celibate—for example, Jeremiah, Elijah, Eliseus and John the Baptist. The Blessed Virgin, who received a very special inspiration of the Holy Spirit to practise virginity, is a first-fruit of the New Testament, which will establish the excellence of virginity over marriage while not taking from the holiness of the married state, which it raises to the level of a sacrament (cf. Vatican II, *Gaudium et spes*, 48).

1:34. Mary believed the archangel's words absolutely; she did not doubt as Zechariah had done (cf. Lk 1:18). Her question, "How can this be?", expresses her readiness to obey the will of God even though at first sight it implied a contradiction: on the one hand, she was convinced that God wished her to remain a virgin; on the other, here was God also announcing that she would become a mother. The archangel announces God's mysterious design, and what had seemed impossible, according to the laws of nature, is explained by a unique intervention on the part of God.

Mary's resolution to remain a virgin was certainly something very unusual, not in line with the practice of righteous people under the Old Covenant, for, as St Augustine explains, "particularly attentive to the propagation and growth of the people of God, through whom the Prince and Saviour of the world might be prophesied and be born, the saints were obliged to make use of the good of matrimony"(*De bono matrimonii*, 9, 9). How-

1:35. The "shadow" is a symbol of the presence of God. When Israel was journeying through the wilderness, the glory of God filled the Tabernacle and a cloud covered the Ark of the Covenant (Ex 40:34–36). And when God gave Moses the tablets of the Law, a cloud covered Mount Sinai (Ex 24:15–16); and also, at the transfiguration of Jesus, the voice of God the Father was heard coming out of a cloud (Lk 9:35).

At the moment of the incarnation the power of God envelopes our Lady—an expression of God's omnipotence. The Spirit of God—which, according to the account in Genesis (1:2), moved over the face of the waters, bringing things to life—now comes down on Mary. And the fruit of her womb will be the work of the Holy Spirit. The Virgin Mary, who herself was conceived without any stain of sin (cf. Pius IX, *Ineffabilis Deus*) becomes, after the incarnation, a new tabernacle of God. This is the mystery we recall every day when saying the Angelus.

33

Mt 1:18–20
Jn 10:36
"The Holy Spirit will come upon you,
and the power of the Most High will overshadow you;
therefore the child to be born[d] will be called holy,
the Son of God.
³⁶And behold, your kinswoman Elizabeth in her old age has also conceived a son; and this is the sixth month with her who was called barren. ³⁷For with God nothing will be impossible." ³⁸And Mary said, "Behold, I am the handmaid of the Lord; let it be to me according to your word." And the angel departed from her.

1:38. Once she learns of God's plan, our Lady yields to God's will with prompt obedience, unreservedly. She realizes the disproportion between what she is going to become—the Mother of God—and what she is—a woman. However, this is what God wants to happen and for him nothing is impossible; therefore no one should stand in his way. So Mary, combining humility and obedience, responds perfectly to God's call: "Behold, I am the handmaid of the Lord; let it be done to me according to your word."

"At the enchantment of this virginal phrase, the Word became flesh" (St J. Escrivá, *Holy Rosary*, first joyful mystery). From the pure body of Mary, God shaped a new body, he created a soul out of nothing, and the Son of God united himself with this body and soul: prior to this he was only God; now he is still God but also man. Mary is now the Mother of God. This truth is a dogma of faith, first defined by the Council of Ephesus (431). At this point she also begins to be the spiritual Mother of all mankind. What Christ says when he is dying—"Behold, your son ..., Behold, your mother" (Jn 19:26–27)—simply promulgates what came about silently at Nazareth. "With her generous 'fiat' (Mary) became, through the working of the Spirit, the Mother of God, but also the Mother of the living, and, by receiving into her

womb the one Mediator, she became the true Ark of the Covenant and true Temple of God" (Paul VI, *Marialis cultus*, 6).

The Gospel shows us the Blessed Virgin as a perfect model of *purity* (the RSV "I have no husband" is a euphemism); of *humility* ("Behold, I am the handmaid of the Lord"); of *candour* and *simplicity* ("How can this be?"); of *obedience* and *lively faith* ("Let it be done to me according to your word"). "Following her example of obedience to God, we can learn to serve delicately without being slavish. In Mary we don't find the slightest trace of the attitude of the foolish virgins, who obey, but thoughtlessly. Our Lady listens attentively to what God wants, ponders what she doesn't fully understand and asks about what she doesn't know. Then she gives herself completely to doing the divine will: 'Behold I am the handmaid of the Lord; let it be done to me according to your word'. Isn't that marvellous? The Blessed Virgin, our teacher in all we do, shows us here that obedience to God is not servile, does not bypass our conscience. We should be inwardly moved to discover the 'freedom of the children of God' (cf. Rom 8:21)" (St Josemaría Escrivá, *Christ Is Passing By*, 173).

1:39–56. We contemplate this episode of our Lady's visit to her cousin St

d. Other ancient authorities add *of you*

34

The Visitation

³⁹In those days Mary arose and went with haste into the hill country, to a city of Judah, ⁴⁰and she entered the house of Zechariah and greeted Elizabeth. ⁴¹And when Elizabeth heard the greeting of Mary, the babe leaped in her womb; and Elizabeth was filled with the Holy Spirit ⁴²and she exclaimed with a loud cry, "Blessed are you among women, and blessed is the fruit of your womb! ⁴³And why is this granted me, that the mother of my Lord should come to me? ⁴⁴For behold, when the voice of your greeting came to my

Lk 1:15, 80

Judg 5:24
Jud 13:23

Elizabeth in the *second joyful mystery* of the Rosary: "Joyfully keep Joseph and Mary company ... and you will hear the traditions of the House of David. ... We walk in haste towards the mountains, to a town of the tribe of Judah (Lk 1:39).

"We arrive. It is the house where John the Baptist is to be born. Elizabeth gratefully hails the Mother of her Redeemer: Blessed are you among women, and blessed is the fruit of your womb. Why should I be honoured with a visit from the mother of my Lord? (Lk 1:42–43).

"The unborn Baptist quivers ... (Lk 1:41). Mary's humility pours forth in the *Magnificat*. ... And you and I, who are proud—who were proud—promise to be humble" (St J. Escrivá, *Holy Rosary*).

1:39. On learning from the angel that her cousin St Elizabeth is soon to give birth and is in need of support, our Lady in her charity hastens to her aid. She has no regard for the difficulties this involves. Although we do not know where exactly Elizabeth was living (it is now thought to be Ain Karim), it certainly meant a journey into the hill country which at that time would have taken four days.

From Mary's visit to Elizabeth Christians should learn to be caring people. "If we have this filial contact with Mary, we won't be able to think just about ourselves and our problems. Selfish personal problems will find no

place in our mind" (St Josemaría Escrivá, *Christ Is Passing By*, 145).

1:42. St Bede comments that Elizabeth blesses Mary using the same words as the archangel "to show that she should be honoured by angels and by men and why she should indeed be revered above all other women" (*In Lucae Evangelium expositio*, in loc.).

When we say the *Hail Mary* we repeat these divine greetings, "rejoicing with Mary at her dignity as Mother of God and praising the Lord, thanking him for having given us Jesus Christ through Mary" (St Pius X, *Catechism*, 333).

1:43. Elizabeth is moved by the Holy Spirit to call Mary "the mother of my Lord", thereby showing that Mary is the Mother of God.

1:44. Although he was conceived in sin—original sin—like other men, St John the Baptist was born sinless because he was sanctified in his mother's womb by the presence of Jesus Christ (then in Mary's womb) and of the Blessed Virgin. On receiving this grace of God St John rejoices by leaping with joy in his mother's womb—thereby fulfilling the archangel's prophecy (cf. Lk 1:15).

St John Chrysostom comments on this scene of the Gospel: "See how new and how wonderful this mystery is. He has not yet left the womb but he speaks

Lk 1:48; 11:28

ears, the babe in my womb leaped for joy. [45]And blessed is she who believed that there would be[e] a fulfilment of what was spoken to her from the Lord."

The Magnificat

1 Sam 2:1–10

[46]And Mary said,
"My soul magnifies the Lord,

---

by leaping; he is not yet allowed to cry out but he makes himself heard by his actions [...]; he has not yet seen the light but he points out the Sun; he has not yet been born and he is keen to act as Precursor. The Lord is present, so he cannot contain himself or wait for nature to run its course: he wants to break out of the prison of his mother's womb and he makes sure he witnesses to the fact that the Saviour is about to come" (*Sermon recorded by Metaphrastrus*).

1:45. Joining the chorus of all future generations, Elizabeth, moved by the Holy Spirit, declares the Lord's Mother to be blessed and praises her faith. No one ever had faith to compare with Mary's; she is the model of the attitude a creature should have towards its Creator —complete submission, total attachment. Through her faith, Mary is the instrument chosen by God to bring about the Redemption; as Mediatrix of all graces, she is associated with the redemptive work of her Son: "This union of the Mother with the Son in the work of salvation is made manifest from the time of Christ's virginal conception up to his death; first when Mary, arising in haste to go to visit Elizabeth, is greeted by her as blessed because of her belief in the promise of salvation and the Precursor leaps with joy in the womb of his mother [...]. The Blessed Virgin advanced in her pilgrimage of faith and faithfully perse-

vered in her union with her Son unto the cross, where she stood (cf. Jn 19:25), in keeping with the divine plan, enduring with her only-begotten Son the intensity of his suffering, associating herself with his sacrifice in her mother's heart, and lovingly consenting to the immolation of this victim which was born of her" (Vatican II, *Lumen gentium*, 57f).

The new Latin text gives a literal rendering of the original Greek when it says "quae credidit" (RSV "she who has believed") as opposed to the Vulgate "quae credidisti" ("you who have believed") which gave more of the sense than a literal rendering.

1:46–55. Mary's *Magnificat* canticle is a poem of singular beauty. It evokes certain passages of the Old Testament with which she would have been very familiar (especially 1 Sam 2:1–10).

Three stanzas may be distinguished in the canticle: in the first (vv. 46–50) Mary glorifies God for making her the Mother of the Saviour, which is why future generations will call her blessed; she shows that the Incarnation is a mysterious expression of God's power and holiness and mercy. In the second (vv. 51–53) she teaches us that the Lord has always had a preference for the humble, resisting the proud and boastful. In the third (vv. 54–55) she proclaims that God, in keeping with his promise, has always taken special care of his chosen people—

e. Or *believed, for there will be*

⁴⁷and my spirit rejoices in God my Saviour,
⁴⁸for he has regarded the low estate of his handmaiden.
For behold, henceforth all generations will call me blessed;
⁴⁹for he who is mighty has done great things for me,
and holy is his name.
⁵⁰And his mercy is on those who fear him
from generation to generation.

Lk 1:38–45
1 Sam 1:11
Ps 113:5–6

Ps 111:9

Ps 103:13, 17

and now does them the greatest honour of all by becoming a Jew (cf. Rom 1:3).

"Our prayer can accompany and imitate this prayer of Mary. Like her, we feel the desire to sing, to acclaim the wonders of God, so that all mankind and all creation may share our joy" (St Josemaría Escrivá, *Christ Is Passing By*, 144).

1:46–47. "The first fruits of the Holy Spirit are peace and joy. And the Blessed Virgin had received within herself all the grace of the Holy Spirit" (St Basil, *In Psalmos homiliae*, on Ps 32). Mary's soul overflows in the words of the *Magnificat*. God's favours cause every humble soul to feel joy and gratitude. In the case of the Blessed Virgin God has bestowed more on her than on any other creature. "Virgin Mother of God, he whom the heavens cannot contain, on becoming man, enclosed himself within your womb" (*Roman Missal*, Antiphon of the common of the Mass for feasts of our Lady). The humble Virgin of Nazareth is going to be the Mother of God; the Creator's omnipotence has never before manifested itself in as complete a way as this.

1:48–49. Mary's expression of humility causes St Bede to exclaim: "It was fitting, then, that just as death entered the world through the pride of our first parents, the entry of Life should be manifested by the humility of Mary" (*In Lucae Evangelium expositio*, in loc.).

"How great is the value of humil-ity!—*Quia respexit humilitatem. ...* It is not of her faith, nor of her charity, nor of her immaculate purity that our Mother speaks in the house of Zachary. Her joyful hymn sings: 'Since he has looked on my humility, all generations will call me blessed'" (St Josemaría Escrivá, *The Way*, 598).

God rewards our Lady's humility by mankind's recognition of her greatness: "All generations will call me blessed." This prophecy is fulfilled every time someone says the Hail Mary, and indeed she is praised on earth continually, without interruption. "From the earliest times the Blessed Virgin is honoured under the title of Mother of God, under whose protection the faithful take refuge together in prayer in all their perils and needs. Accordingly, following the Council of Ephesus, there was a remarkable growth in the cult of the people of God towards Mary, in veneration and love, in invocation and imitation, according to her own prophetic words: 'all generations will call me blessed, for he who is mighty has done great things for me'" (Vatican II, *Lumen gentium*, 66).

1:50. "And his mercy is on these who fear him from generation to generation": "At the very moment of the Incarnation, these words open up a new perspective of salvation history. After the Resurrection of Christ, this perspective is new on both the historical and the eschatological level. From that time on there is a succession of new generations of individuals

37

Ps 33:10; 89:10
2 Sam 22:28
Ps 147:6

Job 12:19

1 Sam 2:5
Ps 34:10; 107:9
Is 41:8

Ps 98:3

Gen 17:7;
18:18; 22:15–18
Mic 7:20

⁵¹He has shown strength with his arm,
    he has scattered the proud in the imagination of their hearts,
⁵²he has put down the mighty from their thrones,
    and exalted those of low degree;
⁵³he has filled the hungry with good things,
    and the rich he has sent empty away.
⁵⁴He has helped his servant Israel,
    in remembrance of his mercy,
⁵⁵as he spoke to our fathers,
    to Abraham and to his posterity for ever."*

in the immense human family, in ever-increasing dimensions; there is also a succession of new generations of the people of God, marked with the sign of the Cross and of the Resurrection and 'sealed' with the sign of the paschal mystery of Christ, the absolute revelation of the mercy that Mary proclaimed on the threshold of her kinswoman's house: 'His mercy is […] from generation to generation' […]. Mary, then, is the one who *has the deepest knowledge of the mystery of God's mercy*. She knows its price, she knows how great it is. In this sense, we call her the *Mother of mercy*: our Lady of mercy, or Mother of divine mercy; in each one of these titles there is a deep theological meaning, for they express the special preparation of her soul, of her whole personality, so that she was able to perceive, through the complex events, first of Israel, then of every individual and of the whole of humanity, that mercy of which 'from generation to generation' people become sharers according to the eternal design of the Most Holy Trinity" (John Paul II, *Dives in misericordia*, 9).

1:51. "The proud": those who want to be regarded as superior to others, whom they look down on. This also refers to those who, in their arrogance, seek to organize society without reference to, or in opposition to, God's law. Even if they

seem to do so successfully, the words of our Lady's canticle will ultimately come true, for God will scatter them as he did those who tried to build the tower of Babel, thinking that they could reach as high as heaven (cf. Gen 11:4).

"When pride takes hold of a soul, it is no surprise to find it bringing along with it a whole string of other vices—greed, self-indulgence, envy, injustice. The proud man is always vainly striving to dethrone God, who is merciful to all his creatures, so as to make room for himself and his ever cruel ways.

"We should beg God not to let us fall into this temptation. Pride is the worst sin of all, and the most ridiculous. ... Pride is unpleasant, even from a human point of view. The person who rates himself better than everyone and everything is constantly studying himself and looking down on other people, who in turn react by ridiculing his foolish vanity" (St Josemaría Escrivá, *Friends of God*, 100).

1:53. This form of divine providence has been experienced countless times over the course of history. For example, God nourished the people of Israel with manna during their forty years in the wilderness (Ex 16:4–35); similarly his angel brought food to Elijah (1 Kings 19:5–8), and to Daniel in the lions' den (Dan 14:31–40); and the widow of Sarepta was given a supply of oil which

⁵⁶And Mary remained with her about three months, and returned to her home.

Birth and circumcision of John the Baptist
⁵⁷Now the time came for Elizabeth to be delivered, and she gave birth to a son. ⁵⁸And her neighbours and kinsfolk heard that the Lord had shown great mercy to her, and they rejoiced with her. ⁵⁹And on the eighth day they came to circumcise the child; and they would have named him Zechariah after his father, ⁶⁰but his mother said, "Not so; he shall be called John." ⁶¹And they said to

Gen 17:12
Lev 12:3

---

miraculously never ran out (1 Kings 17:8ff). So, too, the Blessed Virgin's yearning for holiness was fulfilled by the incarnation of the Word.

God nourished the chosen people with his Law and the preaching of his prophets, but the rest of mankind was left hungry for his word, a hunger now satisfied by the Incarnation. This gift of God will be accepted by the humble; the self-sufficient, having no desire for the good things of God, will not partake of them (cf. St Basil, *In Psalmos homiliae*, on Ps 33).

1:54. God led the people of Israel as he would a child whom he loved tenderly: "the Lord your God bore you, as a man bears his son, in all the way that you went" (Deut 1:31). He did so many times, using Moses, Joshua, Samuel, David etc., and now he gives them a definitive leader by sending the Messiah—moved by his great mercy which takes pity on the wretchedness of Israel and of all mankind.

1:55. God promised the patriarchs of old that he would have mercy on mankind. This promise he made to Adam (Gen 3:15), Abraham (Gen 22:18), David (2 Sam 7:12), etc. From all eternity God had planned and decreed that the Word should become incarnate for the salvation of all mankind. As Christ himself put it,

"God so loved the world that he gave his only Son, that whoever believes in him should not perish but have eternal life" (Jn 3:16).

1:59. Circumcision was a rite established by God under the Old Covenant to mark out those who belonged to his chosen people: he commanded Abraham to institute circumcision as a sign of the Covenant he had made with him and all his descendants (cf. Gen 17:10–14), prescribing that it should be done on the eighth day after birth. The rite was performed either at home or in the synagogue, and, in addition to the actual circumcision, the ceremony included prayers and the naming of the child.

With the institution of Christian Baptism the commandment to circumcise ceased to apply. At the Council of Jerusalem (cf. Acts 15:1ff), the apostles definitively declared that those entering the Church had no need to be circumcised.

St Paul's explicit teaching on the irrelevance of circumcision in the context of the New Alliance established by Christ is to be found in Galatians 5:2ff; 6:12ff; and Colossians 2:11ff.

1:60–63. By naming the child John, Zechariah complies with the instructions God sent him through the angel (cf. Lk 1:13).

her, "None of your kindred is called by this name." ⁶²And they made signs to his father, inquiring what he would have him called. ⁶³And he asked for a writing tablet, and wrote, "His name is John." And they all marvelled. ⁶⁴And immediately his mouth was opened and his tongue loosed, and he spoke, blessing God. ⁶⁵And fear came on all their neighbours. And all these things were talked about through all the hill country of Judea; ⁶⁶and all who heard them laid them up in their hearts, saying, "What then will this child be?" For the hand of the Lord was with him.

Canticle of Zechariah

⁶⁷And his father Zechariah was filled with the Holy Spirit, and prophesied, saying,

Ps 41:13; 72:18;
106:48; 111:9

⁶⁸"Blessed be the Lord God of Israel,
for he has visited and redeemed his people,

1 Sam 2:10
Ps 18:2; 132:17

⁶⁹and has raised up a horn of salvation *for us
in the house of his servant David,

1:64. This miraculous event fulfils the prophecy the angel Gabriel made to Zechariah when he announced the conception and birth of the Baptist (Lk 1:19–20). St Ambrose observes: "With good reason was his tongue loosed, because faith untied what had been tied by disbelief" (*Expositio Evangelii sec. Lucam*, in loc.).

Zechariah's is a case similar to that of St Thomas, who was reluctant to believe in the resurrection of our Lord, and who believed only when Jesus gave him clear proof (cf. Jn 20:24–29). For these two men God worked a miracle and won their belief; but normally he requires us to have faith and to obey him without his working any new miracles. This was why he upbraided Zechariah and punished him, and why he reproached Thomas: "Have you believed because you have seen me? Blessed are those who have not seen and yet believe" (Jn 20:29).

1:67. Zechariah, who was a righteous man (cf. v. 6), received the special grace of prophecy when his son was born—a

gift which led him to pronounce his canticle, called the *Benedictus*, a prayer so full of faith, reverence and piety that the Church has laid it down to be said daily in the Liturgy of the Hours. Prophecy has not only to do with foretelling future events; it also means being moved by the Holy Spirit to praise God. Both aspects of prophecy are to be found in the *Benedictus*.

1:68–79. Two parts can be discerned in the *Benedictus*: in the first (vv. 68–75) Zechariah thanks God for sending the Messiah, the Saviour, as he promised the patriarchs and prophets of Israel. In the second (vv. 76–79) he prophesies that his son will have the mission of being herald of the Most High and precursor of the Messiah, proclaiming God's mercy which reveals itself in the coming of Christ.

1:72–75. Again and again God promised the Old Testament patriarchs that he would take special care of Israel, giving them a land which they would enjoy undisturbed

40

⁷⁰as he spoke by the mouth of his holy prophets from of old, Lk 24:25, 44
⁷¹that we should be saved from our enemies, Ps 106:10
and from the hand of all who hate us;
⁷²to perform the mercy promised to our fathers, Ps 105:8;
 106:45
and to remember his holy covenant, Gen 17:7
⁷³the oath which he swore to our father Abraham, Lev 26:42
⁷⁴to grant us that we, being delivered from the hand of our Lk 1:55
enemies,
might serve him without fear,
⁷⁵in holiness and righteousness before him all the days of our
life.
⁷⁶And you, child, will be called the prophet of the Most High; Mal 3:1
for you will go before the Lord to prepare his ways, Mt 3:3; 11:10
⁷⁷to give knowledge of salvation to his people Jer 31:34
in the forgiveness of their sins, Num 24:17
⁷⁸through the tender mercy of our God, Is 60:1–2
 Jer 23:5–6
when the day shall dawn upon^f us from on high Zech 3:8

---

and many descendants in whom all the peoples of the earth would be blessed. This promise he ratified by means of a covenant or alliance, of the kind commonly made between kings and their vassals in the Near East. God, as Lord, would protect the patriarchs and their descendants, and these would prove their attachment to him by offering him certain sacrifices and by doing him service. See, for example, Genesis 12:13; 17:1–8; 22:16–18 (God's promise, covenant and pledge to Abraham); and Genesis 35:11–12 (where he repeats these promises to Jacob). Zechariah realizes that the events resulting from the birth of John his son, the Precursor of the Messiah, constitute complete fulfilment of these divine purposes.

1:78–79. The "dawning", the "dayspring", is the Messiah, Jesus Christ, coming down from heaven to shed his light upon us: "the sun of righteousness shall rise, with healing on its wings" (Mal 4:2).

Already in the Old Testament we were told about the glory of the Lord, the reflection of his presence—something intimately connected with light. For example, when Moses returned to the encampment after talking with God, his face so shone that the Israelites "were afraid to come near him" (Ex 34:30). St John is making the same reference when he says that "God is light and in him there is no darkness" (1 Jn 1:5) and that there will be no light in heaven "for the glory of God is its light" (cf. Rev 21:23; 22:5).

The angels (cf. Rev 1:11) and the saints (cf. Wis 3:7; Dan 2:3) partake of this divine splendour; our Lady does so in a special way. As a symbol of the Church she is revealed to us in the book of Revelation as "clothed with the sun, with the moon under her feet, and on her head a crown of twelve stars" (12:1).

Even when we live in this world, this divine light reaches us through Jesus Christ who, because he is God, is "the true light that enlightens every man" (Jn

---

f. Or *whereby the dayspring will visit.* Other ancient authorities read *since the dayspring has visited*

Is 9:2; 42:7;
58:8
Mt 4:16

⁷⁹to give light to those who sit in darkness and in the shadow of
   death,
to guide our feet into the way of peace."

Mt 3:1

⁸⁰And the child grew and became strong in spirit, and he was in
the wilderness till the day of his manifestation to Israel.

The birth of Jesus

2 ¹In those days a decree went out from Caesar Augustus that
all the world should be enrolled. ²This was the first enrolment,

---

1:9), as Christ himself tells us: "I am the light of the world; he who follows me will not walk in darkness" (Jn 8:12).

Christians share in this light of God; Jesus tells us: "You are the light of the world" (Mt 5:14). Therefore, we must live as children of the light (cf. Lk 16:8), whose fruit takes the form of "all that is good and right and true" (Eph 5:9); our lives should shine out, thereby helping people to know God and give him glory (cf. Mt 5:16).

1:80. "Wilderness": this must surely refer to the "Judean wilderness" which stretches from the northwestern shores of the Dead Sea to the hill country of Judea. It is not a sand desert but rather a barren steppe with bushes and basic vegetation which suit bees and grasshoppers or wild locusts. It contains many caves which can provide shelter.

2:1. Caesar Augustus was Roman emperor at this time, reigning from 30 BC to AD 14. He is known to have commissioned various censuses, one of which could well be that referred to by the evangelist. Since Rome normally respected local usages, censuses were carried out in line with Jewish custom whereby every householder went to his place of origin to be listed in the census.

2:6–7. The Messiah is born, the Son of God and our Saviour. "He made himself a child [...] to enable you to become a perfect man; he was wrapped in swaddling clothes to free you from the bonds of death [...]. He came down on earth to enable you to rise up to heaven; he had no place in the inn so that you might have many mansions in heaven. He, being rich, became poor for our sake—St Paul says (2 Cor 8:9)—so as to enrich us with his poverty [...]. The tears of this crying child purify men, they wash away my sins" (St Ambrose, *Expositio Evangelii sec. Lucam*, in loc.).

The new-born Child does not yet speak, but he is the eternal Word of the Father. Even from the manger in Bethlehem he teaches us. "We must learn the lessons which Jesus teaches us, even when he is just a newly born child, from the very moment he opens his eyes on this blessed land of men" (St Josemaría Escrivá, *Christ Is Passing By*, 14). The main lesson he gives us concerns humility: "God humbled himself to allow us to get near him, so that we could give our love in exchange for his, so that our freedom might bow, not only at the sight of his power, but also before the wonder of his humility.

"The greatness of this Child who is God! His Father is the God who has made heaven and earth and there he is, in a manger, 'because there was no room at the inn' (Lk 2:7); there was nowhere else for the Lord of all creation" (*Christ Is Passing By*, 18).

when Quirinius was governor of Syria. ³And all went to be enrolled, each to his own city. ⁴And Joseph also went up from Galilee, from the city of Nazareth, to Judea, to the city of David, which is called Bethlehem, because he was of the house and lineage of David, ⁵to be enrolled with Mary, his betrothed, who was with child. ⁶And while they were there, the time came for her to be delivered. ⁷And she gave birth to her first-born* son and wrapped him in swaddling cloths, and laid him in a manger, because there was no place for them in the inn.

Lk 1:27

Mt 1:25

Our hearts should provide Jesus with a place where he can be born spiritually; that is, we should be born to a new life, becoming a new creature (cf. Rom 6:4), keeping that holiness and purity of soul which we were given in Baptism and which is like being born again. We contemplate the birth of our Saviour when we pray the third mystery of the Holy Rosary.

2:7. "First-born son": it is usual for Sacred Scripture to refer to the first male child as "the first-born" whether or not there were other brothers (cf., for example, Ex 13:2; 13:13; Num 15:8; Heb 1:6). The same practice is to be found in ordinary speech; take, for example, this inscription dating from approximately the same time as Christ was born, which was found near Tell-el-Jedvieh (in Egypt) in 1922, which states that a woman named Arsinoe died when giving birth to "her first-born son". Otherwise, as St Jerome explains in his letter *Adversus Helvidium*, 10, "if only he were first-born who was followed by other brothers, he would not deserve the rights of the first-born, which the Law lays down, until the other had been born"—which would be absurd, since the Law ordains that those first-born should be "redeemed" within a month of their birth (cf. Num 18:16).

However, Jesus Christ is first-born in a much deeper sense independent of natural or biological considerations—which

St Bede describes in these words, summarizing a long tradition of the Fathers of the Church: "Truly the Son of God, who was made manifest in the flesh, belongs to a more exalted order not only because he is the Only-begotten of the Father by virtue of the excellence of his divinity; he is also first-born of all creatures by virtue of his fraternity with men: concerning this [his primogeniture] it is said: 'For those whom he foreknew he also predestined to be conformed to the image of his Son, in order that he might be the first-born among many brethren' (Rom 8:29). And concerning the former [his being the Only-begotten] it is said 'we have beheld his glory, glory as of the only Son from the Father' (Jn 1:14). Thus, he is only-begotten by the substance of the Godhead, and first-born through his assumption of humanity; first-born by grace, only-begotten by nature. This is why he is called brother and Lord: brother, because he is the first-born; Lord, because he is the Only-begotten" (*In Lucae Evangelium expositio*, in loc.).

Christian Tradition teaches, as a truth of faith, that Mary remained a virgin after Christ's birth, which is perfectly in keeping with Christ's status as her first-born. See, for example, these words of the Lateran Council of 649: "If anyone does not profess according to the holy Fathers that in the proper and true sense the holy, ever-Virgin, immaculate Mary is the Mother of God, since in this last age not

The adoration of the shepherds

[8]And in that region there were shepherds out in the field, keeping watch over their flock by night. [9]And an angel of the Lord appeared to them, and the glory of the Lord shone around them, and they were filled with fear. [10]And the angel said to them, "Be not afraid; for behold, I bring you good news of a great joy which will come to all the people; [11]for to you is born this day in the city of David a Saviour, who is Christ the Lord. [12]And this will be a

---

with human seed but of the Holy Spirit she properly and truly conceived the divine Word, who was born of God the Father before all ages, and gave him birth without any detriment to her virginity, which remained inviolate even after his birth: let such a one be condemned" (can. 3).

2:8–20. At his birth Christ's divinity and his humanity are perfectly manifested: we see his weakness—the form of a servant (Phil 2:7)—and his divine power. Christian faith involves confessing that Jesus Christ is true God and true man.

The salvation which Christ brought us is offered to everyone, without distinction: "Here there cannot be Greek and Jew, circumcised and uncircumcised, barbarian, Scythian, slave, free man, but Christ is all, and in all" (Col 3:11). That is why, even at his birth, he chose to manifest himself to different kinds of people—the shepherds, the Magi and Simeon and Anna. As St Augustine comments: "The shepherds were Israelites; the Magi, Gentiles. The first lived nearby; the latter, far away. Yet both came to the cornerstone, Christ" (*Sermo de Navitate Domini*, 202).

2:8–9. These shepherds may have been from the neighbourhood of Bethlehem or even have come from further afield in search of pasture for their flocks. It was these simple and humble people who were the first to hear the good news of

Christ's birth. God has a preference for the humble (cf. Prov 3:34); he hides from those who consider themselves wise and understanding and reveals himself to "babes" (cf. Mt 11:25).

2:10–14. The angel announces that the new-born Child is the Saviour, Christ the Lord. He is the *Saviour* because he has come to save us from our sins (cf. Mt 1:21). He is *the Christ*, that is, the Messiah so often promised in the Old Testament, and now born among us in fulfilment of that ancient hope. He is *the Lord*: this shows Christ's divinity, for this is the name God chose to be known by to his people in the Old Testament, and it is the way Christians usually refer to and address Jesus and the way the Church always confesses her faith: "We believe […] in one Lord, Jesus Christ, the only Son of God."

When the angel tells them that the Child has been born in the city of David, he reminds them that this was where the Messiah Redeemer was supposed to be born (cf. Mic 5:2; Mt 2:6), who would be a descendant of David (cf. Ps 110:1–2; Mt 22:42–46).

Christ is the Lord not only of men but also of angels, which is why the angels rejoice at his birth and render him the tribute of adoration: "Glory to God in the highest." And, since men are called to share, like them, in the happiness of heaven, the angels add: "And on earth peace among men with whom he is

sign for you: you will find a babe wrapped in swaddling cloths and lying in a manger." [13]And suddenly there was with the angel a multitude of the heavenly host praising God and saying,
[14]"Glory to God in the highest,
and on earth peace among men with whom he is pleased!"[g]

Lk 19:38
Is 57:19
Ezek 2:14–17

[15]When the angels went away from them into heaven, the shepherds said to one another, "Let us go over to Bethlehem and see this thing that has happened, which the Lord has made known

---

pleased." "They praise the Lord," St Gregory the Great comments, "putting the notes of their hymn in harmony with our redemption; they see us as already sharing in their own happy destiny and rejoice at this" (*Moralia*, 28, 7).

St Thomas explains why the birth of Christ was revealed through angels: "What is in itself hidden needs to be manifested, but not what is in itself manifest. The flesh of him who was born was manifest, but his Godhead was hidden, and therefore it was fitting that this birth should be made known by angels, who are ministers of God. This was why a certain brightness accompanied the angelic apparition, to indicate that he who was just born 'reflects the glory of the Father' (Heb 1:3)" (*Summa theologiae*, 3, 36, 5 ad 1).

The angel also tells the shepherds that Christ is a man: "You will find a babe wrapped in swaddling cloths and lying in a manger" (v. 12)—as foretold in the Old Testament: "To us a child is born, to us a son is given; and the government will be upon his shoulder" (Is 9:6).

2:14. This text can be translated in two ways, which are compatible with each other. One is the version chosen by the RSV; the other, as an RSV note points out: "other ancient authorities read *peace, good will among men*"; a variant is the translation used in the Liturgy: "Peace on

earth to men who are God's friends." Essentially what the text says is that the angels ask for peace and reconciliation with God, which is not something which results from men's merits but rather comes from God's deigning to have mercy on them. The two translations are complementary, for when men respond to God's grace they are fulfilling God's good will, God's love for them: "*Iesus Christus, Deus homo*: Jesus Christ, God-man. This is one of 'the mighty works of God' (Acts 2:11), which we should reflect upon and thank him for. He has come to bring 'peace on earth to men of good will' (Lk 2:14), to all men who want to unite their wills to the holy will of God" (St Josemaría Escrivá, *Christ Is Passing By*, 13).

2:15–18. The birth of the Saviour Messiah is the key event in the history of mankind, but God wanted it to take place so quietly that the world went about its business as if nothing had happened. The only people he tells about it are a few shepherds. It was also to a shepherd, Abraham, that God gave his promise to save mankind.

The shepherds make their way to Bethlehem propelled by the sign they have received. And when they verify it they tell what they heard from the angel and about seeing the heavenly host. They are the first witnesses of the birth of the

g. Other ancient authorities read *peace, good will among men*

45

to us." ¹⁶And they went with haste, and found Mary and Joseph, and the babe lying in a manger. ¹⁷And when they saw it they made known the saying which had been told them concerning this child; ¹⁸and all who heard it wondered at what the shepherds told them. ¹⁹But Mary kept all these things, pondering them in her heart. ²⁰And the shepherds returned, glorifying and praising God for all they had heard and seen, as it had been told them.

Lk 2:51
Dan 7:28

Messiah. "The shepherds were not content with believing in the happy event which the angel proclaimed to them and which, full of wonder, they saw for a fact; they manifested their joy not only to Mary and Joseph but to everyone and, what is more, they tried to engrave it on their memory. 'And all who heard it wondered at what the shepherds told them.' And why would they not have wondered, seeing on earth him who is in heaven, and earth and heaven reconciled; seeing that ineffable Child who joined what was heavenly—divinity—and what was earthly—humanity—creating a wonderful covenant through this union. Not only were they in awe at the mystery of the Incarnation, but also at the great testimony borne by the shepherds, who could not have invented something they had not heard and who publish the truth with a simple eloquence" (Photius, *Ad Amphilochium*, 155).

2:16. The shepherds hasten because they are full of joy and eager to see the Saviour. St Ambrose comments: "No one seeks Christ half-heartedly" (*Expositio Evangelii sec. Lucam*, in loc.). Earlier on, the evangelist observed that our Lady, after the Annunciation, "went in haste" to see St Elizabeth (Lk 1:39). A soul who has given God entry rejoices that God has visited him and his life acquires new energy.

2:19. In very few words this verse tells us a great deal about our Lady. We see the serenity with which she contemplates the wonderful things that are coming true with the birth of her divine Son. She studies them, ponders them and stores them in the silence of her heart. She is a true teacher of prayer. If we imitate her, if we guard and ponder in our hearts what Jesus says to us and what he does in us, we are well on the way to Christian holiness and we shall never lack his doctrine and his grace. Also, by meditating in this way on the teaching Jesus has given us, we shall obtain a deeper understanding of the mystery of Christ, which is how "the Tradition that comes from the apostles makes progress in the Church, with the help of the Holy Spirit. There is a growth in insight into the realities and words that are being passed on. This comes about in various ways. It comes through the contemplation and study of believers who ponder these things in their hearts. It comes from the intimate sense of spiritual realities which they experience. And it comes from the preaching of those who have received, along with their right of succession in the episcopate, the sure charism of truth" (Vatican II, *Dei Verbum*, 8).

2:21. On the meaning and rite of circumcision, see the note on Lk 1:59. "Jesus" means "Yahweh saves" or "Yahweh is salvation," that is, Saviour. This name was given the Child not as the result of any human decision but in keeping with the commandment of God which the angel communicated to the Blessed

The circumcision of Jesus

²¹And at the end of eight days, when he was circumcised, he was
called Jesus, the name given by the angel before he was conceived
in the womb.

Lk 1:59
Lev 12:3ff
Gal 4:4

The purification of Mary and the presentation of Jesus in the temple

²²And when the time came for their purification according to the
law of Moses, they brought him up to Jerusalem to present him to
the Lord ²³(as it is written in the law of the Lord, "Every male that

Lev 12:2–8

Ex 13:2; 12:15

Virgin and to St Joseph (cf. Lk 1:31; Mt 1:21).

The Son of God became incarnate in order to redeem and save all men; so it is very fitting that he be called Jesus, Saviour. We confess this in the Creed: "For us men and for our salvation he came down from heaven." "There were indeed many who were called by this name [...]. But how much more appropriate it is to call by this name our Saviour, who brought light, liberty and salvation, not to one people only, but to all men, of all ages—to men oppressed, not by famine, or Egyptian or Babylonian bondage, but sitting in the shadow of death and fettered by the galling chains of sin and of the devil" (St Pius V, *Catechism*, 1, 36).

2:22–24. The Holy Family goes up to Jerusalem to fulfil the prescriptions of the Law of Moses—the purification of the mother and the presentation and then redemption or buying back of the first-born. According to Leviticus 12:2–8, a woman who bore a child was unclean. The period of legal impurity ended, in the case of a mother of a male child, after forty days, with a rite of purification. Mary most holy, ever-virgin, was exempt from these precepts of the Law, because she conceived without intercourse, nor did Christ's birth undo the virginal integrity of his Mother. However, she

chose to submit herself to the Law, although she was under no obligation to do so.

"Through this example, foolish child, won't you learn to fulfil the holy Law of God, regardless of any personal sacrifice?

"Purification! You and I certainly do need purification. Atonement and, more than atonement, Love. Love as a searing iron to cauterize our soul's uncleanness, and as a fire to kindle with divine flames the wretchedness of our hearts" (St Josemaría Escrivá, *Holy Rosary*, fourth joyful mystery).

Also, in Exodus 13:2, 12–13 it is indicated that every first-born male belongs to God and must be set apart for the Lord, that is, dedicated to the service of God. However, once divine worship was reserved to the tribe of Levi, first-born who did not belong to that tribe were not dedicated to God's service, and to show that they continued to be God's special property, a rite of redemption was performed.

The Law also laid down that the Israelites should offer in sacrifice some lesser victim—for example, a lamb or, if they were poor, a pair of doves or two pigeons. Our Lord, who "though he was rich, yet for your sake he became poor, so that by his poverty you might become rich" (2 Cor 8:9), chose to have a poor man's offering made on his behalf.

Lev 12:8; 5:11
Num 6:9–10

opens the womb shall be called holy to the Lord") [24]and to offer a sacrifice according to what is said in the law of the Lord, "a pair of turtledoves, or two young pigeons."

Simeon's prophecy

Is 40:1; 49:13

[25]Now there was a man in Jerusalem, whose name was Simeon, and this man was righteous and devout, looking for the consolation of Israel, and the Holy Spirit was upon him. [26]And it had been revealed to him by the Holy Spirit that he should not see death before he had seen the Lord's Christ. [27]And inspired by the Spirit[h] he came into the temple; and when the parents brought in the child Jesus, to do for him according to the custom of the law, [28]he took him up in his arms and blessed God and said,

[29]"Lord, now lettest thou thy servant depart in peace,
  according to thy word;

Is 40:5; 52:10

[30]for mine eyes have seen thy salvation
  [31]which thou hast prepared in the presence of all peoples,

Is 42:6; 46:13;
49:6

[32]a light for revelation to the Gentiles,

Acts 13:47

  and for glory to thy people Israel."

2:25–32. Simeon, who is described as a righteous and devout man, obedient to God's will, addresses himself to our Lord as a vassal or loyal servant who, having kept watch all his life in expectation of the coming of his Lord, sees that this moment has "now" come, the moment that explains his whole life. When he takes the Child in his arms, he learns, not through any reasoning process but through a special grace from God, that this Child is the promised Messiah, the Consolation of Israel, the Light of the nations.

Simeon's canticle (vv. 29–32) is also a prophecy. It consists of two stanzas: the first (vv. 29–30) is an act of thanksgiving to God, filled with profound joy for having seen the Messiah. The second (vv. 31–32) is more obviously prophetic and extols the divine blessings which the Messiah is bringing to Israel and to all men. The canticle highlights the fact that Christ brings redemption to all men without exception—something foretold in

many Old Testament prophecies (cf. Gen 22:18; Is 2:6; 42:6; 60:3; Ps 28:2).

It is easy to realize how extremely happy Simeon was—given that many patriarchs, prophets and kings of Israel had yearned to see the Messiah, yet did not see him, whereas he now held him in his arms (cf. Lk 10:24; 1 Pet 1:10).

2:33. The Blessed Virgin and St Joseph marvelled not because they did not know who Christ was; they were in awe at the way God was revealing him. Once again they teach us to contemplate the mysteries involved in the birth of Christ.

2:34–35. After Simeon blesses them, the Holy Spirit moves him to further prophecy about the Child's future and his Mother's. His words become clearer in the light of our Lord's life and death.

Jesus came to bring salvation to all men, yet he will be a sign of contradiction because some people will obstinately

h. Or *in the Spirit*

³³And his father and his mother marvelled at what was said about him; ³⁴and Simeon blessed them and said to Mary his mother, "Behold, this child is set for the fall* and rising of many in Israel, and for a sign that is spoken against ³⁵(and a sword will pierce through your own soul also), that thoughts out of many hearts may be revealed."

Is 8:14
Mt 21:42
1 Pet 2:8
Jn 9:39
Acts 28:22

Jn 19:25

Anna the prophetess

³⁶And there was a prophetess Anna, the daughter of Phanuel, of the tribe of Asher; she was of a great age, having lived with her husband seven years from her virginity, ³⁷and as a widow till she was eighty-four. She did not depart from the temple, worshipping with fasting and prayer night and day. ³⁸And coming up at that very hour she gave thanks to God, and spoke of him to all who were looking for the redemption of Jerusalem.

1 Tim 5:5

Is 52:9

The childhood of Jesus

³⁹And when they had performed everything according to the law of the Lord, they returned to Galilee, to their own city, Nazareth.

---

reject him—and for this reason he will be their ruin. But for those who accept him with faith Jesus will be their salvation, freeing them from sin in this life and raising them up to eternal life.

The words Simeon addresses to Mary announce that she will be intimately linked with her Son's redemptive work. The sword indicates that Mary will have a share in her Son's sufferings; hers will be an unspeakable pain which pierces her soul. Our Lord suffered on the cross for our sins, and it is those sins which forge the sword of Mary's pain. Therefore, we have a duty to atone not only to God but also to his Mother, who is our Mother too.

The last words of the prophecy, "that thoughts out of many hearts may be revealed", link up with v. 34: uprightness or perversity will be demonstrated by whether one accepts or rejects Christ.

2:36–38. Anna's testimony is very similar to Simeon's; like him, she too has been awaiting the coming of the Messiah

her whole life long, in faithful service of God, and she too is rewarded with the joy of seeing him. She spoke of him, that is, of the Child—praising God in her prayer and exhorting others to believe that this Child is the Messiah.

Thus, the birth of Christ was revealed by three kinds of witnesses in three different ways—first, by the shepherds, after the angel's announcement; second, by the Magi, who were guided by a star; third, by Simeon and Anna, who were inspired by the Holy Spirit.

All who, like Simeon and Anna, persevere in piety and in the service of God, no matter how insignificant their lives seem in men's eyes, become instruments the Holy Spirit uses to make Christ known to others. In his plan of redemption God avails of these simple souls to do much good to all mankind.

2:39. Before their return to Nazareth, St Matthew tells us (2:13–23), the Holy Family fled to Egypt where they stayed for some time.

Lk 1:80; 2:52   ⁴⁰And the child grew and became strong, filled with wisdom; and the favour of God was upon him.

The finding in the temple

Ex 12:1ff;
23:14–17   ⁴¹Now his parents went to Jerusalem every year at the feast of the Passover. ⁴²And when he was twelve years old, they went up according to custom; ⁴³and when the feast was ended, as they were returning, the boy Jesus stayed behind in Jerusalem. His parents did not know it, ⁴⁴but supposing him to be in the company they went a day's journey, and they sought him among their kinsfolk and acquaintances; ⁴⁵and when they did not find him, they returned to Jerusalem, seeking him. ⁴⁶After three days they found

---

2:40. "Our Lord Jesus Christ as a child, that is, as one clothed in the fragility of human nature, had to grow and become stronger but as the eternal Word of God he had no need to become stronger or to grow. Hence he is rightly described as full of wisdom and grace" (St Bede, *In Lucae Evangelium expositio*, in loc.).

2:41. Only St Luke (2:41–50) reports the event of the Child Jesus being lost and then found in the temple, which we contemplate in the fifth joyful mystery of the Rosary.

Only males aged twelve and upwards were required to make this journey. Nazareth is about 100 km (60 miles) from Jerusalem as the crow flies, but the hilly nature of the country would have made it a trip of 140 km.

2:43–44. On pilgrimages to Jerusalem, the Jews used to go in two groups—one of men, the other of women. Children could go with either group. This explains how they could go a day's journey before they discovered the Child was missing when the families regrouped to camp.

"Mary is crying. In vain you and I have run from group to group, from caravan to caravan. No one has seen him. Joseph, after fruitless attempts to keep from crying, cries too. ... And you. ... And I.

"Being a common little fellow, I cry my eyes out and wail to heaven and earth ..., to make up for the times when I lost him through my own fault and did not cry" (St Josemaría Escrivá, *Holy Rosary*, fifth joyful mystery).

2:45. The concern which Mary and Joseph show in looking for the Child should encourage us always to seek out Jesus, particularly if we lose him through sin.

"Jesus, may I never lose you again. ... Now you and I are united in misfortune and grief, as we were united in sin. And from the depths of our being come sighs of heartfelt sorrow and burning phrases which the pen cannot and should not record" (*Holy Rosary*, fifth joyful mystery).

2:46–47. The Child Jesus must have been in the courtyard of the temple, which was where the teachers usually taught. Listeners used to sit at their feet, now and again asking questions and responding to them. This was what Jesus did, but his questions and answers attracted the teachers' attention, he was so wise and well-informed.

2:48. Ever since the Annunciation our Lady had known that the Child Jesus was God. This faith was the basis of her gen-

him in the temple, sitting among the teachers, listening to them
and asking them questions; [47]and all who heard him were amazed
at his understanding and his answers. [48]And when they saw him
they were astonished; and his mother said to him, "Son, why have
you treated us so? Behold, your father and I have been looking for
you anxiously." [49]And he said to them, "How is it that you sought
me? Did you not know that I must be in my Father's house?"*
[50]And they did not understand the saying which he spoke to them.

Mt 7:28
Jn 7:15

Jn 2:16

The hidden life of Jesus at Nazareth
[51]And he went down with them and came to Nazareth, and was
obedient to them; and his mother kept all these things in her heart.

Lk 2:19

erous fidelity throughout her life—but there was no reason why it should include detailed knowledge of all the sacrifices God would ask of her, nor of how Christ would go about his mission of redemption: that was something she would discover as time went by, contemplating her Son's life.

2:49. Christ's reply is a form of explanation. His words—his first words to be recorded in the Gospel—clearly show his divine Sonship; and they also show his determination to fulfil the will of his Eternal Father. "He does not upbraid them—Mary and Joseph—for searching for their son, but he raises the eyes of their souls to appreciate what he owes him whose Eternal Son he is" (St Bede, *In Lucae Evangelium expositio*, in loc.). Jesus teaches us that over and above any human authority, even that of our parents, there is the primary duty to do the will of God. "And, once we are consoled by the joy of finding Jesus—three days he was gone!—debating with the teachers of Israel (Lk 2:46), you and I shall be left deeply impressed by the duty to leave our home and family to serve our heavenly Father" (St Josemaría Escrivá, *Holy Rosary*, fifth joyful mystery). See the note on Mt 10:34–37.

2:50. We must remember that Jesus knew in detail the whole course his earthly life would take from his conception onwards (cf. the note on Lk 2:52). This is shown by what he says in reply to his parents. Mary and Joseph realized that his reply contained a deeper meaning which they did not grasp. They grew to understand it as the life of their Child unfolded. Mary's and Joseph's faith and their reverence towards the Child led them not to ask any further questions but to reflect on Jesus' words and behaviour in this instance, as they had done on other occasions.

2:51. The Gospel sums up Jesus' life in Nazareth in just three words: *erat subditus illis*, he was obedient to them. "He obeys Joseph and Mary. God has come to the world to obey, and to obey creatures. Admittedly they two are very perfect creatures—Holy Mary, our mother, greater than whom God alone; and that most chaste man Joseph. But they are only creatures, and yet Jesus, who is God, obeyed them. We have to love God so as to love his will and desire to respond to his calls. They come to us through the duties of our ordinary life—duties of state, profession, work, family, social life, our own and other people's difficulties, friendship, eagerness to do

Prov 3:4 52And Jesus increased in wisdom and in stature,[i] and in favour with God and man.

2. PRELUDE TO THE PUBLIC MINISTRY OF JESUS

John the Baptist preaching in the wilderness

3 1In the fifteenth year of the reign of Tiberius Caesar, Pontius Pilate being governor of Judea, and Herod being tetrarch of

what is right and just" (St Josemaría Escrivá, *Christ Is Passing By*, 17).

Jesus lived like any other inhabitant of Nazareth, working at the same trade as St Joseph and earning his living by the sweat of his brow. "His hidden years are not without significance, nor were they simply a preparation for the years which were to come after—those of his public life. Since 1928 I have understood clearly that God wants our Lord's whole life to be an example for Christians. I saw this with special reference to his hidden life, the years he spent working side by side with ordinary men. Our Lord wants many people to ratify their vocation during years of quiet, unspectacular living. Obeying God's will always means leaving our selfishness behind, but there is no reason why it should entail cutting ourselves off from the normal life of ordinary people who share the same status, work and social position with us.

"I dream—and the dream has come true—of multitudes of God's children, sanctifying themselves as ordinary citizens, sharing the ambitions and endeavours of their colleagues and friends. I want to shout to them about this divine truth: If you are there in the middle of ordinary life, it doesn't mean Christ has forgotten about you or hasn't called you. He has invited you to stay among the activities and concerns of the world. He

wants you to know that your human vocation, your profession, your talents, are not omitted from his divine plans. He has sanctified them and made them a most acceptable offering to his Father" (ibid., 20).

2:52. As far as his human nature was concerned Jesus matured like anyone else. His growth in wisdom should be seen as referring to experiential knowledge—knowledge acquired by his mind from sense experience and general experience of life. It can also be taken as referring to the external expression of his wisdom; in this sense everything he did was done perfectly, in keeping with whatever age he was at the time.

As man Jesus had three kinds of knowledge: 1. *The knowledge of the blessed* (vision of the divine essence) by virtue of the hypostatic union (the union of his human nature with his divine nature in the one person of the Word). This knowledge did not require any increase. 2. *Infused knowledge*, which perfected his intellect and which meant that he knew everything, even hidden things; thus he was able to read men's hearts. Here again his knowledge was complete; it could not grow. 3. *Acquired knowledge*: he acquired new knowledge through sense experience and reflection; logically, this knowledge increased as time went by.

i. Or *years*

52

Galilee, and his brother Philip tetrarch of the region of Ituraea and Trachonitis, and Lysanias tetrarch of Abilene, ²in the high-priesthood of Annas and Caiaphas,* the word of God came to John the son of Zechariah in the wilderness; ³and he went into all the region about the Jordan, preaching a baptism of repentance for the

Mt 3:1–12
Mk 1:2–8

As far as grace, in the strict sense of the word, was concerned, Jesus could not grow. From the first instant of his conception he possessed grace in all its fulness because he was true God by virtue of the hypostatic union. As St Thomas explains: "The end of grace is the union of the rational creature with God. But there can neither be nor be conceived a greater union of the rational creature with God than that which is in the person of Christ [...]. Hence it is clear that the grace of Christ cannot be increased on the part of grace. But neither can it be increased on the part of Christ, since Christ as man was a true and full 'comprehensor' from the first instant of his conception. Hence there could have been no increase of grace in him" (*Summa theologiae*, 3, 7, 12).

However, we can speak of his growing in grace in the sense of the *effects* of grace. In the last analysis, this matter is one of the mysteries of our faith, which our minds cannot fully grasp. How small God would be if we were able fully to fathom this mystery! That Christ should conceal his infinite power and wisdom by becoming a child teaches our pride a great lesson.

3:1. The Gospel identifies very precisely the time and place of the public appearance of John the Baptist, the Precursor of Christ. *Tiberius Caesar* was the second emperor of Rome, and the fifteenth year of his reign corresponds to AD 27 or 29, depending on which of the two possible calculations is correct.

Pontius Pilate was governor or *prae-*

fectus of Judea from AD 26 to 36. His jurisdiction also extended to Samaria and Idumea.

The *Herod* referred to here is Herod Antipas, a son of Herod the Great, who succeeded to part of his father's territory with the title of tetrarch, not king. "Tetrarch" indicated that he exercised his power in subordination to Roman authority. It was Herod Antipas, who died in AD 39, who had St John the Baptist beheaded. On the identity of the four Herods in the New Testament, see the note on Mt 2:1.

Philip, another son of Herod the Great and stepbrother of Herod Antipas, was tetrarch in the territory mentioned here up to AD 34. He married Herodias, who is spoken about in Mark 6:17–19.

3:2. The high priest at the time was *Caiaphas*, who held the position from AD 18 to 36. Annas, his father-in-law, was still so influential that he was considered as the *de facto* head of Jewish religious and political life. That is why, when Christ was arrested, he was first interrogated before Annas (Jn 18:12–24). St Luke therefore is perfectly justified in calling him high priest.

3:2–3. Here St Luke formally introduces St John the Baptist, who appears in his gospel a number of times. When Christ praises the Baptist (cf. Mt 11:7–9) he refers particularly to his strength of will and his commitment to his God-given mission. Humility, austerity, courage and a spirit of prayer figure strongly in John's personality. So faithful was he to his mis-

Is 40:3–5
forgiveness of sins. ⁴As it is written in the book of the words of Isaiah the prophet,
"The voice of one crying in the wilderness:
Prepare the way of the Lord,
make his paths straight.
⁵Every valley shall be filled,
and every mountain and hill shall be brought low,
and the crooked shall be made straight,
and the rough ways shall be made smooth;
Acts 28:28
⁶and all flesh shall see the salvation of God."
Mt 23:33
Jn 3:36
⁷He said therefore to the multitudes that came out to be baptized by him, "You brood of vipers!* Who warned you to flee from the wrath to come? ⁸Bear fruits that befit repentance, and do

---

sion of preparing the way for the Messiah that Christ praises him in a unique way: he is the greatest of those born of woman (cf. Mt 11:11), "a burning and shining lamp" (Jn 5:35). He burned with love, and shone by the witness he bore. Christ was "the true light" (Jn 1:9); the Baptist "came for testimony, to bear witness to the light, that all might believe through him" (Jn 1:7).

John the Baptist appears on the scene preaching the need for repentance. He prepares "the way of the Lord". He is the herald of salvation: but his mission does not go beyond that; he simply announces that salvation is coming. "Among you stands one ... who comes after me, the thong of whose sandal I am not worthy to untie" (Jn 1:26–27). He points Christ out: "Behold, the Lamb of God" (Jn 1:29, 36), behold "the Son of God" (Jn 1:34); and he rejoices to see his own disciples leave him to follow Christ (Jn 1:37): "He must increase, but I must decrease" (Jn 3:30).

3:4–6. In the second part of the Book of Isaiah (chaps. 40–55), which is called the "Book of the Consolation of Israel", the Jewish people are told that they will once again suffer exile and a new exodus in

which their guide will be, not Moses, but God himself; once again they will make their way through the desert to reach a new promised land. St Luke sees the preaching of the Baptist, who announces the arrival of the Messiah, as fulfilling this prophecy.

Because the Lord is imminent, people must prepare themselves spiritually, by doing penance for their sins, to receive the special divine grace the Messiah is bringing. This is what he means by levelling the mountains and making the Lord's path straight.

Every year in its Advent liturgy the Church proclaims the coming of Jesus Christ, our Saviour, exhorting every Christian to purify his or her soul by a new interior conversion.

3:7. The Baptist's question is aimed at getting people to realize that to obtain God's pardon—"to flee from the wrath to come"—it is not enough simply to perform external rites, not even the baptism of John: one's heart needs to be converted if one is to produce fruit of repentance pleasing to God.

3:8. Jews took enormous pride in their noble origin; they did not want to admit

54

not begin to say to yourselves, 'We have Abraham as our father';
for I tell you, God is able from these stones to raise up children to
Abraham. ⁹Even now the axe is laid to the root of the trees; every
tree therefore that does not bear good fruit is cut down and thrown
into the fire."

¹⁰And the multitudes asked him, "What then shall we do?"
¹¹And he answered them, "He who has two coats, let him share
with him who has none; and he who has food, let him do likewise." ¹²Tax collectors also came to be baptized, and said to him,
"Teacher, what shall we do?" ¹³And he said to them, "Collect no
more than is appointed you." ¹⁴Soldiers also asked him, "And we,
what shall we do?" And he said to them, "Rob no one by violence
or by false accusation, and be content with your wages."

---

their sins, for they felt that they alone, being legitimate descendants of Abraham, were predestined to receive the salvation the Messiah would bring, without any need for them to do any other penance than the performance of external penitential practices. This is why John upbraids them, making a play on Hebrew words ("God is able from these stones (*abanim*) to raise up children (*banim*) to Abraham"); if they do not change, they will be shut out of the Kingdom of God; whereas many others, who are not of the line of Abraham according to the flesh, will be made his children by spiritual descent through faith (cf. Mt 8:11; Rom 9:8).

3:12–13. With honesty and courage St John the Baptist lays bare each person's fault. The chief sin of tax collectors lay in their using their privileged position as collaborators of the Roman authorities to acquire personal wealth at the expense of the Jewish people: Rome specified how much Israel as a whole should yield by way of taxes; the tax collectors abused their position by extorting more than was necessary. Take the case of Zacchaeus, for example, who, after his conversion, admits that he acquired wealth unjustly

and, under the influence of grace, promises our Lord to make generous restitution (cf. Lk 19:1–10).

The Baptist's preaching contains a norm of natural justice which the Church also preaches. Public position should be regarded, above all, as an opportunity to serve society, not to obtain personal gain at the expense of the common good and of that justice which people holding such positions are supposed to administer. Certainly, anyone who has fallen into the temptation of unjustly appropriating what belongs to another must not only confess his sin in the sacrament of Penance if he is to obtain pardon; he must also resolve to give back what is not his.

3:14. The Baptist requires of everyone—Pharisees, tax collectors, soldiers—a deep spiritual renewal in the very exercise of their job; they have to act justly and honourably. God asks all of us to sanctify ourselves in our work and in the circumstances in which we find ourselves: "Any honest and worthwhile work can be converted into a divine occupation. In God's service there are no second-class jobs; all of them are important" (St Josemaría Escrivá, *Conversations*, 55).

Jn 1:19–28
Acts 13:25

¹⁵As the people were in expectation, and all men questioned in their hearts concerning John, whether perhaps he were the Christ, ¹⁶John answered them all, "I baptize you with water; but he who is mightier than I is coming, the thong of whose sandal I am not worthy to untie; he will baptize you with the Holy Spirit and with fire. ¹⁷His winnowing fork is in his hand, to clear his threshing floor, and to gather the wheat into his granary, but the chaff he will burn with unquenchable fire."

¹⁸So, with many other exhortations, he preached good news to the people.

John the Baptist imprisoned

Mt 14:3–4
Mk 6:17–18

¹⁹But Herod the tetrarch, who had been reproved by him for Herodias, his brother's wife, and for all the evil things that Herod had done, ²⁰added this to them all, that he shut up John in prison.

3:15–17. Using expressive imagery, John announces Christian Baptism, proclaiming that he is not the Messiah; he, who is on his way, will come with the authority of supreme Judge that belongs to God, and with the dignity of the Messiah, who has no human equal.

3:19–20. John the Baptist preached the moral requirements of the messianic kingdom with charity but without human respect. Preaching the truth can lead one to be a thorn in the side of those who are not ready to change their way of life—to such an extent that they even persecute the preacher, which was what Herod did. "Don't be afraid of the truth, even though the truth may mean your death" (St Josemaría Escrivá, *The Way*, 34).

3:21–22. In its liturgy the Church remembers the first three solemn manifestations of Christ's divinity—the adoration of the Magi (Mt 2:11), the baptism of Jesus (Lk 3:21–22; Mt 3:13–17; Mk 1:9–11) and the first miracle our Lord worked, at the wedding at Cana (Jn 2:11). In the adoration of the Magi God revealed the divinity of Jesus by means of the star. At his baptism the voice of God the Father, coming "from heaven", reveals to John the Baptist and to the Jewish people—and thereby to all men— this profound mystery of Christ's divinity. At the wedding at Cana, Jesus "manifested his glory; and his disciples believed in him" (Jn 2:11). "When he attained to the perfect age," St Thomas Aquinas comments, "when the time came for him to teach, to work miracles and to draw men to himself, then was it fitting for his Godhead to be attested to from on high by the Father's testimony, so that his teaching might be the more credible: 'The Father who sent me has himself borne witness to me' (Jn 5:37)" (*Summa theologiae*, 3, 39, 8 ad 3).

3:21. In Christ's baptism we can find a reflection of the way the sacrament of Baptism affects a person. Christ's baptism was the exemplar of our own. In it the mystery of the Blessed Trinity was revealed, and the faithful, on receiving Baptism, are consecrated by the invocation of and by the power of the Blessed Trinity. Similarly, heaven opening signifies that the power, the effectiveness, of

Jesus is baptized

Mt 3:13–17
Mk 1:9–11
Jn 1:32–34
Ezek 1:1
Lk 9:35
Ps 2:7
Is 42:1

[21]Now when all the people were baptized, and when Jesus also had been baptized and was praying, the heaven was opened, [22]and the Holy Spirit descended upon him in bodily form, as a dove, and a voice came from heaven, "Thou art my beloved Son;[j] with thee I am well pleased."[k]

The ancestry of Jesus

Mt 1:1–17
Lk 4:22

[23]Jesus, when he began his ministry, was about thirty years of age, being the son (as was supposed) of Joseph,* the son of Heli, [24]the son of Matthat, the son of Levi, the son of Melchi, the son of Jannai, the son of Joseph, [25]the son of Mattathias, the son of

---

this sacrament comes from above, from God, and that the baptized have the road to heaven opened up for them, a road which original sin had closed. Jesus' prayer after his baptism teaches us that "after Baptism man needs to pray continually in order to enter heaven; for though sins are remitted through Baptism, there still remains the inclination to sin which assails us from within, and also the flesh and the devil which assail us from without" (St Thomas Aquinas, ibid., 3, 39, 5).

3:23. St Luke tells us our Lord's age at the beginning of his public ministry. His years of "hidden life" are of great significance; they are not an interlude in his work of redemption. In going about his everyday work in Nazareth Jesus is already redeeming the world. "The fact that Jesus grew up and lived just like us shows us that human existence and all the ordinary activity of men have a divine meaning. No matter how much we may have reflected on all this, we should always be surprised when we think of the thirty years of obscurity which made up the greater part of Jesus' life among men. He lived in obscurity, but, for us, that period is full of light. It illuminates our

days and fills them with meaning, for we are ordinary Christians who lead an ordinary life, just like millions of other people all over the world.

"That was the way Jesus lived for thirty years as 'the son of the carpenter' (Mt 13:55). There followed three years of public life spent among the crowds. People were surprised: 'Who is this?' they asked. 'Where has he learned these things?' For he was just like them: he had shared the life of ordinary people. He was 'the carpenter, the son of Mary' (Mk 6:3). And he was God; he was achieving the redemption of mankind and 'drawing all things to himself' (Jn 12:32)" (St J. Escrivá, *Christ Is Passing By*, 14).

Every Christian, then, can and should seek his sanctification in ordinary, everyday things, according to his state in life, his age and his work: "Therefore, all faithful are invited and obliged to holiness and the perfection of their own state of life" (Vatican II, *Lumen gentium*, 42).

3:23–28. Matthew and Luke both record our Lord's genealogy. Matthew (1:1–17) provides it as an introduction to his Gospel, showing Christ's roots in the chosen people, going right back to Abraham; he specifically shows that

---

j. Or *my son* (or *the*) *Beloved* **k.** Other ancient authorities read *today I have begotten thee*

Amos, the son of Nahum, the son of Esli, the son of Naggai, [26]the son of Maath, the son of Mattathias, the son of Semein, the son of Josech, the son of Joda, [27]the son of Joanan, the son of Rhesa, the son of Zerubbabel, the son of Shealtiel,[1] the son of Neri, [28]the son of Melchi, the son of Addi, the son of Cosam, the son of Elmadam, the son of Er, [29]the son of Joshua, the son of Eliezer, the son of Jorim, the son of Matthat, the son of Levi, [30]the son of Simeon, the son of Judah, the son of Joseph, the son of Jonam, the son of Eliakim, [31]the son of Melea, the son of Menna, the son of Mattatha, the son of Nathan, the son of David, [32]the son of Jesse, the son of Obed, the son of Boaz, the son of Sala, the son of Nahshon, [33]the son of Amminadab, the son of Admin, the son of Arni, the son of Hezron, the son of Perez, the son of Judah, [34]the

1 Chron 3:17
Ezra 3:2

1 Sam 16:1–13
2 Sam 5:14
Ruth 4:22
1 Chron 2:1ff
Gen 29:35
Gen 21:2–3;
11:10–26

Jesus is the Messiah announced by the prophets, a descendant of David; he is the king of the Davidic dynasty sent by God in fulfilment of his promises of salvation.

St Luke, on the other hand, writing in the first instance for Christians of Gentile background, underlines the universality of the redemption wrought by Christ; his genealogy, therefore, goes right back to Adam, the father of all men, Gentiles and Jews, linking Christ to all mankind.

St Matthew stresses the messianic character of our Lord, St Luke his priesthood. St Thomas Aquinas, following St Augustine, sees St Luke's genealogy as teaching us about Christ's priesthood: "Luke sets forth Christ's genealogy not at the outset but after Christ's baptism, and not in the descending but in the ascending order, as though giving prominence to the Priest who expiated our sins at the point where the Baptist bore witness to him, saying, 'Behold him who takes away the sins of the world.' And in the ascending order he passes Abraham and continues up to God, to whom we are reconciled by cleansing and expiating" (St Thomas Aquinas, *Summa theologiae*, 3, 31, 3 ad 3).

Some names in these two genealogies differ. Scholars convinced of the absolute historicity of both Gospels have offered various explanations for these differences, but no particular explanation is sponsored by the Church. We must remember that Jews were very careful to keep the record of their genealogical tree—especially Jews of royal or priestly families—to guide them in the exercise of their rights, obligations and functions. For example, after the return from the Babylonian exile, priests and Levites, on production of their genealogy, were permitted to perform their temple functions; others, on the basis of the same evidence, regained possession of land which had previously been theirs; whereas those who, due to the upheaval caused by exile, were unable to prove their descent, were barred from exercising priestly functions and did not regain possession of lands to which they laid claim (cf. Ezra 2:59–62; Neh 7:64ff).

The solutions put forward to explain the differences between the two genealogies hinge on one or other of these two arguments: 1) both evangelists are quoting St Joseph's genealogy, but one follows the

l. Greek *Salathiel*

son of Jacob, the son of Isaac, the son of Abraham, the son of
Terah, the son of Nahor, ³⁵the son of Serug, the son of Reu, the
son of Peleg, the son of Eber, the son of Shelah, ³⁶the son of
Cainan, the son of Arphaxad, the son of Shem, the son of Noah,
the son of Lamech, ³⁷the son of Methuselah, the son of Enoch, the
son of Jared, the son of Mahalaleel, the son of Cainan, ³⁸the son
of Enos, the son of Seth, the son of Adam, the son of God.

1 Chron 1:24–27

1 Chron 1:1–4
Gen 5:3–32

Gen 11:10; 4:25

Gen 5:1–3

Jesus fasts and is tempted in the wilderness

4 ¹And Jesus, full of the Holy Spirit, returned from the Jordan,
and was led by the Spirit ²for forty days in the wilderness,
tempted by the devil. And he ate nothing in those days; and when
they were ended, he was hungry. ³The devil said to him, "If you

Mt 4:1–11
Mk 1:12–13
Lk 3:22

---

levirate law (if someone died without issue his brother had to marry his widow, and the first-born of this marriage was the legal son of the deceased man: cf. Deut 25:5–6) and the other genealogy does not; 2) St Matthew is giving St Joseph's genealogy and St Luke that of the Virgin Mary. In the latter case Joseph would not be properly speaking the son of Heli but rather his son-in-law. However, this second hypothesis does not seem to have any good basis in the Gospel text.

4:1–13. Here we see the devil interfere in Jesus' life for the first time. He acts so very brazenly. Our Lord is about to begin his public ministry, so it is a particularly important point in his work of salvation.

"The whole episode is a mystery which man cannot hope to understand—God submitting to temptation, letting the evil one have his way. But we can meditate upon it, asking our Lord to help us understand the teaching it contains" (St J. Escrivá, *Christ Is Passing By*, 61).

Christ, true God and true man, made himself like us in everything except sin (cf. Phil 2:7; Heb 2:7; 4:15) and voluntarily underwent temptation. "How fortunate we are," exclaims the Curé of Ars, "how lucky to have a God as a model.

Are we poor? We have a God who is born in a stable, who lies in a manger. Are we despised? We have a God who led the way, who was crowned with thorns, dressed in a filthy red cloak and treated as a madman. Are we tormented by pain and suffering? Before our eyes we have a God covered with wounds, dying in unimaginable pain. Are we being persecuted? How can we dare complain when we have a God who is being put to death by executioners? Finally, are we being tempted by the demon? We have our lovable Redeemer; he also was tempted by the demon and was twice taken up by that hellish spirit: therefore, no matter what sufferings, pains or temptations we are experiencing, we always have, everywhere, our God leading the way for us and assuring us of victory as long as we genuinely desire it" (*Selected Sermons*, First Sunday of Lent).

Jesus teaches us therefore that no one should regard himself as incorruptible and proof against temptation; he shows us how we should deal with temptation and exhorts us to have confidence in his mercy, since he himself experienced temptation (cf. Heb 2:18).

For further explanation of this passage, see the notes on Mt 4:3–11.

Deut 8:3 are the Son of God, command this stone to become bread." ⁴And Jesus answered him, "It is written, 'Man shall not live by bread alone.'" ⁵And the devil took him up, and showed him all the kingdoms of the world in a moment of time, ⁶and said to him, "To you I will give all this authority and their glory; for it has been delivered to me, and I give it to whom I will. ⁷If you, then, will worship me, it shall all be yours." ⁸And Jesus answered him, "It is written,

'You shall worship the Lord your God,

Deut 6:13–14   and him only shall you serve.'"

⁹And he took him to Jerusalem, and set him on the pinnacle of the temple, and said to him, "If you are the Son of God, throw yourself down from here; ¹⁰for it is written,

'He will give his angels charge of you, to guard you,'

Ps 91:11–12   ¹¹and

'On their hands they will bear you up,

lest you strike your foot against a stone.'"

¹²And Jesus answered him, "It is said, 'You shall not tempt the

Deut 6:16   Lord your God.'" ¹³And when the devil had ended every tempta-

Heb 4:15   tion, he departed from him until an opportune time.

4:13. Our Lord's temptations sum up every kind of temptation man can experience: "Scripture would not have said", St Thomas comments, "that once all the temptation ended the devil departed from him, unless the matter of all sins were included in the three temptations already related. For the causes of temptation are the causes of desires—namely, lust of the flesh, desire for glory, eagerness for power" (*Summa theologiae*, 3, 41, 4 ad 4).

By conquering every kind of temptation, Jesus shows us how to deal with the snares of the devil. It was as a man that he was tempted and as a man that he resisted: "He did not act as God, bringing his power into play; if he had done so, how could we have availed of his example? Rather, as man he made use of the resources which he has in common with us" (St Ambrose, *Expositio Evangelii sec. Lucam*, in loc.).

He wanted to show us the methods to use to defeat the devil—prayer, fasting, watchfulness, not dialoguing with temptation, having the words of God's Scripture on our lips and putting our trust in the Lord.

"Until an opportune time", that is, until it is time for Jesus to undergo his passion. The devil often appears in the course of our Lord's public life (cf., e.g., Mk 12:28), but it will be at the Passion— "this is your hour, and the power of darkness" (Lk 22:53)—that he will be most clearly seen in his role as tempter. Jesus will forewarn his disciples about this and once more assure them of victory (cf. Jn 12:31; 14:30). Through the passion, death and resurrection of Christ, the devil will be overpowered once and for all. And by virtue of Christ's victory we are enabled to overcome all temptations.

4:16–30. For the Jews the sabbath was a day of rest and prayer, as God commanded (Ex 20:8–11). On that day they

PART ONE

Jesus' ministry in Galilee

3. THE START OF HIS MINISTRY IN GALILEE

[14]And Jesus returned in the power of the Spirit into Galilee, and a report concerning him went out through all the surrounding country. [15]And he taught in their synagogues, being glorified by all.

Mt 4:12–17
Mk 1:14–15

Preaching in Nazareth

[16]And he came to Nazareth, where he had been brought up; and he went to the synagogue, as his custom was, on the sabbath day.* And he stood up to read; [17]and there was given to him the book of the prophet Isaiah. He opened the book and found the place where it was written,

Mt 13:53–58
Mk 6:1–6

   [18]"The Spirit of the Lord is upon me,
      because he has anointed me to preach good news to the poor.

Mt 11:5

---

would gather together to be instructed in Holy Scripture. At the beginning of this meeting they all recited the *Shema*, a summary of the precepts of the Lord, and the "eighteen blessings". Then a passage was read from the Book of the Law—the Pentateuch—and another from the Prophets. The president invited one of those present who was well versed in the Scriptures to address the gathering. Sometimes someone would volunteer and request the honour of being allowed to give this address—as must have happened on this occasion. Jesus avails himself of this opportunity to instruct the people (cf. Lk 4:16ff), as will his apostles later on (cf. Acts 13:5, 14, 42, 44; 14:1; etc.). The sabbath meeting concluded with the priestly blessing, recited by the president or by a priest if there was one present, to which the people answered "Amen" (cf. Num 6:22ff).

4:18–21. Jesus read the passage from Isaiah 61:1–2 where the prophet announces the coming of the Lord, who will free his people of their afflictions. In Christ this prophecy finds its fulfilment, for he is the Anointed, the Messiah whom God has sent to his people in their tribulation. Jesus has been anointed by the Holy Spirit for the mission the Father has entrusted to him. "These phrases, according to Luke (vv. 18–19), are his first messianic declaration. They are followed by the actions and words known through the Gospel. By these actions and words Christ makes the Father present among men" (John Paul II, *Dives in misericordia*, 3).

   The promises proclaimed in vv. 18 and 19 are the blessings God will send his people through the Messiah. According to Old Testament tradition and Jesus' own preaching (cf. the note on Mt 5:3), "the poor" refers not so much to a partic-

He has sent me to proclaim release to the captives
and recovering of sight to the blind,
to set at liberty those who are oppressed,

Lev 25:10 [19]to proclaim the acceptable year of the Lord."

---

ular social condition as to a very religious attitude of indigence and humility towards God, which is to be found in those who, instead of relying on their possessions and merits, trust in God's goodness and mercy. Thus, preaching good news to the poor means bringing them the "good news" that God has taken pity on them. Similarly, the Redemption, the release, which the text mentions, is to be understood mainly in a spiritual, transcendental sense: Christ has come to free us from the blindness and oppression of sin, which, in the last analysis, is slavery imposed on us by the devil. "Captivity can be felt", St John Chrysostom teaches in a commentary on Psalm 126, "when it proceeds from physical enemies, but the spiritual captivity referred to here is worse; sin exerts a more severe tyranny, evil takes control and blinds those who lend it obedience; from this spiritual prison Jesus Christ rescued us" (*Catena aurea*). However, this passage is also in line with Jesus' special concern for those most in need. "Similarly, the Church encompasses with her love all those who are afflicted by human misery and she recognizes in those who are poor and who suffer the image of her poor and suffering Founder. She does all in her power to relieve their need and in them she strives to serve Christ" (Vatican II, *Lumen gentium*, 8).

4:18–19. The words of Isaiah which Christ read out on this occasion describe very graphically the reason why God has sent his Son into the world—to redeem men from sin, to liberate them from slavery to the devil and from eternal death. It

is true that in the course of his public ministry Christ, in his mercy, worked many cures, cast out devils, etc. But he did not cure all the sick people in the world, nor did he eliminate all forms of distress in this life, because pain, which entered the world through sin, has a permanent redemptive value when associated with the sufferings of Christ. Therefore, Christ worked miracles not so much to release the people concerned from suffering, as to demonstrate that he had a God-given mission to bring everyone eternal redemption.

The Church carries on this mission of Christ: "Go therefore and make disciples of all nations, baptizing them in the name of the Father and of the Son and of the Holy Spirit, teaching them to observe all that I have commanded you; and lo, I am with you always, to the close of the age" (Mt 28:19–20). These simple and sublime words, which conclude the Gospel of St Matthew, point out "the obligation to preach the truths of faith, the need for sacramental life, the promise of Christ's continual assistance to his Church. You cannot be faithful to our Lord if you neglect these supernatural demands—to receive instruction in Christian faith and morality and to frequent the sacraments. It is with this mandate that Christ founded his Church [...]. And the Church can bring salvation to souls only if she remains faithful to Christ in her constitution and teaching, both dogmatic and moral.

"Let us reject, therefore, the suggestion that the Church, ignoring the Sermon on the Mount, seeks a purely human happiness on earth, since we

²⁰And he closed the book, and gave it back to the attendant, and sat down; and the eyes of all in the synagogue were fixed on him. ²¹And he began to say to them, "Today this scripture has been fulfilled in your hearing." ²²And all spoke well of him, and wondered

Mt 5:17

Jn 6:42

---

know that her only task is to bring men to eternal glory in heaven. Let us reject any purely naturalistic view that fails to value the supernatural role of divine grace. Let us reject materialistic opinions that exclude spiritual values from human life. Let us equally reject any secularizing theory which attempts to equate the aims of the Church with those of earthly states, distorting its essence, institutions and activities into something similar to those of temporal society" (St J. Escrivá, *In Love with the Church*, 23 and 31).

4:18. The Fathers of the Church see this verse as a reference to the three persons of the Holy Trinity: the Spirit (the Holy Spirit) of the Lord (the Father) is upon me (the Son); cf. Origen, *Homily* 32. The Holy Spirit dwelt in Christ's soul from the very moment of the Incarnation and descended visibly upon him in the form of a dove when he was baptized by John (cf. Lk 3:21–22).

"Because he has anointed me": this is a reference to the anointing Jesus received at the moment of his Incarnation, principally through the grace of the hypostatic union. "This anointing of Jesus Christ was not an anointing of the body as in the case of the ancient kings, priests and prophets; rather it was entirely spiritual and divine, because the fulness of the Godhead dwells in him substantially" (St Pius X, *Catechism*, 77). From this hypostatic union the fulness of all grace derives. To show this, Jesus Christ is said to have been anointed by the Holy Spirit *himself*—not just to have received the graces and gifts of the Spirit, like the saints.

4:19. "The acceptable year": this is a reference to the jubilee year of the Jews, which the Law of God (Lev 25:8) lays down as occurring every fifty years, symbolizing the era of redemption and liberation which the Messiah would usher in. The era inaugurated by Christ, the era of the New Law extending to the end of the world, is "the acceptable year", the time of mercy and redemption, which will be obtained definitively in heaven. The Catholic Church's custom of the "Holy Year" is also designed to proclaim and remind people of the redemption brought by Christ, and of the full form it will take in the future life.

4:20–22. Christ's words in v. 21 show us the authenticity with which he preached and explained the Scriptures: "Today this scripture has been fulfilled in your hearing." Jesus teaches that this prophecy, like the other main prophecies in the Old Testament, refers to him and finds its fulfilment in him (cf. Lk 24:44ff). Thus, the Old Testament can be rightly understood only in the light of the New—as the risen Christ showed the apostles when he opened their minds to understand the Scriptures (cf. Lk 24:45), an understanding which the Holy Spirit perfected on the day of Pentecost (cf. Acts 2:4).

4:22–29. At first the people of Nazareth listened readily to the wisdom of Jesus' words. But they were very superficial; in their narrow-minded pride they felt hurt that Jesus, their fellow-townsman, had not worked in Nazareth the wonders he had worked elsewhere. They presume they have a special entitlement and they

Mt 4:13

Jn 4:44

1 Kings 18:1
Jas 5:17

1 Kings 17:9ff
2 Kings 5:9ff

Mk 1:21–28
Mt 4:13
Jn 2:12
Mt 7:28–29
Jn 7:46

at the gracious words which proceeded out of his mouth; and they said, "Is not this Joseph's son?" ²³And he said to them, "Doubtless you will quote to me this proverb, 'Physician, heal yourself; what we have heard you did at Capernaum, do here also in your own country.'" ²⁴And he said, "Truly, I say to you, no prophet is acceptable in his own country. ²⁵But in truth, I tell you, there were many widows in Israel in the days of Elijah, when the heaven was shut up three years and six months, when there came a great famine over all the land; ²⁶and Elijah was sent to none of them but only to Zarephath, in the land of Sidon, to a woman who was a widow. ²⁷And there were many lepers in Israel in the time of the prophet Elisha; and none of them was cleansed, but only Naaman the Syrian." ²⁸When they heard this, all in the synagogue were filled with wrath. ²⁹And they rose up and put him out of the city, and led him to the brow of the hill on which their city was built, that they might throw him down headlong. ³⁰But passing through the midst of them he went away.

In the synagogue in Capernaum

³¹And he went down to Capernaum, a city of Galilee. And he was teaching them on the sabbath; ³²and they were astonished at his teaching, for his word was with authority. ³³And in the synagogue there was a man who had the spirit of an unclean demon; and he

insolently demand that he perform miracles to satisfy their vanity, not to change their hearts. In view of their attitude, Jesus performs no miracle (his normal response to lack of faith: cf., for example, his meeting with Herod in Lk 23:7–11); he actually reproaches them, using two examples taken from the Old Testament (cf. 1 Kings 17:9 and 2 Kings 5:14), which show that one needs to be well-disposed if miracles are to lead to faith. His attitude so wounds their pride that they are ready to kill him. This whole episode is a good lesson about understanding Jesus. We can understand him only if we are humble and are genuinely resolved to make ourselves available to him.

4:30. Jesus does not take flight but withdraws majestically, leaving the crowd paralysed. As on other occasions men do

him no harm; it was by God's decree that he died on a cross (cf. Jn 18:32) when his hour had come.

4:33–37. Jesus now demonstrates by his actions that authority which was evident in his words.

4:34. The demon tells the truth here when he calls Jesus "the Holy One of God", but Jesus does not accept this testimony from the "father of lies" (Jn 8:44). This shows that the devil usually says something partially true in order to disguise untruth; by sowing confusion in this way, he can more readily deceive people. By silencing and expelling the demon, Jesus teaches us to be prudent and not let ourselves be deceived by half-truths.

4:38–39. In the public life of Jesus we

cried out with a loud voice, [34]"Ah![m] What have you to do with us, Jesus of Nazareth? Have you come to destroy us? I know who you are, the Holy One of God." [35]But Jesus rebuked him, saying, "Be silent, and come out of him!" And when the demon had thrown him down in the midst, he came out of him, having done him no harm. [36]And they were all amazed and said to one another, "What is this word? For with authority and power he commands the unclean spirits, and they come out." [37]And reports of him went out into every place in the surrounding region.

Curing of Peter's mother-in-law

[38]And he arose and left the synagogue, and entered Simon's house. Now Simon's mother-in-law was ill with a high fever, and they besought him for her. [39]And he stood over her and rebuked the fever, and it left her; and immediately she rose and served them.

Mt 8:14–17
Mk 1:21–39

Other cures

[40]Now when the sun was setting, all those who had any that were sick with various diseases brought them to him; and he laid his hands on every one of them and healed them. [41]And demons also came out of many, crying, "You are the Son of God!" But he rebuked them, and would not allow them to speak, because they knew that he was the Christ.

Mt 8:29
Mk 3:11–12

---

find many touching episodes (cf. e.g. Lk 19:1ff; Jn 2:1ff) which show the high regard he had for everyday family life.

Here we can clearly see the effectiveness of prayer on behalf of other people: "No sooner did they pray to the Saviour", St Jerome says, "than he immediately healed the sick; from this we learn that he also listens to the prayers of the faithful for help against sinful passions" (*Expositio in Evangelium sec. Lucam*, in loc.).

St John Chrysostom refers to this total, instantaneous cure: "Since this was a curable type of illness he displayed his power through the way he brought healing, doing what medicine could not do. Even after being cured of fever, patients need time to recover their former strength, but here the cure was instanta-

neous" (*Hom. on St Matthew*, 27).

The Fathers saw in this lady's fever a symbol of concupiscence: "Peter's mother-in-law's fever represents our flesh affected by various illnesses and concupiscences; our fever is passion, our fever is lust, our fever is anger—vices which, although they affect the body, perturb the soul, the mind and the feelings" (St Ambrose, *Expositio evangelii sec. Lucam*, in loc.).

On the practical consequences of this St Cyril says: "Let us receive Jesus Christ, because when he visits us and we take him into our minds and hearts, even our worst passions are extinguished and we are kept safe to serve him, that is, to do what pleases him" (*Hom. 28 in Mattheum*).

m. Or *Let us alone*

65

Jesus preaches in other cities in Judea

⁴²And when it was day he departed and went into a lonely place. And the people sought him and came to him, and would have kept him from leaving them; ⁴³but he said to them, "I must preach the good news of the kingdom of God to the other cities also; for I was sent for this purpose." ⁴⁴And he was preaching in the synagogues of Judea.[n]

Lk 8:1

Mt 4:23

The miraculous catch of fish and the calling of the first disciples

Mt 4:18–22
Mk 1:16–20

5 ¹While the people pressed upon him to hear the word of God, he was standing by the lake of Gennesaret. ²And he saw two

---

4:43. Our Lord again stresses one of the reasons why he has come into the world. St Thomas, when discussing the purpose of the Eucharist, says that Christ "came into the world, first, to make the truth known, as he himself says: 'for this I was born, and for this I have come into the world, to bear witness to the truth' (Jn 18:37). Hence it was not fitting that he should hide himself by leading a solitary life, but rather that he should appear openly and preach in public. For this reason he tells those who wanted to detain him, 'I must preach the good news of the kingdom of God to the other cities also; for I was sent for this purpose.' Secondly, he came in order to free men from sin; as the apostle says, 'Christ Jesus came into the world to save sinners' (1 Tim 1:15). This is why Chrysostom says, 'Although Christ might, while staying in the same place, have drawn all men to himself to hear his preaching, he did not do so—in order to give us the example to go out and seek the lost sheep, as the shepherd does, or as the doctor does, who visits the sick person.' Thirdly, he came so that 'we might obtain access to God' (Rom 5:2)" (*Summa theologiae*, 3, 40, 1, c.).

5:1. "Just as they do today! Can't you see? They want to hear God's message, even though outwardly they may not show it. Some perhaps have forgotten Christ's teachings. Others, through no fault of their own, have never known them and they think that religion is something odd. But of this we can be sure, that in every man's life there comes a time sooner or later when his soul draws the line. He has had enough of the usual explanations. The lies of the false prophets no longer satisfy. Even though they may not admit it at the time, such people are longing to quench their thirst with the teachings of our Lord" (St Josemaría Escrivá, *Friends of God*, 260).

5:3. The Fathers saw in Simon's boat a symbol of the pilgrim Church on earth. "This is the boat which according to St Matthew was in danger of sinking and according to St Luke was filled with fish. Here we can see the difficult beginnings of the Church and its later fruitfulness" (St Ambrose, *Expositio Evangelii sec. Lucam*, in loc.). Christ gets into the boat in order to teach the crowds—and from the barque of Peter, the Church, he continues to teach the whole world.

Each of us can also see himself as this boat Christ uses for preaching. Externally no change is evident: "What has changed? There is a change inside our

---

n. Other ancient authorities read *Galilee*

boats by the lake; but the fishermen had gone out of them and were washing their nets. ³Getting into one of the boats, which was Simon's, he asked him to put out a little from the land. And he sat down and taught the people from the boat. ⁴And when he had ceased speaking, he said to Simon, "Put out into the deep and let down your nets for a catch." ⁵And Simon answered, "Master, we toiled all night and took nothing! But at your word I will let down the nets." ⁶And when they had done this, they enclosed a great shoal of fish; and as their nets were breaking, ⁷they beckoned to their partners in the other boat to come and help them. And they

Jn 21:6

---

soul, now that Christ has come aboard, as he went aboard Peter's boat. Its horizon has opened wider. It feels a greater ambition to serve and an irrepressible desire to tell all creation about the *magnalia Dei* (Acts 2:11), the marvellous doings of our Lord, if only we let him work" (St Josemaría Escrivá, *Friends of God*, 265).

5:4. "When he had finished his catechising, he told Simon: 'Put out into the deep, and lower your nets for a catch' (Lk 5:4). Christ is the master of this boat. He it is who prepares the fishing. It is for this that he has come into the world, to do all he can so that his brothers may find the way to glory and to the love of the Father" (*Friends of God*, 260). To carry this task out, our Lord charges all of them to cast their nets, but it is only Peter he tells to put out into the deep.

This whole passage refers in some way to the life of the Church. In the Church the bishop of Rome, Peter's successor, "is the vicar of Jesus Christ because he represents him on earth and acts for him in the government of the Church" (St Pius X, *Catechism*, 195). Christ is also addressing each one of us, urging us to be daring in apostolate: " '*Duc in altum*—Put out into deep water!' Cast aside the pessimism that makes a coward of you. '*Et laxate retia vestra in capturam*—And lower your nets for a catch.' Don't you see that, as

Peter said: '*In nomine tuo, laxabo rete*— At your word I will lower the net', you can say, Jesus, in your name, I will seek souls!" (St J. Escrivá, *The Way*, 792).

"If you were to fall into the temptation of wondering, 'Who's telling me to embark on this?' we would have to reply, 'Christ himself is telling you, is begging you.' 'The harvest is plentiful enough, but the labourers are few. You must ask the Lord to whom the harvest belongs to send labourers out for the harvesting' (Mt 9:37–38). Don't take the easy way out. Don't say, 'I'm no good at this sort of thing; there are others who can do it; it isn't my line.' No, for this sort of thing, there is no one else: if you could get away with that argument, so could everyone else. Christ's plea is addressed to each and every Christian. No one can consider himself excused, for whatever reason—age, health or occupation. There are no excuses whatsoever. Either we carry out a fruitful apostolate, or our faith will prove barren" (*Friends of God*, 272).

5:5. When Christ gives him these instructions, Peter states the difficulties involved. "A reasonable enough reply. The night hours were their normal time for fishing, and this time the catch had yielded nothing. What was the point of fishing by day? But Peter has faith: 'But at your word I will let down the nets' (Lk 5:5). He decides to act on Christ's sug-

came and filled both the boats, so that they began to sink. ⁸But when Simon Peter saw it, he fell down at Jesus' knees, saying, "Depart from me, for I am a sinful man, O Lord." ⁹For he was astonished, and all that were with him, at the catch of fish which they had taken; ¹⁰and so also were James and John, sons of Zebedee, who were partners with Simon. And Jesus said to Simon, "Do not be afraid; henceforth you will be catching men." ¹¹And when they had brought their boats to land, they left everything and followed him.

Mt 13:47

Mt 19:27

Curing of a leper

Mt 8:1–4
Mk 1:40–45

¹²While he was in one of the cities, there came a man full of leprosy; and when he saw Jesus, he fell on his face and besought

gestion. He undertakes the work relying entirely on the word of our Lord" (St Josemaría Escrivá, *Friends of God*, 261).

5:8. Peter does not want Christ to leave him; aware of his sins, he declares his unworthiness to be near Christ. This reminds us of the attitude of the centurion who confesses his unworthiness to receive Jesus into his house (cf. Mt 8:8). The Church requires her children to repeat these exact words of the centurion before receiving the Blessed Eucharist. She also teaches us to show due external reverence to the Blessed Sacrament when going to Communion: by falling down on his knees Peter also shows that internal adoration of God should also be expressed externally.

5:11. Perfection is not simply a matter of leaving all things but of doing so in order to follow Christ—which is what the apostles did: they gave up everything in order to be available to do what God's calling involved.

We should develop this attitude of availability, for "Jesus is never satisfied 'sharing': he wants all" (St Josemaría Escrivá, *The Way*, 155).

If we don't give ourselves generously we will find it very difficult to follow

Jesus: "Detach yourself from people and things until you are stripped of them. For, says Pope Saint Gregory, the devil has nothing of his own in this world, and he goes into battle naked. If you are clothed when you fight him, you will soon be pulled to the ground, because he will have something to grab on to" (*The Way*, 149).

5:12. The words of the leper are a model prayer. First, they show his faith. "He did not say, 'If you ask God for it ...', but 'If you will'" (St John Chrysostom, *Hom. on St Matthew*, 25). He rounds this off by saying, "You can"—an open confession of Christ's omnipotence. The psalmist expressed this same faith: "Whatever the Lord pleases he does, in heaven and on earth, in the seas and all deeps" (Ps 135:6). Along with this faith he shows confidence in God's mercy. "God is merciful; there is no need therefore to ask him; all we have to do is show him our need" (St Thomas Aquinas, *Comm. on St Matthew*, 8, 1). And St John Chrysostom concludes: "Prayer is perfect when it is joined to faith and confession; the leper showed his faith and confessed his need out loud" (*Hom. on St Matthew*, 25).

"*Domine!*—Lord—*si vis, potes me mundare*—if thou wilt, thou canst make

him, "Lord, if you will, you can make me clean." [13]And he
stretched out his hand, and touched him, saying, "I will; be clean."
And immediately the leprosy left him. [14]And he charged him to
tell no one; but "go and show yourself to the priest, and make an
offering for your cleansing, as Moses commanded, for a proof to
the people."o [15]But so much the more the report went abroad concerning him; and great multitudes gathered to hear and to be
healed of their infirmities. [16]But he withdrew to the wilderness
and prayed.

Lev 13:49;
14:2–32

Mk 1:35

Curing of a paralyzed man

[17]On one of those days, as he was teaching, there were Pharisees
and teachers of the law sitting by, who had come from every vil-

Mt 9:1–8
Mk 2:1–12

---

me clean.' What a beautiful prayer for
you to say often, with the faith of the
poor leper, when there happens to you
what God and you and I know may
happen! You will not have to wait long to
hear the Master's reply: '*Volo, mundare!*
I will be clean!'" (St Josemaría Escrivá,
The Way, 142).

5:13. Jesus listens to the leper's petition
and cures him of his disease. All of us
suffer from spiritual ailments and our
Lord is waiting for us to approach him:
"He is our physician, and he heals our
selfishness, if we let his grace penetrate
to the depths of our soul. Jesus has taught
us that the worst sickness is hypocrisy,
the pride that leads us to hide our own
sins. We have to be totally sincere with
him. We have to tell the whole truth, and
then we have to say, 'Lord, if you will'—
and you are always willing—'you can
make me clean' (Mt 8:2). You know my
weaknesses; I feel these symptoms; I
suffer from these failings. We show him
the wound, with simplicity, and if the
wound is festering, we show the pus too.
Lord, you have cured so many souls; help
me to recognize you as the divine physician, when I have you in my heart or

when I contemplate your presence in the
tabernacle" (St Josemaría Escrivá, *Christ
Is Passing By*, 93).

5:16. The Third Gospel frequently draws
attention to Jesus going off, alone, to
pray (cf. 6:12; 9:18; 11:1). By doing this
Jesus teaches us the need for personal
prayer in all the various situations in
which we find ourselves.

"Forgive me if I insist, but it is very
important to note carefully what the
Messiah did, because he came to show us
the path that leads to the Father. With our
Lord we will discover how to give a
supernatural dimension to all our actions,
even those that seem least important. We
will learn to live every moment of our
lives with a lively awareness of eternity,
and we will understand more deeply
man's need for periods of intimate conversation with his God, so as to get to
know him, to invoke him, to praise him,
to break out into acts of thanksgiving, to
listen to him or, quite simply, to be
with him" (St Josemaría Escrivá, *Friends
of God*, 239).

5:17. A little earlier, beside the lake,
Jesus addressed his teaching to crowds

o. Greek *to them*

69

lage of Galilee and Judea and from Jerusalem; and the power of the Lord was with him to heal.[p] [18]And behold, men were bringing on a bed a man who was paralyzed, and they sought to bring him in and lay him before Jesus;[q] [19]but finding no way to bring him in, because of the crowd, they went up on the roof and let him down with his bed through the tiles into the midst before Jesus. [20]And when he saw their faith he said, "Man, your sins are forgiven you." [21]And the scribes and the Pharisees began to question, saying, "Who is this that speaks blasphemies? Who can forgive sins but God only?" [22]When Jesus perceived their questionings, he answered them, "Why do you question in your hearts? [23]Which is easier, to say, 'Your sins are forgiven you,' or to say, 'Rise and walk'? [24]But that you may know that the Son of man has authority on earth to forgive sins"—he said to the man who was para-

Lk 7:49
Is 43:25; 55:7

Jn 20:21–23

(vv. 1ff). Here his audience includes some of the most educated of Jews. Christ desired not only to teach but also to cure everyone—spiritually and, sometimes, physically, as he will soon do in the case of the paralytic. The evangelist's observation at the end of this verse reminds us that our Lord is ever-ready to use his omnipotence for our good: "'I know the plans I have for you, plans for welfare and not for evil', was God's promise through Jeremiah (29:11). The liturgy applies these words to Jesus, for in him we are clearly shown that God does love us in this way. He did not come to condemn us, to accuse us of meanness and smallness. He came to save us, pardon us, excuse us, bring us peace and joy" (St J. Escrivá, *Christ Is Passing By*, 165). On this occasion also Jesus wanted to benefit all his listeners, even though some of them would not receive this divine gift because they were not well-disposed.

5:19–20. Our Lord is touched when he sees these friends of the paralytic putting their faith into practice: they had gone up onto the roof, taken off some of the tiles

and lowered the bed down in front of Jesus. Friendship and faith combine in obtaining a miraculous cure. The paralytic himself had a like faith: he let himself be carried around, brought up onto the roof and so forth. Seeing such solid faith Jesus gives them even more than they expect: he cures the man's body and, what is much more, cures his soul. Perhaps he does this, as St Bede suggests (cf. *In Lucae Evangelium expositio*, in loc.), to show two things: that the illness was a form of punishment for his sins and therefore the paralytic could only get up once these sins had been forgiven; and that others' faith and prayer can move God to work miracles.

In some way, the paralytic symbolizes everyone whose sins prevent him from reaching God. For example, St Ambrose says: "How great is the Lord who on account of the merits of some pardons others, and while praising the former absolves the latter! [...] Therefore, let you, who judge, learn to pardon; you, who are ill, learn to beg for forgiveness. And if the gravity of your sins causes you to doubt the possibility of

p. Other ancient authorities read *was present to heal them* **q.** Greek *him*

lyzed—"I say to you, rise, take up your bed and go home." ²⁵And immediately he rose before them, and took up that on which he lay, and went home, glorifying God. ²⁶And amazement seized them all, and they glorified God and were filled with awe, saying, "We have seen strange things today."

The calling of Matthew

²⁷After this he went out, and saw a tax collector, named Levi, sitting at the tax office; and he said to him, "Follow me." ²⁸And he left everything, and rose and followed him.

Mt 9:9–18
Mk 2:13–17

²⁹And Levi made him a great feast in his house; and there was a large company of tax collectors and others sitting at table^r with them. ³⁰And the Pharisees and their scribes murmured against his disciples, saying, "Why do you eat and drink with tax collectors

Lk 15:1;
19:6–7

---

being forgiven, have recourse to intercessors, have recourse to the Church, who will pray for you, and the Lord will grant you, out of love for her, what he might have refused you" (*Expositio Evangelii sec. Lucam*, in loc.).

Apostolic work should be motivated by desire to help people find Jesus Christ. Among other things it calls for daring—as we see in the friends of the paralytic; and it also needs the intercession of the saints, whose help we seek because we feel God will pay more attention to them than to us sinners.

5:24. Our Lord is going to perform a public miracle to prove that he is endowed with invisible, spiritual power. Christ, the only Son of the Father, has power to forgive sins because he is God, and he uses this power on our behalf as our Mediator and Redeemer (Lk 22:20; Jn 20:17–18, 28; 1 Tim 2:5–6; Col 2:13–14; Heb 9:14; 1 Jn 1:9; Is 53:4–5). Jesus used this power personally when he was on earth and after ascending into heaven he still uses it, through the apostles and their successors.

A sinner is like a paralytic in God's presence. The Lord is going to free him

of his paralysis, forgiving him his sins and enabling him to walk by giving him grace once more. In the sacrament of Penance, if Jesus Christ "sees us cold, unwilling, rigid perhaps with the stiffness of a dying interior life, his tears will be our life: 'I say to you, my friend, Arise and walk' (cf. Jn 11:43; Lk 5:24), leave that narrow life which is no life at all" (St J. Escrivá, *Christ Is Passing By*, 93).

5:27–29. Levi, better known as Matthew, responds generously and promptly to the call from Jesus. To celebrate and to show how appreciative he is for his vocation he gives a banquet. This passage of the Gospel shows us that a vocation is something about which we should be very grateful and happy. If we see it only in terms of renunciation and giving things up, and not as a gift from God and something which will enhance us and redound to others' benefit, we can easily become depressed, like the rich young man who, not wanting to give up his possessions, went away sad (cf. Lk 18:18ff). Matthew believes in quite the opposite way, as did the Magi who, "when they saw the star, rejoiced exceedingly with great joy" (Mt

r. Greek *reclining*

71

and sinners?" [31]And Jesus answered them, "Those who are well have no need of a physician, but those who are sick; [32]I have not come to call the righteous, but sinners to repentance."

A discussion on fasting

Mt 9:14–17
Mk 2:18–22

Jn 16:20
Lk 17:22

[33]And they said to him, "The disciples of John fast often and offer prayers, and so do the disciples of the Pharisees, but yours eat and drink." [34]And Jesus said to them, "Can you make wedding guests fast while the bridegroom is with them? [35]The days will come, when the bridegroom is taken away from them, and then they will fast in those days." [36]He told them a parable also: "No one tears a piece from a new garment and puts it upon an old garment; if he does, he will tear the new, and the piece from the new will not match the old. [37]And no one puts new wine into old wineskins; if he does, the new wine will burst the skins and it will be spilled, and the skins will be destroyed. [38]But new wine must be put into fresh wineskins. [39]And no one after drinking old wine desires new; for he says, 'The old is good.'"[s]

The law of the sabbath

Mt 12:1–8
Mk 2:23–28
Deut 23:25

6 [1]On a sabbath,[t] while he was going through the grainfields, his disciples plucked and ate some ears of grain, rubbing them in

2:10) and who gave much more importance to adoring the new-born God than to all the inconveniences involved in travelling to see him. See also the notes on Mt 9:9; 9:10–11; 9:12; 9:13; and Mk 2:14; 2:17.

5:32. Since this is how Jesus operates, the only way we can be saved is by admitting before God, in all simplicity, that we are sinners. "Jesus has no time for calculations, for astuteness, for the cruelty of cold hearts, for attractive but empty beauty. What he likes is the cheerfulness of a young heart, a simple step, a natural voice, clean eyes, attention to his affectionate word of advice. That is how he reigns in the soul" (St Josemaría Escrivá, *Christ Is Passing By*, 181).

5:33–35. In the Old Testament God established certain days as days of fasting—the main one being the "day of atonement" (Num 29:7; Acts 27:9). Fasting implied total or partial abstinence from food or drink. Moses and Elijah fasted (Ex 34:28; 1 Kings 19:8) and our Lord himself fasted in the desert for forty days before beginning his public ministry. In the present passage Jesus gives a deeper meaning to the word "fasting"—the deprivation of his physical presence which his apostles would experience after his death. All through his public life Jesus is trying to prepare his disciples for the final parting. At first the apostles were not very robust and Christ's physical presence did them more good than the practice of fasting.

s. Other ancient authorities read *better* **t.** Other ancient authorities read *On the second first sabbath* (on the second sabbath after the first)

their hands. ²But some of the Pharisees said, "Why are you doing what is not lawful to do on the sabbath?" ³And Jesus answered, "Have you not read what David did when he was hungry, he and those who were with him: ⁴how he entered the house of God, and took and ate the bread of the Presence, which it is not lawful for any but the priests to eat, and also gave it to those with him?" ⁵And he said to them, "The Son of man is lord of the sabbath."

1 Sam 21:6

Lev 24:9

Curing of a man with a withered hand
⁶On another sabbath, when he entered the synagogue and taught, a man was there whose right hand was withered. ⁷And the scribes and the Pharisees watched him, to see whether he would heal on the sabbath, so that they might find an accusation against him. ⁸But he knew their thoughts, and he said to the man who had the withered hand, "Come and stand here." And he rose and stood there. ⁹And Jesus said to them, "I ask you, is it lawful on the sabbath to do good or to do harm, to save life or to destroy it?" ¹⁰And he looked around on them all, and said to him, "Stretch out your hand." And he did so, and his hand was restored. ¹¹But they were filled with fury and discussed with one another what they might do to Jesus.

Mt 12:9–14
Mk 3:1–6
Lk 14:1

Christians should sometimes abstain from food. "Fast and abstain from flesh meat when Holy Mother Church so ordains" (St Pius X, *Catechism*, 495). That is the purpose of the fourth commandment of the Church, but it has a deeper meaning, as St Leo the Great tells us: "The merit of our fasts does not consist only in abstinence from food; there is no use in depriving the body of nourishment if the soul does not cut itself off from iniquity and if the tongue does not cease to speak evil" (*Sermo IV in Quadragesima*).

6:1–5. Accused by the Pharisees of breaking the sabbath, Jesus explains the correct way of understanding the sabbath rest, using an example from the Old Testament. And, by stating that he is "Lord of the sabbath" he is openly revealing that he is God himself, for it was God who gave this precept to the

people of Israel. For more on this, see the notes on Mt 12:2 and 12:3–8.

6:10. The Fathers teach us how to discover a deep spiritual meaning in apparently casual things Jesus says. St Ambrose, for example, commenting on the phrase "Stretch out your hand," says: "This form of medicine is common and general. Offer it often, in benefit of your neighbour; defend from injury anyone who seems to be suffering as a result of calumny; stretch out your hand also to the poor man who asks for your help; stretch it out also to the Lord, asking him to forgive your sins; that is how you should stretch your hand out, and that is the way to be cured" (*Expositio Evangelii sec. Lucam*, in loc.).

6:11. The Pharisees do not want to reply to Jesus' question and do not know how to react to the miracle which he goes on

4. JESUS' MIRACLES AND PREACHING IN GALILEE

Jesus chooses twelve apostles

Mk 3:13–19
Mt 10:2–4
Jn 6:70
Acts 1:13

¹²In these days he went out into the hills to pray; and all night he continued in prayer to God. ¹³And when it was day, he called his disciples, and chose from them twelve, whom he named apostles: ¹⁴Simon, whom he named Peter, and Andrew his brother, and James and John, and Philip and Bartholomew, ¹⁵and Matthew, and Thomas, and James the son of Alphaeus, and Simon who was

---

to work. It should have converted them, but their hearts were in darkness and they were full of jealousy and anger. Later on, these people, who kept quiet in our Lord's presence, began to discuss him among themselves, not with a view to approaching him again but with the purpose of doing away with him. In this connexion St Cyril comments: "O Pharisee, you see him working wonders and healing the sick by using a higher power, yet out of envy you plot his death" (*Commentarium in Lucam*, in loc.).

6:12–13. The evangelist writes with a certain formality when describing this important occasion on which Jesus chooses the Twelve, constituting them as the apostolic college: "The Lord Jesus, having prayed at length to the Father, called to himself those whom he willed and appointed twelve to be with him, whom he might send to preach the Kingdom of God (cf. Mk 2:13–19; Mt 10:1–42). These apostles (cf. Lk 6:13) he constituted in the form of a college or permanent assembly, at the head of which he placed Peter, chosen from among them (cf. Jn 21:15–17). He sent them first of all to the children of Israel and then to all peoples (cf. Rom 1:16), so that, sharing in his power, they might make all peoples his disciples and sanctify and govern them (cf. Mt 28:16–20; and par.) and thus

spread the Church and, administering it under the guidance of the Lord, shepherd it all days until the end of the world (cf. Mt 28:20). They were fully confirmed in this mission on the day of Pentecost (cf. Acts 2:1–26) [...]. Through their preaching the Gospel everywhere (cf. Mk 16:20), and through its being welcomed and received under the influence of the Holy Spirit by those who hear it, the apostles gather together the universal Church, which the Lord founded upon the apostles and built upon Blessed Peter their leader, the chief cornerstone being Christ Jesus himself (cf. Rev 21:14; Mt 16:18; Eph 2:20). That divine mission, which was committed by Christ to the apostles, is destined to last until the end of the world (cf. Mt 28:20), since the Gospel, which they were charged to hand on, is, for the Church, the principle of all its life for all time. For that very reason the apostles were careful to appoint successors in this hierarchically constituted society" (Vatican II, *Lumen gentium*, 19–20).

Before establishing the apostolic college, Jesus spent the whole night in prayer. He often made special prayer for his Church (Lk 9:18; Jn 17:1ff), thereby preparing his apostles to be its pillars (cf. Gal 2:9). As his passion approaches, he will pray to the Father for Simon Peter, the head of the Church, and solemnly tell Peter that he has done so: "But I have

called the Zealot, [16]and Judas the son of James, and Judas Iscariot, who became a traitor.

Preaching on the plain

[17]And he came down with them and stood on a level place, with a great crowd of his disciples and a great multitude of people from all Judea and Jerusalem and the sea coast of Tyre and Sidon, who came to hear him and to be healed of their diseases; [18]and those who were troubled with unclean spirits were cured. [19]And all the crowd sought to touch him, for power came forth from him and healed them all.

Mt 4:23; 5:1
Mk 3:7–12

Lk 5:17; 8:46

---

prayed for you that your faith may not fail" (Lk 22:32). Following Christ's example, the Church stipulates that on many occasions liturgical prayer should be offered for the pastors of the Church (the Pope, the bishops in general, and priests) asking God to give them grace to fulfil their ministry faithfully.

Christ is continually teaching us that we need to pray always (Lk 18:1). Here he shows us by his example that we should pray with special intensity at important moments in our lives. "*Pernoctans in oratione Dei*. He spent the whole night in prayer to God.' So St Luke tells of our Lord. And you? How often have you persevered like that? Well, then ..." (St Josemaría Escrivá, *The Way*, 104).

On the need for prayer and the qualities our prayer should have, see the notes on Mt 6:5–6; 7:7–11; 14:22–23; Mk 1:35; Lk 5:16; 11:1–4; 22:41–42.

6:12. Since Jesus is God, why does he pray? There were two wills in Christ, one divine and one human (cf. St Pius X, *Catechism*, 91), and although by virtue of his divine will he was omnipotent, his human will was not omnipotent. When we pray, what we do is make our will known to God; therefore Christ, who is like us in all things but sin (cf. Heb 4:15), also had to pray in a human way (cf. St

Thomas Aquinas, *Summa theologiae*, 3, 21, 1). Reflecting on Jesus at prayer, St Ambrose comments: "The Lord prays not to ask things for himself, but to intercede on my behalf; for although the Father has put everything into the hands of the Son, still the Son, in order to behave in accordance with his condition as man, considers it appropriate to implore the Father for our sake, for he is our Advocate [...]. A Master of obedience, by his example he instructs us concerning the precepts of virtue: 'We have an advocate with the Father'(1 Jn 2:1)" (*Expositio Evangelii sec. Lucam*, in loc.).

6:14–16. Jesus chose for apostles very ordinary people, most of them poor and uneducated; apparently only Matthew and the brothers James and John had social positions of any consequence. But all of them gave up whatever they had, little or much as it was, and all of them, bar Judas, put their faith in the Lord, overcame their shortcomings and eventually proved faithful to grace and became saints, veritable pillars of the Church. We should not feel uneasy when we realize that we too are low in human qualities; what matters is being faithful to the grace God gives us.

6:19. God became man to save us. The divine person of the Word acts through

75

The Beatitudes and the Woes

Mt 5:3–12

Rev 7:16–17
Ps 126:5–6
Is 61:3

²⁰And he lifted up his eyes on his disciples, and said:*
"Blessed are you poor, for yours is the kingdom of God.
²¹"Blessed are you that hunger now, for you shall be satisfied.
"Blessed are you that weep now, for you shall laugh.

---

the human nature which he took on. The cures and casting out of devils which he performed during his life on earth are also proof that Christ actually brings redemption and not just hope of redemption. The crowds of people from Judea and other parts of Israel who flock to him, seeking even to touch him, anticipate, in a way, Christians' devotion to the holy Humanity of Christ.

6:20–49. These thirty verses of St Luke correspond to some extent to the Sermon on the Mount, an extensive account of which St Matthew gives us in chapters 5–7 in his Gospel. It is very likely that in the course of his public ministry in different regions and towns of Israel Jesus preached the same things, using different words on different occasions. Under the inspiration of the Holy Spirit each evangelist would have chosen to report those things which he considered most useful for the instruction of his immediate readers—Christians of Jewish origin in the case of Matthew, Gentile converts in the case of Luke. There is no reason why one evangelist should not have selected certain items and another different ones, depending on his readership, or why one should not have laid special stress on some subjects and shortened or omitted accounts of others.

In this present discourse, we might distinguish three parts—the Beatitudes and the curses (6:20–26); love of one's enemies (6:27–38); and teaching on uprightness of heart (6:39–49).

Some Christians may find it difficult to grasp the need of practising the moral

teaching of the Gospel so radically, in particular Christ's teaching in the Sermon on the Mount. Jesus is very demanding in what he says, but he is saying it to everyone, and not just to his apostles or to those disciples who followed him closely. We are told expressly that "when Jesus finished these sayings, the crowds were astonished at his teaching" (Mt 7:28). It is quite clear that the Master calls everyone to holiness, making no distinction of state-in-life, race or personal circumstances. This teaching on the universal call to holiness was a central point of the teaching of St Josemaría Escrivá de Balaguer. The Second Vatican Council expressed the same teaching with the full weight of its authority: everyone is called to Christian holiness; consider, for example, just one reference it makes, in *Lumen gentium*, 11: "Strengthened by so many and such great means of salvation, all the faithful, whatever their condition or state—though each in his or her own way—are called by the Lord to that perfection of sanctity by which the Father himself is perfect."

In the Sermon on the Mount Jesus is not proposing an unattainable ideal, useful though that might be to make us feel humble in the light of our inability to reach it. No. Christian teaching in this regard is quite clear: what Christ commands, he commands in order to have us do what he says. Along with his commandment comes grace to enable us to fulfil it. Therefore, every Christian is capable of practising the moral teaching of Christ and of attaining the full height of his calling—holiness—not by his own

76

²²"Blessed are you when men hate you, and when they exclude you and revile you, and cast out your name as evil, on account of the Son of man! ²³Rejoice in that day, and leap for joy, for behold, your reward is great in heaven; for so their fathers did to the prophets.
²⁴"But woe to you that are rich, for you have received your consolation.

Jn 15:19; 16:2

Jas 5:1

efforts alone but by means of the grace which Christ has won for us, and with the abiding help of the means of sanctification which he left to his Church. "If anyone plead human weakness to excuse himself for not loving God, it should be explained that He who demands our love pours into our hearts by the Holy Spirit the fervour of his love, and this good Spirit our heavenly Father gives to those that ask him. With reason, therefore, did St Augustine pray: 'Give me what thou command, and command what you please.' As, then, God is ever ready to help us, especially since the death of Christ our Lord, by which the prince of this world was cast out, there is no reason why anyone should be disheartened by the difficulty of the undertaking. To him who loves, nothing is difficult" (St Pius V, *Catechism*, 3, 1, 7).

6:20–26. The eight Beatitudes which St Matthew gives (5:3–12) are summed up in four by St Luke, but with four opposite curses. We can say, with St Ambrose, that Matthew's eight are included in Luke's four (cf. *Expositio Evangelii sec. Lucam*, in loc.). In St Luke they are in some cases stated in a more incisive, more direct form than in the First Gospel, where they are given with more explanation: for example, the first beatitude says simply "Blessed are you poor", whereas in Matthew we read, "Blessed are the poor in spirit", which contains a brief explanation of the meaning of the virtue of poverty.

6:20. "The ordinary Christian has to reconcile two aspects of this life that can at first sight seem contradictory. There is, on the one hand, *true poverty*, which is obvious and tangible and made up of definite things. This poverty should be an expression of faith in God and a sign that the heart is not satisfied with created things and aspires to the Creator; that it wants to be filled with love of God so as to be able to give this same love to everyone. On the other hand, an ordinary Christian is and wants to be *one more among his fellow men*, sharing their way of life, their joys and happiness; working with them, loving the world and all the good things that exist in it; using all created things to solve the problems of human life and to establish a spiritual and material environment which will foster personal and social development [...].

"To my way of thinking, the best examples of poverty are those mothers and fathers of large and poor families who spend their lives for their children and who with their effort and constancy—often without complaining of their needs—bring up their family, creating a cheerful home in which everyone learns to love, to serve and to work" (St Josemaría Escrivá, *Conversations*, 111f).

6:24–26. Our Lord here condemns four things: avarice and attachment to the things of the world; excessive care of the body, gluttony; empty-headed joy and general self-indulgence; flattery, and disordered desire for human glory—four

Is 5:22
²⁵"Woe to you that are full now, for you shall hunger.
"Woe to you that laugh now, for you shall mourn and weep.

Jas 4:4
Mic 2:11
²⁶"Woe to you, when all men speak well of you, for so their fathers did to the false prophets.

Love of enemies

Mt 5:39–48
²⁷"But I say to you that hear, Love your enemies, do good to those who hate you, ²⁸bless those who curse you, pray for those who abuse you. ²⁹To him who strikes you on the cheek, offer the other also; and from him who takes away your cloak do not withhold

common vices which a Christian needs to be on guard against.

6:24. In the same kind of way as in v. 20, which refers to the poor in the sense of those who love poverty, seeking to please God better, so in this verse the "rich" are to be understood as those who strive to accumulate possessions heedless of whether or not they are doing so lawfully, and who seek their happiness in those possessions, as if they were their ultimate goal. But people who inherit wealth or acquire it through honest work can be really poor provided they are detached from these things and are led by that detachment to use them to help others, as God inspires them. We can find in Sacred Scripture a number of people to whom the beatitude of the poor can be applied although they possessed considerable wealth—Abraham, Isaac, Moses, David, Job, for example.

As early as St Augustine's time there were people who failed to understand poverty and riches properly; they reasoned as follows: The Kingdom of heaven belongs to the poor, the Lazaruses of this world, the hungry; all the rich are bad, like this rich man here. This sort of thinking led St Augustine to explain the deep meaning of wealth and poverty according to the spirit of the Gospel: "Listen, poor man, to my comments on your words. When you refer to yourself as Lazarus, that holy man

covered with wounds, I am afraid your pride makes you describe yourself incorrectly. Do not despise rich men who are merciful, who are humble: or, to put it briefly, do not despise poor rich men. Oh, poor man!, be poor yourself; poor, that is, humble [...]. Listen to me, then. Be truly poor, be devout, be humble; if you glory in your ragged and ulcerous poverty, if you glory in likening yourself to that beggar lying outside the rich man's house, then you are only noticing his poverty, and nothing else. What should I notice, you ask? Read the Scriptures and you will understand what I mean. Lazarus was poor, but he to whose bosom he was brought was rich. 'It came to pass, it is written, that the poor man died and he was brought by the angels to Abraham's bosom.' To where? To Abraham's bosom or, let us say, to that mysterious place where Abraham was resting. Read [...] and remember that Abraham was a very wealthy man when he was on earth: he had abundance of money, a large family, flocks, land; yet that rich man was poor, because he was humble. 'Abraham believed God and he was reckoned righteous.' [...] He was faithful, he did good, he received the commandment to offer his son in sacrifice, and he did not refuse to offer what he had received to Him from whom he had received it. He was approved in God's sight and set before us as an example of faith" (*Sermons*, 14).

78

your coat as well. [30]Give to every one who begs from you; and of
him who takes away your goods do not ask them again. [31]And as
you wish that men would do to you, do so to them.
[32]"If you love those who love you, what credit is that to you?
For even sinners love those who love them. [33]And if you do good
to those who do good to you, what credit is that to you? For even
sinners do the same. [34]And if you lend to those from whom you
hope to receive, what credit is that to you? Even sinners lend to
sinners, to receive as much again. [35]But love your enemies, and do
good, and lend, expecting nothing in return;[v] and your reward will

Mt 7:12

Lev 25:35f

Mt 6:14

To sum up: poverty does not consist in something purely external, in having or not having material goods, but in something that goes far deeper, affecting a person's heart and soul; it consists in having a humble attitude to God, in being devout, in having total faith. If a Christian has these virtues and also has an abundance of material possessions, he should be detached from his wealth and act charitably towards others and thus be pleasing to God. On the other hand, if someone is not well-off he is not justified in God's sight on that account, if he fails to strive to acquire those virtues in which true poverty consists.

6:27. "In loving our enemies there shines forth in us some likeness to God our Father, who, by the death of his Son, ransomed from everlasting perdition and reconciled to himself the human race, which previously was most unfriendly and hostile to him" (St Pius V, *Catechism*, 4, 14, 19). Following the example of God our Father, we must desire for everyone (even those who say they are our enemies) eternal life, in the first place; additionally, a Christian has a duty to respect and understand everyone without exception, because of his or her intrinsic dignity as a human person, made in the image and likeness of the Creator.

6:28. Jesus Christ teaches us by example that this is a real precept and not just a pious recommendation; even when nailed to the cross he prayed to his Father for those who had brought him to such a pass: "Father, forgive them; for they know not what they do" (Lk 23:34). In imitation of the Master, St Stephen, the first martyr of the Church, when he was being stoned, prayed to our Lord not to hold the sin against his persecutors (cf. Acts 7:60). In the liturgy of Good Friday the Church offers prayers and suffrages to God on behalf of those outside the Church, asking him to give them the grace of faith; to release from their ignorance those who do not know him; to give Jews the light of the truth; to bring non-Catholic Christians, linked by true charity, into full communion with our Mother the Church.

6:29. Our Lord gives us more examples to show us how we should act if we want to imitate the mercy of God. The first has to do with one of what are traditionally called the "spiritual works of mercy"— forgiving injuries and being patient with other people's defects. This is what he means in the first instance about turning the other cheek.

To understand what our Lord is saying here, St Thomas comments that

v. Other ancient authorities read *despairing of no man*

be great, and you will be sons of the Most High; for he is kind to the ungrateful and the selfish. ³⁶Be merciful, even as your Father is merciful.

Mt 4:24

³⁷"Judge not, and you will not be judged; condemn not, and you will not be condemned; forgive, and you will be forgiven; ³⁸give, and it will be given to you; good measure, pressed down, shaken together, running over, will be put into your lap. For the measure you give will be the measure you get back."

Integrity

Mt 15:14

³⁹He also told them a parable: "Can a blind man lead a blind man? Will they not both fall into a pit? ⁴⁰A disciple is not above his

---

"Holy Scripture needs to be understood in the light of the example of Christ and the saints. Christ did not offer the other cheek to be struck in the house of Annas (Jn 18:22f), nor did St Paul when, as we are told in the Acts of the Apostles, he was beaten in Philippi (Acts 16:22f). Therefore, we should not take it that Christ literally meant that you should offer the other cheek to someone to hit you; what he was referring to was your interior disposition; that is, if necessary we should be ready not to be intolerant of anyone who hurts us, and we should be ready to put up with this kind of treatment, or worse than that. That was how the Lord acted when he surrendered his body to death" (*Comm. on St John*, 18, 37).

6:36. The model of mercy which Christ sets before us is God himself, of whom St Paul says: "Blessed be the God and Father of our Lord Jesus Christ, the Father of mercies and God of all comfort, who comforts us in all our affliction" (2 Cor 1:3–4). "The first quality of this virtue", Fray Luis de Granada explains, "is that it makes men like God and like the most glorious thing in him, his mercy (Lk 6:36). For certainly the greatest perfection a creature can have is to be like his Creator; and the more like him he is,

the more perfect he is. Certainly one of the things which is most appropriate to God is mercy, which is what the Church means when it says that prayer: 'Lord God, to whom it is proper to be merciful and forgiving ...'. It says that this is proper to God, because just as a creature, as creature, is characteristically poor and needy (and therefore characteristically receives and does not give), so, on the contrary, since God is infinitely rich and powerful, to him alone does it belong to give and not to receive, and therefore it is appropriate for him to be merciful and forgiving" (*Book of Prayer and Meditation*, third part, third treatise).

This is the rule a Christian should apply: be compassionate towards other people's afflictions as if they were one's own, and try to remedy them. The Church spells out this rule by giving us a series of corporal works of mercy (visiting and caring for the sick, giving food to the hungry, drink to the thirsty ...) and spiritual works of mercy (teaching the ignorant, correcting the person who has erred, forgiving injuries ...): cf. St Pius X, *Catechism*, 944f.

We should also show understanding towards people who are in error: "Love and courtesy of this kind should not, of course, make us indifferent to truth and goodness. Love, in fact, impels the fol-

teacher, but every one when he is fully taught will be like his Mt 10:24–25
Jn 15:20 teacher. ⁴¹Why do you see the speck that is in your brother's eye, but do not notice the log that is in your own eye? ⁴²Or how can you say to your brother, 'Brother, let me take out the speck that is in your eye,' when you yourself do not see the log that is in your own eye? You hypocrite, first take the log out of your own eye, and then you will see clearly to take out the speck that is in your brother's eye.

⁴³"For no good tree bears bad fruit, nor again does a bad tree bear good fruit; ⁴⁴for each tree is known by its own fruit. For figs are not gathered from thorns, nor are grapes picked from a bramble bush. ⁴⁵The good man out of the good treasure of his heart Mt 12:34–35

lowers of Christ to proclaim to all men the truth which saves. But we must distinguish between the error (which must always be rejected) and the person in error, who never loses his dignity as a person even though he flounders amid false or inadequate religious ideas. God alone is the judge and the searcher of hearts; he forbids us to pass judgment on the inner guilt of others" (Vatican II, *Gaudium et spes*, 28).

6:38. We read in Sacred Scripture of the generosity of the widow of Zarephath, whom God asked to give food to Elijah the prophet even though she had very little left; he then rewarded her generosity by constantly renewing her supply of meal and oil (cf. 1 Kings 17:9ff). The same sort of thing happened when the boy supplied the five loaves and two fish which our Lord multiplied to feed a huge crowd of people (cf. Jn 6:9)—a vivid example of what God does when we give him whatever we have, even if it does not amount to much.

God does not let himself be outdone in generosity: "Go, generously and like a child ask him: 'What can you mean to give me when you ask me for "this"?' " (St Josemaría Escrivá, *The Way*, 153). However much we give God in this life, he will give us more in life eternal.

6:43–44. To distinguish the good tree from the bad tree we need to look at the fruit the tree produces (deeds) and not at its foliage (words). "For there is no lack of people here on earth who, on being approached, turn out to be nothing but large, shiny, glossy leaves. Foliage, just foliage and nothing more. Meanwhile, many souls are looking to us, hoping to satisfy their hunger, which is a hunger for God. We must not forget that we have all the resources we need. We have sufficient doctrine and the grace of God, in spite of our wretchedness" (St Josemaría Escrivá, *Friends of God*, 51).

6:45. Jesus is giving us two similes—that of the tree which, if it is good, produces good fruit, and that of the man, who speaks of those things he has in his heart. "The treasure of the heart is the same as the root of the tree," St Bede explains. "A person who has a treasure of patience and of perfect charity in his heart yields excellent fruit; he loves his neighbour and has all the other qualities Jesus teaches; he loves his enemies, does good to him who hates him, blesses him who curses him, prays for him who calumniates him, does not react against him who attacks him or robs him; he gives to those who ask, does not claim what they have stolen from him, wishes

produces good, and the evil man out of his evil treasure produces evil; for out of the abundance of the heart his mouth speaks.

Mal 1:6
Mt 7:21

[46]"Why do you call me 'Lord, Lord,' and not do what I tell you? [47]Every one who comes to me and hears my words and does them, I will show you what he is like: [48]he is like a man building a house, who dug deep, and laid the foundation upon rock; and when a flood arose, the stream broke against that house, and could not shake it, because it had been well built.[w] [49]But he who hears and does not do them is like a man who built a house on the ground without a foundation; against which the stream broke, and immediately it fell, and the ruin of that house was great."

The centurion's faith

Mt 8:5–13
Jn 4:46

7 [1]After he had ended all his sayings in the hearing of the people he entered Capernaum. [2]Now a centurion had a slave who was dear[x] to him, who was sick and at the point of death. [3]When he heard of Jesus, he sent to him elders of the Jews, asking him to come and heal his slave. [4]And when they came to Jesus,

---

not to judge and does not condemn, corrects patiently and affectionately those who err. But the person who has in his heart the treasure of evil does exactly the opposite: he hates his friends, speaks evil of him who loves him and does all the other things condemned by the Lord" (*In Lucae Evangelium expositio*, 2, 6).

6:46. Jesus asks us to act in a way consistent with being Christians and not to make any separation between the faith we profess and the way we live: "What matters is not whether or not we wear a religious habit; it is whether we try to practise the virtues and surrender our will to God and order our lives as His Majesty ordains, and not want to do our will but his" (St Teresa of Avila, *Interior Castle*, 2, 6).

7:1–10. "They besought him earnestly" (v. 4). Here is an example of the effectiveness of the prayer of petition, which

induces almighty God to work a miracle. In this connexion St Bernard explains what we should ask God for: "As I see it, the petitions of the heart consist in three things [...]. The first two have to do with the present, that is, with things for the body and for the soul; the third is the blessedness of eternal life. Do not be surprised that he says that we should ask God for things for the body: all things come from him, physical as well as spiritual things [...]. However, we should pray more often and more fervently for things our souls need, that is, for God's grace and for virtues" (*Fifth Lenten sermon*, 8f). To obtain his grace—of whatever kind—God himself expects us to ask him assiduously, confidently, humbly and persistently.

What stands out here is the centurion's humility: he did not belong to the chosen people, he was a pagan; but he makes his request through friends, with deep humility. Humility is a route to faith,

---

w. Other ancient authorities read *founded upon the rock*   x. Or *valuable*

they besought him earnestly, saying, "He is worthy to have you do this for him, [5]for he loves our nation, and he built us our synagogue." [6]And Jesus went with them. When he was not far from the house, the centurion sent friends to him, saying to him, "Lord, do not trouble yourself, for I am not worthy to have you come under my roof; [7]therefore I did not presume to come to you. But say the word, and let my servant be healed. [8]For I am a man set under authority, with soldiers under me: and I say to one, 'Go,' and he goes; and to another, 'Come,' and he comes; and to my slave, 'Do this,' and he does it." [9]When Jesus heard this he marvelled at him, and turned and said to the multitude that followed him, "I tell you, not even in Israel have I found such faith." [10]And when those who had been sent returned to the house, they found the slave well.

The son of the widow of Nain restored to life

[11]Soon afterward[y] he went to a city called Nain, and his disciples and a great crowd went with him. [12]As he drew near to the gate of   1 Kings 17:17ff

---

whether to receive faith for the first time or to revive it. Speaking of his own conversion experience, St Augustine says that because he was not humble, he could not understand how Jesus, who was such a humble person, could be God, nor how God could teach anyone by lowering himself to the point of taking on our human condition. This was precisely why the Word, eternal Truth, became man—to demolish our pride, to encourage our love, to subdue all things and thereby be able to raise us up (cf. *Confessions*, 7, 18, 24).

7:6–7. Such is the faith and humility of the centurion that the Church, in its eucharistic liturgy, gives us his very words to express our own sentiments just before receiving Holy Communion; we too should strive to have this interior disposition when Jesus enters under our roof, our soul.

7:11–17. "Jesus crosses paths again with a crowd of people. He could have passed

by or waited until they called him. But he didn't. He took the initiative, because he was moved by a widow's sorrow. She had just lost all she had, her son.

"The evangelist explains that Jesus was moved. Perhaps he even showed signs of it, as when Lazarus died. Jesus Christ was not, and is not, insensitive to the suffering that stems from love. He is pained at seeing children separated from their parents. He overcomes death so as to give life, to reunite those who love one another. But at the same time, he requires that we first admit the pre-eminence of divine love, which alone can inspire genuine Christian living.

"Christ knows he is surrounded by a crowd which will be awed by the miracle and will tell the story all over the countryside. But he does not act artificially, merely to create an effect. Quite simply he is touched by that woman's suffering and cannot but console her. So he goes up to her and says, 'Do not weep.' It is like saying: 'I don't want to see you

y. Other ancient authorities read *Next day*

the city, behold, a man who had died was being carried out, the only son of his mother, and she was a widow; and a large crowd from the city was with her. [13]And when the Lord saw her, he had compassion on her and said to her, "Do not weep." [14]And he came and touched the bier, and the bearers stood still. And he said, "Young man, I say to you, arise." [15]And the dead man sat up, and began to speak. And he gave him to his mother. [16]Fear seized them all; and they glorified God, saying, "A great prophet has arisen among us!" and "God has visited his people!" [17]And this report concerning him spread through the whole of Judea and all the surrounding country.

Messengers from John the Baptist

Mt 11:2–19
Mal 3:1

[18]The disciples of John told him of all these things. [19]And John, calling to him two of his disciples, sent them to the Lord, saying, "Are you he who is to come, or shall we look for another?" [20]And when the men had come to him, they said, "John the Baptist has sent us to you, saying, 'Are you he who is to come, or shall we

---

crying; I have come on earth to bring joy and peace.' And then comes the miracle, the sign of the power of Christ who is God. But first came his compassion, an evident sign of the tenderness of the heart of Christ the man" (St Josemaría Escrivá, *Christ Is Passing By*, 166).

7:15. This mother's joy on being given back her son reminds us of the joy of our Mother the Church when her sinful children return to the life of grace. "The widowed mother rejoiced at the raising of that young man," St Augustine comments. "Our Mother the Church rejoices every day when people are raised again in spirit. The young man had been dead physically; the latter, dead spiritually. The young man's death was mourned visibly; the death of the latter was invisible and unmourned. He seeks them out who knew them to be dead; only he can bring them back to life" (*Sermons*, 98, 2).

7:18–23. "It was not out of ignorance that John enquired about Christ's coming in

the flesh, for he had already clearly professed his belief, saying, 'I have seen and have borne witness that this is the Son of God' (Jn 1:34). That is why he does not ask, 'Are you he who has come?' but rather, 'Are you he who is to come?' thus asking about the future, not about the past. Nor should we think that the Baptist did not know about Christ's future passion, for it was John who said, 'Behold the Lamb of God, who takes away the sins of the world' (Jn 1:29), thus foretelling his future immolation, which other prophets had already foretold, particularly Isaiah (chap. 53) [...]. It can also be replied, with St John Chrysostom, that John made this enquiry not from doubt or ignorance, but because he wished his disciples to be satisfied on this point by Christ. Therefore, Christ gave his reply to instruct these disciples, by pointing to the evidence of his miracles (v. 22)" (St Thomas Aquinas, *Summa theologiae*, 2–2, 2, 7 ad 2).

7:22. In his reply to these disciples of John the Baptist, Jesus points to the miracles

look for another?' " ²¹In that hour he cured many of diseases and
plagues and evil spirits, and on many that were blind he bestowed
sight. ²²And he answered them, "Go and tell John what you have   Is 35:5; 61:1
seen and heard: the blind receive their sight, the lame walk, lepers
are cleansed, and the deaf hear, the dead are raised up, the poor
have good news preached to them. ²³And blessed is he who takes
no offence at me."

²⁴When the messengers of John had gone, he began to speak to
the crowds concerning John: "What did you go out into the
wilderness to behold? A reed shaken by the wind? ²⁵What then did   Mt 3:4
you go out to see? A man clothed in soft raiment? Behold, those
who are gorgeously apparelled and live in luxury are in kings'
courts. ²⁶What then did you go out to see? A prophet? Yes, I tell   Lk 1:76
you, and more than a prophet. ²⁷This is he of whom it is written,   Mal 3:1
'Behold, I send my messenger before thy face,
who shall prepare thy way before thee.'
²⁸I tell you, among those born of women none is greater than   Lk 1:15
John; yet he who is least in the kingdom of God is greater than

---

he has worked, which show that he has
inaugurated the Kingdom of God; he is,
therefore, the promised Messiah. Along
with miracles, one of the signs of the
coming of the Kingdom is the preaching
of salvation to the poor. On the meaning
of "the poor", see the notes on Mt 5:3;
Lk 6:20 and 6:24. Following the Lord's
example, the Church has always taken
special care of those in need. In our own
time the Popes have stressed time and
again the duties of Christians in regard to
poverty caused by man's injustice to
man: "Selfishness and domination are
permanent temptations for men. Likewise
an ever finer discernment is needed, in
order to strike at the roots of newly arising situations of injustice and to establish
progressively a justice which will be less
and less imperfect [...]. The Church
directs her attention to these new 'poor'
—the handicapped, the maladjusted, the
old, various groups on the fringe of society—in order to recognize them, help
them, defend their place and dignity
in a society hardened by competition

and the attraction of success" (Paul VI,
Octogesima adveniens, 15).

7:23. These words refer to the same
thing Simeon prophesied about when he
referred to Christ as a sign that is spoken
against, a sign of contradiction (cf. Lk
2:34). People who reject our Lord, who
are scandalized by him, will not reach
heaven.

7:28. St John the Baptist is the greatest
of the prophets of the Old Testament
because he was the nearest to Christ and
received the unique mission of actually
pointing out the Messiah. Still, he belongs to the time of the promise (the Old
Testament), when the work of redemption lay in the future. Once Christ did
that work (the New Testament), those
who faithfully accept God's gift of grace
are incomparably greater than the righteous of the Old Covenant who were
given, not this grace, but only the
promise of it. Once the work of redemption was accomplished God's grace also

Lk 3:7–12
Mt 21:32

Acts 13:46
he."* ²⁹(When they heard this all the people and the tax collectors justified God, having been baptized with the baptism of John; ³⁰but the Pharisees and the lawyers rejected the purpose of God for themselves, not having been baptized by him.)

Jesus reproaches his contemporaries

³¹"To what then shall I compare the men of this generation, and what are they like? ³²They are like children sitting in the market place and calling to one another,

'We piped to you, and you did not dance;
we wailed, and you did not weep.'

Lk 5:30; 15:2
³³For John the Baptist has come eating no bread and drinking no wine; and you say, 'He has a demon.' ³⁴The Son of man has come eating and drinking; and you say, 'Behold, a glutton and a drunkard, a friend of tax collectors and sinners!' ³⁵Yet wisdom is justified by all her children."

---

reached the righteous of the Old Testament, who were waiting for Christ to open heaven and let them, too, enter.

7:31–34. See the note on Mt 11:16–19.

7:35. The wisdom referred to here is divine wisdom, especially Christ himself (cf. Wis 7:26; Prov 8:22). "Children of Wisdom" is a Hebrew way of saying "wise men"; he is truly wise who comes to know God and love him and be saved by him—in other words, a saint.

Divine wisdom is revealed in the creation and government of the universe and, particularly, in the salvation of mankind. Wise men "justifying" wisdom seems to mean that the wise, the saints, bear witness to Christ by living holy lives: "Let your light so shine before men, that they may see your good works and give glory to your Father who is in heaven" (Mt 5:16).

7:36–40. This woman, moved no doubt by grace, was attracted by Christ's preaching and by what people were saying about him. When dining, people reclined

on low divans leaning on their left arm with their legs tucked under them, away from the table. A host was expected to give his guest a kiss of greeting and offer him water for his feet, and perfumes.

7:41–50. In this short parable of the two debtors Christ teaches us three things —his own divinity and his power to forgive sins; the merit the woman's love deserves; and the discourtesy implied in Simeon's neglecting to receive Jesus in the conventional way. Our Lord was not interested in these social niceties as such but in the affection which they expressed; that was why he felt hurt at Simeon's neglect.

"Jesus notices the omission of the expression of human courtesy and refinement which the Pharisee failed to show him. Christ is *perfectus Deus, perfectus homo (Athanasian Creed)*. He is perfect God, the Second Person of the Blessed Trinity, and perfect man. He comes to save, not to destroy nature. It is from him that we learn that it is unchristian to treat our fellow men badly, for they are creatures of God, made in his image and like-

Forgiveness for a sinful woman

³⁶One of the Pharisees asked him to eat with him, and he went into the Pharisee's house, and sat at table. ³⁷And behold, a woman of the city, who was a sinner, when she learned that he was sitting at table in the Pharisee's house, brought an alabaster flask of ointment, ³⁸and standing behind him at his feet, weeping, she began to wet his feet with her tears; and wiped them with the hair of her head, and kissed his feet, and anointed them with the ointment. ³⁹Now when the Pharisee who had invited him saw it, he said to himself, "If this man were a prophet, he would have known who and what sort of woman this is who is touching him, for she is a sinner." ⁴⁰And Jesus answering said to him, "Simon, I have something to say to you." And he answered, "What is it, Teacher?" ⁴¹"A certain creditor had two debtors; one owed five hundred denarii, and the other fifty. ⁴²When they could not pay, he forgave them both. Now which of them will love him more?" ⁴³Simon

Lk 11:37

Mt 26:7–13
Mk 14:3–9
Jn 12:3–8

Jn 4:19

ness (cf. Gen 1:26)" (St Josemaría Escrivá, *Friends of God*, 73).

Moreover, the Pharisee was wrong to think badly of this sinner and of Jesus: reckoning that Christ did not know anything about her, he complained inwardly. Our Lord, who could read the secret thoughts of men (which showed his divinity), intervened to point out to him his mistake. True righteousness, says St Gregory the Great (cf. *In Evangelia homiliae*, 33), is compassionate; whereas false righteousness is indignant. There are many people like this Pharisee: forgetting that they themselves were or are poor sinners, when they see other people's sin they immediately become indignant, instead of taking pity on them, or else they rush to judge them or sneer at them. They forget what St Paul says: "Let any one who thinks that he stands take heed lest he fall" (1 Cor 10:12); "Brethren, if a man is overtaken in any trespass, you who are spiritual should restore him in a spirit of gentleness [...]. Bear one another's burdens, and so fulfil the law of Christ" (Gal 6:1–2).

We should strive to have charity govern all our judgments. Otherwise, we will easily be unjust towards others. "Let us be slow to judge. Each one see things from his own point of view, and with his own mind, with all its limitations, through eyes that are often dimmed and clouded by passion.... Of what little worth are the judgments of men! Don't judge without sifting your judgment in prayer" (St J. Escrivá, *The Way*, 451).

Charity and humility will allow us to see in the sins of others our own weak and helpless position, and will help our hearts go out to the sorrow of every sinner who repents, for we too would fall into sins as serious or more serious if God in his mercy did not stay by our side.

"It was not the ointment that the Lord loved", St Ambrose comments, "but the affection; it was the woman's faith that pleased him, her humility. And you also, if you desire grace, increase your love; pour over the body of Jesus Christ your faith in the Resurrection, the perfume of the holy Church and the ointment of charity towards others" (*Expositio Evangelii sec. Lucam*, in loc.).

answered, "The one, I suppose, to whom he forgave more." And he said to him, "You have judged rightly." [44]Then turning toward the woman he said to Simon, "Do you see this woman? I entered your house, you gave me no water for my feet, but she has wet my feet with her tears and wiped them with her hair. [45]You gave me no kiss, but from the time I came in she has not ceased to kiss my feet. [46]You did not anoint my head with oil, but she has anointed my feet with ointment. [47]Therefore I tell you, her sins, which are many, are forgiven, for she loved much; but he who is forgiven little, loves little."* [48]And he said to her, "Your sins are forgiven." [49]Then those who were at table with him began to say among themselves, "Who is this, who even forgives sins?" [50]And he said to the woman, "Your faith has saved you; go in peace."

Lk 5:20–21

Lk 8:48;
17:19; 18:42

Lk 4:43

The holy women

8 [1]Soon afterward he went on through cities and villages, preaching and bringing the good news of the kingdom of God.

7:47. Man cannot merit forgiveness for his sins because, since God is the offended party, they are of infinite gravity. We need the sacrament of Penance, in which God forgives us by virtue of the infinite merits of Jesus Christ; there is only one indispensable condition for winning God's forgiveness—our love, our repentance. We are pardoned to the extent that we love; when our heart is full of love there is no longer any room in it for sin because we have made room for Jesus, and he says to us as he said to this woman, "Your sins are forgiven." Repentance is a sign that we love God. But it was God who first loved us (cf.1 Jn 4:10). When God forgives us he is expressing his love for us. Our love for God is, then, always a response to his initiative. By forgiving us God helps us to be more grateful and more loving towards him. "He loves little", St Augustine comments, "who has little forgiven. You say that you have not committed many sins: but why is that the case? [...] The reason is that God was guiding you [...]. There is no sin that one man

commits, which another may not commit also unless God, man's maker, guides him" (*Sermons*, 99, 6). Therefore, we ought to fall ever more deeply in love with our Lord, not only because he forgives us our sins but also because he helps us by means of his grace not to commit them.

7:50. Jesus declares that it was faith that moved this woman to throw herself at his feet and show her repentance; her repentance wins his forgiveness. Similarly, when we approach the sacrament of Penance we should stir up our faith in the fact that it is "not a human but a divine dialogue. It is a tribunal of divine justice and especially of mercy, with a loving judge who 'has no pleasure in the death of the wicked; I desire that the wicked turn back from his way and live' (Ezek 33:11)" (St Josemaría Escrivá, *Christ Is Passing By*, 78).

8:1–3. The Gospel refers a number of times to women accompanying our Lord. Here St Luke gives us the names of three

And the twelve were with him, ²and also some women who had been healed of evil spirits and infirmities: Mary, called Magdalene, from whom seven demons had gone out, ³and Joanna, the wife of Chuza, Herod's steward, and Susanna, and many others, who provided for them[z] out of their means.

Mt 27:55–56
Mk 15:40–41;
16:9

Lk 24:10

Parable of the sower. The meaning of parables

⁴And when a great crowd came together and people from town after town came to him, he said in a parable: ⁵"A sower went out to sow his seed; and as he sowed, some fell along the path, and was trodden under foot, and the birds of the air devoured it. ⁶And some fell on the rock; and as it grew up, it withered away, because it had no moisture. ⁷And some fell among thorns; and the thorns grew with it and choked it. ⁸And some fell into good soil and grew, and yielded a hundredfold." As he said this, he called out, "He who has ears to hear, let him hear."

Mt 13:1–23
Mk 4:1–20

---

of them—Mary, called Magdalene, to whom the risen Christ appeared beside the holy sepulchre (Jn 20:11–18; Mk 16:9); Joanna, a lady of some position, whom we also meet among the women who went to the tomb on the morning of the Resurrection (Lk 24:10), and Susanna, whom the Gospel does not mention again. The role of these women consisted in helping Jesus and his disciples out of their own resources, thereby showing their gratitude for what Christ had done for them, and in cooperating in his ministry.

Men and women enjoy equal dignity in the Church. Within the context of that equality, women certainly have specific characteristics which must necessarily be reflected in their role in the Church: "All the baptised, men and women alike, share equally in the dignity, freedom and responsibility of the children of God. ... Women are called to bring to the family, to society and to the Church, characteristics which are their own and which they alone can give—their gentle warmth and untiring generosity, their love for detail, their quick-wittedness and intuition, their simple and deep piety, their constancy. ... A woman's femininity is genuine only if she is aware of the beauty of this contribution for which there is no substitute—and if she incorporates it into her own life" (St Josemaría Escrivá, *Conversations*, 14 and 87).

The Gospel makes special reference to the generosity of these women. It is nice to know that our Lord availed himself of their charity, and that they responded to him with such refined and generous detachment that Christian women feel filled with a holy and fruitful envy (cf. St J. Escrivá, *The Way*, 981).

8:4–8. Our Lord explains this parable in vv. 11–15. The seed is Jesus himself and his preaching; and the kinds of ground it falls on reflect people's different attitudes to Jesus and his teaching. Our Lord sows the life of grace in souls through the preaching of the Church and through an endless flow of actual graces.

---

z. Other ancient authorities read *him*

Is 6:9–10

⁹And when his disciples asked him what this parable meant, ¹⁰he said, "To you it has been given to know the secrets of the kingdom of God; but for others they are in parables, so that seeing they may not see, and hearing they may not understand. ¹¹Now the parable is this: The seed is the word of God. ¹²The ones along the path are those who have heard; then the devil comes and takes away the word from their hearts, that they may not believe and be saved. ¹³And the ones on the rock are those who, when they hear the word, receive it with joy; but these have no root, they believe for a while and in time of temptation fall away. ¹⁴And as for what fell among the thorns, they are those who hear, but as they go on their way they are choked by the cares and riches and pleasures of life, and their fruit does not mature. ¹⁵And as for that in the good soil, they are those who, hearing the word, hold it fast in an honest and good heart, and bring forth fruit with patience.

8:10–12. Jesus uses parables to teach people the mysteries of the supernatural life and thereby lead them to salvation. However, he foresaw that, due to the bad dispositions of some of his listeners, these parables would lead them to harden their hearts and to reject grace. For a fuller explanation of the purpose of parables see the notes on Mt 13:10–13 and Mk 4:11–12.

8:12. Some people are so immersed in a life of sin that they are like the path on which falls the seed "which suffers from two kinds of hazard: it is trodden on by wayfarers and snatched by birds. The path, therefore, is the heart, which is trodden on by the frequent traffic of evil thoughts, and cannot take in the seed and let it germinate because it is so dried up" (St Bede, *In Lucae Evangelium expositio*, in loc.). Souls hardened by sin can become good soil and bear fruit through sincere repentance and penance. We should note the effort the devil makes to prevent souls from being converted.

8:13. "Many people are pleased by what they hear, and they resolve to do good; but as soon as they experience difficulties they give up the good works they started. Stony ground has not enough soil, which is why the shoots fail to produce fruit. There are many who, when they hear greed criticized, do conceive a loathing for it and extol the scorning of it; but as soon as the soul sees something else that it desires, it forgets what it previously promised. There are also others who when they hear talk against impurity not only desire not to be stained by the filth of the flesh but are even ashamed of the stains that they already bear; but as soon as bodily beauty presents itself to their eyes, their heart is so drawn by desires that it is as if they had done or decided to do nothing against these desires, and they act in a manner deserving condemnation and in a way which they themselves previously condemned when they reflected on their behaviour. Very often we feel compunction for our faults and yet we go back and commit them even after bemoaning them" (St Gregory the Great, *In Evangelia homiliae*, 15).

Parable of the lamp

[16]"No one after lighting a lamp covers it with a vessel, or puts it under a bed, but puts it on a stand, that those who enter may see the light. [17]For nothing is hid that shall not be made manifest, nor anything secret that shall not be known and come to light. [18]Take heed then how you hear; for to him who has will more be given, and from him who has not, even what he thinks that he has will be taken away."

Mk 4:21–25
Mt 5:15

Mt 10:26

Lk 19:26

The true kinsmen of Jesus

[19]Then his mother and his brethren* came to him, but they could not reach him for the crowd. [20]And he was told, "Your mother and your brethren are standing outside, desiring to see you." [21]But he said to them, "My mother and my brethren are those who hear the word of God and do it."

Mt 12:46–50
Mk 3:31–35

8:14. This is the case of people who after receiving the divine seed, the Christian calling, and having stayed on the right path for some time, begin to give up the struggle. These souls run the risk of developing a distaste for the things of God and of taking the easy, and wrong, way of seeking compensations suggested to them by their disordered ambition for power and their desire for material wealth and a comfortable life involving no suffering.

A person in this situation begins to be lukewarm and tries to serve two masters: "It is wrong to have two candles lighted—one to St Michael and another to the devil. We must snuff out the devil's candle: we must spend our lives completely in the service of the Lord. If our desire for holiness is sincere, if we are docile enough to place ourselves in God's hands, everything will go well. For he is always ready to give us his grace" (St Josemaría Escrivá, *Christ Is Passing By*, 59).

8:15. Jesus tells us that the good soil has three features—listening to God's demands with the good disposition of a gen-

erous heart; striving to ensure that one does not water down these demands as time goes by; and, finally, beginning and beginning again and not being disheartened if the fruit is slow to appear. "You cannot 'rise'. It's not surprising: that fall!

"Persevere and you will 'rise'. Remember what a spiritual writer has said: your poor soul is like a bird whose wings are caked with mud. Suns of heaven are needed and personal efforts, small and constant, to shake off those inclinations, those vain fancies, that depression: that mud clinging to your wings. And you will see yourself free. If you persevere, you will 'rise'" (St Josemaría Escrivá, *The Way*, 991).

8:19–21. These words of our Lord show us that fulfilment of the will of God is more important than kinship and that, therefore, our Lady is more united to her Son by virtue of her perfect fulfilment of what God asked of her than by the Holy Spirit's using her to make Christ's body (cf. the notes on Mt 12:48–50 and Mk 3:31–35).

The calming of the storm

Mt 8:18; 23–27
Mk 4:35–41 [22]One day he got into a boat with his disciples and he said to them, "Let us go across to the other side of the lake." So they set out, [23]and as they sailed he fell asleep. And a storm of wind came down on the lake, and they were filling with water, and were in danger. [24]And they went and woke him, saying, "Master, Master, we are perishing!" And he awoke and rebuked the wind and the raging waves; and they ceased, and there was a calm. [25]He said to them, "Where is your faith?" And they were afraid, and they marvelled, saying to one another, "Who then is this, that he commands even wind and water, and they obey him?"

The Gerasene demoniac

Mk 8:28–34
Mk 5:1–20 [26]Then they arrived at the country of the Gerasenes,[a] which is opposite Galilee. [27]And as he stepped out on land, there met him a man from the city who had demons; for a long time he had worn no clothes, and he lived not in a house but among the tombs. [28]When he saw Jesus, he cried out and fell down before him, and said with a loud voice, "What have you to do with me, Jesus, Son of the Most High God? I beseech you, do not torment me." [29]For he had commanded the unclean spirit to come out of the man. (For many a time it had seized him; he was kept under guard, and bound with chains and fetters, but he broke the bonds and was driven by the demon into the desert.) [30]Jesus then asked him, "What is your name?" And he said, "Legion"; for many demons had entered him. [31]And they begged him not to command them to

8:22–25. On this passage see the note on Mt 8:23–27.

8:23. Jesus fell asleep; he was tired. In other passages the Gospel describes similar situations: he sits wearily beside a well (Jn 4:6); he is thirsty and asks the Samaritan woman for a drink (Jn 4:7). Passages of this kind show the humanity of Jesus, true God and true man. "How generous our Lord is in humbling himself and fully accepting his human condition! He does not use his divine power to escape from difficulties or effort. Let's pray that he will teach us to be tough, to love work, to appreciate the human and divine nobility of savouring the consequences of self-giving" (St Josemaría Escrivá, *Christ Is Passing By*, 61).

8:26–39. "Gerasenes": some Greek manuscripts, which the New Vulgate follows, speak of "Gergesenes". But most manuscripts say "Gerasenes" or else "Gadarenes". Gadara (cf. Mt 8:28) and Gerasa (cf. Mk 5:1) were both towns of the Decapolis, adjacent to one another. On the geographical location of these two towns, see the notes on Mt 8:28 and Mk 5:20. On this cure and on the very

a. Other ancient authorities read *Gadarenes*, others *Gergesenes*

depart into the abyss. ³²Now a large herd of swine was feeding there on the hillside; and they begged him to let them enter these. So he gave them leave. ³³Then the demons came out of the man and entered the swine, and the herd rushed down the steep bank into the lake and were drowned.

³⁴When the herdsmen saw what had happened, they fled, and told it in the city and in the country. ³⁵Then people went out to see what had happened, and they came to Jesus, and found the man from whom the demons had gone, sitting at the feet of Jesus, clothed and in his right mind; and they were afraid. ³⁶And those who had seen it told them how he who had been possessed with demons was healed. ³⁷Then all the people of the surrounding country of the Gerasenes[a] asked him to depart from them; for they were seized with great fear; so he got into the boat and returned. ³⁸The man from whom the demons had gone begged that he might be with him; but he sent him away, saying, ³⁹"Return to your home, and declare how much God has done for you." And he went away, proclaiming throughout the whole city how much Jesus had done for him.*

Jairus' daughter is restored to life. Curing of the woman with a haemorrhage

⁴⁰Now when Jesus returned, the crowd welcomed him, for they were all waiting for him. ⁴¹And there came a man named Jairus, who was a ruler of the synagogue; and falling at Jesus' feet he besought him to come to his house, ⁴²for he had an only daughter, about twelve years of age, and she was dying.

Mt 9:18–26
Mk 5:21–43

Lk 7:12

---

different attitudes of the townsfolk and the possessed man, see the notes on Mt 8:28–34 and on Mk 5:1–20 and 5:15–20.

8:40–56. Jesus Christ asks faith of those who approach him; but he does not require us all to show him respect and reverence in exactly the same way. "There are always sick people who, like Bartimaeus, pray with great faith and have no qualms about confessing their faith at the top of their voices. But notice how, among those whom Christ encounters, no two souls are alike. This woman, too, has great faith, but she does not cry aloud; she draws near to Jesus without anyone even noticing. For her it is enough just to touch his garment, because she is quite certain she will be cured. No sooner has she done so than our Lord turns round and looks at her. He already knows what is going on in the depths of her heart and has seen how sure she is: 'Take heart, daughter; your faith has made you well' (Mt 9:22)" (St Josemaría Escrivá, *Friends of God*, 199). For a more detailed description of these two miracles, see the notes on Mt 9:18–26; 9:18; 9:23; 9:24; and Mk 5:21–43; 5:25; 5:30; 5:39; 5:40–42.

As he went, the people pressed round him. [43]And a woman who had had a flow of blood for twelve years and had spent all her living upon physicians[b] and could not be healed by any one, [44]came up behind him, and touched the fringe of his garment; and immediately her flow of blood ceased. [45]And Jesus said, "Who was it that touched me?" When all denied it, Peter[c] said, "Master, the multitudes surround you and press upon you!" [46]But Jesus said, "Some one touched me; for I perceive that power has gone forth from me." [47]And when the woman saw that she was not hidden, she came trembling, and falling down before him declared in the presence of all the people why she had touched him, and how she had been immediately healed. [48]And he said to her, "Daughter, your faith has made you well; go in peace."

[49]While he was still speaking, a man from the ruler's house came and said, "Your daughter is dead; do not trouble the Teacher any more." [50]But Jesus on hearing this answered him, "Do not fear; only believe, and she shall be well." [51]And when he came to the house, he permitted no one to enter with him, except Peter and John and James, and the father and mother of the child. [52]And all were weeping and bewailing her; but he said, "Do not weep; for she is not dead but sleeping." [53]And they laughed at him, knowing that she was dead. [54]But taking her by the hand he called, saying,

Lk 6:19

Lk 7:50

Lk 7:13

8:43–48. Many Fathers (St Ambrose, St Augustine, St Bede etc.) see this woman with the flow of blood (cf. the note on Mk 5:25) as symbolizing the church of the Gentiles which, unlike the Jews, approached our Lord with faith and was healed; she also represents every soul who, repentant for his sins, feels sorrow and shame for his past life, and also reverence towards God and firm confidence in his help.

"This holy woman, refined, devout, most ready to believe, most prudent as can be seen from her modesty—because modesty and faith are present when one recognizes that one is sick and does not despair of forgiveness—discreetly touches the fringe of the Lord's garment, approaches him with faith, believes with devotion and knows, through wisdom, that she has been

cured [...]. Christ is touched through faith, Christ is sighted through faith [...]. Therefore, if we also wish to be healed, let us touch through our faith the fringe of Christ's garment" (St Ambrose, *Expositio Evangelii sec. Lucam*, in loc.).

8:50. St John Chrysostom (*Hom. on St Matthew*, 31) observes that the curing of the woman with the haemorrhage also has the purpose of strengthening Jairus' faith because he was about to be given the news of his daughter's death. The combination of the two miracles reveals God's loving plan to cause those present to have a deeper faith.

"The Lord requires faith of those who invoke him," St Athanasius comments, "not because they really need it (for he is

---

b. Other ancient authorities omit *and had spent all her living upon physicians* **c.** Other ancient authorities add *and those who were with him*

"Child, arise." ⁵⁵And her spirit returned, and she got up at once;
and he directed that something should be given her to eat. ⁵⁶And
her parents were amazed; but he charged them to tell no one what
had happened.

Lk 5:14
Mk 1:44; 7:36
Mt 16:20

5. JESUS TRAVELS WITH HIS APOSTLES

The mission of the apostles

9 ¹And he called the twelve together and gave them power and
authority over all demons and to cure diseases, ²and he sent
them out to preach the kingdom of God and to heal. ³And he said
to them, "Take nothing for your journey, no staff, nor bag, nor
bread, nor money; and do not have two tunics. ⁴And whatever
house you enter, stay there, and from there depart. ⁵And wherever
they do not receive you, when you leave that town shake off the
dust from your feet as a testimony against them." ⁶And they
departed and went through the villages, preaching the gospel and
healing everywhere.

Mt 10:1, 7,
9–11
Mk 6:7–13

Lk 10:5–7

Lk 10:11

Herod's opinion about Jesus

⁷Now Herod the tetrarch heard of all that was done, and he was
perplexed, because it was said by some that John had been raised

Mt 14:1–2
Mk 6:14–16

---

the Lord, he is the giver of faith), but in order that they do not think that he dispenses his graces in an arbitrary way; and so he shows that he favours those who believe him, to ensure that they do not receive his benefits without faith, and if they lose them it only happens through their unfaithfulness. When he does good, Christ wants grace to endure, and when he cures he wants the cure to be permanent" (*Fragmenta in Lucam*, in loc.).

8:53. "They laughed at him": when someone has no faith in God's omnipotence, he tries to measure everything by his own limited understanding and easily fails to grasp supernatural realities: instead of reacting humbly, he tries to make fun of them. St Paul is referring to someone in this position when he says, "The unspiritual man does not receive the

gifts of the Spirit of God, for they are folly to him, and he is not able to understand them because they are spiritually discerned" (1 Cor 2:14).

"There are some who pass through life as through a tunnel, without ever understanding the splendour, the security and the warmth of the sun of faith" (St Josemaría Escrivá, *The Way*, 575).

9:1–4. This is the first mission the apostles were sent on. Jesus wants them to gain experience which will help them in the mission they will have after he ascends into heaven. He charges them to do what he himself did—preach the Kingdom of God and heal the sick. This scene is commented on at greater length in notes on Mt 10:7–8; 10:9–10; and Mk 6:8–9.

9:7–9. Except for the Sadducees, all Jews

Lk 23:8

from the dead, ⁸by some that Elijah had appeared, and by others that one of the old prophets had risen. ⁹Herod said, "John I beheaded; but who is this about whom I hear such things?" And he sought to see him.

Return of the apostles. First miracle of the loaves and fish

Mt 14:13–21
Mk 6:30–44
Jn 6:1–13

¹⁰On their return the apostles told him what they had done. And he took them and withdrew apart to a city called Bethsaida. ¹¹When the crowds learned it, they followed him; and he welcomed them and spoke to them of the kingdom of God, and cured those who had need of healing. ¹²Now the day began to wear away; and the twelve came and said to him, "Send the crowd away, to go into the villages and country round about, to lodge and get provisions; for we are here in a lonely place." ¹³But he said to them, "You give them something to eat." They said, "We have no more than five loaves and two fish—unless we are to go and buy food for all these people." ¹⁴For there were about five thousand men. And he said to his disciples, "Make them sit down in companies, about fifty each." ¹⁵And they did so, and made them all sit down. ¹⁶And taking the five loaves and the two fish he looked up to heaven, and

---

believed in the resurrection of the dead, as revealed by God in Sacred Scripture (cf. Ezek 37:10; Dan 12:2 and 2 Mac 7:9). It was also commonly believed by Jews at the time that Elijah or some other prophet had to appear again (cf. Deut 19:15). This may have been why Herod began to think that perhaps John had come back to life (cf. Mt 14:1–2 and Mk 6:14–16), particularly since Jesus worked miracles and people thought this power was the prerogative of those who had risen from the dead. And yet he was aware that Christ was working miracles even before John died (cf. Jn 2:23); therefore, at first, he was disconcerted. Later, as the fame of Christ's miracles spread, to have some sort of adequate explanation he decided, as the other Gospels tell us, that John must indeed have risen.

9:10–17. Jesus replies to his disciples knowing very well what he is going to do

(cf. Jn 6:5–6)—thereby teaching them little by little to trust in God's omnipotence. On this miracle see the notes on Mt 14:14–21; 15:32; 15:33–38; Mk 6:34; 6:41; 6:42; 8:1–9; and Jn 6:5–9; 6:10; 6:11; 6:12–13.

9:20. "Christ" means "anointed" and is a name indicating honour and office. In the Old Law *priests* were anointed (Ex 29:7 and 40:13), as were *kings* (1 Sam 9:16), because God laid down that they should receive anointing in view of their position; there was also a custom to anoint *prophets* (1 Sam 16:13) because they were interpreters and intermediaries of God. "When Jesus Christ our Saviour came into the world, he assumed the position and obligations of the three offices of priest, king and prophet and was therefore called Christ" (St Pius V, *Catechism*, 1, 3, 7).

9:22. Jesus prophesied his passion and

blessed and broke them, and gave them to the disciples to set
before the crowd. [17]And all ate and were satisfied. And they took
up what was left over, twelve baskets of broken pieces.

2 Kings 4:42–44

Peter's profession of faith

[18]Now it happened that as he was praying alone the disciples were
with him; and he asked them, "Who do the people say that I am?"
[19]And they answered, "John the Baptist; but others say, Elijah; and
others, that one of the old prophets has risen." [20]And he said to
them, "But who do you say that I am?" And Peter answered, "The
Christ of God."

Mt 16:13–20
Mk 8:27–30
Lk 9:7
Jn 6:68–69

First announcement of the Passion

[21]But he charged and commanded them to tell this to no one, [22]say-
ing, "The Son of man must suffer many things, and be rejected by
the elders and chief priests and scribes, and be killed, and on the
third day be raised."

Mt 16:21–23
Mk 8:31–33
Lk 9:44;
18:23–33

The need for self-denial

[23]And he said to all, "If any man would come after me, let him
deny himself and take up his cross daily and follow me. [24]For

Mt 16:24–28
Mk 8:34–39
Lk 14:27
Lk 17:33
Mt 10:39
Jn 12:25

---

death in order to help his disciples
believe in him. It also showed that he was
freely accepting these sufferings he
would undergo. "Christ did not seek to
be glorified: he chose to come without
glory in order to undergo suffering; and
you, who have been born without glory,
do you wish to be glorified? The route
you must take is the one Christ took. This
means recognizing him and it means imitating him both in his ignominy and in
his good repute; thus you will glory in
the Cross, which was his path to glory.
That was what Paul did, and therefore he
gloried in saying, 'Far be it from me to
glory except in the cross of our Lord
Jesus Christ' (Gal 6:14)" (St Ambrose,
Expositio Evangelii sec. Lucam, in loc.).

9:23. "Christ is saying this again, to us,
whispering it in our ears: the cross *each
day*. As St Jerome puts it: 'Not only in
time of persecution or when we have the

chance of martyrdom, but in all circumstances, in everything we do and think, in
everything we say, let us deny what we
used to be and let us confess what we
now are, reborn as we have been in
Christ' (*Epistola* 121, 3) [...]. Do you
see? The *daily* cross. No day without a
cross; not a single day in which we are
not to carry the cross of the Lord, in
which we are not to accept his yoke" (St
Josemaría Escrivá, *Christ Is Passing By*,
58 and 176). "There is no doubt about it:
a person who loves pleasure, who seeks
comfort, who flies from anything that
might spell suffering, who is over-
anxious, who complains, who blames
and who becomes impatient at the least
little thing which does not go his way—a
person like that is a Christian only in
name; he is only a dishonour to his religion, for Jesus Christ has said so:
Anyone who wishes to come after me, let
him deny himself and take up his cross

Mt 10:33

whoever would save his life will lose it; and whoever loses his life for my sake, he will save it. ²⁵For what does it profit a man if he gains the whole world and loses or forfeits himself? ²⁶For whoever is ashamed of me and of my words, of him will the Son of man be ashamed when he comes in his glory and the glory of the Father and of the holy angels. ²⁷But I tell you truly, there are some standing here who will not taste death before they see the kingdom of God."

---

every day of his life, and follow me" (St John Mary Vianney, *Selected Sermons*, Ash Wednesday).

The cross should be present not only in the life of every Christian but also at the crossroads of the world: "How beautiful are those crosses on the summits of high mountains, and crowning great monuments, and on the pinnacles of cathedrals ...! But the Cross must also be inserted in the very heart of the world.

"Jesus wants to be raised on high, there in the noise of the factories and workshops, in the silence of libraries, in the loud clamour of the streets, in the stillness of the fields, in the intimacy of the family, in crowded gatherings, in stadiums.... Wherever there is a Christian striving to lead an honourable life, he should, with his love, set up the Cross of Christ, who attracts all things to himself" (St Josemaría Escrivá, *The Way of the Cross*, XI, 3).

9:25. By this radical statement Jesus teaches us to do everything with a view to eternal life: it is well worth while to devote our entire life on earth to attaining eternal life. "We have been warned that it profits man nothing if he gains the whole world and loses or forfeits himself. Far from diminishing our concern to develop this earth, the expectancy of a new earth should spur us on, for it is here that the body of a new human family grows, foreshadowing in some way the age which is to come. That is why, although we must

be careful to distinguish earthly progress clearly from the increase of the Kingdom of Christ, such progress is of vital concern to the Kingdom of God, insofar as it can contribute to the better ordering of human society" (Vatican II, *Gaudium et spes*, 39).

9:26. Our Lord is well aware how weak people can be when difficult circumstances arise in which they have to confess their faith by word or deed. To overcome this weakness he has given us a special resource—the grace of the sacrament of Confirmation, which strengthens the recipient to be a "a good soldier of Christ Jesus" (2 Tim 2:3) and to be "the aroma of Christ" (2 Cor 2:15) among men, which prevents us being led astray by an environment contrary to Christian faith and morals: "Therefore, the one to be confirmed is anointed on the forehead, where shame shows itself, lest he be ashamed to confess the name of Christ and especially his cross which was, indeed, according to the apostle, a stumbling block to the Jews and to the Gentiles foolishness (cf. 1 Cor 1:23)" (Council of Florence, *Pro Armeniis*; cf. *Lumen gentium*, 11).

This duty to confess the faith applies not only to one's private or family life but also to one's public life: "Nonsectarianism. Neutrality. Old myths that always try to seem new. Have you ever stopped to think how absurd it is to leave one's Catholicism aside on entering a univer-

The Transfiguration

[28]Now about eight days after these sayings he took with him Peter   Mt 17:1–9
and John and James, and went up on the mountain to pray. [29]And   Mk 9:2–9
as he was praying, the appearance of his countenance was altered,
and his raiment became dazzling white. [30]And behold, two men

---

sity, a professional association, a scholarly meeting, or Parliament, like a man leaving his hat at the door?" (St Josemaría Escrivá, *The Way*, 353). See the note on Mt 10:32–33.

9:27. Christ's words in v. 27 may refer to the destruction of Jerusalem (which occurred in the year AD 70) or to his own transfiguration, which took place shortly after this prophecy. If the former, the destruction of Jerusalem would in effect be the external sign indicating the changeover from Jewish rites to Christian rites; some of those present would actually witness this change. The second explanation is based on the fact that the transfiguration is reported in the Synoptic Gospels immediately after these words, as happening about one week later; whence some Fathers' interpretation is that the statement that some would not taste death before they see the Kingdom of God refers precisely to the apostles Peter, James and John, the witnesses of the transfiguration.

9:28–36. By his transfiguration Jesus strengthens his disciples' faith, revealing a trace of the glory his body will have after the Resurrection. He wants them to realize that his passion will not be the end but rather the route he will take to reach his glorification. "For a person to go straight along the road, he must have some knowledge of the end—just as an archer will not shoot an arrow straight unless he first sees the target [...]. This is particularly necessary if the road is hard and rough, the going heavy, and the end

delightful" (St Thomas Aquinas, *Summa theologiae*, 3, 45, 1).

Through the miracle of the transfiguration Jesus shows one of the qualities of glorified bodies—brightness, "by which the bodies of the saints shall shine like the sun, according to the words of our Lord recorded in the Gospel of St Matthew: 'The righteous will shine like the sun in the kingdom of their Father' (Mt 13:43). To remove the possibility of doubt on the subject, he exemplifies this in his transfiguration. This quality the apostle sometimes calls glory, sometimes brightness: He 'will change our lowly body to be like his glorious body' (Phil 3:21); and again, 'It is sown in dishonour, it is raised in glory' (1 Cor 15:43). Of this glory the Israelites beheld some image in the desert, when the face of Moses, after he had enjoyed the presence and conversation of God, shone with such lustre that they could not look on it (cf. Ex 34:29; 2 Cor 3:7). This brightness is a sort of radiance reflected by the body from the supreme happiness of the soul. It is a participation in that bliss which the soul enjoys [...]. This quality is not common to all in the same degree. All the bodies of the saints will be equally impassible; but the brightness of all will not be the same, for, according to the apostle, 'There is one glory of the sun, and another glory of the moon, and another glory of the stars; for star differs from star in glory. So it is with the resurrection of the dead' (1 Cor 15:41f)" (St Pius V, *Catechism*, 1, 12 13). See also the notes on Mt 17:1–13; 17:5; 17:10–13; and Mk 9:2–10; 9:7.

Luke 9:31

[handwritten: Moses represents fulness of the Law]
[handwritten: Elijah represents prophetic courage + witness]
[handwritten: Christ is the fulfillment of the OT]
Jn 1:14

talked with him, Moses and Elijah, [31]who appeared in glory and spoke of his departure, which he was to accomplish at Jerusalem. [32]Now Peter and those who were with him were heavy with sleep but kept awake, and they saw his glory and the two men who stood with him. [33]And as the men were parting from him, Peter said to Jesus, "Master, it is well that we are here; let us make three booths, one for you and one for Moses and one for Elijah"—not knowing what he said. [34]As he said this, a cloud came and overshadowed them; and they were afraid as they entered the cloud.

Lk 3:22
2 Pet 1:15–18
Ps 2:7
Is 42:1

[35]And a voice came out of the cloud, saying, "This is my Son, my Chosen;[d] listen to him!" [36]And when the voice had spoken, Jesus was found alone. And they kept silence and told no one in those days anything of what they had seen.

Curing of an epileptic boy

Mt 17:14–23
Mk 9:14–32

[37]On the next day, when they had come down from the mountain, a great crowd met him. [38]And behold, a man from the crowd cried, "Teacher, I beg you to look upon my son, for he is my only child; [39]and behold, a spirit seizes him and he suddenly cries out;

9:31. "And spoke of his departure": that is, his departure from this world, in other words, his death. It can also be understood as meaning our Lord's ascension.

9:35. "Listen to him!": everything God wishes to say to mankind he has said through Christ, now that the fulness of time has come (cf. Heb 1:2) "Therefore," St John of the Cross explains, "if any now should question God or desire a vision or revelation, not only would he be acting foolishly but he would be committing an offence against God, by not fixing his gaze on Christ with no desire for any new thing. For God could reply to him in this way: 'If I have spoken all things to you in my Word, which is my Son, and I have no other word, what answer can I give you now, or what can I reveal to you that is greater than this? Fix your eyes on him alone, for in him I have spoken and revealed to you all things, and in him you will find even more than what you ask

for and desire [...]. Hear him, for I have no more faith to reveal, nor have I any more things to declare'" (*Ascent of Mount Carmel*, book 2, chap. 22, 5).

9:39. The power of devils over men is limited to what God permits them to have. Within these limits diabolic possession can occur. Diabolic possession involves the devil exercising a certain control over the physical and mental behaviour of the possessed person, with a parallel loss of control on the person's part; a person's body becomes a kind of tool of the devil, thereby suffering the most cruel form of slavery.

When Jesus expels devils from the bodies of possessed people it shows that the Kingdom of God has come, that the devil is beginning to be dislodged from a domain which he obtained as a result of the original sin of Adam and Eve. Our Lord won complete victory over the devil

d. Other ancient authorities read *my Beloved*

it convulses him till he foams, and shatters him, and will hardly leave him. ⁴⁰And I begged your disciples to cast it out, but they could not." ⁴¹Jesus answered, "O faithless and perverse generation, how long am I to be with you and bear with you? Bring your son here." ⁴²While he was coming, the demon tore him and convulsed him. But Jesus rebuked the unclean spirit, and healed the boy, and gave him back to his father. ⁴³And all were astonished at the majesty of God.

Lk 7:15

Second announcement of the Passion
But while they were all marvelling at everything he did, he said to his disciples, ⁴⁴"Let these words sink into your ears; for the Son of man is to be delivered into the hands of men." ⁴⁵But they did not understand this saying, and it was concealed from them, that they should not perceive it; and they were afraid to ask him about this saying.

Lk 9:22; 24:26
Lk 18:34; 24:44
Mk 9:32

Humility and tolerance
⁴⁶And an argument arose among them as to which of them was the greatest. ⁴⁷But when Jesus perceived the thought of their hearts, he

Mk 18:1–5
Mk 9:33–40
Lk 6:8
Mt 9:4
Mt 10:40
Lk 22:26

through his passion and death, but the forces of hell will not be finally subdued until the second coming of Christ, or Parousia, at the end of the world.

9:41. Everyone present, in one way or other, deserved this severe reproach—the disciples, for their imperfect faith in the powers he had given them (cf. Lk 9:1); the boy's father, for his lack of confidence in the disciples; the curious spectators, who were also skeptical and who included some scribes who harassed the apostles (cf. Mk 9:14) and tried to discredit the powers Jesus gave them.

"How long am I to be with you and bear with you?": "By these words Christ means: you are enjoying my company and yet you are forever accusing me and my disciples [...]. He did not say this in anger; rather, he was speaking as a doctor would who is visiting a sick person who does not want to take his prescription and that is why he says: How long will I keep

coming to see you, given that you are not doing what I tell you?" (St Thomas Aquinas, *Comm. on St Matthew*, 17, 17).

9:44. Christ predicts his passion and death a number of times. Initially he does so in veiled terms (Jn 2:19; Lk 5:35) to the crowd; and later, much more explicitly, to his disciples (Lk 9:22), though they fail to understand his words, not because what he says is not clear, but because they do not have the right dispositions. St John Chrysostom comments: "Let no one be scandalized by this imperfection in the apostles; for the Cross had not yet been reached nor the grace of the Spirit given" (*Hom. on St Matthew*, 65).

9:46–48. Jesus takes a child in his arms to give his apostles example and to correct their too-human ambitions, thereby teaching all of us not to make ourselves important. "Don't try to be older. A child, always a child, even when you are dying

took a child and put him by his side, [48]and said to them, "Whoever receives this child in my name receives me, and whoever receives me receives him who sent me; for he who is least among you all is the one who is great."

[49]John answered, "Master, we saw a man casting out demons in your name, and we forbade him, because he does not follow with us." [50]But Jesus said to him, "Do not forbid him; for he that is not against you is for you."

Lk 11:23
Phil 1:18

PART TWO

Jerusalem is paramount in Luke's Gospel

Jesus' ministry on the way to Jerusalem

6. THE JOURNEY BEGINS

Samaritans refuse to receive Jesus   *determined, strongly*

Mt 19:1
Mk 10:32

[51]When the days drew near for him to be received up, he set his face to go to Jerusalem.* [52]And he sent messengers ahead of him,

---

of old age. When a child stumbles and falls, nobody is surprised; his father promptly lifts him up. When the person who stumbles and falls is older, the immediate reaction is one of laughter. Sometimes, after this first impulse, the laughter gives way to pity. But older people have to get up by themselves.

"Your sad experience of each day is full of stumbles and falls. What would become of you if you were not continually more of a child? Don't try to be older. Be a child; and when you stumble, may your Father God pick you up" (St Josemaría Escrivá, *The Way*, 870).

9:49–50. Our Lord corrects the exclusivist and intolerant attitude of the apostles. St Paul later learned this lesson, as we can see from what he wrote during his imprisonment in Rome: "Some

indeed preach Christ from envy and rivalry, but others from good will [...]. What then? Only that in every way, whether in pretence or in truth, Christ is proclaimed; and in that I rejoice" (Phil 1:15, 18). "Rejoice when you see others working in good apostolic activities. And ask God to grant them abundant grace and correspondence to that grace. Then, you, on your way. Convince yourself that it's the only way for you" (St Josemaría Escrivá, *The Way*, 965).

9:51. "When the days drew near for him to be received up": these words refer to the moment when Jesus will leave this world and ascend into heaven. Our Lord will say this more explicitly during the Last Supper: "I come from the Father and have come into the world; again, I am leaving the world and going to the

102

who went and entered a village of the Samaritans, to make ready for him; [53]but the people would not receive him, because his face was set toward Jerusalem.* [54]And when his disciples James and John saw it, they said, "Lord, do you want us to bid fire come down from heaven and consume them?"[e] [55]But he turned and rebuked them.[f] [56]And they went on to another village.

Jn 4:4–9

Mt 18:11
Jn 3:17; 12:47

Requirements for following Jesus

[57]As they were going along the road, a man said to him, "I will follow you wherever you go." [58]And Jesus said to him, "Foxes have holes, and birds of the air have nests; but the Son of man has nowhere to lay his head." [59]To another he said, "Follow me." But

Mt 8:19–22

Father" (Jn 16:28). By making his way resolutely to Jerusalem, towards his cross, Jesus freely complies with his Father's plan for his passion and death to be the route to his resurrection and ascension.

9:52–53. The Samaritans were hostile towards the Jews. This enmity derived from the fact that the Samaritans were descendants of marriages of Jews with Gentiles who repopulated the region of Samaria at the time of the Assyrian captivity (in the eighth century before Christ). There were also religious differences: the Samaritans had mixed the religion of Moses with various superstitious practices, and did not accept the temple of Jerusalem as the only place where sacrifices could properly be offered. They built their own temple on Mount Gerizim, in opposition to Jerusalem (cf. Jn 4:20); this was why, when they realized Jesus was headed for the Holy City, they refused him hospitality.

9:54–56. Jesus corrects his disciples' desire for revenge, because it is out of keeping with the mission of the Messiah,

who has come to save men, not destroy them (cf. Lk 19:10; Jn 12:47). The apostles are gradually learning that zeal for the things of God should not be bitter or violent.

"The Lord does everything in an admirable way [...]. He acts in this way to teach us that perfect virtue retains no desire for vengeance, and that where there is true charity there is no room for anger—in other words, that weakness should not be treated with harshness but should be helped. Indignation should be very far from holy souls, and desire for vengeance very far from great souls" (St Ambrose, *Expositio Evangelii sec. Lucam*, in loc.).

See the RSV footnote at v. 55. These words appear in a considerable number of early Greek manuscripts and other versions and were included in the Clementine Vulgate; but they do not appear in the best and oldest Greek codexes and have not been included in the New Vulgate.

9:57–62. Our Lord spells out very clearly what is involved in following him. Being a Christian is not an easy or

---

e. Other ancient authorities read *as Elijah did* f. Other ancient authorities add *and he said, "You do not know what manner of spirit you are of; for the Son of man came not to destroy men's lives but to save them"*

he said, "Lord, let me first go and bury my father." [60]But he said to him, "Leave the dead to bury their own dead; but as for you, go and proclaim the kingdom of God." [61]Another said, "I will follow you, Lord; but let me first say farewell to those at my home."

Gen 19:17

[62]Jesus said to him, "No one who puts his hand to the plough and looks back is fit for the kingdom of God."

Mt 10:7–16
Mk 6:7–11
Ex 24:1
Mt 9:37–38
Jn 4:35

The mission of the seventy disciples

10 [1]After this the Lord appointed seventy[g] others, and sent them on ahead of him, two by two, into every town and

comfortable affair: it calls for self-denial and for putting God before everything else. See the notes on Mt 8:18–22 and Mt 8:22.

We see here the case of the man who wanted to follow Christ, but on one condition—that he be allowed to say goodbye to his family. Our Lord, seeing that he is rather undecided, gives him an answer which applies to all of us, for we have all received a calling to follow him and we have to try not to receive this grace in vain. "We receive the grace of God in vain, when we receive it at the gate of our heart, and do not let it enter our heart. We receive it without receiving it, that is, we receive it without fruit, since there is no advantage in feeling the inspiration if we do not accept it […]. It sometimes happens that being inspired to do much we consent not to the whole inspiration but only to some part of it, as did those good people in the Gospel, who upon the inspiration which our Lord gave them to follow him wished to make reservations, the one to go first and bury his father, the other to go to take leave of his people" (St Francis de Sales, *Treatise on the Love of God*, book 2, chap. 11).

Our loyalty and fidelity to the mission God has given us should equip us to deal with every obstacle we meet: "There is never reason to look back (cf. Lk

9:62). The Lord is at our side. We have to be faithful and loyal; we have to face up to our obligations and we will find in Jesus the love and the stimulus we need to understand other people's faults and overcome our own" (St Josemaría Escrivá, *Christ Is Passing By*, 160).

10:1–12. Those who followed our Lord and received a calling from him (cf. Lk 9:57–62) included many other disciples in addition to the Twelve (cf. Mk 2:15). We do not know who most of them were; but undoubtedly some of them were with him all along, from when Jesus was baptized by John up to the time of his ascension—for example, Joseph called Barsabbas, and Matthias (cf. Acts 1:21–26). We can also include Cleopas and his companion, to whom the risen Christ appeared on the road to Emmaus (cf. Lk 24:13–35).

From among these disciples, our Lord chooses seventy for a special assignment. Of them, as of the apostles (cf. Lk 9:1–5), he demands total detachment and complete abandonment to divine providence.

From Baptism onwards every Christian is called by Christ to perform a mission. Therefore, the Church, in our Lord's name, "makes to all the laity an earnest appeal in the Lord to give a will-

g. Other ancient authorities read *seventy-two*

104

place where he himself was about to come. ²And he said to them,
"The harvest is plentiful, but the labourers are few; pray therefore
the Lord of the harvest to send out labourers into his harvest. ³Go
your way; behold, I send you out as lambs in the midst of wolves.
⁴Carry no purse, no bag, no sandals; and salute no one on the

Lk 9:3–5

---

ing, noble and enthusiastic response to the voice of Christ, who at this hour is summoning them more pressingly, and to the urging of the Holy Spirit. The younger generation should feel this call to be addressed in a special way to themselves; they should welcome it eagerly and generously. It is the Lord himself, by this Council, who is once more inviting all the laity to unite themselves to him ever more intimately, to consider his interests as their own (cf. Phil 2:5), and to join in his mission as Saviour. It is the Lord who is again sending them into every town and every place where he himself is to come (cf. Lk 10:1). He sends them on the Church's apostolate, an apostolate that is one yet has different forms and methods, an apostolate that must all the time be adapting itself to the needs of the moment; he sends them on an apostolate where they are to show themselves his cooperators, doing their full share continually in the work of the Lord, knowing that in the Lord their labour cannot be lost (cf. 1 Cor 15:58)" (Vatican II, *Apostolicam actuositatem*, 33).

10:3–4. Christ wants to instil apostolic daring into his disciples; this is why he says, "I send you out", which leads St John Chrysostom to comment: "This suffices to give us encouragement, to give us confidence and to ensure that we are not afraid of our assailants" (*Hom. on St Matthew*, 33). The apostles' and disciples' boldness stemmed from their firm conviction that they were on a God-given mission: they acted, as Peter the apostle confidently explained to the Sanhedrin,

in the name of Jesus Christ of Nazareth, "for there is no other name under heaven … by which we must be saved" (Acts 4:12).

"And the Lord goes on," St Gregory the Great adds, "'Carry no purse, no bag, no sandals; and salute no one on the road.' Such should be the confidence the preacher places in God that even if he is not provided with the necessities of life, he is convinced that they will come his way. This will ensure that worry about providing temporal things for himself does not distract him from providing others with eternal things" (*In Evangelia homiliae*, 17). Apostolate calls for generous self-surrender which leads to detachment; therefore, Peter, following our Lord's commandment, when the beggar at the Beautiful Gate asked him for alms (Acts 3:2–3), said, "I have no silver or gold" (ibid., 3:6), "not so as to glory in his poverty", St Ambrose points out, "but to obey the Lord's command. It is as if he were saying, 'You see in me a disciple of Christ, and you ask me for gold? He gave us something much more valuable than gold, the power to act in his name. I do not have what Christ did not give me, but I do have what he did give me: In the name of Jesus Christ, arise and walk' (cf. Acts 3:6)" (*Expositio Evangelii sec. Lucam*, in loc.). Apostolate, therefore, demands detachment from material things and it also requires us to be always available, for there is an urgency about apostolic work.

"And salute no one on the road": "How can it be", St Ambrose asks himself, "that the Lord wishes to get rid of a

road. ⁵Whatever house you enter, first say, 'Peace be to this
house!' ⁶And if a son of peace is there, your peace shall rest upon
him; but if not, it shall return to you. ⁷And remain in the same
house, eating and drinking what they provide, for the labourer
deserves his wages; do not go from house to house. ⁸Whenever
you enter a town and they receive you, eat what is set before you;
⁹heal the sick in it and say to them, 'The kingdom of God has
come near to you.' ¹⁰But whenever you enter a town and they do
not receive you, go into its streets and say, ¹¹'Even the dust of
your town that clings to our feet, we wipe off against you; nevertheless know this, that the kingdom of God has come near.' ¹²I tell
you, it shall be more tolerable on that day for Sodom than for that
town.

1 Pet 4:14
1 Cor 9:5–14
1 Tim 5:18

Lk 9:2–5

Acts 13:51; 18:6

Jesus reproaches cities for their unbelief

¹³"Woe to you, Chorazin! woe to you, Bethsaida! for if the mighty
works done in you had been done in Tyre and Sidon, they would

Mt 11:12–23
Jn 3:6

---

custom so full of kindness? Notice, however, that he does not just say, 'Do not
salute anyone', but adds, 'on the road.'
And there is a reason for this.

"He also commanded Elisha not to
salute anyone he met, when he sent him
to lay his staff on the body of the dead
child (2 Kings 4:29): he gave him this
order so as to get him to do this task
without delay and effect the raising of the
child, and not waste time by stopping to
talk to any passer-by he met. Therefore,
there is no question of omitting the good
manners to greet others; it is a matter of
removing a possible obstacle in the way
of service; when God commands, human
considerations should be set aside, at
least for the time being. To greet a person
is a good thing, but it is better to carry
out a divine instruction which could
easily be frustrated by a delay" (ibid.).

10:6. Everyone is "a son of peace" who
is disposed to accept the teaching of the
Gospel which brings with it God's peace.
Our Lord's recommendation to his disciples to proclaim peace should be a con-

stant feature of all the apostolic action of
Christians: "Christian apostolate is not a
political programme or a cultural alterna-
tive. It implies the spreading of good,
'infecting' others with a desire to love,
sowing peace and joy" (St Josemaría
Escrivá, *Christ Is Passing By*, 124).

Feeling peace in our soul and in our
surroundings is an unmistakeable sign
that God is with us, and a fruit of the
Holy Spirit (cf. Gal 5:22): "Get rid of
those scruples that deprive you of peace.
What robs you of your peace of soul
cannot come from God. When God
comes to you, you will realize the truth
of those greetings: My peace I give to
you … , My peace I leave you … , My
peace be with you … , and this peace you
will feel even in the midst of tribulation"
(St Josemaría Escrivá, *The Way*, 258).

10:7. Our Lord clearly considered poverty
and detachment a key feature in an apostle
(vv. 3–4). But he was aware of his disciples' material needs and therefore stated
the principle that apostolic ministry
deserves its recompense. Vatican Council

have repented long ago, sitting in sackcloth and ashes. ¹⁴But it shall be more tolerable in the judgment for Tyre and Sidon than for you. ¹⁵And you, Capernaum, will you be exalted to heaven? You shall be brought down to Hades.

Is 14:13–15

¹⁶"He who hears you hears me, and he who rejects you rejects me, and he who rejects me rejects him who sent me."

Mt 10:40
Jn 5:23; 12:48;
15:23

The seventy return from their mission
¹⁷The seventyᵍ returned with joy, saying, "Lord, even the demons are subject to us in your name!" ¹⁸And he said to them, "I saw Satan fall like lightning from heaven.* ¹⁹Behold, I have given you authority to tread upon serpents and scorpions, and over all the power of the enemy; and nothing shall hurt you. ²⁰Nevertheless do not rejoice in this, that the spirits are subject to you; but rejoice that your names are written in heaven."

Jn 12:31
Rev 12:8–9
Mk 16:18
Ps 91:13
Ex 32:32
Mt 7:22

II reminds us that we all have an obligation to contribute to the sustenance of those who generously devote themselves to the service of the Church: "Completely devoted as they are to the service of God in the fulfilment of the office entrusted to them, priests are entitled to receive a just remuneration. For 'the labourer deserves his wages' (Lk 10:7), and 'the Lord commanded that they who proclaim the gospel should get their living by the gospel' (1 Cor 9:14). For this reason, insofar as provision is not made from some other source for the just remuneration of priests, the faithful are bound by a real obligation of seeing to it that the necessary provision for a decent and fitting livelihood for the priests is available" (*Presbyterorum ordinis*, 20).

10:16. On the evening of the day of his resurrection, our Lord entrusts his apostles with the mission he received from the Father, endowing them with powers similar to his own (Jn 20:21). Some days later he will confer on Peter the primacy he had already promised him (Jn

21:15–17). The Pope is the successor of Peter, and the bishops the successors of the apostles (cf. *Lumen gentium*, 20). Therefore, "Bishops who teach in communion with the Roman Pontiff are to be revered by all as witnesses of divine and Catholic truth [...]. This loyal submission of the will and intellect must be given, in a special way, to the authentic teaching authority of the Roman Pontiff, even when he does not speak *ex cathedra*" (Vatican II, *Lumen gentium*, 25).

10:20. Our Lord corrects his disciples, making them see that the right reason for rejoicing lies in hope of reaching heaven, not in the power to do miracles which he gave them for their mission. As he said on another occasion, "On that day many will say to me, 'Lord, Lord, did we not prophesy in your name, and cast out demons in your name, and do many mighty works in your name?' And then will I declare to them, 'I never knew you; depart from me, you evildoers'" (Mt 7:22–23). In other words, in the eyes of God doing his holy will at all times is more important than working miracles.

g. Other ancient authorities read *seventy-two*

Jesus gives thanks

Mt 11:25–27
[21]In that same hour he rejoiced in the Holy Spirit and said, "I thank thee, Father, Lord of heaven and earth, that thou hast hidden these things from the wise and understanding and revealed them to babes; yea, Father, for such was thy gracious will.[h] [22]All things have been delivered to me by my Father; and no one knows who the Son is except the Father, or who the Father is except the Son and any one to whom the Son chooses to reveal him."

Mt 13:16–17
1 Pet 1:10
[23]Then turning to the disciples he said privately, "Blessed are the eyes which see what you see! [24]For I tell you that many prophets and kings desired to see what you see, and did not see it, and to hear what you hear, and did not hear it."

10:21. This passage of the Gospel is usually called our Lord's "hymn of joy" and is also to be found in St Matthew (11:25–27). It is one of those moments when Jesus rejoices to see humble people understanding and accepting the word of God.

Our Lord also reveals one of the effects of humility—spiritual childhood. For example, in another passage he says: "Truly, I say to you, unless you turn and become like children, you will never enter the kingdom of heaven" (Mt 18:3). But spiritual childhood does not involve weakness, softness or ignorance: "I have often meditated on this life of spiritual childhood, which is not incompatible with fortitude, because it demands a strong will, proven maturity, an open and firm character [...]. To become children we must renounce our pride and self-sufficiency, recognizing that we can do nothing by ourselves. We must realize that we need grace, and the help of God our Father to find our way and keep to it. To be little, you have to abandon yourself as children do, believe as children believe, beg as children beg" (St Josemaría Escrivá, *Christ Is Passing By*, 10 and 143).

10:22. "This statement is a wonderful help to our faith," St Ambrose comments,

"because when you read 'all' you realize that Christ is all-powerful, that he is not inferior to the Father, or less perfect than he; when you read 'have been delivered to me', you confess that Christ is the Son, to whom everything belongs by right of being one in substance [with the Father] and not by grace of gift" (*Expositio Evangelii sec. Lucam*, in loc.).

Here we see Christ as almighty Lord and God, consubstantial with the Father, and the only one capable of revealing who the Father is. At the same time, we can recognize the divine nature of Jesus only if the Father gives us the grace of faith—as he did to St Peter (cf. Mt 16:17).

10:23–24. Obviously, seeing Jesus with one's own eyes was a wonderful thing for people who believed in him. However, our Lord will say to Thomas, "Blessed are those who have not seen and yet believe" (Jn 20:29). St Peter, for his part, tells us: "Without having seen him you love him; though you do not see him you believe in him and rejoice with unutterable and exalted joy. As the outcome of your faith you obtain the salvation of your souls" (1 Pet 1:8–9).

h. Or *so it was well-pleasing before thee*

7. FURTHER PREACHING

Parable of the good Samaritan

25And behold, a lawyer stood up to put him to the test, saying, "Teacher, what shall I do to inherit eternal life?" 26He said to him, "What is written in the law? How do you read?" 27And he answered, "You shall love the Lord your God with all your heart, and with all your soul, and with all your strength, and with all your mind: and your neighbour as yourself." 28And he said to him, "You have answered right; do this, and you will live."	Mt 22:35–40 Mk 12:28–34 Lk 18:18–20 Deut 6:5 Lev 19:18 Lev 18:5 Mt 19:17

10:25–28. Our Lord's teaching is that the way to attain eternal life is through faithful fulfilment of the Law of God. The Ten Commandments, which God gave Moses on Mount Sinai (Ex 20:1–17), express the natural law in a clear and concrete way. It is part of Christian teaching that the natural law exists, that it is a participation by rational creatures in the Eternal Law and that it is impressed on the conscience of every man when he is created by God (cf. Leo XIII, *Libertas praestantissimum*). Obviously, therefore, the natural law, expressed in the Ten Commandments, cannot change or become outdated, for it is not dependent on man's will or on changing circumstances.

In this passage Jesus praises and accepts the summary of the Law given by the Jewish scribe. This reply, taken from Deuteronomy (6:4ff), was a prayer which the Jews used to say frequently. Our Lord gives the very same reply when he is asked which is the principal commandment of the Law and concludes his answer by saying, "On these two commandments depend all the law and the prophets" (Mt 22:40; cf. also Rom 13:8–9; Gal 5:14).

There is a hierarchy and order in these two commandments constituting the double precept of charity: before everything and above everything comes loving God in himself; in the second place, and as a consequence of the first commandment, comes loving one's neighbour, for God explicitly requires us to do so (1 Jn 4:21; cf. the notes on Mt 22:34–40 and 22:37–38).

This passage of the Gospel also includes another basic doctrine: the Law of God is not something negative—"Do not do this"—but something completely positive—love. Holiness, to which all baptized people are called, does not consist in not sinning, but in loving, in doing positive things, in bearing fruit in the form of love of God. When our Lord describes for us the Last Judgment he stresses this positive aspect of the Law of God (Mt 25:31–46). The reward of eternal life will be given to those who do good.

10:27. "Yes, our only occupation here on earth is that of loving God—that is, to start doing what we will be doing for all eternity. Why must we love God? Well, because our happiness consists in love of God; it can consist in nothing else. So, if we do not love God, we will always be unhappy; and if we wish to enjoy any consolation and relief in our pains, we will attain it only by recourse to love of God. If you want to be convinced of this, go and find the happiest man according to the world; if he does not love God, you

109

²⁹But he, desiring to justify himself, said to Jesus, "And who is my neighbour?" ³⁰Jesus replied, "A man was going down from Jerusalem to Jericho, and he fell among robbers, who stripped him and beat him, and departed, leaving him half dead. ³¹Now by chance a priest was going down that road; and when he saw him he passed by on the other side. ³²So likewise a Levite, when he came to the place and saw him, passed by on the other side. ³³But a Samaritan, as he journeyed, came to where he was; and when he saw him, he had compassion, ³⁴and went to him and bound up his wounds, pouring on oil and wine; then he set him on his own beast and brought him to an inn, and took care of him. ³⁵And the

Is 1:6

---

will find that in fact he is an unhappy man. And, on the contrary, if you discover the man most unhappy in the eyes of the world, you will see that because he loves God he is happy in every way. Oh my God!, open the eyes of our souls, and we will seek our happiness where we truly can find it" (St John Mary Vianney, *Selected Sermons*, Twenty-second Sunday after Pentecost).

10:29–37. In this moving parable, which only St Luke gives us, our Lord explains very graphically who our neighbour is and how we should show charity towards him, even if he is our enemy.

Following other Fathers, St Augustine (*De verbis Domini sermones*, 37) identifies the good Samaritan with our Lord, and the waylaid man with Adam, the source and symbol of all fallen mankind. Moved by compassion, he comes down to earth to cure man's wounds, making them his own (Is 53:4; Mt 8:17; 1 Pet 2:24; 1 Jn 3:5). In fact, we often see Jesus being moved by man's suffering (cf. Mt 9:36; Mk 1:41; Lk 7:13). And St John says: "In this the love of God was made manifest among us, that God sent his only Son into the world, so that we might live through him. In this is love, not that we loved God but that he loved us and sent his Son to be the expiation for our sins. Beloved, if God so

loved us, we also ought to love one another" (1 Jn 4:9–11).

This parable leaves no doubt about who our neighbour is—anyone (without distinction of race or relationship) who needs our help; nor about how we should love him—by taking pity on him, being compassionate towards his spiritual and corporal needs; and it is not just a matter of having the right feelings towards him: we must do something, we must generously serve him.

Christians, who are disciples of Christ, should share his love and compassion, never distancing themselves from others' needs. One way to express love for one's neighbour is to perform the "works of mercy", which get their name from the fact that they are not duties in justice. There are fourteen such works, seven spiritual and seven corporal. The spiritual are: To convert the sinner; To instruct the ignorant; To counsel the doubtful; To comfort the sorrowful; To bear wrongs patiently; To forgive injuries; To pray for the living and the dead. The corporal works are: To feed the hungry; To give drink to the thirsty; To clothe the naked; To shelter the homeless; To visit the sick; To visit the imprisoned; To bury the dead.

10:31–32. Very probably one reason why our Lord used this parable was to

next day he took out two denarii[i] and gave them to the inn-keeper, saying, 'Take care of him; and whatever more you spend, I will repay you when I come back.' [36]Which of these three, do you think, proved neighbour to the man who fell among the robbers?" [37]He said, "The one who showed mercy on him." And Jesus said to him, "Go and do likewise."

Martha and Mary welcome our Lord

[38]Now as they went on their way, he entered a village; and a woman named Martha received him into her house. [39]And she had a sister called Mary, who sat at the Lord's feet and listened to his

Jn 11:1;
12:2–3

---

correct one of the excesses of false piety common among his contemporaries. According to the Law of Moses, contact with dead bodies involved legal impurity, from which one was cleansed by various ablutions (cf. Num 19:11–22; Lev 21:1–4, 11–12). These regulations were not meant to prevent people from helping the injured; they were designed for reasons of hygiene and respect for the dead. The aberration of the priest and the Levite in this parable consisted in this: they did not know for sure whether the man who had been assaulted was dead or not, and they preferred to apply a wrong interpretation of a secondary, ritualistic precept of the Law rather than obey the more important commandment of loving one's neighbour and giving him whatever help one can.

10:38–42. Our Lord was heading for Jerusalem (Lk 9:51) and his journey took him through Bethany, the village where Lazarus, Martha and Mary lived—a family for whom he had a special affection, as we see in other passages of the Gospel (cf. Jn 11:1–45; 12:1–9).

St Augustine comments on this scene as follows: "Martha, who was arranging and preparing the Lord's meal, was busy doing many things, whereas Mary pre-

ferred to find her meal in what the Lord was saying. In a way she deserted her sister, who was very busy, and sat herself down at Jesus' feet and just listened to his words. She was faithfully obeying what the Psalm said: 'Be still, and know that I am God' (Ps 46:10).

"Martha was getting annoyed, Mary was feasting; the former coping with many things, the latter concentrating on one. Both occupations were good" (*Sermon*, 103). Martha has come to be, as it were, the symbol of the active life, and Mary that of the contemplative life. However, for most Christians, called as they are to sanctify themselves in the middle of the world, action and contemplation cannot be regarded as two opposite ways of practising the Christian faith: an active life forgetful of union with God is useless and barren; but an apparent life of prayer which shows no concern for apostolate and the sanctification of ordinary things also fails to please God. The key lies in being able to combine these two lives, without either harming the other. Close union between action and contemplation can be achieved in very different ways, depending on the specific vocation each person is given by God.

Far from being an obstacle, work should be a means and an occasion for a

i. The denarius was a day's wage for a labourer

111

1 Cor 7:35

Mt 6:33

teaching. [40]But Martha was distracted with much serving; and she went to him and said, "Lord, do you not care that my sister has left me to serve alone? Tell her then to help me." [41]But the Lord answered her, "Martha, Martha, you are anxious and troubled about many things; [42]one thing is needful.[j] Mary has chosen the good portion, which shall not be taken away from her."

---

close relationship with our Lord, which is the most important thing in our life.

Following this teaching of our Lord, the ordinary Christian should strive to attain an integrated life—an intense life of piety and external activity, orientated towards God, practised out of love for him and with an upright intention, which expresses itself in apostolate, in everyday work, in doing the duties of one's state in life. "You must understand now more clearly that God is calling you to serve him *in and from* the ordinary, material and secular activities of human life. He waits for us every day, in the laboratory, in the operating room, in the army barracks, in the university chair, in the factory, in the workshop, in the fields, in the home and in all the immense panorama of work. Understand this well: there is something holy, something divine, hidden in the most ordinary situations, and it is up to each one of you to discover it [...]. There is no other way. Either we learn to find our Lord in ordinary, everyday life, or else we shall never find him. That is why I can tell you that our age needs to give back to matter and to the most trivial occurrences and situations their noble and original meaning. It needs to restore them to the service of the Kingdom of God, to spiritualize them, turning them into a means and an occasion for a continuous meeting with Jesus Christ" (St Josemaría Escrivá, *Conversations*, 114).

11:1–4. St Luke gives us a shorter form

of the Lord's Prayer, or Our Father, than St Matthew (6:9–13). In Matthew there are seven petitions, in Luke only four. Moreover, St Matthew's version is given in the context of the Sermon on the Mount and specifically as part of Jesus' teaching on how to pray; St Luke's is set in one of those occasions just after our Lord has been at prayer—two different contexts. There is nothing surprising about our Lord teaching the same thing on different occasions, not always using exactly the same words, not always at the same length, but always stressing the same basic points. Naturally, the Church uses the longer form of the Lord's Prayer, that of St Matthew.

"When the disciples asked the Lord Jesus, 'Teach us to pray,' he replied by saying the words of the Our Father, thereby giving a concrete model which is also a universal model. In fact, everything that can and must be said to the Father is contained in those seven requests which we all know by heart. There is such a simplicity in them that even a child can learn them, but at the same time such a depth that a whole life can be spent meditating on their meaning. Isn't that so? Does not each of those petitions deal with something essential to our life, directing it totally towards God the Father? Doesn't this prayer speak to us about 'our daily bread', 'forgiveness of our sins, since we forgive others' and about protecting us from 'temptation' and 'delivering us from evil'?" (John Paul II, General Audience, 14 March 1979).

j. Other ancient authorities read *few things are meaningful, or only one*

The Our Father

11 ¹He was praying in a certain place, and when he ceased, one of his disciples said to him, "Lord, teach us to pray, as John taught his disciples." ²And he said to them, "When you pray, say: Lk 5:33; 6:12; 9:29

Mt 6:9–13

The first thing our Lord teaches us to ask for is the glorification of God and the coming of his Kingdom. That is what is really important—the Kingdom of God and his justice (cf. Mt 6:33). Our Lord also wants us to pray confidently that our Father will look after our material needs, for "your heavenly Father knows that you need them all" (Mt 6:32). However, the Our Father makes us aspire especially to possess the goods of the Holy Spirit, and invites us to seek forgiveness (and to forgive others) and to avoid the danger of sinning. Finally, the Our Father emphasizes the importance of vocal prayer. "*'Domine, doce nos orare*. Lord, teach us to pray!' And our Lord answered: 'When you pray, say: *Pater noster, qui es in coelis* … Our Father, who art in heaven …'. How can we fail to appreciate the value of vocal prayer!" (St Josemaría Escrivá, *The Way*, 84).

11:1. Jesus often went away to pray (cf. Lk 6:12; 22:39ff). This practice of the Master's causes his disciples to want to learn how to pray. Jesus teaches them to do what he himself does. Thus, when our Lord prays, he begins with the word "Father!": "Father, into thy hands I commit my spirit" (Lk 23:46; see also Mt 11:25; 26:42, 53; Lk 23:34; Jn 11:41; etc.). His prayer on the cross, "My God, my God, …" (Mt 27:46), is not really an exception to this rule, because there he is quoting Psalm 22, the desperate prayer of the persecuted just man.

Therefore, we can say that the first characteristic prayer should have is the simplicity of a son speaking to his Father, "You wrote to me: 'To pray is to talk with God. But about what?' About what? About Him, about yourself: joys, sorrows, successes and failures, noble ambitions, daily worries, even your weaknesses! And acts of thanksgiving and petition—and love and reparation. In short, to get to know him and to get to know yourself: 'to get acquainted!'" (St Josemaría Escrivá, *The Way*, 91).

11:2. "Hallowed be thy name": in this first petition of the Our Father "we pray that God may be known, loved, honoured and served by everyone and by ourselves in particular." This means that we want "unbelievers to come to a knowledge of the true God, heretics to recognize their errors, schismatics to return to the unity of the Church, sinners to be converted and the righteous to persevere in doing good." By this first petition, our Lord is teaching us that "we must desire God's glory more than our own interest and advantage". This hallowing of God's name is attained "by prayer and good example and by directing all our thoughts, affections and actions towards him" (St Pius X, *Catechism*, 290–293).

"Thy kingdom come": "By the Kingdom of God we understand a triple spiritual kingdom—the Kingdom of God in us, which is grace; the Kingdom of God on earth, which is the Catholic Church; and the Kingdom of God in heaven, which is eternal bliss […]. As regards grace, we pray that God reign in us with his sanctifying grace, by which he is pleased to dwell in us as a king in his throne-room, and that he keep us united to him by the virtues of faith, hope and charity, by which he reigns in our

"Father, hallowed be thy name. Thy kingdom come. [3]Give us each day our daily bread;[k] [4]and forgive us our sins, for we ourselves forgive every one who is indebted to us; and lead us not into temptation."

Effective prayer

[5]And he said to them, "Which of you who has a friend will go to him at midnight and say to him, 'Friend, lend me three loaves; [6]for a friend of mine has arrived on a journey, and I have nothing to set before him'; [7]and he will answer from within, 'Do not bother me; the door is now shut, and my children are with me in bed; I cannot

Lk 18:5

---

intellect, in our heart and in our will [...]. As regards the Church, we pray that it extend and spread all over the world for the salvation of men [...]. As regards heaven, we pray that one day we be admitted to that eternal bliss for which we have been created, where we will be totally happy" (ibid., 294–297).

11:3. The Tradition of the Church usually interprets the "bread" as not only material bread, since "man shall not live by bread alone, but by every word that proceeds from the mouth of God" (Mt 4:4; Deut 8:3). Here Jesus wants us to ask God for "what we need each day for soul and body [...]. For our soul we ask God to sustain our spiritual life, that is, we beg him to give us his grace, of which we are continually in need [...]. The life of our soul is sustained mainly by the divine word and by the Blessed Sacrament of the Altar [...]. For our bodies we pray for what is needed to maintain us" (*St Pius X Catechism*, 302–305).

Christian doctrine stresses two ideas in this petition of the Our Father: the first is trust in divine providence, which frees us from excessive desire to accumulate possessions to insure us against the future (cf. Lk 12:16–21); the other idea is that we should take a brotherly interest in

other people's needs, thereby moderating our selfish tendencies.

11:4. "So rigorously does God exact from us forgetfulness of injuries and mutual affection and love, that he rejects and despises the gifts and sacrifices of those who are not reconciled to one another" (*St Pius V Catechism*, 4, 14, 16).

"This, sisters, is something which we should consider carefully; it is such a serious and important matter that God should pardon us our sins, which have merited eternal fire, that we must pardon all trifling things which have been done to us. As I have so few, Lord, even of these triflings things, to offer thee, thy pardoning of me must be a free gift: there is abundant scope here for thy mercy. Blessed be thou, who endurest one that is so poor" (St Teresa of Avila, *Way of Perfection*, chap. 36).

"And leads us not into temptation": it is not a sin to *feel* temptation but to *consent* to temptation. It is also a sin to put oneself voluntarily into a situation which can easily lead one to sin. God allows us to be tempted, in order to test our fidelity, to exercise us in virtue and to increase our merits with the help of grace. In this petition we ask the Lord to give us his grace not to be overcome when put to the

---

k. Or *our bread for the morrow*

get up and give you anything'? ⁸I tell you, though he will not get
up and give him anything because he is his friend, yet because of
his importunity he will rise and give him whatever he needs. ⁹And
I tell you, Ask, and it will be given you; seek, and you will find;   Mt 7:7–11
knock, and it will be opened to you. ¹⁰For every one who asks
receives, and he who seeks finds, and to him who knocks it will be
opened. ¹¹What father among you, if his son asks for¹ a fish, will
instead of a fish give him a serpent; ¹²or if he asks for an egg, will
give him a scorpion? ¹³If you then, who are evil, know how to give
good gifts to your children, how much more will the heavenly
Father give the Holy Spirit to those who ask him!"

test, or to free us from temptation if we
cannot cope with it.

11:5–10. One of the essential features of
prayer is trusting perseverance. By this
simple example and others like it (cf. Lk
18:1–8) our Lord encourages us not to
desist in asking God to hear us. "Persevere in prayer. Persevere even when
your efforts seem sterile. Prayer is always
fruitful" (St J. Escrivá, *The Way*, 101).

11:9–10. "Do you see the effectiveness
of prayer when it is done properly? Are
you not convinced like me that, if we do
not obtain what we ask God for, it is
because we are not praying with faith,
with a heart pure enough, with enough
confidence, or that we are not persevering in prayer the way we should? God
has never refused, nor will ever refuse,
anything to those who ask for his graces
in the way they should. Prayer is the
great recourse available to us to get out
of sin, to persevere in grace, to move
God's heart and to draw upon us all kinds
of blessings from heaven, whether for the
souls or to meet our temporal needs" (St
John Mary Vianney, *Selected Sermons*,
Fifth Sunday after Easter).

11:11–13. Our Lord uses the example of

human parenthood as a comparison to
stress again the wonderful fact that God
is our Father, for God's fatherhood is the
source of parenthood in heaven and on
earth (cf. Eph 3:15). "The God of our
faith is not a distant being who contemplates indifferently the fate of men—their
desires, their struggles, their sufferings.
He is a Father who loves his children so
much that he sends the Word, the Second
Person of the most Blessed Trinity, so
that by taking on the nature of man he
may die to redeem us. He is the loving
Father who now leads us gently to himself, through the action of the Holy Spirit
who dwells in our hearts" (St Josemaría
Escrivá, *Christ Is Passing By*, 84).

11:13. The Holy Spirit is God's best gift
to us, the great promise Christ gives his
disciples (cf. Jn 5:26), the divine fire which
descends on the apostles at Pentecost,
filling them with fortitude and freedom
to proclaim Christ's message (cf. Acts
2). "The profound reality which we see
in the texts of holy Scripture is not a
remembrance from the past, from some
golden age of the Church which has
since been buried in history. Despite the
weaknesses and the sins of every one of
us, it is the reality of today's Church
and the Church of all time. 'I will pray

l. Other ancient authorities insert *bread, will give him a stone; or if he asks for*

The Kingdom of God and the kingdom of Satan

Mt 12:22–30,
43–45
Mk 3:22–27

Mt 16:1
Mk 8:11

Col 2:15
Jn 12:31; 16:33

[14]Now he was casting out a demon that was dumb; when the demon had gone out, the dumb man spoke, and the people marvelled. [15]But some of them said, "He casts out demons by Beelzebul, the prince of demons"; [16]while others, to test him, sought from him a sign from heaven. [17]But he, knowing their thoughts, said to them, "Every kingdom divided against itself is laid waste, and house falls upon house. [18]And if Satan also is divided against himself, how will his kingdom stand? For you say that I cast out demons by Beelzebul. [19]And if I cast out demons by Beelzebul, by whom do your sons cast them out? Therefore they shall be your judges. [20]But if it is by the finger of God that I cast out demons, then the kingdom of God has come upon you. [21]When a strong man, fully armed, guards his own palace, his goods are in peace; [22]but when one stronger than he assails him and overcomes him, he takes away his armour in which he trusted,

---

to the Father,' our Lord told his disciples, 'and he will give you another Counsellor, to be with you for ever' (Jn 14:16). Jesus has kept his promise. He has risen from the dead and, in union with the eternal Father, he sends us the Holy Spirit to sanctify us and to give us life" (St Josemaría Escrivá, *Christ Is Passing By*, 128).

11:14–23. Jesus' enemies remain obstinate despite the evidence of the miracle. Since they cannot deny that he has done something quite extraordinary, they attribute it to the power of the devil, rather than admit that Jesus is the Messiah. Our Lord answers them with a clinching argument: the fact that he expels demons is proof that he has brought the Kingdom of God. The Second Vatican Council reminds us of this truth: "The Lord Jesus inaugurated his Church by preaching the Good News, that is, the coming of the Kingdom of God, promised over the ages of the Scriptures [...]. The miracles of Jesus also demonstrate that the Kingdom has already come on earth: 'If it is by the

finger of God that I cast out demons, then the Kingdom of God has come upon you' (Lk 11:20; cf. Mt 12:28). But principally the Kingdom is revealed in the person of Christ himself, Son of God and Son of man, who came 'to serve and to give his life as a ransom for many' (Mk 10:45)" (*Lumen gentium*, 5).

The strong man well armed is the devil (v. 21), who has enslaved man; but Jesus Christ, one stronger than he, has come and has conquered him and is despoiling him. St Paul will say that Christ "disarmed the principalities and powers and made a public example of them, triumphing over them" (Col 2:15).

After the victory of Christ, the "stronger one", the words of v. 23 are addressed to mankind at large; even if people do not want to recognize it, Jesus Christ has conquered and from now on no one can adopt an attitude of neutrality towards him: he who is not with him is against him.

11:18. Christ's argument is very clear. One of the worst evils that can overtake

and divides his spoil. [23]He who is not with me is against me, and he who does not gather with me scatters.

[24]"When the unclean spirit has gone out of a man, he passes through waterless places seeking rest; and finding none he says, 'I will return to my house from which I came.' [25]And when he comes he finds it swept and put in order. [26]Then he goes and brings seven other spirits more evil than himself, and they enter and dwell there; and the last state of that man becomes worse than the first."

Mt 12:43ff

Jn 5:14

Responding to the word of God

[27]As he said this, a woman in the crowd raised her voice and said to him, "Blessed is the womb that bore you, and the breasts that you sucked!" [28]But he said, "Blessed rather are those who hear the word of God and keep it!"

Mt 12:46–50

---

the Church is disunity among Christians, disunity among believers. We must make Jesus' prayer our own: "That they may be one; even as thou, Father, art in me, and I in thee, that they also may be one in us, so that the world may believe that thou hast sent me" (Jn 17:21).

11:24–26. Our Lord shows us that the devil is relentless in his struggle against man; despite man rejecting him with the help of grace, he still lays his traps, still tries to overpower him. Knowing all this, St Peter advises us to be sober and vigilant, because "your adversary the devil prowls around like a roaring lion, seeking some one to devour. Resist him, firm in your faith" (1 Pet 5:8–9).

Jesus also forewarns us about the danger of being once more defeated by Satan—which would leave us worse off than we were before. The Latin proverb puts it very well: "*corruptio optimi, pessima*" (the corruption of the best is the worst of all). And St Peter, in his inspired text, inveighs against corrupt Christians, whom he compares in a graphic and frightening way to the dog turning back to his own vomit and the sow being

washed and then wallowing in the mire (cf. 2 Pet 2:22).

11:27–28. These words proclaim and praise the Blessed Virgin's basic attitude of soul. As the Second Vatican Council explains: "In the course of her Son's preaching she [Mary] received the words whereby, in extolling a Kingdom beyond the concerns and ties of flesh and blood, he declared blessed those who heard and kept the word of God (cf. Mk 3:35; Lk 11:27–28) as she was faithfully doing (cf. Lk 2:19, 51)" (*Lumen gentium*, 58). Therefore, by replying in this way Jesus is not rejecting the warm praise this good lady renders his Mother; he accepts it and goes further, explaining that Mary is blessed particularly because she has been good and faithful in putting the word of God into practice. "It was a compliment to his Mother on her *fiat*, her 'be it done' (Lk 1:38). She lived it sincerely, unstintingly, fulfilling its every consequence, but never amid fanfare, rather in the hidden and silent sacrifice of each day" (St Josemaría Escrivá, *Christ Is Passing By*, 172). See the note on Luke 1:34–38.

The sign of Jonah

Mt 12:38–42
1 Cor 1:22

[29]When the crowds were increasing, he began to say, "This gener-ation is an evil generation; it seeks a sign, but no sign shall be given to it except the sign of Jonah. [30]For as Jonah became a sign to the men of Nineveh, so will the Son of man be to this genera-

1 Kings 10:1ff

tion. [31]The queen of the South will arise at the judgment with the men of this generation and condemn them; for she came from the ends of the earth to hear the wisdom of Solomon, and behold,

Jn 3:5

something greater than Solomon is here. [32]The men of Nineveh will arise at the judgment with this generation and condemn it; for they repented at the preaching of Jonah, and behold, something greater than Jonah is here.

The lamp of the body, the light of the soul

Mt 5:15

[33]"No one after lighting a lamp puts it in a cellar or under a bushel, but on a stand, that those who enter may see the light.

Mt 6:22–23

[34]Your eye is the lamp of your body; when your eye is sound, your whole body is full of light; but when it is not sound, your body is full of darkness. [35]Therefore be careful lest the light in you be

---

11:29–32. Jonah was the prophet who led the Ninevites to do penance: his actions and preaching they saw as signi-fying that God had sent him (cf. the note on Mt 12:41–42).

11:33–36. Jesus is using metaphors: a person who has good sight can see things well; similarly, a person whose outlook is pure and uncomplicated is in a position to appreciate the things of God.

Those who opposed our Lord saw the things he did and heard what he said, but their viewpoint was distorted and they did not want to recognize God in him. Here we have also a reproach which applies to anyone who is unwilling to accept the Gospel.

11:39–52. In this passage (one of the most severe in the Gospel) Jesus determinedly unmasks the vice which was largely responsible for official Judaism's rejec-tion of his teaching—hypocrisy cloaked in legalism. There are many people who,

under the guise of doing good, keeping the mere letter of the law, fail to keep its spirit; they close themselves to the love of God and neighbour; they harden their hearts and, though apparently very upright, turn others away from fervent pursuit of God—making virtue distaste-ful. Jesus' criticism is vehement because they are worse than open enemies: against open enemies one can defend oneself, but these are enemies it is almost impossible to deal with. The scribes and Pharisees were blocking the way of those who wanted to follow Jesus: they were the most formidable obstacle to the Gospel. Our Lord's invective against the scribes and Pharisees is reported even more fully in chapter 23 of St Matthew. See the note on Mt 23:1–39.

11:40–41. It is not easy to work out what these verses mean. Probably our Lord is using the idea of cleaning the inside and outside of dishes to teach that a person's heart is much more important

darkness. ³⁶If then your whole body is full of light, having no part dark, it will be wholly bright, as when a lamp with its rays gives you light."

Jesus reproaches scribes and Pharisees

³⁷While he was speaking, a Pharisee asked him to dine with him; so he went in and sat at table. ³⁸The Pharisee was astonished to see that he did not first wash before dinner. ³⁹And the Lord said to him, "Now you Pharisees cleanse the outside of the cup and of the dish, but inside you are full of extortion and wickedness. ⁴⁰You fools! Did not he who made the outside make the inside also? ⁴¹But give for alms those things which are within; and behold, everything is clean for you.

⁴²"But woe to you Pharisees! for you tithe mint and rue and every herb, and neglect justice and the love of God; these you ought to have done, without neglecting the others. ⁴³Woe to you Pharisees! for you love the best seat in the synagogues and salutations in the market places. ⁴⁴Woe to you! for you are like graves which are not seen, and men walk over them without knowing it."

Lk 7:36; 14:1

Mt 15:2

Mt 23:1–36

Lk 20:46

---

than what appears on the surface—whereas the Pharisees got it the wrong way round, as so many people tend to do. Jesus is warning us not to be so concerned about "the outside" but rather to give importance to "the inside". Applying this to the case of alms: we have to be generous with those things we are inclined to hoard; in other words, it is not enough just to give a little money (that could be a purely formal, external gesture); love is what we have to give others—love and understanding, refinement, respect for their freedom, deep concern for their spiritual and material welfare; this is something we cannot do unless our interior dispositions are right.

In an address to young people, Pope John Paul II explains what almsgiving really means: "The Greek word for alms, *eleemosyne*, comes from *éleos*, meaning compassion and mercy. Various circumstances have combined to change this meaning so that almsgiving is often regarded as a cold act, with no love in it.

But almsgiving in the proper sense means realizing the needs of others and letting them share in one's own goods. Who would say that there will not always be others who need help, especially spiritual help, support, consolation, fraternity, love? The world is always very poor, as far as love is concerned" (28 March 1979).

11:42. The Law of Moses laid down that the harvest had to be tithed (cf. Lev 27:30–33; Deut 14:22ff; etc.) to provide for the worship offered in the temple. Insignificant products were not subject to this Law.

Rue is a bitter medicinal plant used by the Jews in ancient times. Did it have to be tithed?: the Pharisees, who were so nit-picking, said that it did.

11:44. According to the Old Law, anyone who touched a grave became unclean for seven days (Num 19:16), but with the passage of time a grave could

⁴⁵One of the lawyers answered him, "Teacher, in saying this you reproach us also." ⁴⁶And he said, "Woe to you lawyers also! for you load men with burdens hard to bear, and you yourselves do not touch the burdens with one of your fingers. ⁴⁷Woe to you! for you build the tombs of the prophets whom your fathers killed. ⁴⁸So you are witnesses and consent to the deed of your fathers; for they killed them, and you build their tombs. ⁴⁹Therefore also the Wisdom of God said, 'I will send them prophets and apostles, some of whom they will kill and persecute,' ⁵⁰that the blood of all the prophets, shed from the foundation of the world, may be required of this generation, ⁵¹from the blood of Abel to the blood of Zechariah, who perished between the altar and the sanctuary. Yes, I tell you, it shall be required of this generation. ⁵²Woe to you lawyers! for you have taken away the key of knowledge; you did not enter yourselves, and you hindered those who were entering."

Gen 4:8
2 Chron 24:20

⁵³As he went away from there, the scribes and the Pharisees began to press him hard, and to provoke him to speak of many things, ⁵⁴lying in wait for him, to catch at something he might say.

Lk 20:20

---

become so overgrown that a person could walk on it without noticing. Our Lord uses this comparison to unmask the hypocrisy of the people he is talking to: they are very exact about very small details but they forget their basic duty— justice and the love of God (v. 42). On the outside they are clean but their hearts are full of malice and rottenness (v. 39); they pretend to be just, appearances are all that matters to them; they know that virtue is held in high regard, therefore they strive to appear highly virtuous (v. 43). Duplicity and deceit mark their lives.

11:51. Zechariah was a prophet who died by being stoned in the temple of Jerusalem around the year 800 BC because he accused the people of Israel of being unfaithful to God's law (cf. 2 Chron 24:20–22). The murder of Abel (Gen 4:8) and that of Zechariah were, respectively, the first and last murders reported in these books which the Jews regarded as Scripture. Jesus refers to a Jewish tradition which, in his own time and even later, pointed out the stain of the blood of Zechariah.

The altar referred to here was the altar of holocausts, located outside, in the courtyard of the priests, in front of the temple proper.

11:52. Jesus severely reproaches these doctors of the Law who, given their study and meditation on Scripture, were the very ones who should have recognized Jesus as the Messiah, since his coming had been foretold in the sacred books. However, as we learn from the Gospel, the exact opposite happened. Not only did they not accept Jesus: they obstinately opposed him. As teachers of the Law they should have taught the people to follow Jesus; instead, they blocked the way.

11:53–54. St Luke frequently records this attitude of our Lord's enemies (cf. 6:11; 19:47–48; 20:19–20; 22:2). The people followed Jesus and were enthusiastic

8. ANNOUNCEMENT OF THE END

Various teachings

12 [1] In the meantime, when so many thousands of the multitude had gathered together that they trod upon one another, he began to say to his disciples first, "Beware of the leaven of the Pharisees, which is hypocrisy. [2] Nothing is covered up that will not be revealed, or hidden that will not be known. [3] Whatever you have said in the dark shall be heard in the light, and what you have whispered in private rooms shall be proclaimed upon the housetops.

[4] "I tell you, my friends, do not fear those who kill the body, and after that have no more that they can do. [5] But I will warn you whom to fear: fear him who, after he has killed, has power to cast into hell;[m] yes, I tell you, fear him! [6] Are not five sparrows sold for two pennies? And not one of them is forgotten before God. [7] Why, even the hairs of your head are all numbered. Fear not; you are of more value than many sparrows.

[8] "And I tell you, every one who acknowledges me before men, the Son of man also will acknowledge before the angels of God;

Mt 16:6
Mk 8:15

Mt 10:26–27
Lk 8:17

Mt 10:28–31

Lk 21:18

---

about his preaching and miracles, whereas the Pharisees and scribes would not accept him and would not allow the people to follow him; they tried in every way to discredit him in the eyes of the people (cf. Jn 11:48).

12:3. Most Palestinian houses had a roof in the form of a terrace. There people would meet to chat and while away the time in the hottest part of the day. Jesus points out to his disciples that just as in these get-togethers things said in private became matters of discussion, so too, despite the Pharisees' and scribes' efforts to hide their vices and defects under the veil of hypocrisy, they would become a matter of common knowledge.

12:6–7. Nothing—not even the most insignificant thing—escapes God, his providence and the judgment he will

mete out. For this same reason no one should fear that any suffering or persecution he experiences in following Christ will remain unrewarded in eternity.

The teaching about fear, contained in v. 5, is filled out in vv. 6 and 7, where Jesus tells us that God is a good Father who watches over every one of us—much more than he does over these little ones (whom he also remembers). Therefore, our fear of God should not be servile (based on fear of punishment); it should be a filial fear (the fear of someone who does not want to displease his father), a fear nourished by trust in divine providence.

12:8–9. This follows logically from Christ's previous teaching: worse than physical evils, worse even than death, are evils of the soul, that is, sin. Those who out of fear of temporal suffering deny our

m. Greek *Gehenna*

Lk 9:26
Mt 12:32
Mk 3:28–29

Lk 21:12–15
Mt 10:19–20

⁹but he who denies me before men will be denied before the angels of God. ¹⁰And every one who speaks a word against the Son of man will be forgiven; but he who blasphemes against the Holy Spirit will not be forgiven. ¹¹And when they bring you before the synagogues and the rulers and the authorities, do not be anxious how or what you are to answer or what you are to say; ¹²for the Holy Spirit will teach you in that very hour what you ought to say."

Parable of the rich fool

1 Tim 6:9–10

¹³One of the multitude said to him, "Teacher, bid my brother divide the inheritance with me." ¹⁴But he said to him, "Man, who made me a judge or divider over you?" ¹⁵And he said to them, "Take heed, and beware of all covetousness; for a man's life does not consist in the abundance of his possessions." ¹⁶And he told them a parable, saying, "The land of a rich man brought forth plentifully; ¹⁷and he thought to himself, 'What shall I do, for I

Lord and are unfaithful to the demands of the faith will fall into a greater evil still: they will be denied by Christ himself on the Day of Judgment; whereas those who are penalized in this life because of their faithfulness to Christ will receive the eternal reward of being recognized by him and will come to share his glory.

12:10. Blasphemy against the Holy Spirit consists in maliciously attributing to the devil actions that have God as their origin. A person who does that prevents God's pardon from reaching him: that is why he cannot obtain forgiveness (cf. Mt 12:31; Mk 3:28–30). Jesus understands and excuses the weakness of a person who makes a moral mistake, but he is not similarly indulgent to someone who shuts his eyes and his heart to the wonderful things the Spirit does; that was the way these Pharisees acted who accused Jesus of casting out demons in the name of Beelzebul; it is the way unbelieving people act who refuse to see in Christ's work a sign of the goodness of God, who reject the invitation God offers them and who thereby

put themselves outside the reach of salvation (cf. Heb 6:4–6; 10:26–31). See the note on Mk 3:28–30.

12:13–14. This man is only interested in his own problems; he sees in Jesus only a teacher with authority and prestige who can help sort out his case (cf. Deut 21:17). He is a good example of those who approach religious authorities not to seek advice on the way they should go in their spiritual life, but rather to get them to solve their material problems. Jesus vigorously rejects the man's request—not because he is insensitive to the injustice which may have been committed in this family, but because it is not part of his redemptive mission to intervene in matters of this kind. By his word and example the Master shows us that his work of salvation is not aimed at solving the many social and family problems that arise in human society; he has come to give us the principles and moral standards which should inspire our actions in temporal affairs, but not to give us precise, technical solutions to problems

have nowhere to store my crops?' [18]And he said, 'I will do this: I will pull down my barns, and build larger ones; and there I will store all my grain and my goods. [19]And I will say to my soul, Soul, you have ample goods laid up for many years; take your ease, eat, drink, be merry.' [20]But God said to him, 'Fool! This night your soul is required of you; and the things you have prepared, whose will they be?' [21]So is he who lays up treasure for himself, and is not rich toward God."

Trust in God's fatherly providence
[22]And he said to his disciples, "Therefore I tell you, do not be anxious about your life, what you shall eat, nor about your body, what you shall put on. [23]For life is more than food, and the body more than clothing. [24]Consider the ravens: they neither sow nor reap, they have neither storehouse nor barn, and yet God feeds them. Of how much more value are you than the birds! [25]And which of you by being anxious can add a cubit to his span of life?[n] [26]If then you

Ps 147:9

---

which arise; to that end he has endowed us with intelligence and freedom.

12:15–21. After his statement in v. 15, Jesus tells the parable of the foolish rich man: what folly it is to put our trust in amassing material goods to ensure we have a comfortable life on earth, forgetting the goods of the spirit, which are what really ensure us—through God's mercy—of eternal life.

This is how St Athanasius explained these words of our Lord: "A person who lives as if he were to die every day—given that our life is uncertain by definition—will not sin, for good fear extinguishes most of the disorder of our appetites; whereas he who thinks he has a long life ahead of him will easily let himself be dominated by pleasures" (*Adversus Antigonum*).

12:19. This man's stupidity consisted in making material possession his only aim in life and his only insurance policy. It is

lawful for a person to want to own what he needs for living, but if possession of material resources becomes an absolute, it spells the ultimate destruction of the individual and of society. "Increased possession is not the ultimate goal of nations nor of individuals. All growth is ambivalent. It is essential if man is to develop as a man, but in a way it imprisons man if he considers it the supreme good, and it restricts his vision. Then we see hearts harden and minds close, and men no longer gather together in friendship but out of self-interest, which soon leads to strife and disunity. The exclusive pursuit of possessions thus becomes an obstacle to individual fulfilment and to man's true greatness. Both for nations and for individuals, avarice is the most evident form of moral underdevelopment" (Paul VI, *Populorum progressio*, 19).

12:25. See the note on Mt 6:27. A "cubit", a measurement of length, was approximately half a metre or half a yard.

n. Or *to his stature*

are not able to do as small a thing as that, why are you anxious about the rest? [27]Consider the lilies, how they grow; they neither toil nor spin;[o] yet I tell you, even Solomon in all his glory was not arrayed like one of these. [28]But if God so clothes the grass which is alive in the field today and tomorrow is thrown into the oven, how much more will he clothe you, O men of little faith! [29]And do not seek what you are to eat and what you are to drink, nor be of anxious mind. [30]For all the nations of the world seek these things; and your Father knows that you need them. [31]Instead, seek his[p] kingdom, and these things shall be yours as well.

Lk 22:29
Is 41:14

[32]"Fear not, little flock, for it is your Father's good pleasure to give you the kingdom. [33]Sell your possessions, and give alms; provide yourselves with purses that do not grow old, with a treasure in the heavens that does not fail, where no thief approaches and no moth destroys. [34]For where your treasure is, there will your heart be also.

Mt 6:20–21
Lk 16:9; 18:22

12:27–28. In the history of the people of Israel, it was under King Solomon, who succeeded the great King David on the throne, that the nation reached its high point of cultural and material prosperity: in Jewish tradition, therefore, Solomon was the prototype of earthly power and splendour (cf. Mt 12:42). Jesus stresses here that divine providence looks after all those who accept his call: a person in the grace of God is far more beautiful than the lily, far more splendid than Solomon himself.

12:29–31. Our Lord here sums up his teaching on trust and abandonment to divine providence, contrasting the right attitude (seeking the Kingdom above all else) and the wrong one (seeking only temporal goods). Jesus does not condemn reasonable concern to acquire the necessities of life, but he teaches that one's efforts in this direction should be ordered towards one's last end, the possession of the Kingdom. Therefore he says that earthly things will be given us as an added extra, "not as a good on which you should fix your attention", St Augustine explains, "but as a means of enabling you to reach the true and highest good" (*De Serm. Domini in monte*, 2, 24).

The material instinct to preserve one's life is something divine providence has built into man's make-up. But this instinct should be channelled through well-organized effort and should not take the form of anxious concern which would cause one to forget the most important thing of all—inverting the Christian hierarchy of values by putting material concerns ahead of spiritual welfare.

12:33–34. Our Lord concludes this address by insisting on those imperishable goods to which we should aspire. In this connexion the Second Vatican Council concludes its teaching on the universal call to holiness saying: "Therefore all the faithful are invited and obliged to holiness and the perfection of their own state of life. Accordingly let all of them see that they direct their affections rightly, lest they be hindered in their pursuit of perfect love by

---

o. Other ancient authorities read *Consider the lilies; they neither spin nor weave*   **p.** Other ancient authorities read *God's*

The need for vigilance; the parable of the steward

Mt 24:42–51 Ex 12:11 1 Pet 1:13 Mt 25:1–13

35 "Let your loins be girded and your lamps burning, 36 and be like
men who are waiting for their master to come home from the marriage feast, so that they may open to him at once when he comes
and knocks. 37 Blessed are those servants whom the master finds Jn 13:4ff
awake when he comes; truly, I say to you, he will gird himself and
have them sit at table, and he will come and serve them. 38 If he
comes in the second watch, or in the third, and finds them so,
blessed are those servants! 39 But know this, that if the householder 1 Thess 5:2
had known at what hour the thief was coming, he would have
been awake and[q] would not have left his house to be broken into.
40 You also must be ready; for the Son of man is coming at an hour
you do not expect."

---

the use of worldly things and by an adherence to riches which is contrary to the spirit of evangelical poverty, following the apostle's advice: Let those who use this world not fix their abode in it, for the form of this world is passing away (cf. 1 Cor 7:31)" (*Lumen gentium*, 42).

"When Holy Scripture refers to the heart, it does not refer to some fleeting sentiments of joy or tears. By heart it means the person who directs his whole being, soul and body, to what he considers his good, as Jesus himself indicated: 'For where your treasure is, there will your heart be also' (Mt 6:21)" (St J. Escrivá, *Christ Is Passing By*, 164). Our Lord's teaching is quite clear: man's heart yearns to possess wealth, a good social position, prestigious public or professional appointments, which he sees as providing him with security, contentment and self-affirmation; however, this kind of treasure involves endless worry and disappointment, because there is always a danger of losing it. Jesus does not mean that man should forget about earthly things, but he does teach us that no created thing should become our "treasure", our main aim in life: that should be God, our Creator and Lord, whom we should love and serve as we go about our ordinary affairs, putting our hopes on the eternal joy of heaven. See also the note on Mt 6:19–21.

12:35–39. In the preaching of Christ and of the apostles we are frequently exhorted to be watchful (cf. Mt 24:42; 25:13; Mk 14:34)—for one thing, because the enemy is always on the prowl (cf. 1 Pet 5:8), and also because a person in love is always awake (cf. Song 5:2). This watchfulness expresses itself in a spirit of prayer (cf. Lk 21:36; 1 Pet 4:7) and fortitude in faith (cf. 1 Cor 16:13). See the note on Mt 25:1–13.

12:35. To enable them to do certain kinds of work the Jews used to hitch up the flowing garments they normally wore. "Girding your loins" immediately suggests a person getting ready for work, for effort, for a journey etc. (cf. Jer 1:17; Eph 6:14; 1 Pet 1:13). And "having your lamps burning" indicates the sort of attitude a person should have who is on the watch or is waiting for someone's arrival.

12:40. God has chosen to hide from us the time of our death and the time when the world will come to an end. Immediately

q. Other ancient authorities omit *would have been awake and*

⁴¹Peter said, "Lord, are you telling this parable for us or for all?" ⁴²And the Lord said, "Who then is the faithful and wise steward, whom his master will set over his household, to give them their portion of food at the proper time? ⁴³Blessed is that servant whom his master when he comes will find so doing. ⁴⁴Truly I tell you, he will set him over all his possessions. ⁴⁵But if that servant says to himself, 'My master is delayed in coming,' and begins to beat the menservants and the maidservants, and to eat and drink and get drunk, ⁴⁶the master of that servant will come on a day when he does not expect him and at an hour he does not know, and will punish[r] him, and put him with the unfaithful. ⁴⁷And that servant who knew his master's will, but did not make ready or act according to his will, shall receive a severe beating. ⁴⁸But he who did not know, and did what deserved a beating, shall receive a light beating. Every one to whom much is given, of him will much be required; and of him to whom men commit much they will demand the more.

after death everyone undergoes the particular judgment: "just as it is appointed for men to die once, and after that comes judgment ..." (Heb 9:27). The end of the world is when the general judgment will take place.

12:41–48. After our Lord's exhortation to vigilance, St Peter asks a question (v. 41), the answer to which is the key to understanding this parable. On the one hand, Jesus emphasizes that we simply do not know exactly when God is going to ask us to render an account of our life; on the other—answering Peter's question—our Lord explains that his teaching is addressed to every individual. God will ask everyone to render an account of his doings: everyone has a mission to fulfil in this life and he has to account for it before the judgment seat of God and be judged on what he has produced, be it much or little.

"Since we know neither the day nor the hour, we should follow the advice of the Lord and watch constantly so that, when the single course of our earthly life is completed (cf. Heb 9:27), we may merit to enter with him into the marriage feast and be numbered among the blessed (cf. Mt 25:31–46) and not, like the wicked and slothful servants (cf. Mt 25:26), be ordered to depart into the eternal fire (cf. Mt 25:41)" (Vatican II, *Lumen gentium*, 48).

12:49–50. In the Bible, fire is often used to describe God's burning love for men (cf. Deut 4:24; Ex 13:21–22; etc.). This love finds its highest expression in the Son of God become man: "God so loved the world that he gave his only Son" (Jn 3:16). Jesus voluntarily gave up his life out of love for us, and "greater love has no man than this, that a man lay down his life for his friends" (Jn 15:13).

In these words reported by St Luke, Jesus Christ reveals his abounding desire to give his life for love of us. He calls his death a baptism, because from it he will

r. Or *cut him to pieces*

126

Jesus brings division, not peace

⁴⁹"I came to cast fire upon the earth; and would that it were
already kindled! ⁵⁰I have a baptism to be baptized with; and how   Jn 12:27
I am constrained until it is accomplished! ⁵¹Do you think that I   Mt 10:34–36
have come to give peace on earth? No, I tell you, but rather division; ⁵²for henceforth in one house there will be five divided, three
against two and two against three; ⁵³they will be divided, father   Mic 7:6
against son and son against father, mother against daughter and
daughter against her mother, mother-in-law against daughter-in-
law and daughter-in-law against her mother-in-law."

The signs of the times

⁵⁴He also said to the multitudes, "When you see a cloud rising in   Mt 16:2–3
the west, you say at once, 'A shower is coming'; and so it happens. ⁵⁵And when you see the south wind blowing, you say,
'There will be scorching heat'; and it happens. ⁵⁶You hypocrites!

---

arise victorious never to die again. Our
Baptism is a submersion in Christ's
death, in which we die to sin and are
reborn to the new life of grace: "we were
buried therefore with him by baptism
into death, so that as Christ was raised
from the dead by the glory of the Father,
we too might walk in newness of life"
(Rom 6:4).

Through this new life, we Christians
should become set on fire in the same
way as Jesus set his disciples on fire:
"With the amazing naturalness of the
things of God, the contemplative soul is
filled with apostolic zeal. 'My heart
became hot within me, a fire blazed forth
from my thoughts' (Ps 39:3). What could
this fire be if not the fire that Christ talks
about: 'I came to cast fire upon the earth,
and would that it were already kindled?'
(Lk 12:49). An apostolic fire that
acquires its strength in prayer: there is no
better way than this to carry on, throughout the whole world, the battle of peace
to which every Christian is called to fill
up what is lacking in the sufferings of
Christ (cf. Col 1:24)" (St Josemaría
Escrivá, *Christ Is Passing By*, 120).

12:51–53. God has come into the world
with a message of peace (cf. Lk 2:14)
and reconciliation (cf. Rom 5:11). By
resisting, through sin, the redeeming
work of Christ, we become his oppo-
nents. Injustice and error lead to division
and war. "Insofar as men are sinners, the
threat of war hangs over them and will so
continue until the coming of Christ; but
insofar as they can vanquish sin by
coming together in charity, violence itself
will be vanquished" (Vatican II, *Gaudium et spes*, 78).

During his own life on earth, Christ
was a sign of contradiction (cf. Lk 2:34).
Our Lord is forewarning his disciples
about the contention and division which
will accompany the spread of the Gospel
(cf. Lk 6:20–23; Mt 10:24).

12:56. Jesus' listeners knew from experience how to forecast the weather. However, although they knew the signs of the
Messiah's coming announced by the
prophets, and were hearing his preaching
and witnessing his miracles, they did not
want to draw the logical conclusion; they

You know how to interpret the appearance of earth and sky; but why do you not know how to interpret the present time? [57]"And why do you not judge for yourselves what is right?

Mt 5:25–26 [58]As you go with your accuser before the magistrate, make an effort to settle with him on the way, lest he drag you to the judge, and the judge hand you over to the officer, and the officer put you in prison. [59]I tell you, you will never get out till you have paid the very last copper."

The need for repentance

13 [1]There were some present at that very time who told him of the Galileans whose blood Pilate had mingled with their sacrifices. [2]And he answered them, "Do you think that these Galileans were worse sinners than all the other Galileans, because they suffered thus? [3]I tell you, No; but unless you repent you will all likewise perish. [4]Or those eighteen upon whom the tower in Siloam fell and killed them, do you think that they were worse offenders than all the others who dwelt in Jerusalem? [5]I tell you, No; but unless you repent you will all likewise perish."

Jn 9:2

Ps 7:12

lacked the necessary good will and upright intention, and they just closed their eyes to the light of the Gospel (cf. Rom 1:18ff).

This attitude is also found to be very widespread in our own time, in the form of certain kinds of atheism denounced by the Second Vatican Council: "Those who wilfully try to drive God from their heart and to avoid all questions about religion, not following the biddings of their conscience, are not free from blame" (*Gaudium et spes*, 19).

13:1–5. Our Lord used current events in his teaching. The Galileans referred to here may be the same as mentioned in the Acts of the Apostles (5:37). The episode was fairly typical of the times Jesus lived in, with Pilate sternly suppressing any sign of civil unrest. We do not know anything about the accident at Siloam other than what the Gospel tells us.

The fact that these people died in this way does not mean that they were worse than others, for God does not always punish sinners in this life (cf. Jn 9:3). All of us are sinners, meriting a much worse punishment than temporal misfortune: we merit eternal punishment; but Christ has come to atone for our sins, he has opened the gates of heaven. We must repent of our sins; otherwise God will not free us from the punishment we deserve. "When you meet with suffering, the cross, your thought should be: what is this compared with what I deserve?" (St Josemaría Escrivá, *The Way*, 690).

13:3. "He tells us that, without Holy Baptism, no one will enter the Kingdom of heaven (cf. Jn 3:5); and, elsewhere, that if we do not repent we will all perish (Lk 13:3). This is all easily understood. Ever since man sinned, all his senses rebel against reason; therefore, if we want the flesh to be controlled by the spirit and by reason, it must be mortified; if we do not want the body to be at war with the soul, it and all our senses need

Parable of the barren fig tree

⁶And he told this parable: "A man had a fig tree planted in his vineyard; and he came seeking fruit on it and found none. ⁷And he said to the vinedresser, 'Lo, these three years I have come seeking fruit on this fig tree, and I find none. Cut it down; why should it use up the ground?' ⁸And he answered him, 'Let it alone, sir, this year also, till I dig about it and put on manure. ⁹And if it bears fruit next year, well and good; but if not, you can cut it down.' "

Lk 3:9
Mt 21:19
Mk 11:13

2 Pet 3:9, 15

Jesus cures a woman on the sabbath

¹⁰Now he was teaching in one of the synagogues on the sabbath. ¹¹And there was a woman who had had a spirit of infirmity for eighteen years; she was bent over and could not fully straighten herself. ¹²And when Jesus saw her, he called her and said to her, "Woman, you are freed from your infirmity." ¹³And he laid his hands upon her, and immediately she was made straight, and she praised God. ¹⁴But the ruler of the synagogue, indignant because Jesus had healed on the sabbath, said to the people, "There are six days on which work ought to be done; come on those days and be

Mt 9:18
Mk 7:32

Ex 20:9
Deut 5:13

---

to be chastened; if we desire to go to God, the soul with all its faculties needs to be mortified" (St John Mary Vianney, *Selected Sermons*, Ash Wednesday).

13:6–9. Our Lord stresses that we need to produce plenty of fruit (cf. Lk 8:11–15) in keeping with the graces we have received (cf. Lk 12:48). But he also tells us that God waits patiently for this fruit to appear; he does not want the death of the sinner; he wants him to be converted and to live (Ezek 33:11) and, as St Peter teaches, he is "forbearing towards you, not wishing that any should perish, but that all should reach repentance" (2 Pet 3:9). But God's clemency should not lead us to neglect our duties and become lazy and comfort-seeking, living sterile lives. He is merciful, but he is also just and he will punish failure to respond to his grace.

"There is one case that we should be especially sorry about—that of Christians who could do more and don't; Christians who could live all the consequences of their vocation as children of God, but refuse to do so through lack of generosity. We are partly to blame, for the grace of faith has not been given us to hide but to share with others (cf. Mt 5:15f). We cannot forget that the happiness of these people, in this life and in the next, is at stake. The Christian life is a divine wonder with immediate promises of satisfaction and serenity—but on condition that we know how to recognize the gift of God (cf. Jn 4:10) and be generous, not counting the cost" (St Josemaría Escrivá, *Christ Is Passing By*, 147).

13:10–17. As was the custom, our Lord used go to the synagogue on the sabbath. Noticing this poor woman, he uses his power and mercy to cure her. The ordinary people are delighted, but the ruler of the synagogue, apparently zealous about fulfilling the Law (cf. Ex 20:8; 31:14; Lev 19:3–30), publicly upbraids our Lord. Jesus energetically censures this

healed, and not on the sabbath day." [15]Then the Lord answered
Lk 14:5   him, "You hypocrites! Does not each of you on the sabbath untie
his ox or his ass from the manger, and lead it away to water it?
Lk 19:9   [16]And ought not this woman, a daughter of Abraham whom Satan
bound for eighteen years, be loosed from this bond on the sabbath
day?" [17]As he said this, all his adversaries were put to shame; and
all the people rejoiced at all the glorious things that were done by
him.

Parables of the mustard seed and of the leaven

Mt 13:31–33
Mk 4:30–32   [18]He said therefore, "What is the kingdom of God like? And to
what shall I compare it? [19]It is like a grain of mustard seed which
a man took and sowed in his garden; and it grew and became a
tree, and the birds of the air made nests in its branches."

Ezek 17:23;
31:6   [20]And again he said, "To what shall I compare the kingdom of
God? [21]It is like leaven which a woman took and hid in three measures of meal, till it was all leavened."

---

warped interpretation of the Law and
stresses the need for mercy and understanding, which is what pleases God (cf.
Hos 6:6; Jas 2:13).

13:18–21. The grain of mustard and the
leaven symbolize the Church, which
starts off as a little group of disciples and
steadily spreads with the aid of the Holy
Spirit until it reaches the ends of the
earth. As early as the second century
Tertullian claimed: "We are but of yester-
day and yet we are everywhere" (*Apologeticum*, 37).

Our Lord "with the parable of the
mustard seed encourages them to have
faith and shows them that the Gospel
preaching will spread in spite of everything. The Lord's disciples were the weak-
est of men, but nevertheless, because of
the great power that was in them, the
Gospel has been spread to every part of
the world" (St John Chrysostom, *Hom.
on St Matthew*, 46). Therefore, a Christian should not be discouraged if his apostolic action seems very limited and
insignificant. With God's grace and his

own faithfulness it will keep growing like
the mustard seed, in spite of difficulties:
"In the moments of struggle and tribulation, when perhaps 'the good' fill your
way with obstacles, lift up your apostolic
heart: listen to Jesus as he speaks of the
grain of mustard seed and of the leaven.
And say to him: '*Edissere nobis parabolam*—explain the parable to me.' And
you will feel the joy of contemplating the
victory to come: the birds of the air under
the shelter of your apostolate, now only
in its beginnings, and the whole of the
meal leavened" (St Josemaría Escrivá,
The Way, 695).

13:23–24. Everyone is called to form
part of the Kingdom of God, for he
"desires all men to be saved" (1 Tim 2:4).
"Those who, through no fault of their
own, do not know the Gospel of Christ or
his Church, but who nevertheless seek
God with a sincere heart and, moved by
grace, try in their actions to do his will as
they know it through the dictates of their
conscience: those too may achieve eternal salvation. Nor shall divine providence

The narrow gate

²²He went on his way through towns and villages, teaching, and journeying toward Jerusalem. ²³And some one said to him, "Lord, will those who are saved be few?" And he said to them, ²⁴"Strive to enter by the narrow door; for many, I tell you, will seek to enter and will not be able. ²⁵When once the householder has risen up and shut the door, you will begin to stand outside and to knock at the door, saying, 'Lord, open to us.' He will answer you, 'I do not know where you come from.' ²⁶Then you will begin to say, 'We ate and drank in your presence, and you taught in our streets.' ²⁷But he will say, 'I tell you, I do not know where you come from; depart from me, all you workers of iniquity!' ²⁸There you will weep and gnash your teeth, when you see Abraham and Isaac and Jacob and all the prophets in the kingdom of God and you yourselves thrust out. ²⁹And men will come from east and west, and from north and south, and sit at table in the kingdom of God. ³⁰And behold, some are last who will be first, and some are first who will be last."

Mt 7:13–14
1 Tim 6:12

Mt 25:11–12

Mt 7:22–23
Ps 6:8

Mt 8:11–12

Is 49:12; 59:19
Ps 106:3
Mt 19:30

---

deny the assistance necessary for salvation to those who, without any fault of theirs, have not yet arrived at an explicit knowledge of God, and who, not without grace, strive to lead a good life. Whatever good or truth is found among them is considered by the Church to be a preparation for the Gospel and given by him who enlightens all men that they may at length have life" (Vatican II, *Lumen gentium*, 16).

Certainly, only those who make a serious effort can reach the goal of salvation (cf. Lk 16:16; Mt 11:12). Our Lord tells us so by using the simile of the narrow gate. "A Christian's struggle must be unceasing, for interior life consists in beginning and beginning again. This prevents us from proudly thinking that we are perfect already. It is inevitable that we should meet difficulties on our way. If we did not come up against obstacles, we would not be creatures of flesh and blood. We will always have passions which pull us downwards; we will always have to defend ourselves against more or less self-defeating urges"

(St J. Escrivá, *Christ Is Passing By*, 75).

13:25–28. As at other times, Jesus describes eternal life by using the example of a banquet (cf., e.g., Lk 12:35ff; 14:15ff). Knowing the Lord and listening to his preaching is not enough for getting to heaven; what God judges is how we respond to the grace he gives us: "Not every one who says to me, 'Lord, Lord,' shall enter the kingdom of heaven, but he who does the will of my Father who is in heaven" (Mt 7:21).

13:29–30. Generally speaking, the Jewish people regarded themselves as the sole beneficiaries of the messianic promises made by the prophets; but Jesus proclaims that salvation is open to everyone. The only condition he lays down is that men freely respond to God's merciful call. When Christ died on the cross the veil of the temple was torn in two (Lk 23:45 and par.), a sign of the end of the distinction between Jews and Gentiles. St Paul teaches: "For he [Christ] is our peace, who has made us both one, and

Jesus' reply to Herod

³¹At that very hour some Pharisees came, and said to him, "Get away from here, for Herod wants to kill you." ³²And he said to them, "Go and tell that fox, 'Behold, I cast out demons and perform cures today and tomorrow, and the third day I finish my course. ³³Nevertheless I must go on my way today and tomorrow and the day following; for it cannot be that a prophet should perish away from Jerusalem.'

Jerusalem admonished

Mt 23:27–39

³⁴"O Jerusalem, Jerusalem, killing the prophets and stoning those who are sent to you! How often would I have gathered your children together as a hen gathers her brood under her wings, and you

Jer 22:5
Ps 118:26

would not! ³⁵Behold, your house is forsaken. And I tell you, you will not see me until you say, 'Blessed is he who comes in the name of the Lord.' "

Jesus cures a dropsical man on the sabbath

Lk 6:6–11;
13:10–17

14 ¹One sabbath when he went to dine at the house of a ruler who belonged to the Pharisees, they were watching him.

---

has broken down the dividing wall [...] that he might create in himself one new man in place of the two, so making peace, and might reconcile us both to God in one body through the cross, thereby bringing the hostility to an end" (Eph 2:14–16). Therefore, "all men are called to belong to the new people of God. This people therefore, whilst remaining one and only one, is to be spread throughout the whole world and to all ages in order that the design of God's will may be fulfilled: he made human nature one in the beginning and has decreed that all his children who were scattered should be finally gathered together as one" (Vatican II, *Lumen gentium*, 13).

13:31–33. This episode apparently took place in the Perea region which, like Galilee, was under the jurisdiction of Herod Antipas (cf. Lk 3:1), a son of Herod the Great (cf. the note on Mt 2:1).

On other occasions St Luke mentions that Herod was keen to meet Jesus and see him perform a miracle (cf. Lk 9:9; 23:8). These Pharisees may be giving Jesus the warning just to get him to go away. Jesus calls Herod—and indirectly his accomplices—a "fox", once again showing his rejection of duplicity and hypocrisy.

Jesus' answer shows them he is completely in command of his life and death: he is the Son of God and his Father's will is his only governor (cf. Jn 10:18).

13:34. Jesus here shows the infinite extent of his love. St Augustine explores the meaning of this touching simile: "You see, brethren, how a hen becomes weak with her chickens. No other bird, when it is a mother, shows its maternity so clearly. We see all kinds of sparrows building their nests before our eyes; we see swallows, storks, doves, every day building their nests; but we do not know them to be

²And behold, there was a man before him who had dropsy. ³And Jesus spoke to the lawyers and Pharisees, saying, "Is it lawful to heal on the sabbath, or not?" ⁴But they were silent. Then he took him and healed him, and let him go. ⁵And he said to them, "Which of you, having an ass[s] or an ox that has fallen into a well, will not immediately pull him out on a sabbath day?" ⁶And they could not reply to this.

Mt 12:11

A lesson about humility

⁷Now he told a parable to those who were invited, when he marked how they chose the places of honour, saying to them, ⁸"When you are invited by any one to a marriage feast, do not sit down in a place of honour, lest a more eminent man than you be invited by him; ⁹and he who invited you both will come and say to you, 'Give place to this man,' and then you will begin with shame to take the lowest place. ¹⁰But when you are invited, go and sit in the lowest place, so that when your host comes he may say to you, 'Friend, go up higher'; then you will be honoured in the presence of all who sit at table with you. ¹¹For every one who exalts himself will be humbled, and he who humbles himself will be exalted."

Mt 23:6

Prov 25:6f

Lk 18:14
Mt 23:12

---

parents, except when we see them on their nests. But the hen is so enfeebled over her brood that even if the chickens are not following her, even if you do not see the young ones, you still know her at once to be a mother. With her wings drooping, her feathers ruffled, her note hoarse, in all her limbs she becomes so sunken and abject, that, as I have said, even though you cannot see her young, you can see she is a mother. That is the way Jesus feels" (*In Ioann. Evang.*, 15, 7).

13:35. Jesus shows the deep sorrow he feels over Jerusalem's resistance to the love God had so often shown it. Later St Luke will record Jesus' weeping over Jerusalem (cf. Lk 19:41). See also the note on Mt 23:37–39.

14:1–6. Fanaticism is always evil. It often

causes blindness and leads a person, as in this case, to deny the principles of justice and charity and even basic humanitarianism. We should never be fanatical about anything—no matter how sacred it is.

14:11. Humility is so necessary for salvation that Jesus takes every opportunity to stress its importance. Here he uses the attitudes of people at a banquet to remind us again that it is God who assigns the places at the heavenly banquet. "Together with humility, the realization of the greatness of man's dignity—and of the overwhelming fact that, by grace, we are made children of God—forms a single attitude. It is not our own efforts that save us and give us life; it is the grace of God. This is a truth which must never be forgotten" (St Josemaría Escrivá, *Christ Is Passing By*, 133).

s. Other ancient authorities read *a son*

The right attitude to the poor

[12]He said also to the man who had invited him, "When you give a dinner or a banquet, do not invite your friends or your brothers or your kinsmen or rich neighbours, lest they also invite you in return, and you be repaid. [13]But when you give a feast, invite the poor, the maimed, the lame, the blind, [14]and you will be blessed, because they cannot repay you. You will be repaid at the resurrection of the just."

Deut 14:29

Parable of the invited guests

Mt 22:2–10

[15]When one of those who sat at table with him heard this, he said to him, "Blessed is he who shall eat bread in the kingdom of God!" [16]But he said to him, "A man once gave a great banquet, and invited many; [17]and at the time for the banquet he sent his servant to say to those who had been invited, 'Come; for all is now ready.' [18]But they all alike began to make excuses. The first said to him, 'I have bought a field, and I must go out and see it; I pray you, have me excused.' [19]And another said, 'I have bought five

---

14:14. A Christian acts in the world in the same way anyone else does; but his dealings with his colleagues and others should not be based on pursuit of reward or vainglory: the first thing he should seek is God's glory, desiring heaven as his only reward (cf. Lk 6:32–34).

14:15. In biblical language the expression "to eat bread in the Kingdom of God" means sharing in eternal beatitude, of which this great banquet is a symbol (cf. Is 25:6; Mt 22:1–14).

14:16–24. If God invites someone to know him in faith, he should sacrifice any human interest which gets in the way of replying to God's call, no matter how lawful and noble it be. The objections we tend to put forward, the duties we appeal to, are really just excuses. This is why the ungrateful invitees are blameworthy.

"Compel people to come in": it is not a matter of forcing anyone's freedom—God does not want us to love him under duress—but of helping a person to make

right decisions, to shrug off any human respect, to avoid occasions of sin, to do what he can to discover the truth. ... A person is "compelled to come in" through prayer, the example of a Christian life, friendship—in a word, apostolate. "If, in order to save an earthly life, it is praiseworthy to use force to stop a man from committing suicide, are we not allowed use the same force—holy coercion—to save the Lives (with a capital) of many who are stupidly bent on killing their souls?" (St Josemaría Escrivá, *The Way*, 399).

14:26. These words of our Lord should not disconcert us. Love for God and for Jesus should have pride of place in our lives and we should keep away from anything which obstructs this love: "In this world let us love everyone," St Gregory the Great comments, "even though he be our enemy; but let us hate him who opposes us on our way to God, though he be our relative [...]. We should, then, love our neighbour; we should have char-

yoke of oxen, and I go to examine them; I pray you, have me excused.' [20]And another said, 'I have married a wife, and therefore I cannot come.' [21]So the servant came and reported this to his master. Then the householder in anger said to his servant, 'Go out quickly to the streets and lanes of the city, and bring in the poor and maimed and blind and lame.' [22]And the servant said, 'Sir, what you commanded has been done, and still there is room.' [23]And the master said to the servant, 'Go out to the highways and hedges, and compel people to come in, that my house may be filled. [24]For I tell you, none of these men who were invited shall taste my banquet.' "

Conditions for following Jesus

[25]Now great multitudes accompanied him; and he turned and said to them, [26]"If any one comes to me and does not hate his own father and mother and wife and children and brothers and sisters, yes, and even his own life, he cannot be my disciple.* [27]Whoever does not bear his own cross and come after me, cannot be my dis-

Mt 10:37–38

Deut 33:9–10
Lk 18:29–30
Jn 12:25

Lk 9:23

---

ity towards all—towards relatives and towards strangers—but without separating ourselves from the love of God out of love for them" (*In Evangelia homiliae*, 37, 3). In the last analysis, it is a matter of keeping the proper hierarchy of charity: God must take priority over everything.

This verse must be understood, therefore, in the context of all our Lord's teachings (cf. Lk 6:27–35). These are "hard words. True, 'hate' does not exactly express what Jesus meant. Yet he did put it very strongly, because he doesn't just mean 'love less,' as some people interpret it in an attempt to tone down the sentence. The force behind these vigorous words does not lie in their implying a negative or pitiless attitude, for the Jesus who is speaking here is none other than that Jesus who commands us to love others as we love ourselves and who gives up his life for mankind. These words indicate simply that we cannot be half-hearted when it comes to loving God. Christ's words could be translated

as 'love more, love better', in the sense that a selfish or partial love is not enough: we have to love others with the love of God" (St Josemaría Escrivá, *Christ Is Passing By*, 97). See the notes on Mt 10:34–37; Lk 2:49.

As the Second Vatican Council explains, Christians "strive to please God rather than men, always ready to abandon everything for Christ" (*Apostolicam actuositatem*, 4).

14:27. Christ "by suffering for us not only gave us an example so that we might follow in his footsteps, but he also opened up a way. If we follow that way, life and death become holy and acquire a new meaning" (Vatican II, *Gaudium et spes*, 22).

The way the Christian follows is that of imitating Christ. We can follow him only if we help him bear his cross. We all have experience of suffering, and suffering leads to unhappiness unless it is accepted with a Christian outlook. The Cross is not a tragedy: it is God's way of

ciple. [28]For which of you, desiring to build a tower, does not first sit down and count the cost, whether he has enough to complete it? [29]Otherwise, when he has laid a foundation, and is not able to finish, all who see it begin to mock him, [30]saying, 'This man began to build, and was not able to finish.' [31]Or what king, going to encounter another king in war, will not sit down first and take counsel whether he is able with ten thousand to meet him who comes against him with twenty thousand? [32]And if not, while the other is yet a great way off, he sends an embassy and asks terms of peace. [33]So therefore, whoever of you does not renounce all that he has cannot be my disciple.

Mt 5:13
Mk 9:50

[34]"Salt is good; but if salt has lost its taste, how shall its saltness be restored? [35]It is fit neither for the land nor for the dunghill; men throw it away. He who has ears to hear, let him hear."

---

teaching us that through suffering we can be sanctified, becoming one with Christ and winning heaven as a reward. This is why it is so Christian to love pain: "Let us bless pain. Love pain. Sanctify pain. ... Glorify pain!" (St Josemaría Escrivá, *The Way*, 208).

14:28–35. Our Lord uses different examples to show that if mere human prudence means that a person should try to work out in advance the risks he may run, with all the more reason should a Christian embrace the cross voluntarily and generously, because there is no other way he can follow Jesus Christ: " '*Quia hic homo coepit aedificare et non potuit consummare!*—This man started to build and was unable to finish!' A sad commentary which, if you don't want, need never be made about you: for you possess everything necessary to crown the edifice of your sanctification—the grace of God and your own will" (St Josemaría Escrivá, *The Way*, 324).

14:33. Earlier our Lord spoke about "hating" one's parents and one's very life; now he equally vigorously requires us to be completely detached from pos-

sessions. This verse is a direct application of the two foregoing parables: just as a king is imprudent if he goes to war with an inadequate army, so anyone is foolish who thinks he can follow our Lord without renouncing all his possessions. This renunciation should really bite: our heart has to be unencumbered by anything material if we are to be able to follow in our Lord's footsteps. The reason is, as he tells us later on, that it is impossible to "serve God and mammon" (Lk 16:13). Not infrequently our Lord asks a person to practise total, voluntary poverty; and he asks everyone to practise genuine detachment and generosity in the use of material things. If a Christian has to be ready to give up even life itself, with all the more reason should he renounce possessions: "As a man of God, put the same effort into scorning riches that men of the world put into possessing them" (*The Way*, 633). See the note on Lk 12:33–34.

Besides, for a soul to become filled with God it first must be emptied of everything that could be an obstacle to God's indwelling: "The doctrine that the Son of God came to teach was contempt for all things in order to receive as a reward the Spirit of God in himself. For,

136

9. PARABLES OF GOD'S MERCY

The lost sheep

15 ¹Now the tax collectors and sinners were all drawing near to hear him. ²And the Pharisees and the scribes murmured, saying, "This man receives sinners and eats with them."
³So he told them this parable: ⁴"What man of you, having a hundred sheep, if he has lost one of them, does not leave the ninety-nine in the wilderness, and go after the one which is lost, until he finds it? ⁵And when he has found it, he lays it on his shoulders, rejoicing. ⁶And when he comes home, he calls together his friends

Lk 5:30; 19:7

Mt 18:12–14
Ezek 34:11–16
Lk 19:10

---

as long as the soul does not reject all things, it has no capacity to receive the Spirit of God in pure transformation" (St John of the Cross, *Ascent of Mount Carmel*, book 1, chap. 5, 2).

15:1–32. Jesus' actions manifest God's mercy: he receives sinners in order to convert them. The scribes and Pharisees, who despised sinners, just cannot understand why Jesus acts like this; they grumble about him; and Jesus uses the opportunity to tell these mercy parables. "The Gospel writer who particularly treats of these themes in Christ's teaching is Luke, whose Gospel has earned the title of 'the Gospel of mercy'" (John Paul II, *Dives in misericordia*, 3).

In this chapter St Luke reports three of these parables in which Jesus describes the infinite, fatherly mercy of God and his joy at the conversion of the sinner.

The Gospel teaches that no one is excluded from forgiveness and that sinners can become beloved children of God if they repent and are converted. So much does God desire the conversion of sinners that each of these parables ends with a refrain, as it were, telling of the great joy in heaven over every sinner who repents.

15:1–2. This is not the first time that publicans and sinners approach Jesus (cf. Mt 9:10). They are attracted by the directness of our Lord's preaching and by his call to self-giving and love. The Pharisees in general were jealous of his influence over the people (cf. Mt 26:2–5; Jn 11:47), a jealousy which can also beset Christians; a severity of outlook which does not accept that, no matter how great his sins may have been, a sinner can change and become a saint; a blindness which prevents a person from recognizing and rejoicing over the good done by others. Our Lord criticized this attitude when he replied to his disciples' complaints about others casting out devils in his name: "Do not forbid him; for no one who does a mighty work in my name will be able soon after to speak evil of me" (Mk 9:39). And St Paul rejoiced that others proclaimed Christ and even overlooked the fact they did so out of self-interest, provided Christ was preached (cf. Phil 1:17–18).

15:5–6. Christian tradition, on the basis of this and other Gospel passages (cf. Jn 10:11), applies this parable to Christ, the Good Shepherd, who misses and then seeks out the lost sheep: the Word, by becoming man, seeks out mankind,

and his neighbours, saying to them, 'Rejoice with me, for I have found my sheep which was lost.' [7]Just so, I tell you, there will be more joy in heaven over one sinner who repents than over ninety-nine righteous persons who need no repentance.

The lost coin

[8]"Or what woman, having ten silver coins,[t] if she loses one coin, does not light a lamp and sweep the house and seek diligently until she finds it? [9]And when she has found it, she calls together her friends and neighbours, saying, 'Rejoice with me, for I have found the coin which I had lost.' [10]Just so, I tell you, there is joy before the angels of God over one sinner who repents.''

The prodigal son

[11]And he said, "There was a man who had two sons; [12]and the younger of them said to his father, 'Father, give me the share of

---

which has strayed through sinning. Here is St Gregory the Great's commentary: "He put the sheep on his shoulders because, on taking on human nature, he burdened himself with our sins" (*In Evangelia homiliae*, 2, 14).

The Second Vatican Council applies these verses of St Luke to the way priests should approach their pastoral work: "They should be mindful that by their daily conduct and solicitude they display the reality of a truly priestly and pastoral ministry both to believers and unbelievers alike, to Catholics and non-Catholics; that they are bound to bear witness before all men of the truth and of the life, and as good shepherds seek after those too who, whilst having been baptised in the Catholic Church, have given up the practice of the sacraments, or even fallen away from the faith" (*Lumen gentium*, 28). However, every member of the faithful should show this same kind of concern—expressed in a fraternal way—towards his brothers and sisters, towards everyone on the road to sanctification and salvation.

15:7. This does not mean that our Lord does not value the perseverance of the just: he is simply emphasizing the joy of God and the saints over the conversion of a sinner. This is clearly a call to repentance, to never doubt God's readiness to forgive. "Another fall, and what a fall! ... Must you give up hope? No. Humble yourself and, through Mary, your Mother, have recourse to the merciful Love of Jesus. A *miserere*, have mercy on me, and lift up your heart! And now begin again" (St J. Escrivá, *The Way*, 711).

15:8. This silver coin was a "drachma", of about the same value as a denarius, that is, approximately a day's wage for an agricultural worker (cf. Mt 20:2).

15:11. This is one of Jesus' most beautiful parables, which teaches us once more that God is a kind and understanding Father (cf. Mt 6:8; Rom 8:15; 2 Cor 1:3). The son who asks for his part of the inheritance is a symbol of the person who cuts himself off from God through sin. "Although the word 'mercy' does not

---

t. The drachma, rendered here by *silver coin*, was about a day's wage for a labourer

property that falls to me.' And he divided his living between them.
[13]Not many days later, the younger son gathered all he had and took his journey into a far country, and there he squandered his property in loose living. [14]And when he had spent everything, a great famine arose in that country, and he began to be in want. [15]So he went and joined himself to one of the citizens of that country, who sent him into his fields to feed swine. [16]And he would gladly have fed on[u] the pods that the swine ate; and no one gave him anything. [17]But when he came to himself he said, 'How many of my father's hired servants have bread enough and to spare, but I perish here with hunger! [18]I will arise and go to my father, and I will say to him, "Father, I have sinned against heaven and before you; [19]I am no longer worthy to be called your son; treat me as one of your hired servants." ' [20]And he arose and came

Prov 23:21;
29:3

Jer 3:12–13
Ps 51:4

---

appear, this parable nevertheless express-es the essence of the divine mercy in a particularly clear way" (John Paul II, *Dives in misericordia*, 5).

15:12. "That son, who receives from the father the portion of the inheritance that is due to him and leaves home to squan-der it in a far country 'in loose living', in a certain sense is the man of every period, beginning with the one who was the first to lose the inheritance of grace and original justice. The analogy at this point is very wide-ranging. The parable indirectly touches upon every breach of the covenant of love, every loss of grace, every sin" (*Dives in misericordia*, 5).

15:14–15. At this point in the parable we are shown the unhappy effects of sin. The young man's hunger evokes the anxiety and emptiness a person feels when he is far from God. The prodigal son's predicament describes the enslavement which sin involves (cf. Rom 1:25; 6:6; Gal 5:1): by sinning one loses the free-dom of the children of God (cf. Rom 8:21; Gal 4:31; 5:13) and hands oneself over to the power of Satan.

15:17–21. His memory of home and his conviction that his father loves him cause the prodigal son to reflect and to change his life. "Human life is in some way a constant returning to our Father's house. We return through contrition, through the conversion of heart which means a desire to change, a firm decision to improve our life and which, therefore, is expressed in sacrifice and self-giving. We return to our Father's house by means of that sacra-ment of pardon in which, by confessing our sins, we put on Jesus Christ again and become his brothers, members of God's family" (St Josemaría Escrivá, *Christ Is Passing By*, 64).

15:20–24. God always hopes for the return of the sinner; he wants him to repent. When the young man arrives home his father does not greet him with reproaches but with immense compas-sion, which causes him to embrace his son and cover him with kisses.

15:20. "There is no doubt that in this simple but penetrating analogy the figure of the father reveals to us God as Father. The conduct of the father in the parable

u. Other ancient authorities read *filled his belly with*

to his father. But while he was yet at a distance, his father saw him and had compassion, and ran and embraced him and kissed him. [21]And the son said to him, 'Father, I have sinned against heaven and before you; I am no longer worthy to be called your son.'[v] [22]But the father said to his servants, 'Bring quickly the best robe, and put it on him; and put a ring on his hand, and shoes on his feet; [23]and bring the fatted calf and kill it, and let us eat and make merry; [24]for this my son was dead, and is alive again; he was lost, and is found.' And they began to make merry.

[25]"Now his elder son was in the field; and as he came and drew near to the house, he heard music and dancing. [26]And he called one of the servants and asked what this meant. [27]And he said to him, 'Your brother has come, and your father has killed the fatted calf, because he has received him safe and sound.' [28]But he was angry and refused to go in. His father came out and entreated him, [29]but he answered his father, 'Lo, these many years I have served

Eph 2:1–5
Lk 5:14

---

and his whole behaviour, which manifests his internal attitude, enables us to rediscover the individual threads of the Old Testament vision of mercy in a synthesis which is totally new, full of simplicity and depth. The father of the prodigal son *is faithful to this fatherhood, faithful to the love* that he had always lavished on his son. This fidelity is expressed in the parable not only by his immediate readiness to welcome him home when he returns after having squandered his inheritance; it is expressed even more fully by that joy, that merrymaking for the squanderer after his return, merrymaking which is so generous that it provokes the opposition and hatred of the elder brother, who had never gone far away from his father and had never abandoned the home.

"The father's fidelity to himself [...] is at the same time expressed in a manner particularly charged with affection. We read, in fact, that when the father saw the prodigal son returning home 'he had *compassion*, ran to meet him, threw his arms around his neck and kissed him.' He certainly does this under the influence of a deep affection, and this also explains his generosity towards his son, that generosity which so angers the elder son" (John Paul II, *Dives in misericordia*, 6).

"When God runs towards us, we cannot keep silent, but with St Paul we exclaim, *Abba, Pater*: 'Father, my Father!' (Rom 8:15), for, though he is the creator of the universe, he doesn't mind our not using high-sounding titles, nor worry about our not acknowledging his greatness. He wants us to call him Father; he wants us to savour that word, our souls filling with joy [...].

"God is waiting for us, like the father in the parable, with open arms, even though we don't deserve it. It doesn't matter how great our debt is. Just like the prodigal son, all we have to do is open our heart, to be homesick for our Father's house, to wonder at and rejoice in the gift which God makes us of being able to call ourselves his children, of really being his children, even though our response to him has been so poor" (St Josemaría Escrivá, *Christ Is Passing By*, 64).

v. Other ancient authorities add *treat me as one of your hired servants*

you, and I never disobeyed your command; yet you never gave me a kid, that I might make merry with my friends. [30]But when this son of yours came, who has devoured your living with harlots, you killed for him the fatted calf!' [31]And he said to him, 'Son, you are always with me, and all that is mine is yours. [32]It was fitting to make merry and be glad, for this your brother was dead, and is alive; he was lost, and is found.'"

10. VARIOUS TEACHINGS

The unjust steward

16 [1]He also said to the disciples, "There was a rich man who had a steward, and charges were brought to him that this man was wasting his goods. [2]And he called him and said to him, 'What is this that I hear about you? Turn in the account of your

---

15:25–30. God's mercy is so great that man cannot grasp it: as we can see in the case of the elder son, who thinks his father loves the younger son excessively, his jealousy prevents him from understanding how his father can do so much to celebrate the recovery of the prodigal; it cuts him off from the joy that the whole family feels. "It's true that he was a sinner. But don't pass so final a judgment on him. Have pity in your heart, and don't forget that he may yet be an Augustine, while you remain just another mediocrity" (St Josemaría Escrivá, *The Way*, 675).

We should also consider that if God has compassion towards sinners, he must have much much more towards those who strive to be faithful to him. St Thérèse of Lisieux understood this very well: "What joy to remember that our Lord is just; that he makes allowances for all our shortcomings, and knows full well how weak we are. What have I to fear then? Surely the God of infinite justice who pardons the prodigal son with such mercy will be just with me 'who am always with Him'" (*The Autobiography of a Saint*, chap. 8).

15:32. "Mercy, as Christ has presented it in the parable of the prodigal son, has *the interior form of the love* that in the New Testament is called *agape*. This love is able to reach down to every prodigal son, to every human misery, and above all to every form of moral misery, to sin. When this happens, the person who is the object of mercy does not feel humiliated, but rather is found again and 'restored to value'. The father first and foremost expresses to him his joy, that he has been 'found again' and that he has 'returned to life'. This joy indicates a good that has remained intact: even if he is a prodigal, a son does not cease to be truly his father's son; it also indicates a good that has been found again, which in the case of the prodigal son was his return to the truth about himself" (John Paul II, *Dives in misericordia*, 6).

16:1–8. The unfaithful steward manages to avoid falling on hard times. Of course, our Lord presumes that we realize the immorality of the man's behaviour. What he emphasizes and praises, however, is his shrewdness and effort: he tries to

141

stewardship, for you can no longer be steward.' ³And the steward said to himself, 'What shall I do, since my master is taking the stewardship away from me? I am not strong enough to dig, and I am ashamed to beg. ⁴I have decided what to do, so that people may receive me into their houses when I am put out of the stewardship.' ⁵So, summoning his master's debtors one by one, he said to the first, 'How much do you owe my master?' ⁶He said, 'A hundred measures of oil.' And he said to him, 'Take your bill, and sit down quickly and write fifty.' ⁷Then he said to another, 'And how much do you owe?' He said, 'A hundred measures of wheat.' He said to him, 'Take your bill, and write eighty.' ⁸The master commended the dishonest steward for his prudence; for the sons of this worldʷ are wiser in their own generation than the sons of light.* ⁹And I tell you, make friends for yourselves by means of

Lk 14:14
Mt 6:20; 10:40

derive maximum material advantage from his former position as steward. In saving our soul and spreading the Kingdom of God, our Lord wants us to apply at least the same ingenuity and effort as people put into their worldly affairs or their attempts to attain some human ideal. The fact that we can count on God's grace does not in any way exempt us from the need to employ all available legitimate human resources even if that means strenuous effort and heroic sacrifice. "What zeal people put into their earthly affairs: dreaming of honours, striving for riches, bent on sensuality! Men and women, rich and poor, old and middle-aged and young and even children: all of them alike. When you and I put the same zeal into the affairs of our souls, we will have a living and working faith. And there will be no obstacle that we cannot overcome in our apostolic works" (St J. Escrivá, The Way, 317).

16:9–11. "Unrighteous mammon" means temporal goods which have been obtained in some unjust, unrighteous way. However, God is very merciful: even this unjust wealth can enable a

person to practise virtue by making restitution, by paying for the damage done and then by striving to help his neighbour by giving alms, by creating work opportunities etc. This was the case with Zacchaeus, the chief tax collector, who undertook to restore fourfold anything he had unjustly taken, and also to give half his wealth to the poor. On hearing that, our Lord specifically declared that salvation had that day come to that house (cf. Lk 19:1–10).

Our Lord speaks out about faithfulness in very little things, referring to riches—which really are insignificant compared with spiritual wealth. If a person is faithful and generous and is detached in the use he makes of these temporal riches, he will, at the end of his life, receive the reward of eternal life, which is the greatest treasure of all, and a permanent one. Besides, by its very nature human life is a fabric of little things: anyone who fails to give them their importance will never be able to achieve great things. "Everything in which we poor little men take a part—even holiness—is a fabric of small trifles which, depending upon one's intention,

w. Greek age

unrighteous mammon, so that when it fails they may receive you into the eternal habitations.

¹⁰"He who is faithful in a very little is faithful also in much; and he who is dishonest in a very little is dishonest also in much. ¹¹If then you have not been faithful in the unrighteous mammon, who will entrust to you the true riches? ¹²And if you have not been faithful in that which is another's, who will give you that which is your own? ¹³No servant can serve two masters; for either he will hate the one and love the other, or he will be devoted to the one and despise the other. You cannot serve God and mammon."

¹⁴The Pharisees, who were lovers of money, heard all this, and they scoffed at him. ¹⁵But he said to them, "You are those who justify yourselves before men, but God knows your hearts; for what is exalted among men is an abomination in the sight of God.

Lk 19:17

Mt 6:24

Mt 23:14
Lk 18:9–14
Mt 23:28
Ps 7:9
Prov 6:16–17

---

can form a splendid tapestry of heroism or of degradation, of virtue or of sin.

"The epic legends always related extraordinary adventures, but never fail to mix them with homely details about the hero. May you always attach great importance—faithfully—to the little things" (St J. Escrivá, *The Way*, 826).

The parable of the unjust steward is a symbol of man's life. Everything we have is a gift from God, and we are his stewards or managers, who sooner or later will have to render an account to him.

16:12. "That which is another's" refers to temporal things, which are essentially impermanent. "That which is your own" refers to goods of the spirit, values which endure, which are things we really do possess because they will go with us into eternal life. In other words: how can we be given heaven if we have proved unfaithful, irresponsible, during our life on earth?

16:13–14. In the culture of that time "service" involved such commitment to one's master that a servant could not take on any other work or serve any other master.

Our service to God, our sanctification, requires us to direct all our actions towards him. A Christian does not divide up his time, allocating some of it to God and some of it to worldly affairs: everything he does should become a type of service to God and neighbour—by doing things with upright motivation, and being just and charitable.

The Pharisees jeered at what Jesus was saying, in order to justify their own attachment to material things. Sometimes people make fun of total commitment to God and detachment from material things because they themselves are not ready to practise virtue; they cannot even imagine other people really having this generosity: they think they must have ulterior motives. See also the note on Mt 6:24.

16:15. "Abomination": the original Greek word means worship of idols and, by derivation, the horror this provoked in a true worshipper of God. So the expression conveys God's disgust with the attitude of the Pharisees who, by wanting to be exalted, are putting themselves, like idols, in the place of God.

143

The law and the Gospel

Mt 11:12–13   16"The law and the prophets were until John; since then the good news of the kingdom of God is preached, and every one enters it
Mt 5:18   violently. 17But it is easier for heaven and earth to pass away, than for one dot of the law to become void.
Mt 5:32; 19:9   18"Every one who divorces his wife and marries another commits adultery, and he who marries a woman divorced from her husband commits adultery.

16:16–17. John the Baptist marks, as it were, the final point of the Old Covenant, the last of the prophets who had been preparing the way for the coming of the Messiah. With Jesus the new and definitive stage in the history of salvation has arrived; however, the moral precepts of the Old Law remain in force; they are brought to perfection by Jesus.

"Every one enters it violently": for an interpretation of these words see the note on the parallel text in Matthew (11:12).

16:18. Our Lord's teaching on the indissolubility of marriage is very clear: once a man and a woman contract a true marriage neither can marry again while the other is alive. This matter is the subject of commentaries on Matthew 5:31–32 and 19:9, to which the reader is referred. Here we will simply add that adultery is a very serious transgression of the natural moral order, frequently and expressly condemned in Sacred Scripture (e.g., Ex 20:14; Lev 20:10; Deut 5:18, 22:22; Prov 6:32; Rom 13:9; 1 Cor 6:9; Heb 13:4; etc.). The Magisterium of the Church has constantly taught this same doctrine: "Endorsed by mutual fidelity and, above all, consecrated by Christ's sacrament, this love abides faithfully in mind and body in prosperity and adversity and hence excludes both adultery and divorce" (Vatican II, *Gaudium et spes*, 49).

16:19–31. This parable disposes of two errors—that which denied the survival of the soul after death and, therefore, retribution in the next life; and that which interpreted material prosperity in this life as a reward for moral rectitude, and adversity as punishment. The parable shows that, immediately after death, the soul is judged by God for all its acts—the "particular judgment"—and is rewarded or punished; and that divine revelation is by itself sufficient for men to be able to believe in the next life.

In another area, the parable teaches the innate dignity of every human person, independent of his social, financial, cultural or religious position. And respect for this dignity implies that we must help those who are experiencing any material or spiritual need: "Wishing to come down to topics that are practical and of some urgency, the Council lays stress on respect for the human person: everyone should look upon his neighbour (without any exception) as another self, bearing in mind above all his life and the means necessary for living it in a dignified way lest he follow the example of the rich man who ignored Lazarus, the poor man" (Vatican II, *Gaudium et spes*, 27).

Another practical consequence of respect for others is proper distribution of material resources and protection of human life, even unborn life, as Paul VI pleaded with the General Assembly of the United Nations: "Respect for life, even with regard to the great problem of the birth rate, must find here in your assembly its highest affirmation and its

144

Lazarus and the rich man

[19]"There was a rich man, who was clothed in purple and fine linen and who feasted sumptuously every day. [20]And at his gate lay a poor man named Lazarus, full of sores, [21]who desired to be fed with what fell from the rich man's table; moreover the dogs came and licked his sores. [22]The poor man died and was carried by the angels to Abraham's bosom. The rich man also died and was buried; [23]and in Hades, being in torment, he lifted up his eyes, and

---

most reasoned defence. You must strive to multiply bread so that it suffices for the tables of mankind, and not rather favour an artificial control of birth, which would be irrational, in order to diminish the number of guests at the banquet of life" (Address to the UN, 4 October 1965).

16:21. Apparently this reference to the dogs implies not that they alleviated Lazarus' sufferings but increased them, in contrast with the rich man's pleasure: to the Jews dogs were unclean and therefore not generally used as domestic animals.

16:22–26. Earthly possessions, as also suffering, are ephemeral things: death marks their end, and also the end of our testing-time, our capacity to sin or to merit reward for doing good; and immediately after death we begin to enjoy our reward or to suffer punishment, as the case may be. The Magisterium of the Church has defined that the souls of all who die in the grace of God enter heaven, immediately after death or after first undergoing a purging, if that is necessary. "We believe in eternal life. We believe that the souls of all those who die in the grace of Christ—whether they must still make expiation in the fire of purgatory, or whether from the moment they leave their bodies they are received by Jesus into Paradise like the good thief—go to form that people of God which succeeds death, death which will

be totally destroyed on the day of the resurrection when these souls are reunited with their bodies" (Paul VI, *Creed of the People of God*, 28).

The expression "Abraham's bosom" refers to the place or state "into which the souls of the just, before the coming of Christ the Lord were received, and where, without experiencing any sort of pain, but supported by the blessed hope of redemption, they enjoyed peaceful repose. To liberate these holy souls, who, in the bosom of Abraham were expecting the Saviour, Christ the Lord descended into hell" (St Pius V, *Catechism*, 1, 6, 3).

16:22. "Both the rich man and the beggar died and were carried before Abraham, and there judgment was rendered on their conduct. And the Scripture tells us that Lazarus found consolation, but that the rich man found torment. Was the rich man condemned because he had riches, because he abounded in earthly possessions, because he 'dressed in purple and linen and feasted sumptuously every day'? No, I would say that it was not for this reason. The rich man was condemned because he did not pay attention to the other man, because he failed to take notice of Lazarus, the person who sat at his door and who longed to eat the scraps from his table. Nowhere does Christ condemn the mere possession of earthly goods as such. Instead, he pronounces very harsh words against those who use their possessions in a selfish

Lk 6:24

saw Abraham far off and Lazarus in his bosom. [24]And he called out, 'Father Abraham, have mercy upon me, and send Lazarus to dip the end of his finger in water and cool my tongue; for I am in anguish in this flame.' [25]But Abraham said, 'Son, remember that you in your lifetime received your good things, and Lazarus in like manner evil things, but now he is comforted here, and you are in anguish. [26]And besides all this, between us and you a great chasm has been fixed, in order that those who would pass from here to you may not be able, and none may cross from there to us.' [27]And he said, 'Then I beg you, father, to send him to my father's house, [28]for I have five brothers, so that he may warn them, lest they also come into this place of torment.' [29]But Abraham said, 'They have Moses and the prophets; let them hear them.' [30]And he said, 'No, father Abraham; but if some one goes

2 Tim 3:16

way, without paying attention to the needs of others [...].

"The parable of the rich man and Lazarus must always be present in our memory; it must form our conscience. Christ demands openness to our brothers and sisters in need—openness from the rich, the affluent, the economically advantaged; openness to the poor, the underdeveloped and the disadvantaged. Christ demands an openness that is more than benign attention, more than token actions or half-hearted efforts that leave the poor as destitute as before or even more so [...].

"We cannot stand idly by, enjoying our own riches and freedom, if, in any place, the Lazarus of the twentieth century stands at our doors. In the light of the parable of Christ, riches and freedom mean a special responsibility. Riches and freedom create a special obligation. And so, in the name of the solidarity that binds us all together in a common humanity, I again proclaim the dignity of every human person: the rich man and Lazarus are both human beings, both of them equally created in the image and likeness of God, both of them equally redeemed by Christ, at a great price, the

price of the 'precious blood of Christ' (1 Pet 1:19)" (John Paul II, Homily in Yankee Stadium, 2 October 1979).

16:24–31. The dialogue between the rich man and Abraham is a dramatization aimed at helping people remember the message of the parable: strictly speaking, there is no room in hell for feelings of compassion towards one's neighbour: in hell hatred presides. "When Abraham said to the rich man 'between us and you a great chasm has been fixed', he showed that after death and resurrection there will be no scope for any kind of penance. The impious will not repent and enter the Kingdom, nor will the just sin and go down into hell. This is the unbridgable abyss" (Aphraates, *Demonstratio*, 20; *De sustentatione egenorum*, 12). This helps us understand what St John Chrysostom says: "I ask you and I beseech you and, falling at your feet, I beg you: as long as we enjoy the brief respite of life, let us repent, let us be converted, let us become better, so that we will not have to lament uselessly like that rich man when we die and tears can do us no good. For even if you have a father or a son or a friend or anyone else who might have influence

to them from the dead, they will repent.' ³¹He said to him, 'If they do not hear Moses and the prophets, neither will they be convinced if some one should rise from the dead'."

Jn 5:46;
11:45–53

On leading others astray

17 ¹And he said to his disciples, "Temptations to sinˣ are sure to come; but woe to him by whom they come! ²It would be better for him if a millstone were hung round his neck and he were cast into the sea, than that he should cause one of these little ones to sin.ʸ

Mt 18:6–7

Forgiving offences

³Take heed to yourselves; if your brother sins, rebuke him, and if he repents, forgive him; ⁴and if he sins against you seven times in

Mt 18:15

Mt 18:21–22

with God, no one will be able to set you free, for your own deeds condemn you" (*Hom. on 1 Cor*).

17:1–3. Our Lord condemns scandal, that is, "any saying, action or omission which constitutes for another an occasion of sin" (St Pius X, *Catechism*, 417). Jesus is teaching two things here: the first is that scandal will *in fact* happen; the second, that it is a grave sin, as shown by the punishment it earns.

The reason why it is so serious a sin is that it "tends to destroy God's greatest work, that of Redemption, through souls being lost; it kills one's neighbour's soul by taking away the life of grace, which is more precious than the life of the body, and it is the cause of a multitude of sins. This is why God threatens with the most severe punishment those who cause others to stumble" (ibid., 418). See the notes on Mt 18:6–7; 18:8; 18:10.

"Take heed to yourselves": a serious warning, meaning that we should not be a cause of scandal to others nor should we be influenced by the bad example others give us.

People who enjoy authority of any kind (parents, teachers, politicians, writ-

ers, artists, etc.) can more easily be a cause of scandal. We need to be on the alert in this respect in view of our Lord's warning, "Take heed to yourselves."

17:2. Millstones were circular in shape with a large hole in the centre. Our Lord's description, therefore, was very graphic: it meant that the person's head just fitted through the hole and then he could not get the stone off.

17:3–4. In order to be a Christian one must always, genuinely, forgive others. Also, one has to correct an erring brother to help him change his behaviour. But fraternal correction should always be done in a very refined way, full of charity; otherwise we would humiliate the person who has committed the fault, whereas we should not humiliate him but help him to be better.

Forgiving offences—which is something we should always do—should not be confused with giving up rights which have been unjustly violated. One can claim rights without any kind of hatred being implied; and sometimes charity and justice require us to exercise our rights. "Let's not confuse the rights of the

x. Greek *stumbling blocks*   y. Greek *stumble*

the day, and turns to you seven times, and says, 'I repent,' you must forgive him."

The power of faith

Mk 9:24

Mt 13:31; 17:20; 21:21

[5]The apostles said to the Lord, "Increase our faith!" [6]And the Lord said, "If you had faith as a grain of mustard seed, you could say to this sycamine tree, 'Be rooted up, and be planted in the sea,' and it would obey you.

Humble service

[7]"Will any one of you, who has a servant ploughing or keeping sheep, say to him when he has come in from the field, 'Come at once and sit down at table'? [8]Will he not rather say to him, 'Prepare supper for me, and gird yourself and serve me, till I eat and drink; and afterward you shall eat and drink'? [9]Does he thank the servant because he did what was commanded? [10]So you also, when you have done all that is commanded you, say, 'We are unworthy servants; we have only done what was our duty.'"

---

office you hold with your rights as a person. The former can never be waived" (St Josemaría Escrivá, *The Way*, 407).

Sincere forgiveness leads us to forget the particular offence and to extend the hand of friendship, which in turn helps the offender to repent.

The Christian vocation is a calling to holiness, but one of its essential requirements is that we show apostolic concern for the spiritual welfare of others: Christianity cannot be practised in an isolated, selfish way. Thus, "if any one among you wanders from the truth and some one brings him back, let him know that whoever brings back a sinner from the error of his way will save his soul from death and will cover a multitude of sins" (Jas 5:19–20).

17:5. "Increase our faith!": a good ejaculatory prayer for every Christian. "*Omnia possibilia sunt credenti.* Everything is possible for anyone who has faith.' The words are Christ's. How is it that you don't say to him with the apostles: '*Adauge nobis fidem!* Increase my faith!'?" (*The Way*, 588).

17:6. "I'm not one for miracles. I have told you that in the holy Gospel I can find more than enough to confirm my faith. But I can't help pitying those Christians—pious people, 'apostles' many of them—who smile at the idea of extraordinary ways, of supernatural events. I feel the urge to tell them: Yes, this is still the age of miracles: we too would work them if we had faith!" (*The Way*, 583).

17:7–10. Jesus is not approving this master's abusive and arbitrary behaviour. He is using an example very familiar to his audience to show the attitude a person should have towards his Creator: everything, from our very existence to the eternal happiness promised us, is one huge gift from God. Man is always in debt to God; no matter what service he renders him he can never adequately repay the gifts God has given him. There is no sense in a creature adopting a proud atti-

Cure of ten lepers

[11]On the way to Jerusalem he was passing along between Samaria and Galilee. [12]And as he entered a village, he was met by ten lepers, who stood at a distance [13]and lifted up their voices and said, "Jesus, Master, have mercy on us." [14]When he saw them he said to them, "Go and show yourselves to the priests." And as they went they were cleansed. [15]Then one of them, when he saw that he was healed, turned back, praising God with a loud voice; [16]and he fell on his face at Jesus' feet, giving him thanks. Now he was a Samaritan. [17]Then said Jesus, "Were not ten cleansed? Where are the nine? [18]Was no one found to return and give praise to God except this foreigner?" [19]And he said to him, "Rise and go your way; your faith has made you well."

Lev 13:34ff

Lk 5:14

Lk 7:50

The coming of the Kingdom of God

[20]Being asked by the Pharisees when the kingdom of God was coming, he answered them, "The kingdom of God is not coming

Jn 18:36

---

tude towards God. What Jesus teaches us here we see being put into practice by our Lady, who replied to God's messenger, "Behold, I am the handmaid of the Lord" (Lk 1:38).

17:11–19. The setting of this episode explains how a Samaritan could be in the company of Jews. There was no love lost between Jews and Samaritans (cf. Jn 4:9), but shared pain, in the case of these lepers, overcame racial antipathy.

The Law of Moses laid down, to prevent the spread of the disease, that lepers should live away from other people and should let it be known that they were suffering from this disease (cf. Lev 13:45–46). This explains why they did not come right up to Jesus and his group, but instead begged his help by shouting from a distance. Before curing them our Lord orders them to go to the priests to have their cure certified (cf. Lev 14:2ff), and to perform the rites laid down. The lepers' obedience is a sign of their faith in Jesus' words. And, in fact, soon after setting out they are cleansed.

However, only one of them, the Samaritan, who returns praising God and showing his gratitude for the miracle, is given a much greater gift than the cure of leprosy. Jesus says as much: "Your faith has made you well" (v.19) and praises the man's gratefulness. The Gospel records this event to teach us the value of gratefulness: "Get used to lifting your heart to God, in acts of thanksgiving, many times a day. Because he gives you this and that. Because you have been despised. Because you haven't what you need or because you have.

"Because he made his Mother so beautiful, his Mother who is also your Mother. Because he created the sun and the moon and this animal and that plant. Because he made that man eloquent and you he left tongue-tied. ...

"Thank him for everything, because everything is good" (St Josemaría Escrivá, *The Way*, 268).

17:20–21. Like many Jews of their time, the Pharisees imagined the establishment of the Kingdom of God in terms of exter-

149

Luke 17:21

Mt 24:23   with signs to be observed;* [21]nor will they say, 'Lo, here it is!' or 'There!' for behold, the kingdom of God is in the midst of you."[z]

The day of Christ's coming

[22]And he said to the disciples, "The days are coming when you will desire to see one of the days of the Son of man, and you will

Lk 21:8   not see it. [23]And they will say to you, 'Lo, there!' or 'Lo, here!'

Mt 24:26–27   Do not go, do not follow them. [24]For as the lightning flashes and lights up the sky from one side to the other, so will the Son of man

Lk 9:22   be in his day.[a] [25]But first he must suffer many things and be

Mt 24:37–39   rejected by this generation. [26]As it was in the days of Noah, so

Gen 7:7–23   will it be in the days of the Son of man. [27]They ate, they drank, they married, they were given in marriage, until the day when Noah entered the ark, and the flood came and destroyed them all.

---

nal, political authority; whereas Jesus teaches that it is something eminently spiritual, supernatural, which has been happening ever since Jesus' coming, although its climax will be after his second coming or Parousia at the end of the world; its effect is to be seen, above all, in men's hearts, although it is also something visible and external, just as the Church has a visible dimension.

The presence of the Kingdom of God in each soul is something one perceives through the affections and inspirations communicated by the Holy Spirit. St Thérèse of Lisieux says this about her own experience: "The Doctor of doctors teaches us without the sound of words. I have never heard him speak, and yet I know he is within my soul. Every moment he is guiding and inspiring me, and, just at the moment I need them, 'lights' till then unseen are granted me. Most often it is not at prayer that they come but while I go about my daily duties" (*The Autobiography of a Saint*, chap. 8).

17:22. After the apostles receive the Holy Spirit on the day of Pentecost they

will devote their whole lives to preaching boldly the message of Jesus Christ, and winning all men over to the Lord. This will lead them to experience many severe contradictions; they will suffer so much that they will yearn to see even "one of the days of the Son of man", that is, one of the days of the victory of Jesus Christ. But this day will not arrive until the Lord's second coming.

17:23–36. These words of our Lord are a prophecy about the last coming of the Son of man. We should remember that prophecy often involves events on different levels, many symbols, a terminology of its own; the *chiaroscuro* which they create gives us insight into future events, but the concrete details only become clear when the events actually occur. Our Lord's last coming will be something sudden and unexpected; it will catch many people unprepared. Jesus illustrates this by giving examples from sacred history: as in the time of Noah (cf. Gen 6:9–9:7) and that of Lot (cf. Gen 18:16–19, 27) divine judgment will be visited on men without warning.

However, it is useful to recall here

z. Or *within you*   a. Other ancient authorities omit *in his day*

[28]Likewise as it was in the days of Lot—they ate, they drank, they bought, they sold, they planted, they built, [29]but on the day when Lot went out from Sodom fire and brimstone rained from heaven and destroyed them all— [30]so will it be on the day when the Son of man is revealed. [31]On that day, let him who is on the housetop, with his goods in the house, not come down to take them away; and likewise let him who is in the field not turn back. [32]Remember Lot's wife. [33]Whoever seeks to gain his life will lose it, but whoever loses his life will preserve it. [34]I tell you, in that night there will be two men in one bed; one will be taken and the other left. [35]There will be two women grinding together; one will be taken and the other left."[b] [37]And they said to him, "Where, Lord?" He said to them, "Where the body is, there the eagles[c] will be gathered together."

Gen 18:20

Gen 19:15, 24–26

Mt 24:17–18

Lk 9:24

Mt 20:40–41

Job 39:30
Mt 24:28

---

that everyone will find himself before the divine Judge immediately when he dies, at the particular judgment. Thus Jesus' teaching has also a present urgency about it: *here and now* a disciple should scrutinize his own conduct, for the Lord can call him when he least expects.

17:33. "Will preserve it": what the Greek word literally means is "will engender (his life)", that is to say, "will give true life to the soul". Thus our Lord seems to mean the following: he who wants to save his life at all costs, making it his basic value, will lose eternal life; whereas he who is ready to lose his earthly life—that is, to resist even to death the enemies of God and of his soul—will obtain eternal happiness through this struggle. In content this passage is almost identical with Luke 9:24.

17:36. In the Vulgate this verse reads: "Una assumetur, et altera relinquetur. Duo in agro; unus assumetur, et alter relinquetur" ("One will be taken and the other left. Two men will be in the field; one will be taken and the other left").

These words seem to be an addition to Luke, taken from Matthew 24:40; they do not appear in the better Greek manuscripts, which is why the New Vulgate omits them. See the RSV note.

17:37. "Where, Lord?" The Pharisees had asked Jesus when the Kingdom of God was coming (v. 20). Now, after hearing the Messiah's explanation the disciples, out of natural curiosity, ask him, "Where ... will this take place?" Jesus replies with a phrase which sounds very much like a proverb and which, precisely because it is enigmatic, suggests that he does not want to give a clear answer to their question. And so our Lord's short discourse on the coming of the Kingdom of God and of Christ opens and closes with questions put by his listeners, superficial questions which he uses to teach them something which they will later come to understand.

"Where the body is, there the eagles will gather": the Greek text uses a word which could mean either eagle or vulture. In any event the proverb indicates the speed with which birds of prey swoop

b. Other ancient authorities add v. 36 *"two men will be in the field; one will be taken and the other left"*
c. Or *vultures*

151

Rom 12:13
Col 4:2
1 Thess 5:17

Lk 11:7–8

Persevering prayer. Parable of the unjust judge

18 ¹And he told them a parable, to the effect that they ought always to pray and not lose heart. ²He said, "In a certain city there was a judge who neither feared God nor regarded man; ³and there was a widow in that city who kept coming to him and saying, 'Vindicate me against my adversary.' ⁴For a while he refused; but afterward he said to himself, 'Though I neither fear God nor regard man, ⁵yet because this widow bothers me, I will vindicate her, or she will wear me out by her continual coming.'"

---

down on their victims—apparently referring to the sudden, unexpected way the second coming or last judgment will happen. Holy Scripture also deals with this subject in other passages: "But as to the times and the seasons, brethren, you have no need to have anything written to you. For you yourselves know well that the day of the Lord will come like a thief in the night" (1 Thess 5:1–2). Once more Jesus is exhorting us to be watchful: we should never neglect the most important thing in life—eternal salvation. "All that, which worries you for the moment, is of relative importance. What is of absolute importance is that you be happy, that you be saved" (St Josemaría Escrivá, *The Way*, 297). So curious are the Pharisees and the disciples about the time and place of the last coming that they are distracted from Jesus' main point; the same thing happens to us: for example, we can spend a lot of time pondering the circumstances of the deaths of people we know, and fail to grasp the warning these deaths contain—that this life is going to end one way or another and that after it we too will meet God.

18:1–8. The parable of the unjust judge is a very eloquent lesson about the effectiveness of persevering, confident prayer. It also forms a conclusion to Jesus' teaching about watchfulness, contained in the previous verses (17:23–26). Comparing God with a person like this makes the

point even clearer: if even an unjust judge ends up giving justice to the man who keeps on pleading his case, how much more will God, who is infinitely just, and who is our Father, listen to the persevering prayer of his children. God, in other words, gives justice to his elect if they persist in seeking his help.

18:1. "They ought always to pray and not lose heart." Why must we pray? "1. *We must pray first and foremost because we are believers.* Prayer is in fact the recognition of our limitation and our dependence: we come from God, we belong to God and we return to God! We cannot, therefore, but abandon ourselves to him, our Creator and Lord, with full and complete confidence [...]. Prayer, therefore, is first of all an act of intelligence, a feeling of humility and gratitude, an attitude of trust and abandonment to him who gave us life out of love. Prayer is a mysterious but real dialogue with God, a dialogue of confidence and love.

"2. *We, however, are Christians, and therefore we must pray as Christians.* For the Christian, in fact, prayer acquires a particular characteristic, which completely changes its innermost nature and innermost value. The Christian is a disciple of Jesus; he is one who really believes that Jesus is the Word Incarnate, the Son of God who came among us on this earth. As a man, the life of Jesus was a continual prayer, a continual act of

⁶And the Lord said, "Hear what the unrighteous judge says. ⁷And will not God vindicate his elect, who cry to him day and night? Will he delay long over them? ⁸I tell you, he will vindicate them speedily. Nevertheless, when the Son of man comes, will he find faith on earth?"

Jer 5:3

Parable of the Pharisee and the tax collector
⁹He also told this parable to some who trusted in themselves that they were righteous and despised others: ¹⁰"Two men went up into

worship and love of the Father and since the maximum expression of prayer is sacrifice, the summit of Jesus' prayer is the Sacrifice of the Cross, anticipated by the Eucharist at the Last Supper and handed down by means of the Holy Mass throughout the centuries. Therefore, the Christian knows that his prayer is that of Jesus; every prayer of his starts from Jesus; it is he who prays in us, with us, for us. All those who believe in God, pray; but the Christian prays in Jesus Christ: Christ is our prayer!

"3. *Finally, we must also pray because we are frail and guilty.* It must be humbly and realistically recognized that we are poor creatures, confused in ideas, tempted by evil, frail and weak, in continual need of inner strength and consolation. Prayer gives the strength for great ideals, to maintain faith, charity, purity and generosity. Prayer gives the courage to emerge from indifference and guilt, if unfortunately one has yielded to temptation and weakness. Prayer gives light to see and consider the events of one's own life and of history in the salvific perspective of God and eternity. Therefore, do not stop praying! Let not a day pass without your having prayed a little! Prayer is a duty, but it is also a great joy, because it is a dialogue with God through Jesus Christ! Every Sunday, Holy Mass: if it is possible for you, sometimes during the week. Every day, morning and evening prayers, and at the

most suitable moments!" (John Paul II, Audience with young people, 14 March 1979).

18:8. Jesus combines his teaching about perseverance in prayer with a serious warning about the need to remain firm in the faith: faith and prayer go hand in hand. St Augustine comments, "In order to pray, let us believe; and for our faith not to weaken, let us pray. Faith causes prayer to grow, and when prayer grows our faith is strengthened" (*Sermon*, 115).

Our Lord has promised his Church that it will remain true to its mission until the end of time (cf. Mt 28:20); the Church, therefore, cannot go off the path of the true faith. But not everyone will remain faithful: some will turn their backs on the faith of their own accord. This is the mystery which St Paul describes as "the rebellion" (2 Thess 2:3) and which Jesus Christ announces on other occasions (cf. Mt 24:12–13). In this way our Lord warns us, to help us stay watchful and persevere in the faith and in prayer even though people around us fall away.

18:9–14. Our Lord here rounds off his teaching on prayer. In addition to being persevering and full of faith, prayer must flow from a humble heart, a heart that repents of its sins: *Cor contritum et humiliatum, Deus, non despicies* (Ps 51:17), the Lord, who never despises a contrite

Is 58:2–3
Lk 16:15

Mt 23:23
Ps 51:1

Lk 14:11
Mt 23:12
Ezra 21:31

the temple to pray, one a Pharisee and the other a tax collector. [11]The Pharisee stood and prayed thus with himself, 'God, I thank thee that I am not like other men, extortioners, unjust, adulterers, or even like this tax collector. [12]I fast twice a week, I give tithes of all that I get.' [13]But the tax collector, standing far off, would not even lift up his eyes to heaven, but beat his breast, saying, 'God, be merciful to me a sinner!' [14]I tell you, this man went down to his house justified rather than the other; for every one who exalts himself will be humbled, but he who humbles himself will be exalted."

Jesus blesses the children

Mt 19:13–15
Mk 10:13–16

[15]Now they were bringing even infants to him that he might touch them; and when the disciples saw it, they rebuked them. [16]But

---

and humble heart, resists the proud and gives his grace to the humble (cf. 1 Pet 5:5; Jas 4:6).

The parable presents two opposite types—the Pharisee, who is so meticulous about external fulfilment of the Law; and the tax collector, who in fact is looked on as a public sinner (cf. Lk 19:7). The Pharisee's prayer is not pleasing to God, because his pride causes him to be self-centred and to despise others. He begins by giving thanks to God, but obviously it is not true gratitude, because he boasts about all the good he has done and he fails to recognize his sins; since he regards himself as righteous, he has no need of pardon, he thinks; and he remains in his sinful state; to him also apply these words spoken by our Lord to a group of Pharisees on another occasion: "If you were blind, you would have no guilt; but now that you say, 'We see,' your guilt remains" (Jn 9:41). The Pharisee went down from the temple, therefore, unjustified.

But the tax collector recognizes his personal unworthiness and is sincerely sorry for his sins: he has the necessary dispositions for God to pardon him. His ejaculatory prayer wins God's forgiveness: "It is not without reason that some have said that prayer justifies; for repen-

tant prayer or supplicant repentance, raising up the soul to God and re-uniting it to his goodness, without doubt obtains pardon in virtue of the holy love which gives it this sacred movement. And therefore we ought all to have very many such ejaculatory prayers, said as an act of loving repentance and with a desire of obtaining reconciliation with God, so that by thus laying our tribulation before our Saviour, we may pour out our souls before and within his pitiful heart, which will receive them with mercy" (St Francis de Sales, *Treatise on the Love of God*, book 2, chap. 20).

18:15. The adverb "even" or "also" suggests that mothers were bringing little children to meet our Lord at the same time as others brought sick people to him. "That he might touch them": the sight of the curing of the sick naturally led the people to bring their children to Jesus, to be assured of good health by being touched by him—in the same way as the lady with the issue of blood thought she could be cured by touching him (cf. Mt 9:20–22). The parallel text in St Matthew (19:13) is a little more specific: "Children were brought to him that he might lay his hands on them and pray," that is, to have him bless them.

Jesus called them to him, saying, "Let the children come to me, and do not hinder them; for to such belongs the kingdom of God. [17]Truly, I say to you, whoever does not receive the kingdom of God like a child shall not enter it."

Mt 18:3

The rich young man. Christian poverty and renunciation
[18]And a ruler asked him, "Good Teacher, what shall I do to inherit eternal life?" [19]And Jesus said to him, "Why do you call me good? No one is good but God alone. [20]You know the commandments: 'Do not commit adultery, Do not kill, Do not steal, Do not bear false witness, Honour your father and mother.'" [21]And he said, "All these I have observed from my youth." [22]And when Jesus heard it, he said to him, "One thing you still lack. Sell all that you

Mt 19:16–29
Mk 10:17–30
Ex 20:12–16
Deut 5:16–20

Mt 6:20
Lk 12:33

18:15–17. The episode of Jesus and the children corroborates the teaching about humility contained in the parable of the Pharisee and the tax collector. "Why, then, does he say that children are fit for the Kingdom of heaven? Perhaps because usually they are without malice, nor are they deceptive, nor do they dare to avenge themselves; they have no experience of lust, do not covet riches and are not ambitious. But the virtue of all this does not lie in ignorance of evil, but in its rejection; it does not consist in not being able to sin but rather in not consenting to sin. Therefore, the Lord is not referring to childhood as such, but to the innocence which children have in their simplicity" (St Ambrose, *Expositio Evangelii sec. Lucam*, in loc.).

Receiving the Kingdom of God like children, becoming children before God, means "renouncing our pride and self-sufficiency, recognizing that we can do nothing by ourselves. We must realize that we need grace, the help of God our Father, to find our way and keep to it. To be little, you have to abandon yourself as children do, believe as children believe, beg as children beg" (St Josemaría Escrivá, *Christ Is Passing By*, 143).

18:18–27. The story of this man (Mt 19:20 tells us he was a young man) is a sad one; he trades his vocation as an apostle for material possessions. So too today, if the Lord calls us to complete self-giving, we can answer "No" and give preference to money, honour, comfort, professional prestige; in a word, to selfishness.

"You say of that friend of yours that he frequents the sacraments, that he is clean-living and a good student. But that he won't 'respond'; when you speak to him of sacrifice and apostolate, he becomes sad and tries to avoid you.

"Don't worry. It's not a failure of your zeal. It is, to the letter, the scene related by the Evangelist: 'If you wish to be perfect, go and sell what you own and give the money to the poor' (sacrifice), 'and then come, follow me' (apostolate).

"The young man also *abiit tristis*, went away sad; he was not willing to respond to grace" (St Josemaría Escrivá, *The Way*, 807).

18:22. The words "Come, follow me" are much more expressive in the original. A more exact translation might be: "Come on, follow me": Jesus does not offer him a gentle invitation: he imperiously calls him to follow him immediately.

have and distribute to the poor, and you will have treasure in heaven; and come, follow me." [23]But when he heard this he became sad, for he was very rich. [24]Jesus looking at him said, "How hard it is for those who have riches to enter the kingdom of God! [25]For it is easier for a camel to go through the eye of a needle than for a rich man to enter the kingdom of God." [26]Those who heard it said, "Then who can be saved?" [27]But he said, "What is impossible with men is possible with God." [28]And Peter said, "Lo, we have left our homes and followed you." [29]And he said to them, "Truly, I say to you, there is no man who has left house or wife or brothers or parents or children, for the sake of the king-dom of God, [30]who will not receive manifold more in this time, and in the age to come eternal life."

18:24–26. The image of the camel and the eye of a needle is exaggeration for the sake of effect—to show how enormously difficult it is for a rich man attached to his riches to enter the Kingdom of heaven.

"Earthly goods are not bad, but they are debased when man sets them up as idols, when he adores them. They are ennobled when they are converted into instruments for good, for just and chari-table Christian undertakings. We cannot seek after material goods as if they were a treasure. ... Our treasure is Christ and all our love and desire must be centred on him, 'for where our treasure is, there will our hearts be also' (Mt 6:21)" (St J. Escrivá, *Christ Is Passing By*, 35).

18:27. A Christian should show daring in things to do with his sanctification and apostolate. He should not reckon on his own resources but on God's infinite power.

18:28–30. Jesus gives an answer which completely satisfies Peter and the other disciples. His words reassure those who, after giving up everything to follow the Lord, may feel at some point a certain nostalgia for the things they have left behind. Jesus' promise far exceeds what the world can give. Our Lord wants us to be happy in this world also; those who follow him generously obtain, even in this life, a joy and a peace which far exceeds human joys and consolations. To these, a foretaste of the happiness of heaven, is added eternal beatitude. Com-menting on this passage St Josemaría Escrivá says in *The Way* (670): "Try to find on earth anyone who repays so gen-erously!" On the nature of this promised reward see also Mk 10:28–30 and the note on same.

18:31–34. The apostles simply cannot understand Jesus' words; they have too human an idea of what the Messiah would be like and they do not want to accept his being handed over for execu-tion. Later on, when they receive the Holy Spirit, they will realize very clearly that "what God foretold by the mouth of all the prophets, that his Christ should suffer, he thus fulfilled" (Acts 3:18). So, "suffering is part of God's plans. This is the truth, however difficult it may be for us to understand it" (St J. Escrivá, *Christ Is Passing By*, 168). If we cultivate the Holy Spirit, he will help us understand the meaning of suffering and the scope it

Third announcement of the Passion

Mt 20:17–19
Mk 10:32–34
Lk 9:22–24

³¹And taking the twelve, he said to them, "Behold, we are going up to Jerusalem, and everything that is written of the Son of man by the prophets will be accomplished. ³²For he will be delivered to the Gentiles, and will be mocked and shamefully treated and spit upon; ³³they will scourge him and kill him, and on the third day he will rise." ³⁴But they understood none of these things; this saying was hid from them, and they did not grasp what was said.

Mk 9:22

Curing of the blind man of Jericho

Mt 20:29–34
Mk 10:46–52

³⁵As he drew near to Jericho, a blind man was sitting by the roadside begging; ³⁶and hearing a multitude going by, he inquired what this meant. ³⁷They told him, "Jesus of Nazareth is passing

---

gives for co-redemption. And we should ask him to make us realize that only if we decide to place the cross in the centre of our lives will we experience true joy and true peace of soul. See the note on Lk 14:27.

St John Chrysostom points out that Christ's passion "had been foretold by Isaiah when he said, 'I gave my back to the smiters, and my cheeks to those who pulled out the beard; I hid not my face from shame and spitting' (Is 50:6), and the same prophet even foretold the punishment of the Cross with these words: 'He poured out his soul unto death, and was numbered with the transgressors' (Is 53:12). And therefore the text adds, 'They will scourge him and kill him'; but David had also announced his resurrection when he said, 'Thou dost not let thy godly one see the Pit' (Ps 16:10). In fulfilment of this the Lord adds, 'And on the third day he will rise'" (*Hom. on St Matthew*, 66).

18:35–43. The blind man of Jericho is quick to use the opportunity presented by Christ's presence. We should not neglect the Lord's graces, for we do not know whether he will offer them to us again. St Augustine described very succinctly the urgency with which we should respond

to God's gift, to his passing us on the road: *"Timeo Jesum praetereuntem et non redeuntem*: I fear Jesus may pass by and not come back." For, at least on some occasion, in some way, Jesus passes close to everyone.

The blind man of Jericho acclaims Jesus as the Messiah—he gives him the messianic title of Son of David—and asks him to meet his need, to make him see. His is an active faith; he shouts out, he persists, despite the people getting in his way. And he manages to get Jesus to hear him and call him. God wanted this episode to be recorded in the Gospel, to teach us how we should believe and how we should pray—with conviction, with urgency, with constancy, in spite of the obstacles, with simplicity, until we manage to get Jesus to listen to us.

"Lord, let me receive my sight": this simple ejaculatory prayer should be often on our lips, flowing from the depths of our heart. It is a very good prayer to use in moments of doubt and vacillation, when we cannot understand the reason behind God's plans, when the horizon of our commitment becomes clouded. It is even a good prayer for people who are sincerely trying to find God but who do not yet have the great gift of faith. See also the note on Mk 10:46–52.

by." ³⁸And he cried, "Jesus, Son of David, have mercy on me!" ³⁹And those who were in front rebuked him, telling him to be silent; but he cried out all the more, "Son of David, have mercy on me!" ⁴⁰And Jesus stopped, and commanded him to be brought to him; and when he came near, he asked him, ⁴¹"What do you want me to do for you?" He said, "Lord, let me receive my sight." ⁴²And Jesus said to him, "Receive your sight; your faith has made you well." ⁴³And immediately he received his sight and followed him, glorifying God; and all the people, when they saw it, gave praise to God.

The conversion of Zacchaeus

19 ¹He entered Jericho and was passing through. ²And there was a man named Zacchaeus; he was a chief tax collector, and rich. ³And he sought to see who Jesus was, but could not, on account of the crowd, because he was small of stature. ⁴So he ran on ahead and climbed up into a sycamore tree to see him, for he

19:1–10. Jesus Christ is the Saviour of mankind; he has healed many sick people, has raised the dead to life and, particularly, has brought forgiveness of sin and the gift of grace to those who approach him in faith. As in the case of the sinful woman (cf. Lk 7:36–50), here he brings salvation to Zacchaeus, for the mission of the Son of man is to save that which was lost.

Zacchaeus was a tax collector and, as such, was hated by the people, because the tax collectors were collaborators of the Roman authorities and were often guilty of abuses (cf. the note on Mt 5:46). The Gospel implies that this man also had things to seek forgiveness for (cf. vv. 7–10). Certainly he was very keen to see Jesus (no doubt moved by grace) and he did everything he could to do so. Jesus rewards his efforts by staying as a guest in his house. Moved by our Lord's presence Zacchaeus begins to lead a new life.

The crowd begin to grumble against Jesus for showing affection to a man they consider to be an evildoer. Our Lord makes no excuses for his behaviour: he explains that this is exactly why he has come—to seek out sinners. He is putting into practice the parable of the lost sheep (cf. Lk 15:4–7), which was already prophesied in Ezekiel: "I will seek the lost, and I will bring back the strayed, and I will bind up the crippled, and I will strengthen the weak" (34:16).

19:4. Zacchaeus wants to see Jesus, and to do so he has to go out and mix with the crowd. Like the blind man of Jericho he has to shed any kind of human respect. In our own search for God we should not let false shame or fear of ridicule prevent us from using the resources available to us to meet our Lord. "Convince yourself that there is no such thing as ridicule for whoever is doing what is best" (St Josemaría Escrivá, *The Way*, 392).

19:5–6. This is a very good example of the way God acts to save men. Jesus calls Zacchaeus personally, using his name, suggesting he invite him home. The Gospel states that Zacchaeus does so promptly and joyfully. This is how we

was to pass that way. [5]And when Jesus came to the place, he looked up and said to him, "Zacchaeus, make haste and come down; for I must stay at your house today." [6]So he made haste and came down, and received him joyfully. [7]And when they saw it they all murmured, "He has gone in to be the guest of a man who is a sinner." [8]And Zacchaeus stood and said to the Lord, "Behold, Lord, the half of my goods I give to the poor; and if I have defrauded any one of anything, I restore it fourfold." [9]And Jesus said to him, "Today salvation has come to this house, since he also is a son of Abraham. [10]For the Son of man came to seek and to save the lost."

Lk 15:2

Ex 22:1
Num 5:6–7

Ezra 34:16
Jn 3:17
1 Tim 1:15

Parable of the pounds
[11]As they heard these things, he proceeded to tell a parable, because he was near to Jerusalem, and because they supposed that the kingdom of God was to appear immediately. [12]He said therefore, "A nobleman went into a far country to receive kingly power[d] and then return. [13]Calling ten of his servants, he gave them

Mt 25:14–30
Lk 24:21
Acts 1:6

should respond when God calls us by means of grace.

19:8. Responding immediately to grace, Zacchaeus makes it known that he will restore fourfold anything he obtained unjustly—thereby going beyond what is laid down in the Law of Moses (cf. Ex 21:37f). And in generous compensation he gives half his wealth to the poor. "Let the rich learn", St Ambrose comments, "that evil does not consist in having wealth, but in not putting it to good use; for just as riches are an obstacle to evil people, they are also a means of virtue for good people" (*Expositio Evangelii sec. Lucam*, in loc.). Cf. the note on Lk 16:9–11.

19:10. Jesus' ardent desire to seek out a sinner fills us with hope of attaining eternal salvation. "He chooses a chief tax collector: who can despair when such a man obtains grace?" (St Ambrose, *Expositio Evangelii sec. Lucam*, in loc.).

19:11. The disciples had a wrong con-

cept of the Kingdom of heaven: they thought it was about to happen and they saw it in earthly terms. They envisaged Jesus conquering the Roman tyrant and immediately establishing the Kingdom in the holy city of Jerusalem, and that when that happened they would hold privileged positions in the Kingdom. There is always a danger of Christians failing to grasp the transcendent, supernatural character of the Kingdom of God in this world, that is, the Church, which "has but one sole purpose—that the Kingdom of God may come and the salvation of the human race may be accomplished" (Vatican II, *Gaudium et spes*, 45).

Through this parable our Lord teaches us that, although his reign has begun, it will only be fully manifested later on. In the time left to us we should use all the resources and graces God gives us, in order to merit the reward.

19:13. The "mina", here translated as "pound", was worth about 35 grammes of gold. This parable is very like the

d. Greek *a kingdom*

Ps 2:2f

ten pounds,[e] and said to them, 'Trade with these till I come.' [14]But his citizens hated him and sent an embassy after him, saying, 'We do not want this man to reign over us.' [15]When he returned, having received the kingly power,[d] he commanded these servants, to whom he had given the money, to be called to him, that he might know what they had gained by trading. [16]The first came before him, saying, 'Lord, your pound has made ten pounds more.' [17]And he said to him, 'Well done, good servant! Because you have been faithful in a very little, you shall have authority over ten cities.' [18]And the second came, saying, 'Lord, your pound has made five pounds.' [19]And he said to him, 'And you are to be over five cities.' [20]Then another came, saying, 'Lord, here is your pound, which I kept laid away in a napkin; [21]for I was afraid of you, because you are a severe man; you take up what you did not lay down, and reap what you did not sow.' [22]He said to him, 'I will condemn you out of your own mouth, you wicked servant! You knew that I was a severe man, taking up what I did not lay down and reaping what I did not sow? [23]Why then did you not put my money into the bank, and at my coming I should have collected it with interest?' [24]And he said to those who stood by, 'Take the pound from him, and give it to him who has the ten pounds.'

Lk 16:10

---

parable of the talents reported in St Matthew (cf. 25:14–30).

19:14. The last part of this verse, although it has a very specific context, reflects the attitude of many people who do not want to bear the sweet yoke of our Lord and who reject him as king. "There are millions of people in the world who reject Jesus Christ in this way; or rather they reject his shadow, for they do not know Christ. They have not seen the beauty of his face; they do not realize how wonderful his teaching is. This sad state of affairs makes me want to atone to our Lord. When I hear that endless clamour—expressed more in ignoble actions than in words—I feel the need to cry out, 'He must reign!' (1 Cor 15:25)" (St J. Escrivá, *Christ Is Passing By*, 179).

19:17. God counts on our fidelity in little things, and the greater our effort in this regard the greater the reward we will receive: "Because you have been *in pauca fidelis*, faithful in small things, come and join in your master's happiness. The words are Christ's. *In pauca fidelis!* ... Now will you neglect little things, if heaven itself is promised to those who keep them?" (St Josemaría Escrivá, *The Way*, 819).

19:24–26. God expects us to strive to put to good use the gifts we have received—and he lavishly rewards those who respond to his grace. The king in the parable is shown to be very generous towards these servants—and generous in rewarding those who managed to increase the money they were given. But he is very

---

e. The mina, rendered here by *pound*, was about three months' wages for a labourer   **d.** Greek *a kingdom*

²⁵(And they said to him, 'Lord, he has ten pounds!') ²⁶'I tell you, that to every one who has will more be given; but from him who has not, even what he has will be taken away. ²⁷But as for these enemies of mine, who did not want me to reign over them, bring them here and slay them before me.'"

Lk 8:18
Mt 13:12

Ps 2:9
Is 63:1–6
1 Cor 15:25

PART THREE

The Jerusalem ministry

11. CLEANSING OF THE TEMPLE. CONTROVERSIES

The Messiah enters the Holy City
²⁸And when he had said this, he went on ahead, going up to Jerusalem. ²⁹When he drew near to Bethphage and Bethany, at the mount that is called Olivet, he sent two of the disciples, ³⁰saying,

Mt 21:1–9
Mk 11:1–10
Jn 12:12–16

severe towards the lazy servant who was also the recipient of a gift from his lord, who did not let it erode but guarded it carefully—and for this his king criticizes him: he failed to fulfil the just command the king gave him when he gave him the money: "Trade till I come." If we appreciate the treasures the Lord has given us—life, the gift of faith, grace—we will make a special effort to make them bear fruit—by fulfilling our duties, working hard and doing apostolate. "Don't let your life be barren. Be useful. Make yourself felt. Shine forth with the torch of your faith and your love. With your apostolic life, wipe out the trail of filth and slime left by the corrupt sowers of hatred. And set aflame all the ways of the earth with the fire of Christ that you bear in your heart" (St Josemaría Escrivá, *The Way*, 1).

19:28. Normally in the Gospels when there is mention of going to the Holy City it is in terms of "going up" to Jerusalem (cf. Mt 20:18; Jn 7:8), probably because geographically the city is located on Mount Zion. Besides, since the temple was the religious and political centre, going up to Jerusalem had also a sacred meaning of ascending to the holy place, where sacrifices were offered to God.

Particularly in the Gospel of St Luke, our Lord's whole life is seen in terms of a continuous ascent towards Jerusalem, where his self-surrender reaches its highpoint in the redemptive sacrifice of the cross. Here Jesus is on the point of entering the city, conscious of the fact that his passion and death are imminent.

19:30–35. Jesus makes use of a donkey for his entry into Jerusalem, thereby ful-

"Go into the village opposite, where on entering you will find a colt tied, on which no one has ever yet sat; untie it and bring it here. ³¹If any one asks you, 'Why are you untying it?' you shall say this, 'The Lord has need of it.'" ³²So those who were sent went away and found it as he had told them. ³³And as they were untying the colt, its owners said to them, "Why are you untying the colt?" ³⁴And they said, "The Lord has need of it." ³⁵And they brought it to Jesus, and throwing their garments on the colt they set Jesus upon it. ³⁶And as he rode along, they spread their garments on the road. ³⁷As he was now drawing near, at the descent of the Mount of Olives, the whole multitude of the disciples began to rejoice and praise God with a loud voice for all the mighty works that they had seen, ³⁸saying, "Blessed is the King who comes in the name of the Lord! Peace in heaven and glory in the highest!" ³⁹And some of the Pharisees in the multitude said to him, "Teacher, rebuke your disciples." ⁴⁰He answered, "I tell you, if these were silent, the very stones would cry out."

Ps 118:26
Lk 2:14

---

filling an ancient prophecy: "Rejoice greatly, O daughter of Zion! Shout aloud, O daughter of Jerusalem! Lo, your king comes to you; triumphant and victorious is he, humble and riding on an ass, on a colt the foal of an ass" (Zech 9:9).

The people, and particularly the Pharisees, were quite aware of this prophecy. Therefore, despite its simplicity of form, there was a certain solemnity about the whole episode which impressed those present, stirring the hearts of the people and irritating the Pharisees. By fulfilling the prophecy our Lord was showing everyone that he was the Messiah prophesied in the Old Testament. Other aspects of this episode are commented on in connexion with Mk 11:3.

19:38. Christ is greeted with the prophetic words referring to the enthronement of the Messiah, contained in Psalm 118:26: "Blessed be he who enters in the name of the Lord!" But the people also acclaim him as king. This is a great messianic demonstration, which infuriates the Pharisees. One of the accla-

mations, "Peace in heaven and glory in the highest", echoes the announcement made by the angel to the shepherds on Christmas night (cf. Lk 2:14).

19:40. To the reproaches of the Pharisees, who are scandalized by the people's shouts, our Lord replies in a phrase which sounds like a proverb: so obvious is his messiahship that if men refused to recognize it nature would proclaim it. In fact, when his friends were cowed on the hill of Calvary the earth trembled and the rocks split (cf. Mt 27:51). At other times our Lord imposed silence on those who want to proclaim him King or Messiah, but now he adopts a different attitude: the moment has come for his dignity and his mission to be made public.

19:41–44. When the procession reaches a place where there is a good view of the city, they are disconcerted by Jesus' unexpected weeping. Our Lord explains why he is weeping, by prophesying the destruction of the city which he loved so much: not one stone will remain on

Jesus weeps over Jerusalem

⁴¹And when he drew near and saw the city he wept over it, ⁴²saying, "Would that even today you knew the things that make for peace! But now they are hid from your eyes. ⁴³For the days shall come upon you, when your enemies will cast up a bank about you and surround you, and hem you in on every side, ⁴⁴and dash you to the ground, you and your children within you, and they will not leave one stone upon another in you; because you did not know the time of your visitation."*

Ps 137:9

Jesus in the temple

⁴⁵And he entered the temple and began to drive out those who sold, ⁴⁶saying to them, "It is written, 'My house shall be a house of prayer'; but you have made it a den of robbers."

⁴⁷And he was teaching daily in the temple. The chief priests and the scribes and the principal men of the people sought to destroy him; ⁴⁸but they did not find anything they could do, for all the people hung upon his words.

Mt 21:12–16
Mk 11:15–18
Jn 2:13–16
Is 56:7
Jer 7:11

Jn 18:20

---

another, and its inhabitants will be massacred—a prophecy which was fulfilled in the year 70, when Titus razed the city and the temple was destroyed.

These historical events will be a punishment for Jerusalem failing to recognize the time of its visitation, that is, for closing its gates to the salvific coming of the Redeemer. Jesus loved the Jews with a very special love: they were the first to whom the Gospel was preached (cf. Mt 10:5–6); to them he directed his ministry (cf. Mt 15:24); he showed by his word and by his miracles that he was the Son of God and the Messiah foretold in the Scriptures. But the Jews for the most part failed to appreciate the grace the Lord was offering them; their leaders led them to the extreme of calling for Jesus to be crucified. Jesus visits every one of us; he comes as our Saviour; he teaches us through the preaching of the Church; he gives us forgiveness and grace through the sacraments. We should not reject our Lord, we should not remain indifferent to his visit.

19:45–48. Jesus' indignation shows his zeal for the glory of his Father, to be recognized at this time in the temple itself. He inveighs against the traders for engaging in business which has nothing to do with divine worship (cf. Mt 21:12; Mk 11:15). Even the priests allowed some of these abuses to go on—perhaps because they benefitted from them in the form of taxes. The traders did perform services necessary for divine worship but this was vitiated by their excessive desire for gain, turning the temple into a marketplace.

"My house shall be a house of prayer": Jesus uses these words from Isaiah (56:7; cf. Jer 7:11) to underline the purpose of the temple. Jesus' behaviour shows the respect the temple of Jerusalem deserved; how much more reverence should be shown our churches, where Jesus himself is really present in the Blessed Eucharist (cf. the notes on Mt 21:12–13; and Mk 11:15–18).

Jesus' authority

Mt 21:23–27
Mk 11:27–33

20 ¹One day, as he was teaching the people in the temple and preaching the gospel, the chief priests and the scribes with the elders came up ²and said to him, "Tell us by what authority you do these things, or who it is that gave you this authority." ³He answered them, "I also will ask you a question; now tell me, ⁴Was the baptism of John from heaven or from men?" ⁵And they discussed it with one another, saying, "If we say, 'From heaven,' he will say, 'Why did you not believe him?' ⁶But if we say, 'From men,' all the people will stone us; for they are convinced that John was a prophet." ⁷So they answered that they did not know whence it was. ⁸And Jesus said to them, "Neither will I tell you by what authority I do these things."

Parable of the wicked tenants

Mt 21:33–46
Mk 12:1–12
Is 5:1

⁹And he began to tell the people this parable: "A man planted a vineyard, and let it out to tenants, and went into another country

---

20:1–40. Our Lord's public ministry is coming to an end. He has gone up from Jericho to Jerusalem on his last journey. He will stay in the city and its environs until his death. He has made his entry as Messiah into the temple and has cleansed it. And with the authority of the Messiah he now preaches in the courtyards of the temple. In this chapter the evangelist narrates a series of arguments provoked by Pharisees and Sadducees—about Jesus' authority (v. 18), about the lawfulness of giving tribute to Caesar (vv. 20–26), and about the resurrection of the dead (vv. 27–40). The chapter ends with our Lord countering, by asking them how they interpret Psalm 110:1, and by telling the parable of the murderous tenants (Lk 20:9–18). The apostles remembered with special poignancy these events prior to the Saviour's passion and death, whose transcendent meaning they later grasped in the light of the events of Easter. Jesus' long journey from Galilee to Jerusalem has reached its destination; but the authorities in the Holy City reject the Messiah and Saviour. However, there the salvation of mankind will be achieved thanks to the sacrifice of the Son of God.

20:1–8. To these sly questions Jesus replies immediately and very much to the point.

The question, "By what authority do you do these things", refers to everything our Lord has done. Therefore, the technical term "authority" must be taken in all its depth of meaning: What is the nature of Jesus' authority and power. Because of the evil motivation behind the question, our Lord avoids giving a direct answer, countering instead by asking a question about John's baptism. When the priests and scribes give an evasive reply our Lord simply closes the discussion: he asserts that he has the authority and he refuses to say how he got it. A few days later, when in the presence of the whole Sanhedrin he is solemnly asked if he is the Messiah and Son of God, he will reply by saying quite clearly that he is, thereby showing the basis of his authority and explaining why he has acted in the way he has (cf. Mt 26:63–64 and Lk 22:66–71).

for a long while. [10]When the time came, he sent a servant to the tenants, that they should give him some of the fruit of the vineyard; but the tenants beat him, and sent him away empty-handed. [11]And he sent another servant; him also they beat and treated shamefully, and sent him away empty-handed. [12]And he sent yet a third; this one they wounded and cast out. [13]Then the owner of the vineyard said, 'What shall I do? I will send my beloved son; it may be they will respect him.' [14]But when the tenants saw him, they said to themselves, 'This is the heir; let us kill him, that the inheritance may be ours.' [15]And they cast him out of the vineyard and killed him. What then will the owner of the vineyard do to them? [16]He will come and destroy those tenants, and give the vineyard to others." When they heard this, they said, "God forbid!" [17]But he looked at them and said, "What then is this that is written:

'The very stone which the builders rejected
has become the head of the corner'?

2 Chron 36:15–17

Ps 118:22

20:9–19. As the days of his passion draw near, our Lord spells out to the priests and scribes the seriousness of the sin they are committing by rejecting him, and the terrible consequences which will follow. That is the purpose of this parable, whose central theme is deeply rooted in Sacred Scripture and is very familiar to his listeners: the people of Israel are the vineyard of the Lord. Of the many places where this comparison is to be found in the Old Testament (Hos 10:1; Jer 10:21; 12:10; Ezek 19:10–14; Ps 80:7–18) one has special resonance—the Song of the vineyard which instead of yielding good grapes yielded only sour grapes (Is 5:1–7); our Lord's words seem to evoke that ancient prophetic complaint: "What more was there to do for my vineyard, that I have not done in it?" Every character in the Gospel parable is very easy to identify: the vineyard is Israel; the tenants are the leaders of Israel; the servants sent by the lord to the vineyard are the prophets, so often ill-treated; the son is Jesus Christ, the only Son of the Father. Jesus alludes to his death on the outskirts of the city; the tenants cast him out of the vineyard—Jerusalem—and put him to death. The owner of the vineyard is God. The leading priests and scribes understand what the end of the parable means and they are horrified, which is why they cry, "God forbid!" For our Lord is saying that the owner of the vineyard will put the tenants to death and hand over the vineyard to others: the leaders of the people will be rejected. To underline the teaching in the parable our Lord concludes by applying to himself the words of Psalm 118:22: "The stone which the builders rejected has become the head of the corner." The parable contains a clear lesson for all of us: it is a grave sin to reject the Lord, to despise God's grace. If our heart becomes hardened, like those priests and scribes, we will inevitably hear from our Lord's lips similar words of rejection.

The passage ends on a sad note: wounded in their pride by the clarity of what Jesus says, their hearts became even more hardened, to the point of planning to kill him.

Is 8:14   [18]Every one who falls on that stone will be broken to pieces; but when it falls on any one it will crush him." [19]The scribes and chief priests tried to lay hands on him at that very hour, but they feared the people; for they perceived that he had told this parable against them.

Tribute to Caesar

Mt 22:15–22
Mk 12:13–17
Lk 11:54

[20]So they watched him, and sent spies, who pretended to be sincere, that they might take hold of what he said, so as to deliver him up to the authority and jurisdiction of the governor. [21]They asked him, "Teacher, we know that you speak and teach rightly, and show no partiality, but truly teach the way of God. [22]Is it lawful for us to give tribute to Caesar, or not?" [23]But he perceived their craftiness, and said to them, [24]"Show me a coin.[f] Whose likeness and inscription has it?" They said, "Caesar's." [25]He said to them, "Then render to Caesar the things that are Caesar's, and to God the things that are God's." [26]And they were not able in the

---

20:20–26. The leaders of the people are trying to find some grounds for laying charges against Jesus, so they put to him two mischievous questions—about the legitimacy of Roman authority in Palestine and about the resurrection of the dead (vv. 21–39).

Their question about paying tribute to Caesar is malicious: if our Lord answers "Yes", they will be able to accuse him of collaboration with the Romans, whom the Jews hated because they were invaders; if he answers "No," it will allow them to report him to Pilate, the Roman ruler, as a rebel.

Our Lord's reply takes the people by surprise, it is so simple, profound and prudent. It emphasizes a duty which obliges everyone—that of giving God his due. "Render to God the things that are God's." This phrase is the key to understanding Jesus' reply in all its depth: recognition of God's sovereignty comes before everything else.

Because he is true God and true man,

Christ has authority over everything, even over temporal realities, but during his life on earth "he refrained from exercising that authority, and although he himself disdained to possess or to care for earthly things, he did not, nor does he today, interfere with those who possess them" (Pius XI, *Quas primas*). Our Lord acts in this way to make sure that his Kingdom—which is spiritual—is not confused with an earthly kingdom.

At the same time Jesus' answer provides the key to the right relationship between Church and State. Each must have its own independence and sphere of action, and both should cooperate in those matters which by their very nature require the action of both authorities, as the Second Vatican Council teaches: "The political community and the Church are autonomous and independent of each other in their own fields. Nevertheless, both are devoted to the personal vocation of man, though under different titles. This service will redound the

---

f. Greek *denarius*

presence of the people to catch him by what he said; but marvelling at his answer they were silent.

The resurrection of the dead

[27]There came to him some Sadducees, those who say that there is no resurrection, [28]and they asked him a question, saying, "Teacher, Moses wrote for us that if a man's brother dies, having a wife but no children, the man[g] must take the wife and raise up children for his brother. [29]Now there were seven brothers; the first took a wife, and died without children; [30]and the second [31]and the third took her, and likewise all seven left no children and died. [32]Afterward the woman also died. [33]In the resurrection, therefore, whose wife will the woman be? For the seven had her as wife."

[34]And Jesus said to them, "The sons of this age marry and are given in marriage; [35]but those who are accounted worthy to attain to that age and to the resurrection from the dead neither marry nor are given in marriage, [36]for they cannot die any more, because

Mt 22:23–33, 46
Mk 12:18–27, 34
Gen 38:8
Deut 25:5–6

Phil 3:11

1 Jn 3:1–2

---

more effectively to the welfare of all insofar as both institutions practise better cooperation according to the local and prevailing situation" (*Gaudium et spes*, 76).

Jesus also teaches us here that we have a duty to fulfil our obligations as citizens. In this connexion St Paul exhorted the Romans: "Pay all of them their dues, taxes to whom taxes are due, revenue to whom revenue is due, respect to whom respect is due, honour to whom honour is due" (Rom 13:7).

This was also how the first Christians acted: "As we have been instructed by him [Jesus], we before all others try everywhere to pay your appointed officials the ordinary and special taxes" (St Justin, *Apology*, 1, 17, 1).

20:27–40. The Sadducees did not believe in the resurrection of the body or the immortality of the soul. They came along to ask Jesus a question which is apparently unanswerable. According to the levirate law (cf. Deut 25:5ff), if a man

died without issue, his brother was duty bound to marry his widow to provide his brother with descendants. The consequences of this law would seem to give rise to a ridiculous situation at the resurrection of the dead.

Our Lord replies by reaffirming that there will be a resurrection; and by explaining the properties of those who have risen again, the Sadducees' argument simply evaporates. In this world people marry in order to continue the species: that is the primary aim of marriage. After the resurrection there will be no more marriage because people will not die any more.

Quoting Holy Scripture (Ex 3:2, 6) our Lord shows the grave mistake the Sadducees make, and he argues: God is not the God of the dead but of the living, that is to say, there exists a permanent relationship between God and Abraham, Isaac and Jacob, who have been dead for years. Therefore, although these just men have died as far as their bodies are concerned, they are alive, truly alive, in God—

g. Greek *his brother*

they are equal to angels and are sons of God, being sons of the
resurrection. ³⁷But that the dead are raised, even Moses showed,
in the passage about the bush, where he calls the Lord the God of
Abraham and the God of Isaac and the God of Jacob.* ³⁸Now he
is not God of the dead, but of the living; for all live to him." ³⁹And
some of the scribes answered, "Teacher, you have spoken well."
⁴⁰For they no longer dared to ask him any question.

Ex 3:2–6

Rom 14:8

The divinity of the Messiah

⁴¹But he said to them, "How can they say that the Christ is David's
son? ⁴²For David himself says in the Book of Psalms,

Mt 22:41–45
Mk 12:35–37
Ps 110:1
Jn 7:42

> 'The Lord said to my Lord,
>   Sit at my right hand,
> ⁴³till I make thy enemies a stool for thy feet.'

⁴⁴David thus calls him Lord; so how is he his son?"

Jesus condemns the scribes

⁴⁵And in the hearing of all the people he said to his disciples,
⁴⁶"Beware of the scribes, who like to go about in long robes, and
love salutations in the market places and the best seats in the synagogues and the places of honour at feasts, ⁴⁷who devour widow's
houses and for a pretence make long prayers. They will receive
the greater condemnation."

Mt 23:5ff
Mk 12:38–40
Lk 11:43

---

their souls are immortal—and they are awaiting the resurrection of their bodies.

See also the notes on Mt 22:23–33 and Mk 12:18–27.

20:41–44. Jesus states that not only is he the son of David but also he is Lord and God; he quotes Psalm 110: the Messiah, a descendant of David, seated at the right hand of God, is called Lord by David himself. In this way Jesus alludes to the mystery of his incarnation: he is David's son according to the flesh, and he is God and Lord because he is the Father's Son, equal to him in everything; which explains why he is David's Lord even though he was born long after David.

21:1–4. Our Lord, surrounded by his disciples, watches people putting offerings into the treasury. This was a place in the women's courtyard, where there were collection boxes for the offerings of the faithful. Just then, something happens whose significance Jesus wants his disci- ples to notice: a poor widow puts in two coins, of very little value. He describes this as the greatest offering of all, praising the giving of alms for this purpose, particularly by people who give part of what they need. Our Lord is moved by this tiny offering because in her case it implies a big sacri- fice. "The Lord does not look", St John Chrysostom comments, "at the amount offered but at the affection with which it is offered" (*Hom. on Heb*, 1). Generosity is of the essence of almsgiving. This woman teaches us that we can move God's heart if we give him all we can, which will always amount to very little even if we give our very lives. "How little a life is to offer to God!" (St J. Escrivá, *The Way*, 420).

168

The widow's mite

21 ¹He looked up and saw the rich putting their gifts into the treasury; ²and he saw a poor widow put in two copper coins. ³And he said, "Truly I tell you, this poor widow has put in more than all of them; ⁴for they all contributed out of their abundance, but she out of her poverty put in all the living that she had."

Mk 12:41–44

2 Cor 8:12

Lk 12:15

12. THE ESCHATOLOGICAL DISCOURSE

Announcement of the destruction of the temple

⁵And as some spoke of the temple, how it was adorned with noble stones and offerings, he said, ⁶"As for these things which you see, the days will come when there shall not be left here one stone upon another that will not be thrown down."

Mt 24:1–21
Mk 13:1–19
Lk 19:44

The beginning of tribulation. Persecution on account of the Gospel

⁷And they asked him, "Teacher, when will this be, and what will be the sign when this is about to take place?" ⁸And he said, "Take heed that you are not led astray; for many will come in my name, saying, 'I am he!' and, 'The time is at hand!' Do not go after

Dan 7:22

21:5–36. The disciples are in awe of the magnificence of the temple, and Jesus uses the occasion to give a long discourse, known as the "eschatological discourse" because it has to do with the last days of the world. The account given here is very similar to those in the other Synoptic Gospels. The discourse deals with three inter-connected subjects—the destruction of Jerusalem (which took place some forty years later), the end of the world, and the second coming of Christ in glory and majesty. Jesus, who also predicts here the persecution the Church will experience, exhorts his disciples to be patient, to pray and be watchful.

Our Lord speaks here in the style and language of prophecy, using images taken from the Old Testament; in this discourse, also, we find prophecies that will be fulfilled very soon, mixed in with

others that have to do with the end of the world. It is not our Lord's intention to satisfy people's curiosity about future events, but to protect them from being discouraged and scandalized about what is going to happen in the days immediately ahead. This explains his exhortations in vv. 8, 9 and 36.

21:8. On hearing that Jerusalem is going to be destroyed, the disciples ask what sign will be given as a warning of these events (vv. 5–7). Jesus answers by telling them "not to be led astray," that is to say, not to expect any warning; not to be misled by false prophets; to stay faithful to him. These false prophets will come along claiming to be the Messiah ("I am he!"). Our Lord's reply in fact refers to two events which in the Jewish mind were interrelated—the destruction of the Holy City and the end of the world. This

Dan 2:28 them. ⁹And when you hear of wars and tumults, do not be terrified; for this must first take place, but the end will not be at
once."

Is 19:2
2 Chron 15:6 ¹⁰Then he said to them, "Nation will rise against nation, and
kingdom against kingdom; ¹¹there will be great earthquakes, and
in various places famines and pestilences; and there will be terrors

Lk 12:11 and great signs from heaven. ¹²But before all this they will lay
their hands on you and persecute you, delivering you up to the
synagogues and prisons, and you will be brought before kings and
governors for my name's sake. ¹³This will be a time for you to

Mt 10:19 bear testimony. ¹⁴Settle it therefore in your minds, not to meditate
beforehand how to answer; ¹⁵for I will give you a mouth and

Acts 6:10 wisdom, which none of your adversaries will be able to withstand
or contradict. ¹⁶You will be delivered up even by parents and
brothers and kinsmen and friends, and some of you they will put

Mt 10:21–22
Lk 12:7
Heb 10:36 to death; ¹⁷you will be hated by all for my name's sake. ¹⁸But not
a hair of your head will perish. ¹⁹By your endurance you will gain
your lives.

---

is why he goes on to speak of both events and implies that there will be a long gap between the two; the destruction of the temple and of Jerusalem are a kind of sign or symbol of the catastrophes which will mark the end of the world.

21:9–11. Our Lord does not want his disciples to confuse just any catastrophe —famine, earthquake, war—or even persecution with the signals of the end of the world. He exhorts them quite clearly: "Do not be terrified," because although all this has to happen, "the end will not be at once;" in spite of difficulties of all kinds the Gospel will spread to the ends of the earth. Difficulties should not paralyse the preaching of the faith.

21:19. Jesus foretells all kinds of persecution. Persecution itself is something inevitable: "all who desire to live a godly life in Christ Jesus will be persecuted" (2 Tim 3:12). His disciples will have need to remember the Lord's warning at the Last Supper: "'A servant is not greater

than his master.' If they persecuted me, they will persecute you" (Jn 15:20). However, these persecutions are part of God's providence: they happen because he lets them happen, which he does in order to draw greater good out of them. Persecution provides Christians with an opportunity to bear witness to Christ; without it the blood of martyrs would not adorn the Church. Moreover, our Lord promises to give special help to those who suffer persecution, and he tells them not to be afraid: he will give them of his own wisdom to enable them to defend themselves; he will not permit a hair of their heads to perish, that is, even apparent misfortune and loss will be for them a beginning of heaven.

From Jesus' words we can also deduce the obligation of every Christian to be ready to lose his life rather than offend God. Only those will attain salvation who persevere until the end in faithfulness to the Lord. The three Synoptic Gospels locate his exhortation to perseverance in this discourse (cf. Mt 24:13;

The great tribulation in Jerusalem

20"But when you see Jerusalem surrounded by armies, then know that its desolation has come near. 21Then let those who are in Judea flee to the mountains, and let those who are inside the city depart, and let not those who are out in the country enter it; 22for these are days of vengeance, to fulfil all that is written. 23Alas for those who are with child and for those who give suck in those days! For great distress shall be upon the earth and wrath upon this people; 24they will fall by the edge of the sword, and be led captive among all nations; and Jerusalem will be trodden down by the Gentiles, until the times of the Gentiles* are fulfilled.

Deut 32:35
Hos 9:7
1 Thess 2:16
Deut 28:64
Zech 12:3
Is 63:18
Ps 79:1
Dan 8:10;
9:26; 12:7
Rom 11:25

The coming of the Son of man

25"And there will be signs in sun and moon and stars, and upon the earth distress of nations in perplexity at the roaring of the sea and the waves, 26men fainting with fear and foreboding of what is coming on the world; for the powers of the heavens will be shaken. 27And then they will see the Son of man coming in a

Mt 24:29–30
Mk 13:24–26
Ps 65:7
Is 34:4
Dan 7:13
Mt 26:64

Mk 13:13) and St Matthew gives it elsewhere (Mt 10:22) as does St Peter (1 Pet 5:9)—all of which underlines the importance for every Christian of this warning from our Lord.

21:20–24. Jesus gives quite a detailed prophecy of the destruction of the Holy City. When the Christians living there saw the armies getting closer, they remembered this prophecy and fled to Transjordan (cf. Eusebius, *Ecclesiastical History*, 3, 5). Christ had advised them to flee as soon as possible because this is the time when God would punish Jerusalem for its sins, as the Old Testament predicted (Is 5:5–6).

Catholic tradition sees Israel as symbolizing the Church. In fact, in the Book of Revelation the Church triumphant is called the new Jerusalem (cf. Rev 21:2). Therefore, by applying this passage to the Church, the sufferings the Holy City experiences can symbolize the contradictions the pilgrim Church will experience

due to the sins of men, for "she herself takes her place among the creatures which groan and travail yet and await the revelation of the children of God" (Vatican II, *Lumen gentium*, 48).

21:24. "The times of the Gentiles" means the period in which the Gentiles, who do not belong to the Jewish people, will become members of the new people of God, the Church, until the Jews themselves are converted at the end of the world (cf. Rom 11:11–32).

21:25–26. Jesus refers to the dramatic changes in natural elements when the world is coming to an end. "The power of the heavens will be shaken"; that is to say, the whole universe will tremble at the Lord's coming in power and glory.

21:27–28. Applying to himself the prophecy of Daniel (7:13–14), our Lord speaks of his coming in glory at the end of time. Mankind will see the power and

171

cloud with power and great glory. [28]Now when these things begin to take place, look up and raise your heads, because your redemption is drawing near."

The end will surely come; the lesson of the fig tree

Mt 24:32–35
Mk 13:28–31

[29]And he told them a parable: "Look at the fig tree, and all the trees; [30]as soon as they come out in leaf, you see for yourselves and know that the summer is already near. [31]So also, when you see these things taking place, you know that the kingdom of God is near. [32]Truly, I say to you, this generation will not pass away till

Lk 16:17

all has taken place. [33]Heaven and earth will pass away, but my words will not pass away.

Lk 17:27
Mt 29:49
Is 5:11–13

The need for vigilance

[34]"But take heed to yourselves lest your hearts be weighed down with dissipation and drunkenness and cares of this life, and that

glory of the Son of man, coming to judge the living and the dead. Christ will deliver this judgment in his human capacity. Sacred Scripture describes the solemnity of this event, when the sentence passed on each person in the particular judgment will be confirmed, and God's justice and mercy to men throughout history will shine out for all to see. "It was necessary not only that rewards should await the just and punishments the wicked, in the life to come, but that they should be awarded by a public and general judgment. Thus they will become better known and will be rendered more conspicuous to all, and a tribute of praise will be offered by all to the justice and providence of God" (St Pius V, *Catechism*, 1, 8, 4).

This coming of the Lord is, then, a day of terror for evildoers and of joy for those who have remained faithful. The disciples should hold their heads high because their redemption is at hand. It is the day they will receive their reward. The victory won by Christ on the cross— victory over sin, over the devil and over death—will now be seen clearly, with all

its implications. Therefore St Paul recommends that we be "awaiting our blessed hope, the appearing of the glory of our great God and Saviour Jesus Christ" (Tit 2:13).

"He [Christ] ascended into heaven whence he will come again to judge the living and the dead, each according to his merits. Those who have responded to the love and compassion of God will go into eternal life. Those who have refused them to the end will be consigned to the fire that is never extinguished" (Paul VI, *Creed of the People of God*, 12).

21:31. The Kingdom of God, announced by John the Baptist (cf. Mt 3:2) and described by our Lord in so many parables (cf. Mt 13; Lk 13:18–20), is already present among the apostles (Lk 17:20–21), but it is not yet fully manifest. Jesus here describes what it will be like when the Kingdom comes in all its fulness, and he invites us to pray for this very event in the Our Father: "Thy Kingdom come." "The Kingdom of God, which had its beginnings here on earth in the Church of Christ, is not of

day come upon you suddenly like a snare; ³⁵for it will come upon all who dwell upon the face of the whole earth. ³⁶But watch at all times, praying that you may have strength to escape all these things that will take place, and to stand before the Son of man."

Is 24:17
1 Thess 5:3

Mk 13:33

Jesus teaches in the temple

³⁷And every day he was teaching in the temple, but at night he went out and lodged on the mount called Olivet. ³⁸And early in the morning all the people came to him in the temple to hear him.

Jn 8:1f

Mk 12:37

---

this world, whose form is passing, and its authentic development cannot be measured by the progress of civilization, of science and of technology. The true growth of the Kingdom of God consists in an ever deepening knowledge of the unfathomable riches of Christ, in an ever stronger hope in eternal blessings, in an ever more fervent response to the love of God, and in an ever more generous acceptance of grace and holiness by men" (*Creed of the People of God*, 27). At the end of the world everything will be subjected to Christ and God will reign for ever more (cf. 1 Cor 15:24, 28).

21:32. Everything referring to the destruction of Jerusalem was fulfilled some forty years after our Lord's death—which meant that Jesus' contemporaries would be able to verify the truth of this prophecy. But the destruction of Jerusalem is a symbol of the end of the world; therefore, it can be said that the generation to which our Lord refers did see the end of the world, in a symbolic way. This verse can also be taken to refer to the generation of believers, that is, not just the particular generation of those Jesus was addressing (cf. the note on Mt 24:32–35).

21:34–36. At the end of his discourse Jesus emphasizes that every Christian needs to be vigilant: we do not know the day nor the hour in which he will ask us to render an account of our lives. Therefore, we must at all times be trying to do God's will, so that death, whenever it comes, will find us ready. For those who act in this way, sudden death never takes them by surprise. As St Paul recommends: "You are not in darkness, brethren, for that day to sur-prise you like a thief" (1 Thess 5:4). Vigilance consists in making a constant effort not to be attached to the things of this world (the concupiscence of the flesh, the concupiscence of the eyes and the pride of life: cf. 1 Jn 2:16) and in being assiduous in prayer, which keeps us close to God. If we live in this way, the day we die will be a day of joy and not of terror, for with God's help our vigilance will mean that our souls are ready to receive the visit of the Lord; they are in the state of grace: in meeting Christ we will not be meeting a judge who will find us guilty; instead he will embrace us and lead us into the house of his Father to remain there forever. "Does your soul not burn with the desire to make your Father God happy when he has to judge you?" (St Josemaría Escrivá, *The Way*, 746).

13. THE PASSION, DEATH AND RESURRECTION OF JESUS

Mk 26:1–5
Mk 14:1–2
Lk 20:19

Mt 26:14–15
Mk 14:10–11

Jn 13:2–27

Judas' treachery

22 ¹Now the feast of Unleavened Bread drew near, which is called the Passover. ²And the chief priests and the scribes were seeking how to put him to death; for they feared the people. ³Then Satan entered into Judas called Iscariot, who was of the number of the twelve; ⁴he went away and conferred with the chief priests and captains how he might betray him to them. ⁵And they were glad, and engaged to give him money. ⁶So he agreed and sought an opportunity to betray him to them in the absence of the multitude.

22:1–38. These verses report the events immediately prior to our Lord's passion, events rich in meaning. The three Synoptic Gospels all give more or less the same account, but St Luke omits certain details and adds others which fill out Mark's or Matthew's account. Take, for example, the reporting of the institution of the Eucharist: while being substantially the same in the three Synoptics and often word for word, the Matthew and Mark accounts (cf. Mt 26:26–29; Mk 14:22–25) are quite different from that of Luke taken together with the First Letter to the Corinthians (cf. Lk 22:15–20; 1 Cor 11:23–25).

22:1. The feast of the Passover, the most solemn of all the Jewish feasts, was instituted by God to commemorate the exodus of the Israelites from Egypt and to remind them of their former slavery from which he saved them (Deut 16:3). It began with the passover supper on the evening of the fourteenth day of the month of Nisan (March-April), a little after sundown, and went on until 22 Nisan, the feast of the unleavened bread. The Mosaic Law laid down (Ex 12:15–20) that on the evening of 14 Nisan the Jews had to remove any trace of leaven from their houses and eat unleavened bread for the duration of the feast—reminding them that when the moment came to leave Egypt they had to leave in such a hurry that they had no time to prepare leavened bread to take with them (Ex 12:34).

All this was a prefigurement of the renewal which Christ would bring about: "Cleanse out the old leaven that you may be a new lump, as you really are unleavened. For Christ, our paschal lamb, has been sacrificed. Let us, therefore, celebrate the festival, not with the old leaven, the leaven of malice and evil, but with the unleavened bread of sincerity and truth" (1 Cor 5:7–8).

22:3–6. Even prior to the Passion, one can sense that the behaviour of Jesus' enemies was being orchestrated by the spirit of evil, Satan. This is particularly true where Judas is concerned. Corrupt human will alone cannot explain the torrent of hatred unleashed against Jesus.

The passion of our Lord marks the climax of the struggle between God and the powers of evil. After the third temptation in the desert the devil "departed from him until an opportune time" (Lk 4:13). The time has now come: it is the hour of Christ's enemies and of the power of darkness (cf. Lk 22:53), and it is also the hour of God's definitive vic-

Preparations for the Last Supper

[7]Then came the day of Unleavened Bread, on which the passover lamb had to be sacrificed. [8]So Jesus[h] sent Peter and John, saying, "Go and prepare the passover for us, that we may eat it." [9]They said to him, "Where will you have us prepare it?" [10]He said to them, "Behold, when you have entered the city, a man carrying a jar of water will meet you; follow him into the house which he enters, [11]and tell the householder, 'The Teacher says to you, Where is the guest room, where I am to eat the passover with my disciples?' [12]And he will show you a large upper room furnished; there make ready." [13]And they went, and found it as he had told them; and they prepared the passover.

Mt 26:17–20
Mk 14:12–17
Ex 12:18–20

Lk 19:32

The institution of the Eucharist

[14]And when the hour came, he sat at table, and the apostles with him. [15]And he said to them, "I have earnestly desired to eat this

---

tory, for he "decreed that man should be saved through the wood of the cross. The tree of man's defeat became his tree of victory; where life was lost, there life has been restored" (*Roman Missal*, Preface of the Triumph of the Cross).

22:7–13. This scene took place on 14 Nisan. Every Israelite was familiar with the details of preparations for the Passover: it involved a rite which Jewish tradition, based on God-given regulations contained in the Law (cf. the note on Lk 22:1), had spelt out in minute detail—the unleavened loaves, bitter herbs, and the lamb to be sacrificed in the courtyard of the temple in the late afternoon. Peter and John, therefore, were perfectly acquainted with all these details; the only enquiry concerns where the supper is to be held, and our Lord tells them exactly how to find the place.

The disciples think that all that is involved is the Passover meal; but Jesus is also thinking about the institution of the Holy Eucharist and the Sacrifice of the New Alliance, which will take the place of the sacrifices of the Old Testament.

22:14. The Last Supper is beginning, the meal at which our Lord is going to institute the Holy Eucharist, a mystery of faith and love: "We must therefore approach this mystery, above all, with humble reverence, not following human arguments, which ought to be hushed, but in steadfast adherence to divine revelation" (Paul VI, *Mysterium fidei*).

22:15. St John, the beloved disciple, sums up in a single phrase the sentiments welling up in Jesus' soul at the Last Supper: "when Jesus knew that his hour had come to depart out of this world to the Father, having loved his own who were in the world, he loved them to the end" (Jn 13:1). Our Lord expresses his burning desire to spend the hours prior to his death with those whom he loves most on earth and, as happens when people are taking leave of their nearest and dearest, very affectionate words are exchanged (cf. Theophylact, *Enarratio in Evangel-*

h. Greek *he*

175

passover with you before I suffer; [16]for I tell you I shall not eat it[i] until it is fulfilled in the kingdom of God." [17]And he took a cup,

---

ium Ioannis, in loc.). His love is not confined to the apostles; he is thinking of all men and women. He knows that this Passover meal marks the beginning of his passion. He is going to anticipate the Sacrifice of the New Testament, which will bring such benefits to mankind.

To fulfil his Father's will, Jesus must necessarily go away, but his love, impelling him to stay with his own, moves him to institute the Eucharist, in which he stays behind, in which he remains really and truly present. "Think," St J. Escrivá writes, "of the human experience of two people who love each other, and yet are forced to part. They would like to stay together forever, but duty—in one form or another—forces them to separate. They are unable to fulfil their desire of remaining close to each other, so man's love—which, great as it may be, is limited—seeks a symbolic gesture. People who make their farewells exchange gifts or perhaps a photograph with a dedication so ardent that it seems almost enough to burn that piece of paper. They can do no more, because a creature's power is not so great as its desire.

"What we cannot do, our Lord is able to do. Jesus Christ, perfect God and perfect man, leaves us not a symbol but a reality. He himself stays with us. He will go to the Father, but he will also remain among men. He will leave us, not simply a gift that will make us remember him, not an image that becomes blurred with time, like a photograph that soon fades and yellows, and has no meaning except for those who were contemporaries. Under the appearances of bread and wine, he is really present, with his body and blood, with his soul and divinity" (*Christ Is Passing By*, 83).

22:16–20. This text contains the three basic truths of faith having to do with the sublime mystery of the Eucharist: 1) the institution of this sacrament and Jesus Christ's real presence in it; 2) the institution of the Christian priesthood; and 3) the Eucharist as the Sacrifice of the New Testament or Holy Mass (cf. the note on Mt 26:26–29). St Luke's account is substantially the same as that in the First Gospel, but it is enhanced by his more detailed description of some points (cf. the note on v.17).

Regarding the real presence of Christ in this sacrament, Paul VI stated: "In reliance on this belief of the Church, the Council of Trent 'openly and simply professes that in the bountiful sacrament of the Holy Eucharist, after the consecration of the bread and wine, our Lord and Saviour Jesus Christ, true God and true man, is contained truly, really and substantially under the appearance of the objects that the senses can perceive' (*De SS. Eucharistia*, chap. 1). Therefore our Saviour is not only present according to his humanity at the right hand of the Father, after his natural mode of existence, but at the same time he is present in the sacrament of the Eucharist also by that form of existence which is possible to God, though we can hardly express it in words. With thoughts enlightened by faith we can reach it and we must believe it with the greatest constancy" (*Mysterium fidei*). In contemplating this ineffable mystery, Christian souls have always perceived its grandeur as deriving from the fact of Christ's real presence in it. The sacrament of the Eucharist is not only an efficacious sign of Christ's loving presence in an intimate union with the faith-

i. Other ancient authorities read *never eat it again*

176

ful: in it he is present corporeally and substantially, as God and as man. Certainly, in order to penetrate this mystery one needs to have faith, because "there is no difficulty about Christ being present in the Sacrament as a sign; the real difficulty lies in his being as truly in the Sacrament as he is in heaven; therefore, it is very meritorious to believe this" (St Bonaventure, *In IV Sent.*, d.10, q.1, a.1). This mystery cannot be perceived by the senses: it can only be grasped by faith in the words of our Saviour who, being truth itself (cf. Jn 14:6), cannot deceive or be deceived: thus, in a hymn which is traditionally attributed to St Thomas Aquinas, the *Adoro te devote*, the Christian people sing: "Seeing, touching, tasting are in thee deceived; how says trusty hearing? that shall be believed; what God's Son has told me, take for truth I do; Truth himself speaks truly or there's nothing true" (translated by G.M. Hopkins).

"If no one is to misunderstand this mode of presence, which oversteps the laws of nature and constitutes the greatest miracle of all in its kind, our minds must be docile and we must follow the voice of the Church through her teaching and prayer. This voice continually re-echoes the voice of Christ. It informs us that Christ becomes present in this sacrament precisely by a change of the bread's whole substance into his body and the wine's whole substance into his blood. This is clearly remarkable, a singular change, and the Catholic Church gives it the suitable and accurate name of transubstantiation" (Paul VI, *Mysterium fidei*).

After instituting the Eucharist, our Lord instructs the apostles to perpetuate what he has done: the Church has always taken Christ's words "Do this in remembrance of me" to mean that he thereby made the apostles and their successors priests of the New Covenant who would renew the Sacrifice of Calvary in an unbloody manner in the celebration of Holy Mass.

This means that at the centre of Christ's entire activity stands the bloody Sacrifice he offered on the cross—the Sacrifice of the New Covenant, prefigured in the sacrifices of the Old Law, in the offerings made by Abel (Gen 4:4), by Abraham (Gen 15:10; 22:13), by Melchizedek (Gen 14:18–20; Heb 7:1–28). The Last Supper is the very Sacrifice of Calvary performed in advance of the event through the words of the Consecration. Similarly the Mass renews this sacrifice which was offered once for all on the altar of the cross. Christ alone is the victim and the priest at Supper, Calvary and Mass; the only thing that varies is the way he is offered.

"We believe that the Mass which is celebrated by the priest in the person of Christ in virtue of the power he receives in the sacrament of Order, and which is offered by him in the name of Christ and of the members of his Mystical Body, is indeed the Sacrifice of Calvary sacramentally realized on our altars" (Paul VI, *Creed of the People of God*, 24).

22:16. The words "I shall not eat it [this Passover] until it is fulfilled in the kingdom of heaven," as also those in v. 18, "I shall not drink of the fruit of this vine until the kingdom of God comes," do not mean that Jesus Christ will eat the paschal lamb once his Kingdom is established, but simply that this was the last time he will celebrate the Jewish Passover. Announcing the New Passover, which is now imminent and which will last until his second coming, Jesus once and for all replaces the ancient rite with his redemptive sacrifice, which marks the beginning of the Kingdom.

22:17. The Passover meal always followed a very specific pattern. Before eating the lamb, the senior person explained, in reply

and when he had given thanks he said, "Take this, and divide it among yourselves; [18]for I tell you that from now on I shall not drink of the fruit of the vine until the kingdom of God comes." [19]And he took bread, and when he had given thanks he broke it and gave it to them, saying, "This is my body which is given for you. Do this in remembrance of me." [20]And likewise the cup after supper, saying, "This cup which is poured out for you is the new covenant in my blood.[j]

Mt 26:26–29
Mk 14:22–25
1 Cor 11:23–25
Acts 27:35
Ex 12:14
Ex 24:8
Jer 31:31
Zech 9:11

The treachery of Judas foretold

[21]"But behold the hand of him who betrays me is with me on the table. [22]For the Son of man goes as it has been determined; but

Mt 26:21–25
Mk 14:18–21

to a question from the youngest present, the religious meaning of what was happening. Then the meal proceeded, interspersed with hymns and psalms. At the end came a solemn prayer of thanksgiving. Throughout the meal, marking its main stages, the diners drank four glasses of wine mixed with water. St Luke refers to two of these, the second being that which our Lord consecrated.

22:19. We should note how plainly our Lord speaks: he does not say "here is my body," or "this is the symbol of my body," but "this is my body": that is, "this bread is no longer bread, it is my body". "Some men, accordingly, not paying heed to these things, have contended that Christ's body and blood are present in this sacrament only as in a sign: this is to be rejected as heretical, since it is contrary to Christ's words" (St Thomas Aquinas, *Summa theologiae*, 3, 75, 1). Jesus' words when he promised the Eucharist reinforce what he says here: "I am the living bread which came down from heaven; if any one eats of this bread, he will live for ever; and the bread which I shall give for the life of the world

is my flesh [...]. He who eats my flesh and drinks my blood has eternal life, and I will raise him up at the last day" (Jn 6:51, 54).

"Do this in remembrance of me." The solemn Magisterium of the Church teaches us the meaning and scope of these words: "If anyone says that by the words, 'Do this in remembrance of me' Christ did not make his apostles priests, or that he did not decree that they and other priests should offer his body and blood: let him be condemned" (Council of Trent, *De SS. Missae sacrificio*, c. 2).

22:24–30. This was not the first time the apostles brought up this question about which of them was the greatest. It came up when they were going towards Capernaum, after Jesus' second announcement of his passion. At that time Jesus used a child as an example of humility (cf. Mt 18:1–5; Mk 9:33–37; Lk 9:46–48). A little later, when the mother of James and John made her special request, the same subject arose: the other apostles were very annoyed with the sons of Zebedee, and our Lord intervened and put himself forward as an example: "The

j. Some ancient authorities omit *which is given for you. Do this in remembrance of me.* [20]*And likewise the cup after supper, saying, "This cup which is poured out for you is the new covenant in my blood*

woe to that man by whom he is betrayed!" [23]And they began to question one another, which of them it was that would do this.

Jn 13:18–30

A dispute among the apostles

[24]A dispute also arose among them, which of them was to be regarded as the greatest. [25]And he said to them. "The kings of the Gentiles exercise lordship over them; and those in authority over them are called benefactors. [26]But not so with you; rather let the greatest among you become as the youngest, and the leader as one who serves. [27]For which is the greater, one who sits at table, or one who serves? Is it not the one who sits at table? But I am among you as one who serves.

Lk 9:46ff
Mt 20:25–27
Mk 10:42–44

Jn 13:4–14

Son of man also came not to be served but to serve, and to give his life as a ransom for many" (Mk 10:45; cf. Mt 20:25–28).

The apostles failed to grasp what Jesus meant. They continue to be blinded by their human outlook and the same argument starts again. Jesus had invited them to have a greater sense of responsibility by telling them that one of their number was going to betray him (vv. 21 and 22) and by charging them to renew the Eucharistic Sacrifice (v. 19). As on other occasions when the apostles boasted about their personal merits, Jesus reminds them again of the example of his own life: he was their Teacher and Lord (cf. Jn 13:13) and yet he acted as if he were the least among them and served them. To respond to a calling from God a person needs humility, which expresses itself in the form of a spirit of service. "You want to hear all that I think of 'your way'? Very well, then … , listen: if you respond to the call, you will do your utmost in your work for Christ; if you become a man of prayer, you will be granted the grace necessary to respond and, hungry for sacrifice, you will seek out the hardest tasks. … And you will be happy here, and unspeakably happy hereafter" (St J. Escrivá, *The Way*, 235).

The reward which Jesus promises those who stay faithful to him far exceeds anything human ambition can envisage: the apostles will share in divine friendship in the Kingdom of heaven and they will sit on twelve thrones to judge the twelve tribes of Israel. Christ's word and example are a basic norm of government in the Church; the Second Vatican Council explains our Lord's commandment as follows: "The bishops, vicars and legates of Christ, govern the particular Church assigned to them by their counsels, exhortations and example, but over and above that also by the authority and sacred power which indeed they exercise exclusively for the spiritual development of their flock in truth and holiness, keeping in mind that he who is greater should become as the lesser, and he who is the leader as the servant (cf. Lk 22:26–27)" (*Lumen gentium*, 27).

22:25–27. By spreading Jesus' teaching about humility and service to others, we promote the true brotherhood of man. Pope Paul VI pointed this out in his address to the United Nations: "Allow us to say this to you, as the representative of a religion which accomplishes salvation through the humility of its divine Found-

Jn 6:67
Lk 12:32
Mt 19:28

²⁸"You are those who have continued with me in my trials; ²⁹as my Father appointed a kingdom for me, so do I appoint for you ³⁰that you may eat and drink at my table in my kingdom, and sit on thrones judging the twelve tribes of Israel.

Mt 26:31–35
Mk 14:27–31
Jn 13:36–38
2 Cor 2:11
Amon 9:9

Jn 17:11–20

Peter's denial foretold

³¹"Simon, Simon, behold, Satan demanded to have you,ᵏ that he might sift youᵏ like wheat, ³²but I have prayed for you that your faith may not fail; and when you have turned again, strengthen your brethren." ³³And he said to him, "Lord, I am ready to go with you to prison and to death." ³⁴He said, "I tell you, Peter, the cock will not crow this day, until you three times deny that you know me."

---

er: men cannot be brothers if they are not humble. It is pride, no matter how legitimate it may seem to be, which provokes tension and struggles for prestige, for predominance, colonialism, selfishness; it is pride that disrupts brotherhood" (no. 4).

22:31–34. Jesus had previously told Peter that he was going to give him a specially important mission among the apostles—that of being the cornerstone, the foundation, of the Church he would found. " 'So you are Simon the son of John? You shall be called Cephas' (which means Peter)" (Jn 1:42), Jesus told him on the bank of the Jordan. Later, in Caesarea Philippi, after his profession of faith in the divinity of the Redeemer, Christ again referred to him as being a rock, as having a mission to strengthen the Church: "And I tell you, you are Peter, and on this rock I will build my church, and the powers of death shall not prevail against it" (Mt 16:18). Now, at this very solemn moment, when his death approaches and he has just instituted the Sacrifice of the New Testament, our Lord renews his promise to Peter to give him the primacy: Peter's faith, despite his fall, cannot fail because it is supported by the efficacious prayer of our Lord himself.

Jesus is giving Peter a privilege

which is both personal and transferable. Peter will publicly deny his Lord in the high priest's house, but he will not lose his faith. As St John Chrysostom comments, it is as if our Lord were saying to Peter, "I have not prayed that you may not deny me but that your faith may not fail" (*Hom. on St Matthew*, 3). And Theophylact adds: "For, although St Peter would have to experience ups and downs he still had the hidden seed of faith, and he [Christ] adds, 'And when you have turned again, strengthen your brethren', as if to say, 'After you repent; confirm then your brethren, for I have made you the leader of the apostles; this is the task given you: you with me are the strength and the rock of my Church.' This should be taken not only as applying to the disciples who were present there, for them to be strengthened by Peter: it also refers to all the faithful who would follow, until the end of the world" (*Enarratio in Evangelium Lucae*, in loc.).

And, as it turned out, as a result of our Lord's prayer, Peter's faith did not fail and he recovered from his fall; he confirmed his brothers and was indeed the cornerstone of the Church.

Our Lord's prayer was effective in respect not only to Peter but also to his successors: their faith will not fail. This

---

k. The Greek word for *you* here is plural; in verse 32 it is singular

Appeal to the apostles

³⁵And he said to them, "When I sent you out with no purse or bag   Lk 9:3; 10:4
or sandals, did you lack anything?" They said, "Nothing." ³⁶He
said to them, "But now, let him who has a purse take it, and likewise a bag. And let him who has no sword sell his mantle and buy
one. ³⁷For I tell you that this scripture must be fulfilled in me,   Is 53:12
'And he was reckoned with transgressors'; for what is written
about me has its fulfilment." ³⁸And they said, "Look, Lord, here
are two swords." And he said to them, "It is enough."

Jesus' prayer and agony in the garden

³⁹And he came out, and went, as was his custom, to the Mount of   Mt 26:30; 36–46
Olives; and the disciples followed him. ⁴⁰And when he came to   Mk 14:26; 32–42

indefectibility of the faith of the bishop of Rome, the successor of St Peter, is to be seen as ensuring that he stay committed to the faith, a commitment guaranteed by the charism of infallibility: "This infallibility, with which the divine Redeemer wished to endow his Church in defining doctrine pertaining to faith and morals, is co-extensive with the deposit of revelation, which must be religiously guarded and loyally and courageously expounded. The Roman Pontiff, head of the college of bishops, enjoys this infallibility in virtue of his office, when, as supreme pastor and teacher of all the faithful—who confirms his brethren in the faith (cf. Lk 22:32)—he proclaims in an absolute decision a doctrine pertaining to faith or morals" (Vatican II, *Lumen gentium*, 25).

Therefore, when the Pope speaks *ex cathedra* (cf. Vatican I, *Pastor aeternus*, chap. 4) "he enjoys that infallibility with which the divine Redeemer wished to provide his Church ... and therefore the definitions of the Roman Pontiff are irreformable by their very nature" (see also the note on Mt 16:13–20).

"The supreme power of the Roman Pontiff and his infallibility, when he speaks *ex cathedra*, are not a human invention: they are based on the explicit foundational will of Christ [...]. No one in the Church enjoys absolute power by himself, as man. In the Church there is no leader other than but Christ. And Christ constituted a vicar of his—the Roman Pontiff—for his wayfaring spouse on earth [...]. Love for the Pope must be in us a beautiful passion, because in him we see Christ" (St J. Escrivá, *In Love with the Church*, 13).

22:36–38. Jesus announces his passion by applying to himself the Isaiah prophecy about the Servant of Yahweh (Is 53:12)—"he was numbered with the transgressors"—and pointing out that all the other prophecies about the sufferings of the Redeemer will find fulfilment in him. The testing-time is imminent and our Lord is speaking symbolically when he talks about making provision and buying weapons to put up a fight. The apostles take him literally, and this leads him to express a certain indulgent understanding: "It is enough." "Just in the same way as we," Theophylact says, "when we are speaking to someone and see that he does not understand, say: 'Very well, leave it'" (*Enarratio in Evangelium Lucae*, in loc.).

22:39–71. Our Lord's passion is the out-

Lk 21:37
Jn 18:1

Mt 6:10

1 Kings 19:5-7
Jn 12:29

the place he said to them, "Pray that you may not enter into temptation." ⁴¹And he withdrew from them about a stone's throw, and knelt down and prayed, ⁴²"Father, if thou art willing, remove this cup from me; nevertheless not my will, but thine, be done." ⁴³And there appeared to him an angel from heaven, strengthening him.

---

standing proof of God's love for men: "God so loved the world that he gave his only Son, that whoever believes in him should not perish but have eternal life" (Jn 3:16). It also proves beyond doubt that Christ, true God and true man, loves us, as he said himself: "Greater love has no man than this, that a man lay down his life for his friends" (Jn 15:13).

"Do you want to accompany Jesus closely, very closely? ... Open the Holy Gospel and read the Passion of our Lord. But don't just read it: live it. There is a big difference. To read is to recall something that happened in the past; to live is to find oneself present at an event that is happening here and now, to be someone taking part in those scenes. Then, allow your heart to open wide; let it place itself next to our Lord. And when you notice it trying to slip away—when you see that you are a coward, like the others—ask forgiveness for your cowardice and mine" (St Josemaría Escrivá, *The Way of the Cross*, IX, 3).

22:39-40. It was Jesus' custom to retire to the garden of Gethsemane, on the Mount of Olives, in order to pray; this seems to be implied by both St John (Jn 18:1) and St Luke (21:37). This explains how Judas knew the place (Jn 18:1-2).

As soon as he reaches the garden our Lord prepares to face his agony. Before going aside to pray, he asks his disciples to pray as well because very soon they will be tempted to lose faith when they see him being arrested (cf. Mt 26:31). At the Last Supper Jesus had told them this would happen; now he warns them that if

they are not watchful and prayerful they will not be able to resist the temptation. He also wants his apostles to keep him company when he suffers—which is why, when he comes back and finds them sleeping, he sorrowfully complains to Peter: "Could you not watch with me one hour?" (Mt 26:40).

We should stay close to our Lord and keep him company, even at times of difficulty and tribulation; the command Jesus gives here shows us how to go about this—by prayer and vigilance.

22:41. Jesus prays kneeling down. Many Gospel passages refer to our Lord's prayer but this is the only time his posture is described. It may well be that he knelt at other times also. Kneeling is an external expression of a humble attitude towards God.

22:42. Jesus Christ is perfect God and perfect man: as God he is equal to the Father, as man less than the Father. And therefore as man he could pray, he had to pray—as he did throughout his life. Now, when his spiritual suffering is so intense that he is in agony, our Lord addresses his Father with a prayer which shows both his trust and his anguish: he calls him, with immense affection, "Abba", Father, and asks him to remove this cup of bitterness. What causes our Lord his intense pain? Foreknowledge of all the sufferings involved in his passion, which he freely undergoes; and the weight of all the sins of mankind, the unfaithfulness of the chosen people and abandonment by his disciples. Christ's sensitive soul felt

⁴⁴And being in an agony he prayed more earnestly; and his sweat became like great drops of blood falling down upon the ground.[1] ⁴⁵And when he rose from prayer, he came to the disciples and found them sleeping for sorrow, ⁴⁶and he said to them, "Why do you sleep? Rise and pray that you may not enter into temptation."

the full impact of all this. So intense is our Redeemer's anguish that he actually sweats blood, an indication of the extent of his human capacity to suffer.

In this connexion St Thomas More comments: "The fear of death and torments carries no stigma of guilt but rather is an affliction of the sort Christ came to suffer, not to escape. We should not immediately consider it cowardice for someone to feel fear and horror at the thought of torments [...]. But to flee because of a fear of torture and death when the circumstances make it necessary to fight, or to give up all hope of victory and surrender to the enemy—that, to be sure, is a capital crime according to the military code. But otherwise, no matter how much the heart of the soldier is agitated and stricken by fear, if he still comes forward at the command of the general, goes on, fights and defeats the enemy, he has no reason to fear that his former fear might lessen his reward in any way. As a matter of fact, he ought to receive even more praise because of it, since he had to overcome not only the enemy but also his own fear, which is often harder to conquer than the enemy itself" (*De tristitia Christi*, in loc.).

Jesus perseveres in his prayer: "Not my will, but thine, be done"—which shows that he had a human will and that it was in total harmony with the divine will. This prayer of our Lord is also a perfect lesson in abandonment to and union with the Will of God—features which should be found in our own prayer, particularly in moments of diffi-

culty. "Are things going against you? Are you going through a rough time? Say very slowly, as if relishing it, this powerful and manly prayer: 'May the most just and most lovable will of God be done, be fulfilled, be praised and eternally exalted above all things. Amen, Amen.' I assure you that you will find peace" (St Josemaría Escrivá, *The Way*, 691).

22:43. In the Gospel we often see angels play a part in our Lord's life. An angel announces the mystery of the Incarnation to the Blessed Virgin (Lk 1:26); choirs of angels sing God's praises when Jesus is born in Bethlehem (Lk 2:13); angels minister to him after he is tempted in the wilderness (Mt 4:11); and now the Father sends an angel to comfort him in his agony.

Our Lord, who is God, accepts this consolation. The Creator of all, who is never in need of the help of his creatures, is ready to accept, as man, consolation and help from those who can give it.

In addition to aiding Jesus in his work as Redeemer, angels also minister to the Church in a special way. We often see them act in the early days of the Church (cf. Acts 5:19; 7:30; 8:26; 12:7; 27:23; etc.). God has given angels the mission of accompanying men and helping them as they make their way on earth towards their heavenly goal. The angels, says Paul VI, "intercede for us and come to the aid of our weakness in brotherly care" (*Creed of the People of God*, 29). Their caring presence should move us to rely constantly on our guardian angels, to

[1] Other ancient authorities omit verses 43 and 44

Arrest of Jesus

Mt 26:47–56
Mk 14:43–49
Jn 18:2–11
⁴⁷While he was still speaking, there came a crowd, and the man called Judas, one of the twelve, was leading them. He drew near to Jesus to kiss him; ⁴⁸but Jesus said to him, "Judas, would you betray the Son of man with a kiss?" ⁴⁹And when those who were about him saw what would follow, they said, "Lord, shall we strike with the sword?" ⁵⁰And one of them struck the slave of the high priest and cut off his right ear. ⁵¹But Jesus said, "No more of this!" And he touched his ear and healed him. ⁵²Then Jesus said to the chief priests and captains of the temple and elders, who had come out against him,* "Have you come out as against a robber, Jn 7:30; 18:20 with swords and clubs? ⁵³When I was with you day after day in the temple, you did not lay hands on me. But this is your hour, and the power of darkness."

---

have recourse to them in our needs and to show them reverence.

22:47–48. Judas now gives the prearranged sign (cf. Mt 26:48); he comes forward to kiss our Lord—a form of friendly greeting normal among the Jews. When greeting someone like this, one would say *Shalom*, "peace". In contemplating this sad betrayal by an apostle, Jesus treats Judas in a very gentle way and yet shows up the malice and ugliness of his treachery: for the last time he tries to win Judas back.

There is no limit to the goodness of a merciful God, and not even the greatest sinner should despair of obtaining forgiveness. "Even to Judas," St Thomas More comments, "God gave many opportunities of coming to his senses. He did not deny him his companionship. He did not take away from him the dignity of his apostleship. He did not even take the purse-strings from him, even though he was a thief. He admitted the traitor to the fellowship of his beloved disciples at the last supper. He deigned to stoop down at the feet of the betrayer and to wash with his most innocent and sacred hands Judas' dirty feet, a fit symbol of his filthy mind [...]. Finally when Judas, coming with his crew to seize him, offered him a

kiss, a kiss that was in fact the terrible token of his treachery, Christ received him calmly and gently [...]. Therefore, since God showed his great mercy, in so many ways even toward Judas, an apostle turned traitor, since he invited him to forgiveness so often and did not allow him to perish except through despair alone, certainly there is no reason why, in this life, anyone should despair of any imitator of Judas. Rather, according to that holy advice of the apostle, 'Pray for one another, that you may be healed' (Jas 5:16), if we see anyone wandering wildly from the right road, let us hope that he will one day return to the path, and meanwhile let us pray humbly and incessantly that God will hold out to him chances to come to his senses, and likewise that with God's help he will eagerly seize them, and having seized them will hold fast and not throw them away out of malice or let them slip away from him through wretched sloth" (*De tristitia Christi*, in loc.).

22:51. St Luke, who was a physician (cf. Col 4:15), here by divine inspiration records the last miracle worked by Jesus before his death. Ever merciful, Jesus restores to Malchus the ear Peter cut off

Peter's denials

⁵⁴Then they seized him and led him away, bringing him into the high priest's house. Peter followed at a distance; ⁵⁵and when they had kindled a fire in the middle of the courtyard and sat down together, Peter sat among them. ⁵⁶Then a maid, seeing him as he sat in the light and gazing at him, said, "This man also was with him." ⁵⁷But he denied it, saying, "Woman, I do not know him." ⁵⁸And a little later some one else saw him and said, "You also are one of them." But Peter said, "Man, I am not." ⁵⁹And after an interval of about an hour still another insisted, saying, "Certainly this man also was with him; for he is a Galilean." ⁶⁰But Peter said, "Man, I do not know what you are saying." And immediately, while he was still speaking, the cock crowed. ⁶¹And the Lord turned and looked at Peter. And Peter remembered the word

Mt 26:57f; 69–75
Mk 14:53f;
66–72
Jn 18:12–18, 25–27

(cf. Jn 18:10)—thereby showing that he is still in control of events, even in the present situation. Careless of his own safety he cures one of the people who have come to arrest him. Also, Jesus, who is giving himself up to death in obedience to his Father, refuses to have violence used in his defence. In fulfilment of the prophecies he offers no resistance, he goes like a sheep to the slaughter (cf. Is 53:7).

22:52–53. The "captains of the temple" were a military corps charged with policing the temple precincts; they reported to the high priest. To them, as well as to the priests and elders, our Lord addresses these words.

"This is your hour," that is, the time when you, the prince of darkness, can unleash all your hatred against me: our Lord shows that he knows his death is at hand. Previous attempts to arrest him had failed; but this one will succeed, because, as he explains, God allows it to happen. This is the hour the Father has fixed to accomplish the redemption of mankind; therefore, Jesus freely lets himself be taken prisoner.

22:55–62. Peter, who has been following the throng of people hustling our Lord,

enters the house of the high priest. While Jesus is undergoing his first trial the saddest event in the apostle's life takes place. The evangelists give vivid accounts of the scene. Peter is in a state of shock and is all confused. Inevitably, that night, people would have spoken about Jesus and his disciples a number of times. In conversation Peter says three times that he does not know Jesus, that he is not a follower of his. He does want to continue to follow our Lord, but wanting is not enough: he has a duty not to disguise the fact that he is a disciple, even though it is obviously risky to do so; that is why his denial is a grave sin. No one is justified in denying or disguising his faith, the fact that he is a Christian, a follower of Christ.

After the cock crows Jesus' glance meets Peter's. The apostle is moved by this silent and tender gesture. Peter realizes the seriousness of his sin and the fact that it fulfils our Lord's prophecy about his betrayal. "He went out and wept bitterly." Tears like these are the natural reaction of a noble heart moved by God's grace; this lovesorrow, this contrition, when it is sincere, leads a person to make the firm resolution to do anything necessary to erase the least trace of the sin he has committed.

of the Lord, how he had said to him, "Before the cock crows today, you will deny me three times." ⁶²And he went out and wept bitterly.

Jesus abused by the guards

Mt 26:67–68
Mk 14:65

⁶³Now the men who were holding Jesus mocked him and beat him; ⁶⁴they also blindfolded him and asked him, "Prophesy! Who is it that struck you?" ⁶⁵And they spoke many other words against him, reviling him.

Jesus before the chief priests

Mk 26:59–66
Mk 14:55–64

Jn 8:45; 10:24

Dan 7:13
Ps 110:1

⁶⁶When day came, the assembly of the elders of the people gathered together, both chief priests and scribes; and they led him away to their council, and they said, ⁶⁷"If you are the Christ, tell us." But he said to them, "If I tell you, you will not believe; ⁶⁸and if I ask you, you will not answer. ⁶⁹But from now on the Son of

---

22:66–71. Our Lord's first trial, which took place at night, was aimed at establishing the charges to be laid against him (Mt 26:59–66; Mk 14:53–64). Now, as day dawns, the Sanhedrin trial begins: this trial was required because Jewish custom forbade night trials on serious charges—which meant that any decisions taken at such trials had no legal validity. The authorities want to charge Jesus with a crime carrying the death penalty, and they decide to establish that he has committed blasphemy; but the evidence is so inconsistent that it fails to provide a pretext for condemning him. Therefore the Sanhedrin endeavours to get our Lord to say something which will compromise him. Although he knows that his reply provides the Pharisees with the pretext they are looking for, Jesus solemnly states, to the indignation of those present, not only that he is the Messiah but that he is the Son of God, equal to the Father; and he emphasizes that in him the ancient prophecies are being fulfilled (cf. Dan 7:13; Ps 110:1). The members of the Sanhedrin know exactly what our Lord's

answer means and, tearing their garments to show their horror, they call for his death: he deserves death because he has committed the blasphemy of claiming to be on the same level as God.

Recognizing Jesus would involve their doing an about-turn in their attitude towards him—which they would have found very embarrassing. They are too proud to change, and they close the door on faith—a lesson to us all not to let pride blind us to our mistakes and sins.

23:1–2. Jesus underwent two trials—a religious one, following the Jewish system, and a civil one, following the Roman.

In the first trial, the Jewish authorities condemned Jesus to death on religious grounds for claiming to be the Son of God; but they could not carry out the sentence because the Romans reserved to themselves the exercise of the death penalty. The Sanhedrin now arranges a new trial before Pilate in order to get the Romans to execute the sentence they themselves have already passed. Events are moving to fulfil Jesus' prophecy that

man shall be seated at the right hand of the power of God." [70]And they all said, "Are you the Son of God, then?" And he said to them, "You say that I am." [71]And they said, "What further testimony do we need? We have heard it ourselves from his own lips."

Jesus before Pilate

23 [1]Then the whole company of them arose, and brought him before Pilate. [2]And they began to accuse him, saying, "We found this man perverting our nation, and forbidding us to give tribute to Caesar, and saying that he himself is Christ a king."* [3]And Pilate asked him, "Are you the King of the Jews?" And he answered him, "You have said so." [4]And Pilate said to the chief priests and the multitudes, "I find no crime in this man." [5]But they were urgent, saying, "He stirs up the people, teaching throughout all Judea, from Galilee even to this place."

Mt 27:2, 11–31
Mk 15:1–20
Jn 18:28–19:6
Lk 20:25

1 Tim 6:13

he will die at the hands of the Gentiles (cf. Lk 18:32).

Due to the fact that the Romans were very tolerant of religious customs of subject peoples—and took no interest in them provided they did not lead to public unrest—the Jewish leaders alter the charges they bring against Jesus: from now on they accuse him of political crimes—of inciting rebellion against the Romans and of seeking to become king. And they present these charges in such a way that a verdict favourable to the accused might be interpreted in Rome as a treacherous act: "If you release this man, you are not Caesar's friend; every one who makes himself a king sets himself against Caesar" (Jn 19:12).

23:2. To give their charges a veneer of credibility, they produce half-truths, taken out of context and interpreted in the worst possible light. Jesus had taught: "Render therefore to Caesar the things that are Caesar's, and to God the things that are God's" (Mt 22:21; cf. the note on same), and in his preaching he stated that by virtue of being the Messiah he was King as well as Prophet and Priest; but he also preached that his was a spiritual kingship and therefore he energetically rejected all the people's attempts to proclaim him king (cf. Jn 6:15).

23:3–4. Jesus openly confesses that he is King, but from what he says he makes quite clear the spiritual nature of this kingship (Jn 18:33–38). Pilate becomes convinced that he is guilty of no crime (Jn 18:38; 19:4) and that all the charges brought against him are groundless (Mt 27:18). However, instead of efficiently delivering judgment in favour of the accused, he temporizes; he tries to gain popularity at Jesus' expense and settles for indicating that he is convinced of his innocence—as if inviting the accusers to back off; but this only encourages them to become vociferous and complicates the situation.

By behaving in this way Pilate becomes the classic example of a compromiser: "A man, a 'gentleman', ready to compromise would condemn Jesus to death again" (St Josemaría Escrivá, *The Way*, 393).

187

Jesus before Herod

Lk 3:1   ⁶When Pilate heard this, he asked whether the man was a Galilean. ⁷And when he learned that he belonged to Herod's jurisdiction, he sent him over to Herod, who was himself in Jerusalem

Lk 9:9   at that time. ⁸When Herod saw Jesus, he was very glad, for he had long desired to see him, because he had heard about him, and he was hoping to see some sign done by him. ⁹So he questioned him

Acts 25:7   at some length; but he made no answer. ¹⁰The chief priests and the scribes stood by, vehemently accusing him. ¹¹And Herod with his soldiers treated him with contempt and mocked him; then, arraying him in gorgeous apparel, he sent him back to Pilate. ¹²And

Acts 4:27   Herod and Pilate became friends with each other that very day, for before this they had been at enmity with each other.

Jesus is condemned to death

¹³Pilate then called together the chief priests and the rulers and the

Acts 28:18-19   people, ¹⁴and said to them, "You brought me this man as one who was perverting the people; and after examining him before you, behold, I did not find this man guilty of any of your charges

---

23:7. Herod Antipas normally went up to Jerusalem for the Passover, staying in his own palace in the centre of the city. By sending Jesus to Herod Pilate is trying to rid himself of a troublesome case and build up a friendship useful to his own political career.

23:8–11. Our Lord adopts a very different attitude to Herod Antipas compared with his attitude to Pilate. Herod was superstitious, sensual and adulterous. In spite of his regard for John the Baptist, he had him beheaded to keep his oath to Salome (cf. Mk 6:14–29). Now he tries to get Jesus to perform a miracle, as if Jesus were a magician putting on a show for Herod's entertainment. Jesus does not reply to his flattery. Our Lord's attitude is simple, stately and also severe. His eloquent silence is a perfect example of the way to deal with behaviour of this type. Herod reacts by dressing Jesus in a rich robe, to make fun of him.

23:12. Psalm 2 said this in prophecy of the Messiah: "The kings of the earth set themselves, and the rulers take counsel together, against the Lord and his anointed." These words are now fulfilled to the letter, as the Book of the Acts points out: "For truly in this city there were gathered together against thy holy servant Jesus, whom thou didst anoint, both Herod and Pontius Pilate, with the Gentiles and the people of Israel, to do whatever thy hand and thy plan had predestined to take place" (Acts 4:27f).

23:17. Verse 17—"Necesse autem habebat dimittere eis per diem festum, unum" (in the Old Vulgate)—has not been included in the New Vulgate because it is absent from most of the better Greek manuscripts.

23:24–25. Jesus condemned to death and made to carry the cross (cf. Jn 19:16–17) is devoutly contemplated by Christians in the first and second stations

against him;* [15]neither did Herod, for he sent him back to us.
Behold, nothing deserving death has been done by him; [16]I will
therefore chastise him and release him."[m]

[18]But they all cried out together, "Away with this man, and
release to us Barabbas"—[19]a man who had been thrown into
prison for an insurrection started in the city, and for murder.
[20]Pilate addressed them once more, desiring to release Jesus; [21]but
they shouted out, "Crucify, crucify him!" [22]A third time he said to
them, "Why, what evil has he done? I have found in him no crime
deserving death; I will therefore chastise him and release him."
[23]But they were urgent, demanding with loud cries that he should
be crucified. And their voices prevailed. [24]So Pilate gave sentence
that their demand should be granted. [25]He released the man who Mt 17:12
had been thrown into prison for insurrection and murder, whom
they asked for; but Jesus he delivered up to their will.

The crucifixion and death of Jesus

[26]And as they led him away, they seized one Simon of Cyrene, Mt 27:32
who was coming in from the country, and laid on him the cross, Mk 15:21

---

of the Way of the Cross. Pilate at last gives in to the Sanhedrin and condemns our Lord to the most ignominous form of punishment, death by crucifixion.

It was customary for people condemned to crucifixion to be made to carry the instrument of their own death. Our Lord fulfils in his own person the prophecies of Isaiah: "By oppression and judgment he was taken away; [...] he was cut off out of the land of the living, stricken for the transgression of my people? And they made his grave with the wicked" (Is 53:8–9).

23:26. Christian piety contemplates this episode of the Passion in the fifth station of the Way of the Cross. The soldiers force Simon to help Jesus carry the cross, not because they feel pity for our Lord, but because they realize that he is getting weaker and weaker and they are afraid he may die before reaching Calvary. According to tradition, preserved in the third, seventh and ninth stations, Jesus fell three times under the weight of the cross; but he got up again and lovingly embraced it once more in obedience to his heavenly Father's will, seeing in the cross the altar on which he would give his life as a propitiatory Victim for the salvation of mankind.

However, our Lord chose to be helped by Simon of Cyrene in order to show us that we—whom Simon represents—have to become co-redeemers with him. "Love for God invites us to take up the cross and feel on our own shoulders the weight of humanity. It leads us to fulfill the clear and loving plans of the Father's will in all the circumstances of our work and life" (St Josemaría Escrivá, *Christ Is Passing By*, 97). God the Father, in his providence,

m. Here, or after verse 19, other ancient authorities add verse 17, *Now he was obliged to release one man to them at the festival*

Rev 1:7

Lk 11:27; 21:23

to carry it behind Jesus. [27]And there followed him a great multitude of the people, and of women who bewailed and lamented him. [28]But Jesus turning to them said, "Daughters of Jerusalem, do not weep for me, but weep for yourselves and for your children. [29]For behold, the days are coming when they will say, 'Blessed are the barren, and the wombs that never bore, and the

---

gave his Son this small consolation in the midst of his terrible suffering—just as he sent an angel to comfort him in his agony in Gethsemane (Lk 22:43).

Other aspects of this scene of the Gospel are commented on in notes on Mt 27:32 and Mk 15:21.

23:27–31. The piety of these women shows that Jesus had friends as well as enemies. If we bear in mind that Jewish traditions, as recorded in the Talmud, forbade wailing for people condemned to death, we will appreciate the value of these women's gesture.

"Among the people watching our Lord as he passes by are a number of women who are unable to restrain their compassion and break into tears, perhaps recalling those glorious days spent with Jesus, when everyone exclaimed in amazement: *bene omnia fecit* (Mk 7:37), he has done all things well.

"But our Lord wishes to channel their weeping towards a more supernatural motive, and he invites them to weep for sins, which are the cause of the Passion and which will draw down the rigour of divine justice: 'Daughters of Jerusalem, do not weep for me, but weep for yourselves and for your children. ... For if they do this when the wood is green, what will happen when it is dry?' (Lk 23:28, 31).

"Your sins, my sins, the sins of all men, rise up. All the evil we have done and the good that we have neglected to do. The desolate panorama of the countless crimes and iniquities which we

would have committed, if he, Jesus, had not strengthened us with the light of his most loving glance. How little a life is for making atonement!" (St Josemaría Escrivá, *The Way of the Cross*, VIII).

Christian devotion also includes in the Way of the Cross a pious tradition that a woman, called Veronica (Berenice), approached Jesus and wiped his face with a linen cloth—a brave action on her part, in view of the hostility of the crowd (*sixth station*). And another station, the *fourth*, venerates Jesus' meeting with his blessed Mother on the way to Calvary, a sorrowful meeting which fulfils Simeon's prophecy to the Blessed Virgin (cf. Lk 2:35).

On the way to Calvary the only people who give Jesus consolation are women—evidencing their bravery and religious sensitivity during this painful time in Jesus' life; whereas only one man—John—is to be seen.

In spite of his awful suffering, Jesus is mindful of the terrible times which are approaching. His words in response to the women's lament are a prophecy about the destruction of Jerusalem, which will come about within a few years.

The "green wood" refers to the just and innocent; the "dry wood", to the sinner, the guilty one. Jesus, the Son of God, is the only truly just and innocent man.

23:33. The crucifixion is contemplated in the eleventh station of the Way of the Cross. The soldiers nail Jesus' hands and feet to the beams. The purpose of this

breasts that never gave suck!' ³⁰Then they will begin to say to the mountains, 'Fall on us'; and to the hills, 'Cover us.' ³¹For if they do this when the wood is green, what will happen when it is dry?"* ³²Two others also, who were criminals, were led away to be put to death with him. ³³And when they came to the place which is called The Skull, there they crucified him, and the criminals,

Hos 10:8
Rev 6:16; 9:6

1 Pet 4:17f

Mt 27:33–56
Mk 15:22–41
Jn 19:17–30

---

punishment is to bring on a slow death, involving maximum suffering: "Now they are crucifying our Lord, and with him two thieves, one on his right and one on his left. Meanwhile, Jesus says: 'Father, forgive them; for they know not what they do' (Lk 23:34).

"It is Love that has brought Jesus to Calvary. And once on the Cross, all his gestures and all his words are of love, a love both calm and strong. With a gesture befitting an Eternal Priest, without father or mother, without lineage (cf. Heb 7:3), he opens his arms to the whole human race.

"With the hammerblows with which Jesus is being nailed, there resound the prophetic words of Holy Scripture: 'They have pierced my hands and my feet. I can count all my bones, and they stare and gloat over me' (Ps 22:17–18). 'My people, what have I done to you? In what have I wearied you? Answer me!' (Mic 6:3).

"And we, our soul rent with sorrow, say to Jesus in all sincerity: I am yours and I give my whole self to you; gladly do I nail myself to your Cross, ready to be in the crossroads of this world a soul dedicated to you, to your glory, to the work of Redemption, the co-redemption of the whole human race" (St Josemaría Escrivá, *The Way of the Cross*, XI).

"It is good for us to try to understand better the meaning of Christ's death. We must get beyond external appearances and clichés. [...] Let us, above all, come close to Jesus in his death and to his cross which stands out in silhouette

above the summit of Golgotha. But we must approach him sincerely and with the interior recollection that is a sign of Christian maturity. The divine and human events of the Passion will then pierce our soul as words spoken to us by God to uncover the secrets of our heart and show us what he expects of our lives" (St Josemaría Escrivá, *Christ Is Passing By*, 101).

Jesus' terrible suffering on the cross clearly shows the gravity of the sins of men, of my sin. This gravity is measured by the infinite greatness and honour of God, the offended one. God, who is infinitely merciful and at the same time infinitely just, exercised both these attributes: his infinite justice required an infinite reparation, of which mere man was incapable; his infinite mercy found the solution: the second person of the Trinity, taking on human nature, becoming truly man while not ceasing to be true God, suffered the punishment which was man's due. In this way, by being represented in Jesus' sacred humanity, men would be able to make sufficient atonement to God's justice. No words can express God's love for us as manifested on the cross. A living faith in the mystery of our redemption will lead us to respond with gratitude and love: "We believe that our Lord Jesus Christ redeemed us by the sacrifice on the Cross from original sin and from all those personal sins to which we confess, so that the truth of the apostle's words is vindicated that where sin increased, grace abounded all the more" (Paul VI, *Creed of the People of God*, 17).

Mt 5:44
Is 53:12
Ps 22:18

Ps 22:7

Ps 69:21

one on the right and one on the left. ³⁴And Jesus said, "Father, forgive them; for they know not what they do." ⁿ And they cast lots
to divide his garments. ³⁵And the people stood by, watching; but
the rulers scoffed at him, saying, "He saved others; let him save
himself, if he is the Christ of God, his Chosen One!" ³⁶The soldiers also mocked him, coming up and offering him vinegar, ³⁷and
saying, "If you are the King of the Jews, save yourself!" ³⁸There
was also an inscription over him,° "This is the King of the Jews."

23:34. Jesus addresses the Father in a
tone of supplication (cf. Heb 5:7). We
can distinguish two parts in his
prayer—his simple request: "Father,
forgive them," and the excuse he offers,
"for they know not what they do." We
can see him as one who practises what
he preaches (cf. Acts 1:1) and as a
model whom we should imitate. He had
taught us that we have a duty to forgive
offences (cf. Mt 6:12–15; 18:21–35),
and even to love our enemies (cf. Mt
5:44–45; Rom 12:14, 20), because he
had come into the world to offer himself as a victim "for the forgiveness of
sins" (Mt 26:28; cf. Eph 1:7) and to
enable us to obtain pardon.

The excuse which Jesus offers may at
first take us by surprise: "for they know
not what they do." His love, his perfect
mercy and justice make maximum
allowance for factors rendering our sins
less heinous. It is quite clear that the
people directly responsible were perfectly aware that they were condemning
an innocent person to death, that they
were guilty of homicide; but they did not
realize, in these moments of passion, that
they were also committing deicide. This
is what St Peter means when he tells the
Jews, encouraging them to repent, that
they acted "in ignorance" (Acts 3:17),
and St Paul adds that if they had understood the hidden wisdom of God "they

would not have crucified the Lord of
glory" (1 Cor 2:8). Jesus in his mercy
excuses them on the grounds of ignorance.

In any sinful action there are always
areas of darkness, passion, blindness,
which without taking away a person's
freedom and responsibility do enable him
to carry out an evil action through being
attracted by apparently good aspects
which that action involves; and this does
lessen the evil that we do.

Christ teaches us to forgive those
who offend us and to look for excuses for
them, thereby leaving open the door to
the hope of their pardon and repentance;
only God can be the ultimate judge of
men. This heroic charity was practised by
Christians from the very beginning.
Thus, the first martyr, St Stephen, dies
begging God to pardon his executioners
(cf. Acts 7:60). "Force yourself, if necessary, always to forgive those who offend
you, from the very first moment. For the
greatest injury or offence that you can
suffer from them is as nothing compared
with what God has pardoned you" (St
Josemaría Escrivá, *The Way*, 452).

23:35–37. The Roman governor's soldiers join the Jewish people and their
leaders in mocking Jesus; thus, everyone—Jews and Gentiles—contributed to
making Christ's passion even more bitter.

---

n. Other ancient authorities omit the sentence *And Jesus ... what they do* **o.** Other ancient authorities
add *in letters of Greek and Latin and Hebrew*

³⁹One of the criminals who were hanged railed at him, saying, "Are you not the Christ? Save yourself and us!" ⁴⁰But the other rebuked him, saying, "Do you not fear God, since you are under the same sentence of condemnation? ⁴¹And we indeed justly; for we are receiving the due reward of our deeds; but this man has done nothing wrong." ⁴²And he said, "Jesus, remember me when you come in your kingly power."ᵖ ⁴³And he said to him, "Truly, I say to you, today you will be with me in Paradise."

Mt 16:28

But we should not forget that we too make a mockery of our Lord every time we fall into sin or fail to respond sufficiently to grace. This is why St Paul says that those who sin "crucify the Son of God on their own account and hold him up to contempt" (Heb 6:6).

23:39–43. The episode of the two thieves invites us to admire the designs of divine providence, of grace and human freedom. Both thieves are in the same position—in the presence of the Eternal High Priest as he offers himself in sacrifice for them and for all mankind. One of them hardens his heart, despairs and blasphemes, while the other repents, prays with confidence to Christ and is promised immediate salvation. "The Lord," St Ambrose comments, "always grants more than one asks: the thief only asked him to remember him, but the Lord says to him, 'Truly, I say to you, today you will be with me in Paradise.' Life consists in dwelling with Jesus Christ, and where Jesus Christ is there is his Kingdom" (*Expositio Evangelii sec. Lucam*, in loc.). "It is one thing for man to judge someone he does not know; another, for God, who can see into a person's conscience. Among men, confession is followed by punishment; whereas confession to God is followed by salvation" (St John Chrysostom, *De Cruce et latrone*).

While we make our way through life, we all sin, but we can all repent also. God is always waiting for us with his arms wide open, ready to forgive us. Therefore, no one should despair: everyone should try to have a strong hope in God's mercy. But no one may presume that he will be saved, for none of us can be absolutely certain of our final perseverance (cf. Council of Trent, *De Iustificatione*, can. 16). This relative uncertainty is a spur God gives us to be ever vigilant; this vigilance in turn helps us progress in the work of our sanctification as Christians.

23:42. "Many times have I repeated that verse of the Eucharistic hymn: *Peto quod petivit latro poenitens*, and it always fills me with emotion: to ask like the penitent thief did! He recognized that he himself deserved that awful punishment.... And with a word he stole Christ's heart and 'opened up for himself' the gates of heaven" (St Josemaría Escrivá, *The Way of the Cross*, XII, 4).

23:43. In responding to the good thief, Jesus reveals that he is God, for he has power over man's eternal destiny; and he also shows that he is infinitely merciful and does not reject the soul who sincerely repents. Similarly by these words Jesus reveals to us a basic truth of faith: "We believe in eternal life. We believe

p. Greek *kingdom*

Amos 8:9
Ex 36:35
Ps 31:5
Acts 7:59

Lk 7:16

[44]It was now about the sixth hour, and there was darkness over the whole land[q] until the ninth hour, [45]while the sun's light failed;[r] and the curtain of the temple was torn in two. [46]Then Jesus, crying with a loud voice, said, "Father, into thy hands I commit my spirit!" And having said this he breathed his last. [47]Now when the centurion saw what had taken place, he praised God, and said, "Certainly this man was innocent!" [48]And all the multitudes who

that the souls of all those who die in the grace of Christ—whether they must still make expiation in the fire of purgatory, or whether from the moment they leave their bodies they are received by Jesus Christ into Paradise like the good thief— go to form that People of God which succeeds death, death which will be totally destroyed on the day of the Resurrection when these souls are reunited with their bodies" (Paul VI, *Creed of the People of God*, 28).

23:45. The darkening of the sun is a sign of the magnitude and gravity of the Lord's death (cf. the note on Mk 15:33). The tearing of the curtain of the temple shows the end of the Old Covenant and the beginning of the New Covenant, sealed in the blood of Christ (cf. the note on Mk 15:38).

23:46. The Way of the Cross contemplates Jesus' death as the twelfth station. Christ's life is totally influenced by the fact that he is the only Son of the Father: "I came from the Father and have come into the world; again, I am leaving the world and going to the Father" (Jn 16:28). All along, his only desire was to do the will of him who sent him (cf. Jn 4:34), who, as Christ himself says, "is with me; he has not left me alone, for I always do what is pleasing to him" (Jn 8:29).

At this, the climax of his life on earth, when he is apparently left totally on his own, Christ makes an act of supreme confidence, throws himself into his Father's arms, and freely gives up his life. He was not forced to die nor did he die against his will; he died because he wanted to die. "It was the peculiar privilege of Christ the Lord to have died when he himself decreed to die, and to have died not so much by external violence as by internal assent. Not only his death, but also its time and place, were ordained by him. For thus Isaiah wrote: 'He was offered because it was his own will' (Is 53:7). The Lord, before his Passion, declared the same of himself, 'I lay down my life, that I may take it again. No one takes it from me, but I lay it down of my own accord. I have power to lay it down, and I have power to take it again' (Jn 10:17f)" (St Pius V, *Catechism*, 1, 6, 7).

"We know", says St Paul, "that our old self was crucified with him so that the sinful body might be destroyed, and we might no longer be enslaved to sin.— The death he died he died to sin, once for all. ... So you also must consider yourselves dead to sin and alive to God in Christ Jesus" (Rom 6:6, 10f). Therefore, Vatican II explains, "This work of redeeming mankind [...] Christ the Lord achieved principally by the paschal mystery of his blessed Passion, Resurrection from the dead, and glorious Ascension, whereby 'dying, he destroyed our death, and rising, he restored our life.' For it was

q. Or *earth*   r. Or *the sun was eclipsed*. Other ancient authorities read the *sun was darkened*

assembled to see the sight, when they saw what had taken place, returned home beating their breasts. [49]And all his acquaintances and the women who had followed him from Galilee stood at a distance and saw these things.

Ps 88:8; 37:12
Lk 8:2–3

The burial

[50]Now there was a man named Joseph from the Jewish town of Arimathea. He was a member of the council, a good and righteous

Mt 27:57–61
Mk 15:42–47
Jn 19:38–42
Lk 2:25, 38

from the side of Christ as he slept the sleep of death upon the Cross that there came forth 'the wondrous sacrament of the whole Church' " (*Sacrosanctum Concilium*, 5).

23:47. The three Synoptic Gospels all report the profound reaction of the centurion, the reaction of an upright man who, helped by grace, studies these events with an openness to the mystery of the supernatural. The parallel accounts in Matthew 27:54 and Mark 15:39 show more clearly that the centurion recognized the divinity of Jesus Christ. See the note on Mk 15:39.

23:48. Jesus' redemptive death on the cross immediately begins to draw people towards God by way of repentance: as he made his way to Calvary there was the probable conversion of Simon of Cyrene and the lamentations of the women of Jerusalem; at the cross, the repentance of the good thief, the effect of grace on the Roman centurion, and the compunction felt by the crowd reported in this verse. Jesus had prophesied, "When I am lifted up from the earth, I will draw all men to myself" (Jn 12:32). This prophecy begins to come true on Golgotha, and it will continue to be fulfilled until the end of time.

"On the Cross hangs our Lord's—now lifeless—body. The people, 'when they saw what had taken place, returned home beating their breasts' (Lk 23:48).

"Now that you have repented, promise Jesus that, with his help, you will not crucify him again. Say it with faith. Repeat, over and over again: I will love you, my God, because ever since you were born, ever since you were a child, you abandoned yourself in my arms, defenceless, trusting in my loyalty" (St Josemaría Escrivá, *The Way of the Cross*, XII, 5).

23:49. We should note here the presence of a number of women, some of whose names have been recorded by St Matthew (27:56) and St Mark (15:40–41)—Mary Magdalene, Mary the mother of James and Joseph, and Salome. The soldiers would not have allowed them to approach the cross while Jesus was alive; but the women would have waited, watching from a distance, and then come up close to it, and unashamedly stood there (cf. Jn 19:25), impelled by their deep love for Jesus. "Woman is stronger than man, and more faithful, in the hour of trial: Mary of Magdala and Mary Cleophas and Salome! With a group of valiant women like these, closely united to our Lady of Sorrows, what work for souls could be done in the world!" (St Josemaría Escrivá, *The Way*, 982).

23:50–54. St John's Gospel tells us that "Nicodemus also, who had at first come to him by night, came bringing a mixture of myrrh and aloes, about a hundred pounds' weight" (Jn 19:39). "Joseph of

man, [51]who had not consented to their purpose and deed, and he was looking for the kingdom of God. [52]This man went to Pilate and asked for the body of Jesus. [53]Then he took it down and wrapped it in a linen shroud, and laid him in a rock-hewn tomb, where no one had ever yet been laid. [54]It was the day of Preparation, and the sabbath was beginning.[s] [55]The women who had come with him from Galilee followed, and saw the tomb, and how his body was laid; [56]then they returned, and prepared spices and ointments.

Ex 12:16;
20:10
Lev 23:8

On the sabbath they rested according to the commandment.

Arimathea and Nicodemus visit Jesus secretly in ordinary times and in the time of triumph. But they are courageous in the face of authority, declaring their love for Christ *audacter*—boldly—in the time of cowardice. Learn from them" (*The Way*, 841).

"With them I too will go up to the foot of the Cross; I will press my arms tightly round the cold Body, the corpse of Christ, with the fire of my love ...; I will unnail it, with my reparation and mortifications ...; I will wrap it in the new winding-sheet of my clean life, and I will bury it in the living rock of my breast, where no one can tear it away from me, and there, Lord, take your rest!

"Were the whole world to abandon you and to scorn you ..., *serviam!*, I will serve you, Lord" (St Josemaría Escrivá, *The Way of the Cross*, XIV, 1).

Joseph of Arimathea's and Nicodemus' love for our Lord leads them to ignore the dangers—the hatred of their colleagues in the Sanhedrin, possible reprisals from fanatics. They show the body of Jesus utmost reverence, doing everything required for its pious burial and thereby giving an example to every disciple of Christ who should be ready to risk honour, position and wealth for love for his Lord. In the thirteenth and fourteenth stations of the Cross Christian

piety contemplates the descent from the cross, and the noble actions of these two men, whose respect God chose to reward by inscribing their names in the Gospel text (cf. the note on Mt 15:43–46).

23:55–56. These holy women—who were familiar with the material poverty of our Lord when he was born in Bethlehem, and in the course of his public ministry and on the cross—do not skimp in showing veneration for the body of the Lord. When the Christian people generously endow eucharistic worship they are simply showing that they have learned well the lesson taught by these first disciples.

24:1–4. The affection which led the holy women to make the necessary preparations for the embalming of Jesus' body was, perhaps, an intuition of faith which the Church would express more elaborately much later on: "We firmly believe that when his soul was dissociated from his body, his divinity continued always united both to his body in the sepulchre and to his soul in limbo" (St Pius V, *Catechism*, 1, 5, 6).

24:5–8. True faith concerning the resurrection of Jesus teaches that he truly died, that is, his soul was separated from his

s. Greek *was dawning*

The resurrection of Jesus. The empty tomb

24 ¹But on the first day of the week, at early dawn, they went to the tomb, taking the spices which they had prepared. ²And they found the stone rolled away from the tomb, ³but when they went in they did not find the body.ᵗ ⁴While they were perplexed about this, behold, two men stood by them in dazzling apparel; ⁵and as they were frightened and bowed their faces to the ground, the men said to them, "Why do you seek the living among the dead? He is not here, but has risen.ᵘ ⁶Remember how he told you, while he was still in Galilee, ⁷that the Son of man

Mt 28:1–8
Mk 16:1–8
Jn 20:1–13

Rom 1:4

Acts 1:10

Rev 1:18

body, and his body was in the grave for three days; and that then by his own power his body and soul were united once more, never again to be separated (cf. St Pius V, *Catechism*, 1, 6, 7).

Although this is a strictly supernatural mystery there are some elements in it which come within the category of sense experience—death, burial, the empty tomb, appearances, etc.—and in this sense it is a demonstrable fact and one which has been verified (cf. St Pius X, *Lamentabili*, 36–37).

Jesus Christ's resurrection completes the work of Redemption. "For just as by dying he endured all evil to deliver us from evil, so was he glorified in rising again to advance us towards good things, according to Romans 4:25 which says that 'he was put to death for our trespasses and raised for our justification'" (St Thomas Aquinas, *Summa theologiae*, 3, 53, 1, c.).

"'Christ is alive.' This is the great truth which fills our faith with meaning. Jesus, who died on the cross, has risen. He has triumphed over death; he has overcome sorrow, anguish and the power of darkness. 'Do not be amazed' was how the angels greeted the women who came to the tomb. 'Do not be amazed. You seek Jesus of Nazareth, who was crucified. He has risen; he is

not here' (Mk 16:6). 'This is the day which the Lord has made; let us rejoice and be glad in it' (Ps 118:24).

"Easter is a time of joy—a joy not confined to this period of the liturgical year, for it should always be present in the Christian's heart. For Christ is alive. He is not someone who has gone, someone who existed for a time and then passed on, leaving us a wonderful example and a great memory.

"No, Christ is alive, Jesus is the Emmanuel: God with us. His resurrection shows us that God does not abandon his own. He promised he would not: 'Can a woman forget her sucking child, that she should have no compassion on the son of her womb? Even these may forget, yet I will not forget you' (Is 49:15). And he has kept his promise. His delight is still to be with the children of men (cf. Prov 8:31)" (St Josemaría Escrivá, *Christ Is Passing By*, 102).

Through Baptism and the other sacraments, a Christian becomes part of the redemptive mystery of Christ, part of his death and resurrection: "You were buried with him in baptism, in which you were also raised with him through faith in the working of God, who raised him from the dead" (Col 2:12). "If then you have been raised with Christ, seek the things that are above, where Christ is, seated at

t. Other ancient authorities add *of the Lord Jesus* u. Other ancient authorities omit *He is not here, but has risen*

Lk 8:2–3

must be delivered into the hands of sinful men, and be crucified, and on the third day rise." [8]And they remembered his words, [9]and returning from the tomb they told all this to the eleven and to all the rest. [10]Now it was Mary Magdalene and Joanna and Mary the mother of James and the other women with them who told this to the apostles; [11]but these words seemed to them an idle tale, and they did not believe them. [12]But Peter rose and ran to the tomb; stooping and looking in, he saw the linen cloths by themselves; and he went home wondering at what had happened.[v]

The road to Emmaus

Mk 16:12–13

[13]That very day two of them were going to a village named Emmaus, about seven miles[w] from Jerusalem, [14]and talking with

---

the right hand of God. Set your minds on things that are above, not on things that are on earth. For you have died, and your life is hid with Christ in God" (Col 3:1–3).

24:9–12. The first people to whom the angel announced the birth of Christ were the shepherds at Bethlehem; and the first to be told of his resurrection are these devout women: one further sign of God's preference for simple and sincere souls is the fact that he gives them this honour which the world would not appreciate (cf. Mt 11:25). But it is not only their simplicity and kindness and sincerity that attracts him: poor people (such as shepherds) and women were looked down on in those times, and Jesus loves anyone who is humbled by the pride of men. The women's very simplicity and goodness lead them to go immediately to Peter and the apostles to tell them everything they have seen and heard. Peter, whom Christ promised to make his vicar on earth (cf. Mt 16:18), feels he must take the initiative in checking out their story.

24:13–35. In the course of their conver-

sation with Jesus, the disciples' mood changes from sadness to joy; they begin to hope again, and feel the need to share their joy with others, thus becoming heralds and witnesses of the risen Christ.

This is an episode exclusive to St Luke, who describes it in a masterly way. It shows our Lord's zeal for souls. "As he is walking along, Christ meets two men who have nearly lost all hope. They are beginning to feel that life has no meaning for them. Christ understands their sorrow; he sees into their heart and communicates to them some of the life he carries within himself. When they draw near the village, he makes as if he is going on, but the two disciples stop him and practically force him to stay with them. They recognize him later when he breaks the bread. The Lord, they exclaimed, has been with us! 'And they said to each other: "Did not our hearts burn within us while he talked to us on the road, while he opened to us the scriptures?"' (Lk 24:32). Every Christian should make Christ present among men. He ought to act in such a way that those who know him sense 'the aroma of Christ' (cf. 2 Cor 2:15). Men should be

---

v. Other ancient authorities omit verse 12   **w.** Greek *sixty stadia*; other ancient authorities read *a hundred and sixty stadia*

198

each other about all these things that had happened. ¹⁵While they were talking and discussing together, Jesus himself drew near and went with them. ¹⁶But their eyes were kept from recognizing him. ¹⁷And he said to them, "What is this conversation which you are holding with each other as you walk?" And they stood still, looking sad. ¹⁸Then one of them, named Cleopas, answered him, "Are you the only visitor to Jerusalem who does not know the things that have happened there in these days?" ¹⁹And he said to them, "What things?" And they said to him, "Concerning Jesus of Nazareth, who was a prophet mighty in deed and word before God and all the people, ²⁰and how our chief priests and rulers delivered him up to be condemned to death, and crucified him. ²¹But we had hoped that he was the one to redeem Israel. Yes, and besides all

Mt 18:20

Lk 24:31

Mt 21:11
Acts 2:22

Lk 1:68; 2:38;
19:11
Acts 1:6

---

able to recognize the Master in his disciples" (St Josemaría Escrivá, *Christ Is Passing By*, 105).

24:13–27. Jesus' conversation with the two disciples on the road to Emmaus gives us a very good idea of the disillusionment felt by his disciples after his apparent total failure. Cleopas' words summarize Christ's life and mission (v. 19), his passion and death (v. 20), the despair felt by his disciples (v. 21), and the events of that Sunday morning (v. 22).

Earlier, Jesus had said to the Jews: "You search the scriptures, because you think that in them you have eternal life; and it is they that bear witness to me" (Jn 5:39). In saying this he indicated the best way for us to get to know him. Pope Paul VI points out that today also frequent reading of and devotion to Holy Scripture is a clear inspiration of the Holy Spirit: "The progress made in biblical studies, the increasing dissemination of the Sacred Scriptures, and above all the example of tradition and the interior action of the Holy Spirit are tending to cause the modern Christian to use the Bible ever increasingly as the basic prayerbook and to draw from it genuine inspiration and unsurpassable examples" (*Marialis cultus*, 30).

Because the disciples are so downhearted, Jesus patiently opens for them the meaning of all the scriptural passages concerning the Messiah. "Was it not necessary that the Christ should suffer these things and enter into his glory?": with these words he disabuses them of the notion of an earthly and political Messiah and shows them that Christ's mission is a supernatural one—to save all mankind.

Holy Scripture contained the prophecy that God would bring about salvation through the redemptive passion and death of the Messiah. The Cross does not mean failure: it is the route chosen by God for Christ to achieve definitive victory over sin and death (cf. 1 Cor 1:23–24). Many of our Lord's contemporaries failed to understand his supernatural mission because they misinterpreted the Old Testament texts. No one knew the meaning of Sacred Scripture like Jesus. And, after him, only the Church has the mission and responsibility of conserving Scripture and interpreting it correctly: "all that has been said about the manner of interpreting Scripture is ultimately subject to the judgment of the Church which exercises the divinely conferred commission and ministry of watching over and interpreting the Word of God" (Vatican II, *Dei Verbum*, 12).

this, it is now the third day since this happened. ²²Moreover, some women of our company amazed us. They were at the tomb early in the morning ²³and did not find his body; and they came back saying that they had even seen a vision of angels, who said that he was alive. ²⁴Some of those who were with us went to the tomb, and found it just as the women had said; but him they did not see." ²⁵And he said to them, "O foolish men, and slow of heart to believe all that the prophets have spoken! ²⁶Was it not necessary that the Christ should suffer these things and enter into his glory?" ²⁷And beginning with Moses and all the prophets, he interpreted to them in all the scriptures the things concerning himself.

²⁸So they drew near to the village to which they were going. He appeared to be going further, ²⁹but they constrained him, saying, "Stay with us, for it is toward evening and the day is now

Jn 20:3–10

Deut 18:15
Ps 22
Is 53

24:28–35. The Master's presence and words restore the disciples' spirits and give them new and lasting hope. "There were two disciples on their way to Emmaus. They were walking along at a normal pace, like so many other travellers on that road. And there, without any fuss, Jesus appears to them, and walks with them, his conversation helping to alleviate their tiredness. I can well imagine the scene, just as dusk is falling. A gentle breeze is blowing. All around are fields ripe with wheat, and venerable olive trees, their branches shimmering in the soft glowing light.

"Jesus joins them as they go along their way. Lord, how great you are, in everything! But you move me even more when you come down to our level, to follow us and to seek us in the hustle and bustle of each day. Lord, grant us a childlike spirit, pure eyes and a clear head so that we may recognize you when you come without any outward sign of your glory.

"The journey ends when they reach the village. The two disciples who, without realizing it, have been deeply stirred by the words and love shown by God made man, are sorry to see him leaving. For Jesus 'appeared to be going further'

(Lk 24:28). This Lord of ours never forces himself on us. He wants us to turn to him freely, when we begin to grasp the purity of his Love which he has placed in our souls. We have to hold him back ('they constrained him') and beg him: 'Stay with us, for it is towards evening and the day is now far spent' (Lk 24:29).

"That's just like us—always short on daring, perhaps because we are insincere, or because we feel embarrassed. Deep down, what we are really thinking is: 'Stay with us, because our souls are shrouded in darkness and You alone are the light. You alone can satisfy this longing that consumes us.' For 'we know full well which among all things fair and honourable is the best—to possess God for ever' (St Gregory Nazianzen, *Epistolae*, 212).

"And Jesus stays. Our eyes are opened, as were those of Cleopas and his companion, when Christ breaks the bread; and, though he vanishes once more from sight, we too will find strength to start out once more—though night is falling—to tell the others about him, because so much joy cannot be kept in one heart alone.

"The road to Emmaus—our God has filled this name with sweetness. Now the

far spent." So he went in to stay with them. ³⁰When he was at table with them, he took the bread and blessed, and broke it, and gave it to them. ³¹And their eyes were opened and they recognized him; and he vanished out of their sight. ³²They said to each other, "Did not our hearts burn within us while he talked to us on the road, while he opened to us the scriptures?" ³³And they rose that same hour and returned to Jerusalem; and they found the eleven gathered together and those who were with them, ³⁴who said, "The Lord has risen indeed, and has appeared to Simon!" ³⁵Then they told what had happened on the road, and how he was known to them in the breaking of the bread.

Lk 22:19

Lk 24:16

1 Cor 15:4–5

Jesus appears to the disciples in the upper room
³⁶As they were saying this, Jesus himself stood among them, and said to them, "Peace to you!"ˣ ³⁷But they were startled and fright-

Mk 16:14–18
Jn 20:19–23
1 Cor 15:5
Mt 14:26

---

entire world has become an Emmaus, for the Lord has opened up all the divine paths of the earth" (St Josemaría Escrivá, *Friends of God*, 313f).

24:32. "If you are an apostle, these words of the disciples of Emmaus should rise spontaneously to the lips of your professional companions when they meet you along the way of their lives" (St Josemaría Escrivá, *The Way*, 917).

24:33–35. The disciples now feel the need to return to Jerusalem immediately; there they find the apostles and some other disciples gathered together with Peter, to whom Jesus has appeared.

In sacred history, Jerusalem was the place where God chose to be praised in a very special way and where the prophets carried out their main ministry. God willed that Christ should suffer, die and rise again in Jerusalem, and from there the Kingdom of God begins to spread (cf. Lk 24:47; Acts 1:8). In the New Testament the Church of Christ is described as "the Jerusalem above" (Gal 4:26), "the heavenly Jerusalem" (Heb 12:22) and "new Jerusalem" (Rev 21:2).

The Church began in the Holy City. Later on, St Peter, not without a special intervention of Providence, moved to Rome, thereby making that city the centre of the Church. Just as Peter strengthened these first disciples in the faith, so too Christians of all generations have recourse to the See of Peter to strengthen their faith and thereby build up the unity of the Church: "Take away the Pope and the Catholic Church would no longer be catholic. Moreover, without the supreme, effective and authoritative pastoral office of Peter the unity of Christ's Church would collapse. It would be vain to look for other principles of unity in place of the true one established by Christ himself [...]. We would add that this cardinal principle of holy Church is not a supremacy of spiritual pride and a desire to dominate mankind, but a primacy of service, ministration and love. It is no vapid rhetoric which confers on Christ's vicar the title: 'Servant of the servants of God'" (Paul VI, *Ecclesiam suam*, 83).

24:36–43. This appearance of the risen Jesus is reported by St Luke and St John

x. Other ancient authorities omit *and said to them, "Peace to you!"*

1 Jn 1:1

Jn 21:5–10
Acts 10:41

Lk 9:22–45;
18:31–33
Jn 5:46

ened, and supposed that they saw a spirit. [38]And he said to them, "Why are you troubled, and why do questionings rise in your hearts?* [39]See my hands and my feet, that it is I myself; handle me, and see; for a spirit has not flesh and bones as you see that I have." [40]And when he had said this, he showed them his hands and his feet.[y] [41]And while they still disbelieved for joy, and wondered, he said to them, "Have you anything here to eat?" [42]They gave him a piece of broiled fish, [43]and he took it and ate before them.

[44]Then he said to them, "These are my words which I spoke to you, while I was still with you, that everything written about me

---

(cf. Jn 20:19–23). St John reports the institution of the sacrament of Penance, whereas St Luke puts the stress on the disciples' difficulty in accepting the miracle of the resurrection, despite the angels' testimony to the women (cf. Mt 28:5–7; Mk 16:5–7; Lk 24:4–11) and despite the witness of those who had already seen the risen Lord (cf. Mt 28:9–10; Mk 16:9–13; Lk 24:13ff; Jn 20:11–18).

Jesus appears all of a sudden, when the doors are closed (cf. Jn 20:19), which explains their surprised reaction. St Ambrose comments that "he penetrated their closed retreat not because his nature was incorporeal, but because he had the quality of a resurrected body" (*Expositio Evangelii sec. Lucam*, in loc.). "Subtility", which is one of the qualities of a glorifed body, means that "the body is totally subject to the soul and ever ready to obey its wishes" (St Pius V, *Catechism*, 1, 12, 13), with the result that it can pass through material obstacles without any difficulty.

This scene showing Christ's condescension to confirm for them the truth of his resurrection has a charm all of its own.

24:41–43. Although his risen body is in-

capable of suffering, and therefore has no need of food to nourish it, our Lord confirms his disciples' faith in his resurrection by giving them these two proofs—inviting them to touch him and eating in their presence. "For myself, I know and believe that our Lord was in the flesh even after the Resurrection. And when he came to Peter and his companions, he said to them: 'Here, feel me and see that I am not a bodiless ghost.' They touched him and believed, and were convinced that he was flesh and spirit [...]. Moreover, after the Resurrection, he ate and drank with them like a man of flesh and blood, though spiritually one with the Father" (St Ignatius of Antioch, *Letter to the Christians at Smyrna*, 3, 1–3).

24:44–49. St Matthew stresses that the Old Testament prophecies are fulfilled in Christ, because his immediate audience was Jews, who would accept this as proof that Jesus was indeed the promised Messiah. St Luke does not usually argue along these lines because he is writing for Gentiles; however, in this epilogue he does report, in a summarized way, Christ's statement to the effect that everything foretold about him had come true. By doing so he shows the unity of Old

y. Other ancient authorities omit verse 40

in the law of Moses and the prophets and the psalms must be fulfilled." ⁴⁵Then he opened their minds to understand the scriptures,
⁴⁶and said to them, "Thus it is written, that the Christ should suffer
and on the third day rise from the dead, ⁴⁷and that repentance and
forgiveness of sins should be preached in his name to all nations,ᶻ
beginning from Jerusalem. ⁴⁸You are witnesses of these things.
⁴⁹And behold, I send the promise of my Father upon you; but stay
in the city, until you are clothed with power from on high."

1 Tim 3:16
Acts 17:30

Jn 15:26; 16:7
Acts 1:4

The ascension of our Lord
⁵⁰Then he led them out as far as Bethany, and lifting up his hands
he blessed them. ⁵¹While he blessed them, he parted from them,

Mk 16:19
Acts 1:4–15

and New Testaments and that Jesus is
truly the Messiah.

St Luke also refers to the promise of
the Holy Spirit (cf. Jn 14:16–17, 26;
15:26; 16:7ff), whose fulfilment on the
day of Pentecost he will narrate in detail
in the Book of the Acts (cf. Acts 2:1–4).

24:46. From St Luke's account we have
seen how slow the apostles were to grasp
Jesus' prophecy of his death and resurrection (cf. 9:45; 18:34). Now that the
prophecy is fulfilled Jesus reminds them
that it was necessary for the Christ to
suffer and to rise from the dead (cf. Acts
2:1–4).

The Cross is a mystery, in our own
life as well as in Christ's: "Jesus suffers
to carry out the will of the Father. And
you, who also want to carry out the most
holy will of God, following the steps of
the Master, can you complain if you meet
suffering on your way?" (St Josemaría
Escrivá, *The Way*, 213).

24:49. "I send the promise of my Father
upon you," that is, the Holy Spirit who,
some days later, at Pentecost, would
come down upon them in the cenacle (cf.
Acts 2:1–4) as the Father's gift to them
(cf. Lk 11:13).

24:50–53. St Luke, who will report our
Lord's ascension in the Acts of the
Apostles, here gives a summary account
of this mystery which marks the end of
Jesus' visible presence on earth. St
Thomas Aquinas explains that it was
inappropriate for Christ to remain on
earth after the Resurrection, whereas it
was appropriate that he should ascend
into heaven, because, although his risen
body was already a glorified one, it now
receives an increase in glory due to the
dignity of the place to which it ascends
(cf. *Summa theologiae*, 3, 57, 1).

"Our Lord's Ascension also reminds
us of another fact. The same Christ, who
encourages us to carry out our task in the
world, awaits us in heaven. In other
words, our life on earth, which we love, is
not definitive. 'Here we have no lasting
city, but we seek the city which is to
come' (Heb 13:14), a changeless home,
where we may live forever. [...] Christ
awaits us. We are 'citizens of heaven'
(Phil 3:20), and at the same time fully-
fledged citizens of this earth, in the midst
of difficulties, injustices and lack of
understanding, but also in the midst of the
joy and serenity that comes from knowing that we are children of God" (St J.
Escrivá, *Christ Is Passing By*, 126).

z. Or *nations. Beginning from Jerusalem you are witnesses*

Jn 14:28;
16:22

and was carried up into heaven.^a [52]And they worshipped him, and^b returned to Jerusalem with great joy, [53]and were continually in the temple blessing God.

We have come to the end of St Luke's narrative. Words cannot express the gratitude and love we feel when we reflect on Christ's life among us. Let us offer God our desire to be ever more faithful children and disciples of his, as we savour this summary of Christ's life given us by the Magisterium: "We believe in our Lord Jesus Christ, who is the Son of God. He is the eternal Word born of the Father before time began [...]. He dwelt among us full of grace and truth. He announced and established the Kingdom of God, enabling us to know the Father. He gave us the commandment that we should love one another as he loved us. He taught us the way of the Gospel Beatitudes, according to which we were to be poor in spirit and humble, bearing suffering in patience, thirsting after justice, merciful, clean of heart, peaceful, enduring persecution for justice's sake. He suffered under Pontius Pilate, the Lamb of God taking to himself the sins of the world, and he died for us, nailed to the Cross, saving us by his redeeming blood. After he had been buried he rose from the dead of his own power, lifting us up by his Resurrection to that sharing in the divine life which is grace. He ascended into heaven whence he will come again to judge the living and the dead, each according to his merits. Those who have responded to the love and compassion of God will go into eternal life. Those who have refused them to the end will be consigned to the fire that is never extinguished. And of his kingdom there will be no end" (Paul VI, *Creed of the People of God*, 11f).

---

a. Other ancient authorities omit *and was carried up into heaven* **b.** Other ancient authorities omit *worshipped him, and*

New Vulgate Text

EVANGELIUM SECUNDUM LUCAM

[1] [1]Quoniam quidem multi conati sunt ordinare narrationem, quae in nobis completae sunt, rerum, [2]sicut tradiderunt nobis, qui ab initio ipsi viderunt et ministri fuerunt verbi, [3]visum est et mihi, adsecuto a principio omnia, diligenter ex ordine tibi scribere, optime Theophile, [4]ut cognoscas eorum verborum, de quibus eruditus es, firmitatem. [5]Fuit in diebus Herodis regis Iudaeae sacerdos quidam nomine Zacharias de vice Abiae et uxor illi de filiabus Aaron, et nomen eius Elisabeth. [6]Erant autem iusti ambo ante Deum, incedentes in omnibus mandatis et iustificationibus Domini, irreprehensibiles. [7]Et non erat illis filius eo quod esset Elisabeth sterilis, et ambo processissent in diebus suis. [8]Factum est autem, cum sacerdotio fungeretur in ordine vicis suae ante Deum, [9]secundum consuetudinem sacerdotii sorte exiit, ut incensum poneret ingressus in templum Domini; [10]et omnis multitudo erat populi orans foris hora incensi. [11]Apparuit autem illi angelus Domini stans a dextris altaris incensi; [12]et Zacharias turbatus est videns, et timor irruit super eum. [13]Ait autem ad illum angelus: «Ne timeas, Zacharia, quoniam exaudita est deprecatio tua, et uxor tua Elisabeth pariet tibi filium, et vocabis nomen eius Ioannem. [14]Et erit gaudium tibi et exsultatio, et multi in nativitate eius gaudebunt: [15]erit enim magnus coram Domino et vinum et siceram non bibet et Spiritu Sancto replebitur adhuc ex utero matris suae [16]et multos filiorum Israel convertet ad Dominum Deum ipsorum. [17]Et ipse praecedet ante illum in spiritu et virtute Eliae, *ut convertat corda patrum in filios* et incredibiles ad prudentiam iustorum, parare Domino plebem perfectam». [18]Et dixit Zacharias ad angelum: «Unde hoc sciam? Ego enim sum senex et uxor mea processit in diebus suis». [19]Et respondens angelus dixit ei: «Ego sum Gabriel, qui adsto ante Deum, et missus sum loqui ad te et haec tibi evangelizare. [20]Et ecce eris tacens et non poteris loqui usque in diem, quo haec fiant, pro eo quod non credidisti verbis meis, quae implebuntur in tempore suo». [21]Et erat plebs exspectans Zachariam, et mirabantur quod tardaret ipse in templo. [22]Egressus autem non poterat loqui ad illos, et cognoverunt quod visionem vidisset in templo; et ipse erat innuens illis et permansit mutus. [23]Et factum est ut impleti sunt dies officii eius, abiit in domum suam. [24]Post hos autem dies concepit Elisabeth uxor eius et occultabat se mensibus quinque dicens: [25]«Sic mihi fecit Dominus in diebus, quibus respexit auferre opprobrium meum inter homines». [26]In mense autem sexto missus est angelus Gabriel a Deo in civitatem Galilaeae, cui nomen Nazareth, [27]ad virginem desponsatam viro, cui nomen erat Ioseph de domo David, et nomen virginis Maria. [28]Et ingressus ad eam dixit: «Ave, gratia plena, Dominus tecum». [29]Ipsa autem turbata est in sermone eius et cogitabat qualis esset ista salutatio. [30]Et ait angelus ei: «Ne timeas, Maria; invenisti enim gratiam apud Deum. [31]Et ecce concipies in utero et paries filium, et vocabis nomen eius Iesum. [32]Hic erit magnus et Filius Altissimi vocabitur, et dabit illi Dominus Deus sedem David patris eius, [33]et regnabit super domum Iacob in aeternum, et regni eius non erit finis». [34]Dixit autem Maria ad angelum: «Quomodo fiet istud, quoniam virum non cognosco?». [35]Et respondens angelus dixit ei: «Spiritus Sanctus superveniet in te, et virtus Altissimi obumbrabit tibi: ideoque et quod nascetur sanctum, vocabitur Filius Dei. [36]Et ecce Elisabeth cognata tua et ipsa concepit filium in senecta sua, et hic mensis est sextus illi, quae vocatur sterilis, [37]quia *non erit impossibile apud Deum omne verbum»*. [38]Dixit autem Maria: «Ecce ancilla Domini; fiat mihi secundum verbum tuum». Et discessit ab illa angelus. [39]Exsurgens autem Maria in diebus illis abiit in montana cum festinatione in civitatem Iudae [40]et intravit in domum Zachariae et salutavit Elisabeth. [41]Et factum est ut audivit salutationem Mariae Elisabeth, exsultavit infans in utero eius, et repleta est Spiritu Sancto Elisabeth [42]et exclamavit voce magna et dixit: «Benedicta tu inter mulieres, et benedictus fructus ventris tui. [43]Et unde hoc mihi, ut veniat mater Domini mei ad me? [44]Ecce enim ut facta est vox salutationis tuae in auribus meis, exsultavit in gaudio infans in utero meo. [45]Et beata, quae credidit, quoniam perficientur ea, quae dicta sunt ei a Domino». [46]Et ait Maria: «Magnificat *anima mea Dominum,* / [47]et *exsultavit* spiritus meus *in Deo salvatore meo,* / [48]quia *respexit humilitatem ancillae* suae. / Ecce enim ex hoc beatam me dicent omnes generationes, / [49]quia fecit mihi magna, qui potens est, / et sanctum nomen eius, / [50]et

misericordia eius in progenies et progenies / timentibus eum. / ^{51}Fecit potentiam in brachio suo, / dispersit superbos mente cordis sui; / ^{52}deposuit potentes de sede / et exaltavit humiles; / ^{53}esurientes implevit bonis / et divites dimisit inanes. / ^{54}Suscepit Israel puerum suum, / recordatus misericordiae, / ^{55}sicut locutus est ad patres nostros, / Abraham et semini eius in saecula». ^{56}Mansit autem Maria cum illa quasi mensibus tribus et reversa est in domum suam. ^{57}Elisabeth autem impletum est tempus pariendi, et peperit filium. ^{58}Et audierunt vicini et cognati eius quia magnificavit Dominus misericordiam suam cum illa, et congratulabantur ei. ^{59}Et factum est in die octavo venerunt circumcidere puerum et vocabant eum nomine patris eius Zachariam. ^{60}Et respondens mater eius dixit: «Nequaquam, sed vocabitur Ioannes». ^{61}Et dixerunt ad illam: «Nemo est in cognatione tua, qui vocetur hoc nomine». ^{62}Innuebant autem patri eius quem vellet vocari eum. ^{63}Et postulans pugillarem scripsit dicens: «Ioannes est nomen eius». Et mirati sunt universi. ^{64}Apertum est autem ilico os eius et lingua eius, et loquebatur benedicens Deum. ^{65}Et factus est timor super omnes vicinos eorum, et super omnia montana Iudaeae divulgabantur omnia verba haec. ^{66}Et posuerunt omnes, qui audierant, in corde suo dicentes: «Quid putas puer iste erit?». Etenim manus Domini erat cum illo. ^{67}Et Zacharias pater eius impletus est Spiritu Sancto et prophetavit dicens: ^{68}«*Benedictus Dominus, Deus Israel,* / quia visitavit et fecit redemptionem plebi suae / ^{69}et erexit cornu salutis nobis / in domo David pueri sui, / ^{70}sicut locutus est per os sanctorum, / qui a saeculo sunt, prophetarum eius, / ^{71}salutem ex inimicis nostris / et de manu omnium, qui oderunt nos; / ^{72}ad faciendam misericordiam cum patribus nostris / et memorari testamenti sui sancti, / ^{73}iusiurandum, quod iuravit ad Abraham patrem nostrum, / daturum se nobis, / ^{74}ut sine timore, de manu inimicorum liberati, / serviamus illi / ^{75}in sanctitate et iustitia coram ipso / omnibus diebus nostris. / ^{76}Et tu, puer, propheta Altissimi vocaberis: / praeibis enim *ante faciem Domini parare vias eius,* / ^{77}ad dandam scientiam salutis plebi eius / in remissionem peccatorum eorum, / ^{78}per viscera misericordiae Dei nostri, / in quibus visitabit nos oriens ex alto, / ^{79}*illuminare his, qui in tenebris et in umbra mortis sedent,* / ad dirigendos pedes nostros in viam pacis». ^{80}Puer autem crescebat et confortabatur spiritu et erat in deserto usque in diem ostensionis suae ad Israel. **[2]** ^{1}Factum est autem in diebus illis exiit edictum a Caesare Augusto, ut describeretur universus orbis. ^{2}Haec descriptio prima facta est praeside Syriae Quirino. ^{3}Et ibant omnes, ut profiterentur, singuli in suam civitatem. ^{4}Ascendit autem et Ioseph a Galilaea de civitate Nazareth in Iudaeam in civitatem David, quae vocatur Bethlehem, eo quod esset de domo et familia David, ^{5}ut profiteretur cum Maria desponsata sibi, uxore praegnante. ^{6}Factum est autem cum essent ibi, impleti sunt dies, ut pareret, ^{7}et peperit filium suum primogenitum; et pannis eum involvit et reclinavit eum in praesepio, quia non erat eis locus in deversorio. ^{8}Et pastores erant in regione eadem vigilantes et custodientes vigilias noctis supra gregem suum. ^{9}Et angelus Domini stetit iuxta illos, et claritas Domini circumfulsit illos, et timuerunt timore magno. ^{10}Et dixit illis angelus: «Nolite timere; ecce enim evangelizo vobis gaudium magnum, quod erit omni populo, ^{11}quia natus est vobis hodie Salvator, qui est Christus Dominus, in civitate David. ^{12}Et hoc vobis signum: invenietis infantem pannis involutum et positum in praesepio». ^{13}Et subito facta est cum angelo multitudo militiae caelestis laudantium Deum et dicentium: ^{14}«Gloria in altissimis Deo, et super terram pax in hominibus bonae voluntatis». ^{15}Et factum est ut discesserunt ab eis angeli in caelum, pastores loquebantur ad invicem: «Transeamus usque Bethlehem et videamus hoc verbum, quod factum est, quod Dominus ostendit nobis». ^{16}Et venerunt festinantes et invenerunt Mariam et Ioseph et infantem positum in praesepio. ^{17}Videntes autem notum fecerunt verbum, quod dictum erat illis de puero hoc. ^{18}Et omnes, qui audierunt, mirati sunt de his, quae dicta erant a pastoribus ad ipsos. ^{19}Maria autem conservabat omnia verba haec conferens in corde suo. ^{20}Et reversi sunt pastores glorificantes et laudantes Deum in omnibus, quae audierant et viderant, sicut dictum est ad illos. ^{21}Et postquam consummati sunt dies octo, ut circumcideretur, vocatum est nomen eius Iesus, quod vocatum est ab angelo, priusquam in utero conciperetur. ^{22}Et postquam impleti sunt dies purgationis eorum secundum legem Moysis, tulerunt illum in Hierosolymam, ut sisterent Domino, ^{23}sicut scriptum est in lege Domini: «*Omne masculinum adaperiens vulvam sanctum Domino vocabitur*», ^{24}et ut darent hostiam secundum quod dictum est in lege Domini: *par turturum aut duos pullos columbarum*. ^{25}Et ecce homo erat in Ierusalem, cui nomen Simeon, et homo iste iustus et timoratus, exspectans consolationem Israel, et Spiritus Sanctus erat super eum, ^{26}et responsum acceperat ab Spiritu Sancto non visurum se mortem nisi prius videret Christum Domini. ^{27}Et venit in Spiritu in templum. Et cum inducerent puerum Iesum parentes eius, ut facerent secundum consuetudinem legis pro eo, ^{28}et ipse accepit eum in ulnas suas et benedixit Deum et dixit: ^{29}«Nunc dimittis servum tuum, Domine, / secundum verbum tuum in pace, / ^{30}quia viderunt oculi mei / salutare tuum, / ^{31}quod parasti / ante faciem omnium populorum, / ^{32}lumen ad revelationem gentium / et gloriam plebis tuae Israel». ^{33}Et erat pater eius et mater mirantes super his, quae dicebantur de illo. ^{34}Et benedixit illis Simeon et dixit ad Mariam matrem eius: «Ecce positus est hic in ruinam et resurrectionem multorum in Israel et in signum, cui contradicetur [35]—et tuam ipsius animam pertransiet gladius— ut revelentur ex multis cordibus cogitationes». [36]Et erat Anna prophetissa, filia Phanuel, de tribu Aser. Haec processerat in diebus multis et vixerat cum viro annis septem a virginitate sua; [37]et haec vidua usque ad annos octoginta quattuor, quae non discedebat de templo, ieiuniis et obsecrationibus serviens nocte ac die. [38]Et haec ipsa hora superveniens confitebatur Deo et loquebatur de illo omnibus, qui exspectabant redemptionem Ierusalem. [39]Et ut perfecerunt omnia secundum legem Domini, reversi sunt in Galilaeam in civitatem suam Nazareth. [40]Puer autem crescebat et confortabatur plenus sapientia; et gratia Dei erat super illum. [41]Et ibant parentes eius per omnes annos in Ierusalem in die festo Paschae. [42]Et cum factus esset annorum duodecim, ascendentibus illis secundum consuetudinem diei festi, [43]consummatisque diebus, cum redirent, remansit puer Iesus in Ierusalem, et non cognoverunt parentes eius. [44]Existimantes autem illum esse in comitatu, venerunt iter diei et requirebant eum inter cognatos et notos [45]et non invenientes regressi sunt in Ierusalem requirentes eum. [46]Et factum est post triduum invenerunt illum in templo sedentem in medio doctorum, audientem illos et interrogantem eos; [47]stupebant autem omnes, qui eum audiebant, super prudentia et responsis eius. [48]Et videntes eum admirati sunt, et dixit Mater eius ad illum: «Fili, quid fecisti nobis sic? Ecce pater tuus et ego dolentes quaerebamus te». [49]Et ait ad illos: «Quid est quod me quaerebatis? Nesciebatis quia in his, quae Patris mei sunt, oportet me esse?». [50]Et ipsi non intellexerunt verbum, quod locutus est ad illos. [51]Et descendit cum eis et venit Nazareth et erat subditus illis. Et mater eius conservabat omnia verba in corde suo. [52]Et Iesus *proficiebat* sapientia et aetate *et gratia apud Deum et homines.*   **[3]** [1]Anno autem quinto decimo imperii Tiberii Caesaris, procurante Pontio Pilato Iudaeam, tetrarcha autem Galilaeae Herode, Philippo autem fratre eius tetrarcha Ituraeae et Trachonitidis regionis, et Lysania Abilinae tetrarcha, [2]sub principe sacerdotum Anna et Caipha, factum est verbum Dei super Ioannem Zachariae filium in deserto. [3]Et venit in omnem regionem circa Iordanem praedicans baptismum paenitentiae in remissionem peccatorum, [4]sicut scriptum est in libro sermonum Isaiae prophetae: «*Vox clamantis in deserto: / "Parate viam Domini, / rectas facite semitas eius. / [5]Omnis vallis implebitur / et omnis mons et collis humiliabitur; / et erunt prava in directa, / et aspera in vias planas: / [6]et videbit omnis caro salutare Dei"».* [7]Dicebat ergo ad turbas, quae exibant, ut baptizarentur ab ipso: «Genimina viperarum, quis ostendit vobis fugere a ventura ira? [8]Facite ergo fructus dignos paenitentiae et ne coeperitis dicere in vobis ipsis: "Patrem habemus Abraham"; dico enim vobis quia potest Deus de lapidibus istis suscitare Abrahae filios. [9]Iam enim et securis ad radicem arborum posita est; omnis ergo arbor non faciens fructum bonum exciditur et in ignem mittitur». [10]Et interrogabant eum turbae dicentes: «Quid ergo faciemus?». [11]Respondens autem dicebat illis: «Qui habet duas tunicas, det non habenti; et qui habet escas, similiter faciat». [12]Venerunt autem et publicani, ut baptizarentur, et dixerunt ad illum: «Magister, quid faciemus?». [13]At ille dixit ad eos: «Nihil amplius quam constitutum est vobis, faciatis». [14]Interrogabant autem eum et milites dicentes: «Quid faciemus et nos?». Et ait illis: «Neminem concutiatis, neque calumniam faciatis et contenti estote stipendiis vestris». [15]Existimante autem populo et cogitantibus omnibus in cordibus suis de Ioanne, ne forte ipse esset Christus, [16]respondit Ioannes dicens omnibus: «Ego quidem aqua baptizo vos. Venit autem fortior me, cuius non sum dignus solvere corrigiam calceamentorum eius; ipse vos baptizabit in Spiritu Sancto et igni, [17]cuius ventilabrum in manu eius ad purgandam aream suam et ad congregandum triticum in horreum suum, paleas autem comburet igni inexstinguibili». [18]Multa quidem et alia exhortans evangelizabat populum. [19]Herodes autem tetrarcha, cum corriperetur ab illo de Herodiade uxore fratris sui et de omnibus malis, quae fecit Herodes, [20]adiecit et hoc supra omnia et inclusit Ioannem in carcere. [21]Factum est autem cum baptizaretur omnis populus et Iesu baptizato et orante, apertum est caelum, [22]et descendit Spiritus Sanctus corporali specie sicut columba super ipsum; et vox de caelo facta est: «Tu es Filius meus dilectus; in te complacui mihi». [23]Et ipse Iesus erat incipiens quasi annorum triginta, ut putabatur, filius Ioseph, qui fuit Heli, [24]qui fuit Matthat, qui fuit Levi, qui fuit Melchi, qui fuit Iannae, qui fuit Ioseph, [25]qui fuit Matthathiae, qui fuit Amos, qui fuit Nahum, qui fuit Esli, qui fuit Naggae, [26]qui fuit Maath, qui fuit Matthathiae, qui fuit Semei, qui fuit Iosech, qui fuit Ioda, [27]qui fuit Ioanna, qui fuit Resa, qui fuit Zorobabel, qui fuit Salathiel, qui fuit Neri, [28]qui fuit Melchi, qui fuit Addi, qui fuit Cosam, qui fuit Elmadam, qui fuit Her, [29]qui fuit Iesu, qui fuit Eliezer, qui fuit Iorim, qui fuit Matthat, qui fuit Levi, [30]qui fuit Simeon, qui fuit Iudae, qui fuit Ioseph, qui fuit Iona, qui fuit Eliachim, [31]qui fuit Melea, qui fuit Menna, qui fuit Matthatha, qui fuit Nathan, qui fuit David, [32]qui fuit Iesse, qui fuit Obed, qui fuit Booz, qui fuit Salmon, qui fuit Naasson, [33]qui fuit Aminadab, qui fuit Admin, qui fuit Arni, qui fuit Esrom, qui fuit Phares, qui fuit Iudae, [34]qui fuit Iacob, qui fuit Isaac, qui fuit Abrahae, qui fuit Thare, qui fuit Nachor, [35]qui fuit Seruch, qui fuit Ragau, qui fuit Phaleg, qui fuit Heber, qui fuit Sala, [36]qui fuit Cainan, qui fuit Arphaxad, qui fuit Sem, qui fuit Noe, qui fuit Lamech, [37]qui fuit Mathusala, qui fuit Henoch, qui fuit Iared, qui fuit Malaleel, qui fuit Cainan,

[38]qui fuit Enos, qui fuit Seth, qui fuit Adam, qui fuit Dei. **[4]** [1]Iesus autem plenus Spiritu Sancto regressus est ab Iordane et agebatur in Spiritu in deserto [2]diebus quadraginta et tentabatur a Diabolo. Et nihil manducavit in diebus illis et, consummatis illis, esuriit. [3]Dixit autem illi Diabolus: «Si Filius Dei es, dic lapidi huic, ut panis fiat». [4]Et respondit ad illum Iesus: «Scriptum est: *"Non in pane solo vivet homo"*». [5]Et sustulit illum et ostendit illi omnia regna orbis terrae in momento temporis; [6]et ait ei Diabolus: «Tibi dabo potestatem hanc universam et gloriam illorum, quia mihi tradita est, et, cui volo, do illam: [7]tu ergo, si adoraveris coram me, erit tua omnis». [8]Et respondens Iesus dixit illi: «Scriptum est: *"Dominum Deum tuum adorabis et illi soli servies"*». [9]Duxit autem illum in Ierusalem et statuit eum supra pinnam templi et dixit illi: «Si Filius Dei es, mitte te hinc deorsum. [10]Scriptum est enim: *"Angelis suis mandabit de te, / ut conservent te"* / [11]et: *"In manibus tollent te, / ne forte offendas ad lapidem pedem tuum"*». [12]Et respondens Iesus ait illi: «Dictum est: *"Non tentabis Dominum Deum tuum"*». [13]Et consummata omni tentatione, Diabolus recessit ab illo usque ad tempus. [14]Et regressus est Iesus in virtute Spiritus in Galilaeam. Et fama exiit per universam regionem de illo. [15]Et ipse docebat in synagogis eorum et magnificabatur ab omnibus. [16]Et venit Nazareth, ubi erat nutritus, et intravit secundum consuetudinem suam die sabbati in synagogam et surrexit legere. [17]Et traditus est illi liber prophetae Isaiae; et ut revolvit librum, invenit locum, ubi scriptum erat: [18]*«Spiritus Domini super me; / propter quod unxit me / evangelizare pauperibus, / misit me praedicare captivis remissionem / et caecis visum, / dimittere confractos in remissione, / [19]praedicare annum Domini acceptum»*. [20]Et cum plicuisset librum, reddidit ministro et sedit; et omnium in synagoga oculi erant intendentes in eum. [21]Coepit autem dicere ad illos: «Hodie impleta est haec Scriptura in auribus vestris». [22]Et omnes testimonium illi dabant et mirabantur in verbis gratiae, quae procedebant de ore ipsius, et dicebant: «Nonne hic filius est Ioseph?». [23]Et ait illis: «Utique dicetis mihi hanc similitudinem: "Medice, cura teipsum; quanta audivimus facta in Capharnaum, fac et hic in patria tua"». [24]Ait autem: «Amen dico vobis: Nemo propheta acceptus est in patria sua. [25]In veritate autem dico vobis: Multae viduae erant in diebus Eliae in Israel, quando clausum est caelum annis tribus et mensibus sex, cum facta est fames magna in omni terra; [26]et ad nullam illarum missus est Elias nisi in Sarepta Sidoniae ad mulierem viduam. [27]Et multi leprosi erant in Israel sub Eliseo propheta; et nemo eorum mundatus est nisi Naaman Syrus». [28]Et repleti sunt omnes in synagoga ira haec audientes [29]et surrexerunt et eiecerunt illum extra civitatem et duxerunt illum usque ad supercilium montis, supra quem civitas illorum erat aedificata, ut praecipitarent eum. [30]Ipse autem transiens per medium illorum ibat. [31]Et descendit in Capharnaum civitatem Galilaeae. Et docebat illos sabbatis, [32]et stupebant in doctrina eius, quia in potestate erat sermo ipsius. [33]Et in synagoga erat homo habens spiritum daemonii immundi; et exclamavit voce magna: [34]«Sine; quid nobis et tibi, Iesu Nazarene? Venisti perdere nos? Scio te qui sis: Sanctus Dei». [35]Et increpavit illi Iesus dicens: «Obmutesce et exi ab illo!». Et cum proiecisset illum daemonium in medium, exiit ab illo nihilque illum nocuit. [36]Et factus est pavor in omnibus; et colloquebantur ad invicem dicentes: «Quod est hoc verbum, quia in potestate et virtute imperat immundis spiritibus, et exeunt?». [37]Et divulgabatur fama de illo in omnem locum regionis. [38]Surgens autem de synagoga introivit in domum Simonis. Socrus autem Simonis tenebatur magna febri; et rogaverunt illum pro ea. [39]Et stans super illam imperavit febri, et dimisit illam; et continuo surgens ministrabat illis. [40]Cum sol autem occidisset, omnes, qui habebant infirmos variis languoribus, ducebant illos ad eum; at ille singulis manus imponens curabat eos. [41]Exibant autem daemonia a multis clamantia et dicentia: «Tu es Filius Dei». Et increpans non sinebat ea loqui, quia sciebant ipsum esse Christum. [42]Facta autem die, egressus ibat in desertum locum; et turbae requirebant eum et venerunt usque ad ipsum et detinebant illum, ne discederet ab eis. [43]Quibus ille ait: «Et aliis civitatibus oportet me evangelizare regnum Dei, quia ideo missus sum». [44]Et erat praedicans in synagogis Iudaeae. **[5]** [1]Factum est autem cum turba urgeret illum ut audiret verbum Dei, et ipse stabat secus stagnum Genesareth [2]et vidit duas naves stantes secus stagnum; piscatores autem descenderant de illis et lavabant retia. [3]Ascendens autem in unam navem, quae erat Simonis, rogavit eum a terra reducere pusillum; et sedens docebat de navicula turbas. [4]Ut cessavit autem loqui, dixit ad Simonem: «Duc in altum et laxate retia vestra in capturam». [5]Et respondens Simon dixit: «Praeceptor, per totam noctem laborantes nihil cepimus; in verbo autem tuo laxabo retia». [6]Et cum hoc fecissent, concluserunt piscium multitudinem copiosam; rumpebantur autem retia eorum. [7]Et annuerunt sociis, qui erant in alia navi, ut venirent et adiuvarent eos; et venerunt, et impleverunt ambas naviculas, ita ut mergerentur. [8]Quod cum videret Simon Petrus, procidit ad genua Iesu dicens: «Exi a me, quia homo peccator sum, Domine». [9]Stupor enim circumdederat eum et omnes, qui cum illo erant, in captura piscium, quos ceperant; [10]similiter autem et Iacobum et Ioannem, filios Zebedaei, qui erant socii Simonis. Et ait ad Simonem Iesus: «Noli timere; ex hoc iam homines eris capiens». [11]Et subductis ad terram navibus, relictis omnibus, secuti sunt illum. [12]Et factum est cum esset

in una civitatum, et ecce vir plenus lepra; et videns Iesum et procidens in faciem rogavit eum dicens: «Domine, si vis, potes me mundare». [13]Et extendens manum tetigit illum dicens: «Volo, mundare!»; et confestim lepra discessit ab illo. [14]Et ipse praecepit illi, ut nemini diceret, sed: «Vade, ostende te sacerdoti et offer pro emundatione tua, sicut praecepit Moyses, in testimonium illis». [15]Perambulabat autem magis sermo de illo, et conveniebant turbae multae, ut audirent et curarentur ab infirmitatibus suis; [16]ipse autem secedebat in desertis et orabat. [17]Et factum est in una dierum, et ipse erat docens, et erant pharisaei sedentes et legis doctores, qui venerant ex omni castello Galilaeae et Iudaeae et Ierusalem; et virtus Domini erat ei ad sanandum. [18]Et ecce viri portantes in lecto hominem, qui erat paralyticus, et quaerebant eum inferre et ponere ante eum. [19]Et non invenientes qua parte illum inferrent prae turba, ascenderunt supra tectum et per tegulas summiserunt illum cum lectulo in medium ante Iesum. [20]Quorum fidem ut vidit, dixit: «Homo, remittuntur tibi peccata tua». [21]Et coeperunt cogitare scribae et pharisaei dicentes: «Quis est hic, qui loquitur blasphemias? Quis potest dimittere peccata nisi solus Deus?». [22]Ut cognovit autem Iesus cogitationes eorum, respondens dixit ad illos: «Quid cogitatis in cordibus vestris? [23]Quid est facilius, dicere: "Dimittuntur tibi peccata tua", an dicere: "Surge et ambula"? [24]Ut autem sciatis quia Filius hominis potestatem habet in terra dimittere peccata —ait paralytico—: Tibi dico: Surge, tolle lectulum tuum et vade in domum tuam». [25]Et confestim surgens coram illis tulit, in quo iacebat, et abiit in domum suam magnificans Deum. [26]Et stupor apprehendit omnes, et magnificabant Deum, et repleti sunt timore dicentes: «Vidimus mirabilia hodie». [27]Et post haec exiit et vidit publicanum nomine Levi sedentem ad teloneum et ait illi: «Sequere me». [28]Et relictis omnibus, surgens secutus est eum. [29]Et fecit ei convivium magnum Levi in domo sua; et erat turba multa publicanorum et aliorum, qui cum illis erant discumbentes. [30]Et murmurabant pharisaei et scribae eorum adversus discipulos eius dicentes: «Quare cum publicanis et peccatoribus manducatis et bibitis?». [31]Et respondens Iesus dixit ad illos: «Non egent, qui sani sunt, medico, sed qui male habent. [32]Non veni vocare iustos sed peccatores in paenitentiam». [33]At illi dixerunt ad eum: «Discipuli Ioannis ieiunant frequenter et obsecrationes faciunt, similiter et pharisaeorum; tui autem edunt et bibunt». [34]Quibus Iesus ait: «Numquid potestis convivas nuptiarum, dum cum illis est sponsus, facere ieiunare? [35]Venient autem dies, et cum ablatus fuerit ab illis sponsus, tunc ieiunabunt in illis diebus». [36]Dicebat autem et similitudinem ad illos: «Nemo abscindit commissuram a vestimento novo et immittit in vestimentum vetus; alioquin et novum rumpet, et veteri non convenit commissura a novo. [37]Et nemo mittit vinum novum in utres veteres; alioquin rumpet vinum novum utres, et ipsum effundetur, et utres peribunt; [38]sed vinum novum in utres novos mittendum est. [39]Et nemo bibens vetus vult novum; dicit enim: "Vetus melius est!"». [6] [1]Factum est autem in sabbato cum transiret per sata, et vellebant discipuli eius spicas et manducabant confricantes manibus. [2]Quidam autem pharisaeorum dixerunt: «Quid facitis, quod non licet in sabbatis?». [3]Et respondens Iesus ad eos dixit: «Nec hoc legistis, quod fecit David, cum esurisset ipse et qui cum eo erant? [4]Quomodo intravit in domum Dei et panes propositionis sumpsit et manducavit et dedit his, qui cum ipso erant, quos non licet manducare nisi tantum sacerdotibus?». [5]Et dicebat illis: «Dominus est sabbati Filius hominis». [6]Factum est autem in alio sabbato ut intraret in synagogam et doceret; et erat ibi homo, et manus eius dextra erat arida. [7]Observabant autem illum scribae et pharisaei si sabbato curaret, ut invenirent accusare illum. [8]Ipse vero sciebat cogitationes eorum et ait homini, qui habebat manum aridam: «Surge et sta in medium». Et surgens stetit. [9]Ait autem ad illos Iesus: «Interrogo vos si licet sabbato bene facere an male, animam salvam facere an perdere?». [10]Et circumspectis omnibus illis, dixit illi: «Extende manum tuam». Et fecit, et restituta est manus eius. [11]Ipsi autem repleti sunt insipientia et colloquebantur ad invicem quidnam facerent Iesu. [12]Factum est autem in illis diebus, exiit in montem orare et erat pernoctans in oratione Dei. [13]Et cum dies factus esset, vocavit discipulos suos et elegit Duodecim ex ipsis, quos et apostolos nominavit: [14]Simonem, quem et cognominavit Petrum, et Andream fratrem eius et Iacobum et Ioannem et Philippum et Bartholomaeum [15]et Matthaeum et Thomam et Iacobum Alphaei et Simonem, qui vocatur Zelotes, [16]et Iudam Iacobi et Iudam Iscarioth, qui fuit proditor. [17]Et descendens cum illis stetit in loco campestri, et turba multa discipulorum eius, et multitudo copiosa plebis ab omni Iudaea et Ierusalem et maritima Tyri et Sidonis, [18]qui venerunt, ut audirent eum et sanarentur a languoribus suis; et qui vexabantur a spiritibus immundis, curabantur. [19]Et omnis turba quaerebant eum tangere, quia virtus de illo exibat et sanabat omnes. [20]Et ipse, elevatis oculis suis in discipulos suos, dicebat: «Beati pauperes, quia vestrum est regnum Dei. [21]Beati, qui nunc esuritis, quia saturabimini. Beati, qui nunc fletis, quia ridebitis. [22]Beati eritis, cum vos oderint homines et cum separaverint vos et exprobraverint et eiecerint nomen vestrum tamquam malum propter Filium hominis. [23]Gaudete in illa die et exsultate, ecce enim merces vestra multa in caelo; secundum haec enim faciebant prophetis patres eorum. [24]Verumtamen vae vobis divitibus, quia habetis consolationem vestram! [25]Vae vobis, qui saturati estis nunc, quia esurietis! Vae vobis, qui ridetis nunc, quia lugebitis et flebitis! [26]Vae, cum bene vobis dixerint omnes homines! Secundum haec enim faciebant pseudoprophetis patres eorum. [27]Sed vobis dico, qui auditis: Diligite inimicos vestros, bene facite his, qui vos oderunt; [28]benedicite maledicentibus vobis, orate pro calumniantibus vos. [29]Ei qui te percutit in maxillam, praebe et alteram; et ab eo, qui aufert tibi vestimentum, etiam tunicam noli prohibere. [30]Omni petenti te tribue; et ab eo, qui aufert, quae tua sunt, ne repetas. [31]Et prout vultis, ut faciant vobis homines, facite illis similiter. [32]Et si diligitis eos, qui vos diligunt, quae vobis est gratia? Nam et peccatores diligentes se diligunt. [33]Et si bene feceritis his, qui vobis bene faciunt, quae vobis est gratia? Siquidem et peccatores idem faciunt. [34]Et si mutuum dederitis his, a quibus speratis recipere, quae vobis gratia est? Nam et peccatores peccatoribus fenerantur, ut recipiant aequalia. [35]Verumtamen diligite inimicos vestros et bene facite et mutuum date nihil desperantes; et erit merces vestra multa, et eritis filii Altissimi, quia ipse benignus est super ingratos et malos. [36]Estote misericordes, sicut et Pater vester misericors est. [37]Et nolite iudicare et non iudicabimini; et nolite condemnare et non condemnabimini. Dimittite et dimittemini; [38]date, et dabitur vobis: mensuram bonam, confertam, coagitatam, supereffluentem dabunt in sinum vestrum; eadem quippe mensura, qua mensi fueritis, remetietur vobis». [39]Dixit autem illis et similitudinem: «Numquid potest caecus caecum ducere? Nonne ambo in foveam cadent? [40]Non est discipulus super magistrum; perfectus autem omnis erit sicut magister eius. [41]Quid autem vides festucam in oculo fratris tui, trabem autem, quae in oculo tuo est, non consideras? [42]Quomodo potes dicere fratri tuo: "Frater, sine eiciam festucam, quae est in oculo tuo", ipse in oculo tuo trabem non videns? Hypocrita, eice primum trabem de oculo tuo et tunc perspicies, ut educas festucam, quae est in oculo fratris tui. [43]Non est enim arbor bona faciens fructum malum, neque iterum arbor mala faciens fructum bonum. [44]Unaquaeque enim arbor de fructu suo cognoscitur; neque enim de spinis colligunt ficus, neque de rubo vindemiant uvam. [45]Bonus homo de bono thesauro cordis profert bonum, et malus homo de malo profert malum: ex abundantia enim cordis os eius loquitur. [46]Quid autem vocatis me: "Domine, Domine", et non facitis, quae dico? [47]Omnis, qui venit ad me et audit sermones meos et facit eos, ostendam vobis cui similis sit: [48]similis est homini aedificanti domum, qui fodit in altum et posuit fundamentum supra petram; inundatione autem facta, illisum est flumen domui illi, et non potuit eam movere, bene enim aedificata erat. [49]Qui autem audivit et non fecit, similis est homini aedificanti domum suam supra terram sine fundamento, in quam illisus est fluvius, et continuo cecidit, et facta est ruina domus illius magna». [7] [1]Cum autem implesset omnia verba sua in aures plebis, intravit Capharnaum. [2]Centurionis autem cuiusdam servus male habens erat moriturus, qui illi erat pretiosus. [3]Et cum audisset de Iesu, misit ad eum seniores Iudaeorum, rogans eum, ut veniret et salvaret servum eius. [4]At illi cum venissent ad Iesum, rogabant eum sollicite dicentes: «Dignus est, ut hoc illi praestes: [5]diligit enim gentem nostram et synagogam ipse aedificavit nobis». [6]Iesus autem ibat cum illis. At cum iam non longe esset a domo, misit centurio amicos dicens ei: «Domine, noli vexari; non enim dignus sum, ut sub tectum meum intres, [7]propter quod et meipsum non sum dignum arbitratus, ut venirem ad te; sed dic verbo, et sanetur puer meus. [8]Nam et ego homo sum sub potestate constitutus, habens sub me milites, et dico huic: "Vade", et vadit; et alii: "Veni", et venit; et servo meo: "Fac hoc", et facit». [9]Quo audito, Iesus miratus est eum et conversus sequentibus se turbis dixit: «Dico vobis, nec in Israel tantam fidem inveni!». [10]Et reversi, qui missi fuerant domum, invenerunt servum sanum. [11]Et factum est deinceps, ivit in civitatem, quae vocatur Naim, et ibant cum illo discipuli eius et turba copiosa. [12]Cum autem appropinquaret portae civitatis, et ecce defunctus efferebatur filius unicus matri suae, et haec vidua erat, et turba civitatis multa cum illa. [13]Quam cum vidisset Dominus, misericordia motus super ea dixit illi: «Noli flere!». [14]Et accessit et tetigit loculum; hi autem, qui portabant, steterunt. Et ait: «Adulescens, tibi dico: Surge!». [15]Et resedit, qui erat mortuus, et coepit loqui; et dedit illum matri suae. [16]Accepit autem omnes timor, et magnificabant Deum dicentes: «Propheta magnus surrexit in nobis» et: «Deus visitavit plebem suam». [17]Et exiit hic sermo in universam Iudaeam de eo et omnem circa regionem. [18]Et nuntiaverunt Ioanni discipuli eius de omnibus his. [19]Et convocavit duos de discipulis suis Ioannes et misit ad Dominum dicens: «Tu es qui venturus es, an alium exspectamus?». [20]Cum autem venissent ad eum viri, dixerunt: «Ioannes Baptista misit nos ad te dicens: 'Tu es qui venturus es, an alium exspectamus?'». [21]In ipsa hora curavit multos a languoribus et plagis et spiritibus malis et caecis multis donavit visum. [22]Et respondens dixit illis: «Euntes nuntiate Ioanni, quae vidistis et audistis: *caeci vident*, claudi ambulant, leprosi mundantur et surdi audiunt, mortui resurgunt, *pauperes evangelizantur*; [23]et beatus est, quicumque non fuerit scandalizatus in me». [24]Et cum discessissent nuntii Ioannis, coepit dicere de Ioanne ad turbas: «Quid existis in desertum videre? Arundinem vento moveri? [25]Sed quid existis videre? Hominem mollibus vestimentis indutum? Ecce, qui in veste pretiosa sunt et deliciis, in domibus regum sunt. [26]Sed quid existis videre? Prophetam? Utique, dico vobis, et plus quam prophetam. [27]Hic est, de quo scriptum est: "*Ecce mitto angelum meum ante faciem tuam, / qui praeparabit viam tuam ante te*". [28]Dico vobis: Maior inter natos mulierum Ioanne nemo est; qui autem minor est in regno Dei, maior est illo. [29]Et omnis populus audiens et publicani iustificaverunt Deum, baptizati baptismo Ioannis; [30]pharisaei autem et legis periti consilium Dei spreverunt in semetipsos, non baptizati ab eo. [31]Cui ergo similes dicam homines generationis huius, et cui similes sunt? [32]Similes sunt pueris sedentibus in foro et loquentibus ad invicem, quod dicit: "Cantavimus vobis tibiis, et non saltastis; / lamentavimus, et non plorastis!". [33]Venit enim Ioannes Baptista neque manducans panem neque bibens vinum, et dicitis: 'Daemonium habet!'; [34]venit Filius hominis manducans et bibens, et dicitis: 'Ecce homo devorator et bibens vinum, amicus publicanorum et peccatorum!'. [35]Et iustificata est sapientia ab omnibus filiis suis». [36]Rogabat autem illum quidam de pharisaeis, ut manducaret cum illo; et ingressus domum pharisaei discubuit. [37]Et ecce mulier, quae erat in civitate peccatrix, ut cognovit quod accubuit in domo pharisaei, attulit alabastrum unguenti [38]et stans retro secus pedes eius flens lacrimis coepit rigare pedes eius et capillis capitis sui tergebat, et osculabatur pedes eius et unguento ungebat. [39]Videns autem pharisaeus, qui vocaverat eum, ait intra se dicens: «Hic si esset propheta sciret utique quae et qualis mulier, quae tangit eum, quia peccatrix est». [40]Et respondens Iesus dixit ad illum: «Simon, habeo tibi aliquid dicere». At ille ait: «Magister, dic». [41]«Duo debitores erant cuidam feneratori: unus debebat denarios quingentos, alius quinquaginta. [42]Non habentibus illis, unde redderent, donavit utrisque. Quis ergo eorum plus diliget eum?». [43]Respondens Simon dixit: «Aestimo quia is, cui plus donavit». At ille dixit ei: «Recte iudicasti». [44]Et conversus ad mulierem, dixit Simoni: «Vides hanc mulierem? Intravi in domum tuam: aquam pedibus meis non dedisti; haec autem lacrimis rigavit pedes meos et capillis suis tersit. [45]Osculum mihi non dedisti; haec autem, ex quo intravi, non cessavit osculari pedes meos. [46]Oleo caput meum non unxisti; haec autem unguento unxit pedes meos. [47]Propter quod dico tibi: Remissa sunt peccata eius multa, quoniam dilexit multum; cui autem minus dimittitur, minus diligit». [48]Dixit autem ad illam: «Remissa sunt peccata tua». [49]Et coeperunt, qui simul accumbebant, dicere intra se: «Quis est hic, qui etiam peccata dimittit?». [50]Dixit autem ad mulierem: «Fides tua te salvam fecit; vade in pace!».

[8] [1]Et factum est deinceps, et ipse iter faciebat per civitatem et castellum praedicans et evangelizans regnum Dei, et Duodecim cum illo [2]et mulieres aliquae, quae erant curatae ab spiritibus malignis et infirmitatibus, Maria, quae vocatur Magdalene, de qua daemonia septem exierant, [3]et Ioanna uxor Chuza, procuratoris Herodis, et Susanna et aliae multae, quae ministrabant eis de facultatibus suis. [4]Cum autem turba plurima conveniret et de singulis civitatibus properarent ad eum, dixit per similitudinem: [5]«Exiit, qui seminat, seminare semen suum. Et dum seminat ipse, aliud cecidit secus viam et conculcatum est, et volucres caeli comederunt illud. [6]Et aliud cecidit super petram et natum aruit, quia non habebat umorem. [7]Et aliud cecidit inter spinas, et simul exortae spinae suffocaverunt illud. [8]Et aliud cecidit in terram bonam et ortum fecit fructum centuplum». Haec dicens clamabat: «Qui habet aures audiendi, audiat». [9]Interrogabant autem eum discipuli eius quae esset haec parabola. [10]Quibus ipse dixit: «Vobis datum est nosse mysteria regni Dei, ceteris autem in parabolis, ut *videntes non videant et audientes non intellegant*. [11]Est autem haec parabola: Semen est verbum Dei. [12]Qui autem secus viam, sunt qui audiunt; deinde venit Diabolus et tollit verbum de corde eorum, ne credentes salvi fiant. [13]Qui autem supra petram: qui cum audierint, cum gaudio suscipiunt verbum; et hi radices non habent, qui ad tempus credunt, et in tempore tentationis recedunt. [14]Quod autem in spinis cecidit: hi sunt, qui audierunt et a sollicitudinibus et divitiis et voluptatibus vitae euntes suffocantur et non referunt fructum. [15]Quod autem in bonam terram: hi sunt, qui in corde bono et optimo audientes verbum retinent et fructum afferunt in patientia. [16]Nemo autem lucernam accendens operit eam vaso aut subtus lectum ponit, sed supra candelabrum ponit, ut intrantes videant lumen. [17]Non enim est occultum, quod non manifestetur, nec absconditum, quod non cognoscatur et in palam veniat. [18]Videte ergo quomodo auditis: qui enim habet, dabitur illi; et quicumque non habet, etiam quod putat se habere, auferetur ab illo». [19]Venerunt autem ad illum mater et fratres eius, et non poterant adire ad eum prae turba. [20]Et nuntiatum est illi: «Mater tua et fratres tui stant foris volentes te videre». [21]Qui respondens dixit ad eos: «Mater mea et fratres mei hi sunt, qui verbum Dei audiunt et faciunt». [22]Factum est autem in una dierum, et ipse ascendit in navem et discipuli eius, et ait ad illos: «Transfretemus trans stagnum». Et ascenderunt. [23]Navigantibus autem illis, obdormivit. Et descendit procella venti in stagnum, et complebantur et periclitabantur. [24]Accedentes autem suscitaverunt eum dicentes: «Praeceptor, praeceptor, perimus!». At ille surgens increpavit ventum et tempestatem aquae, et cessaverunt, et facta est tranquillitas. [25]Dixit autem illis: «Ubi est fides vestra?». Qui timentes mirati sunt dicentes ad invicem: «Quis putas hic est, quia et ventis imperat et aquae, et oboediunt ei?». [26]Enavigaverunt autem ad regionem Gergesenorum, quae est contra Galilaeam. [27]Et cum egressus esset ad terram, occurrit illi vir quidam de civitate, qui habebat daemonia et iam tempore multo vestimento non induebatur, neque

in domo manebat sed in monumentis. [28]Is ut vidit Iesum, exclamans procidit ante illum et voce magna dixit: «Quid mihi et tibi est, Iesu, Fili Dei Altissimi? Obsecro te, ne me torqueas». [29]Praecipiebat enim spiritui immundo, ut exiret ab homine. Multis enim temporibus arripiebat illum, et vinciebatur catenis et compedibus custoditus; et ruptis vinculis, agebatur a daemonio in deserta. [30]Interrogavit autem illum Iesus dicens: «Quod tibi nomen est?». At ille dixit: «Legio», quia intraverunt daemonia multa in eum. [31]Et rogabant eum, ne imperaret illis, ut in abyssum irent. [32]Erat autem ibi grex porcorum multorum pascentium in monte; et rogaverunt eum, ut permitteret eis in illos ingredi. Et permisit illis. [33]Exierunt ergo daemonia ab homine et intraverunt in porcos, et impetu abiit grex per praeceps in stagnum et suffocatus est. [34]Quod ut viderunt factum, qui pascebant, fugerunt et nuntiaverunt in civitatem et in villas. [35]Exierunt autem videre, quod factum est, et venerunt ad Iesum, et invenerunt hominem sedentem, a quo daemonia exierant, vestitum ac sana mente ad pedes Iesu, et timuerunt. [36]Nuntiaverunt autem illis hi, qui viderant, quomodo sanus factus esset, qui a daemonio vexabatur. [37]Et rogaverunt illum omnis multitudo regionis Gergesenorum, ut discederet ab ipsis, quia timore magno tenebantur. Ipse autem ascendens navem reversus est. [38]Et rogabat illum vir, a quo daemonia exierant, ut cum eo esset. Dimisit autem eum dicens: [39]«Redi domum tuam et narra quanta tibi fecit Deus». Et abiit per universam civitatem praedicans quanta illi fecisset Iesus. [40]Cum autem rediret Iesus, excepit illum turba; erant enim omnes exspectantes eum. [41]Et ecce venit vir, cui nomen Iairus, et ipse princeps synagogae erat, et cecidit ad pedes Iesu rogans eum, ut intraret in domum eius, [42]quia filia unica erat illi fere annorum duodecim, et haec moriebatur. Et dum iret, a turbis comprimebatur. [43]Et mulier quaedam erat in fluxu sanguinis ab annis duodecim, quae in medicos erogaverat omnem substantiam suam, nec ab ullo potuit curari; [44]accessit retro et tetigit fimbriam vestimenti eius, et confestim stetit fluxus sanguinis eius. [45]Et ait Iesus: «Quis est qui me tetigit?». Negantibus autem omnibus, dixit Petrus: «Praeceptor, turbae te comprimunt et affligunt». [46]At dixit Iesus: «Tetigit me aliquis; nam et ego novi virtutem de me exisse». [47]Videns autem mulier quia non latuit, tremens venit et procidit ante eum et ob quam causam tetigerit eum indicavit coram omni populo et quemadmodum confestim sanata sit. [48]At ipse dixit illi: «Filia, fides tua te salvam fecit. Vade in pace». [49]Adhuc illo loquente, venit quidam e domo principis synagogae dicens: «Mortua est filia tua; noli amplius vexare magistrum». [50]Iesus autem, audito hoc verbo, respondit ei: «Noli timere; crede tantum, et salva erit». [51]Et cum venisset domum, non permisit intrare secum quemquam nisi Petrum et Ioannem et Iacobum et patrem puellae et matrem. [52]Flebant autem omnes et plangebant illam. At ille dixit: «Nolite flere; non est enim mortua, sed dormit». [53]Et deridebant eum scientes quia mortua esset. [54]Ipse autem tenens manum eius clamavit dicens: «Puella, surge!». [55]Et reversus est spiritus eius, et surrexit continuo; et iussit illi dari manducare. [56]Et stupuerunt parentes eius, quibus praecepit, ne alicui dicerent, quod factum erat. **[9]** [1]Convocatis autem Duodecim, dedit illis virtutem et potestatem super omnia daemonia et langueres curarent, [2]et misit illos praedicare regnum Dei et sanare infirmos; [3]et ait ad illos: «Nihil tuleritis in via, neque virgam neque peram neque panem neque pecuniam, neque duas tunicas habeatis. [4]Et in quamcumque domum intraveritis, ibi manete et inde exite. [5]Et quicumque non receperint vos, exeuntes de civitate illa pulverem pedum vestrorum excutite in testimonium supra illos». [6]Egressi autem circumibant per castella evangelizantes et curantes ubique. [7]Audivit autem Herodes tetrarcha omnia, quae fiebant, et haesitabat, eo quod diceretur a quibusdam: «Ioannes surrexit a mortuis»; [8]a quibusdam vero: «Elias apparuit»; ab aliis autem: «Propheta unus de antiquis surrexit». [9]Et ait Herodes: «Ioannem ego decollavi; quis autem est iste, de quo audio ego talia?». Et quaerebat videre eum. [10]Et reversi apostoli narraverunt illi, quaecumque fecerunt. Et assumptis illis, secessit seorsum ad civitatem, quae vocatur Bethsaida. [11]Quod cum cognovissent turbae, secutae sunt illum. Et excepit illos et loquebatur illis de regno Dei, et eos, qui cura indigebant, sanabat. [12]Dies autem coeperat declinare; et accedentes Duodecim dixerunt illi: «Dimitte turbam, ut euntes in castella villasque, quae circa sunt, divertant et inveniant escas, quia hic in loco deserto sumus». [13]Ait autem ad illos: «Vos date illis manducare». At illi dixerunt: «Non sunt nobis plus quam quinque panes et duo pisces, nisi forte nos eamus et emamus in omnem hanc turbam escas». [14]Erant enim fere viri quinque milia. Ait autem ad discipulos suos: «Facite illos discumbere per convivia ad quinquagenos». [15]Et ita fecerunt et discumbere fecerunt omnes. [16]Acceptis autem quinque panibus et duobus piscibus, respexit in caelum et benedixit illis et fregit et dabat discipulis suis, ut ponerent ante turbam. [17]Et manducaverunt et saturati sunt omnes; et sublatum est, quod superfuit illis, fragmentorum cophini duodecim. [18]Et factum est cum solus esset orans, erant cum illo discipuli, et interrogavit illos dicens: «Quem me dicunt esse turbae?». [19]At illi responderunt et dixerunt: «Ioannem Baptistam, alii autem Eliam, alii vero: Propheta unus de prioribus surrexit». [20]Dixit autem illis: «Vos autem quem me esse dicitis?». Respondens Petrus dixit: «Christum Dei». [21]At ille increpans illos praecepit, ne cui dicerent hoc, [22]dicens: «Oportet Filium hominis multa pati et reprobari a senioribus et principibus sacerdotum et scribis et occidi et tertia die resurgere». ²³Dicebat autem ad omnes: «Si quis vult post me venire, abneget semetipsum et tollat crucem suam cotidie et sequatur me. ²⁴Qui enim voluerit animam suam salvam facere, perdet illam; qui autem perdiderit animam suam propter me, hic salvam faciet illam. ²⁵Quid enim proficit homo, si lucretur universum mundum, se autem ipsum perdat vel detrimentum sui faciat? ²⁶Nam qui me erubuerit et meos sermones, hunc Filius hominis erubescet, cum venerit in gloria sua et Patris et sanctorum angelorum. ²⁷Dico autem vobis vere: Sunt aliqui hic stantes, qui non gustabunt mortem, donec videant regnum Dei». ²⁸Factum est autem post haec verba fere dies octo, et assumpsit Petrum et Ioannem et Iacobum et ascendit in montem, ut oraret. ²⁹Et facta est, dum oraret, species vultus eius altera, et vestitus eius albus refulgens. ³⁰Et ecce duo viri loquebantur cum illo, et erant Moyses et Elias, ³¹qui visi in gloria dicebant exodum eius, quem completurus erat in Ierusalem. ³²Petrus vero et qui cum illo gravati erant somno; et evigilantes viderunt gloriam eius et duos viros, qui stabant cum illo. ³³Et factum est cum discederent ab illo, ait Petrus ad Iesum: «Praeceptor, bonum est nos hic esse; et faciamus tria tabernacula: unum tibi et unum Moysi et unum Eliae», nesciens quid diceret. ³⁴Haec autem illo loquente, facta est nubes et obumbravit eos; et timuerunt intrantibus illis in nubem. ³⁵Et vox facta est de nube dicens: «Hic est Filius meus electus; ipsum audite». ³⁶Et dum fieret vox, inventus est Iesus solus. Et ipsi tacuerunt et nemini dixerunt in illis diebus quidquam ex his, quae viderant. ³⁷Factum est autem in sequenti die, descendentibus illis de monte, occurrit illi turba multa. ³⁸Et ecce vir de turba exclamavit dicens: «Magister, obsecro te, respice in filium meum, quia unicus est mihi; ³⁹et ecce spiritus apprehendit illum, et subito clamat et dissipat eum cum spuma et vix discedit ab eo dilanians eum; ⁴⁰et rogavi discipulos tuos, ut eicerent illum, et non potuerunt». ⁴¹Respondens autem Iesus dixit: «O generatio infidelis et perversa, usquequo ero apud vos et patiar vos? Adduc huc filium tuum». ⁴²Et cum accederet, elisit illum daemonium et dissipavit. Et increpavit Iesus spiritum immundum et sanavit puerum et reddidit illum patri eius. ⁴³Stupebant autem omnes in magnitudine Dei. Omnibusque mirantibus in omnibus, quae faciebat, dixit ad discipulos suos: ⁴⁴«Ponite vos in auribus vestris sermones istos: Filius enim hominis futurum est ut tradatur in manus hominum». ⁴⁵At illi ignorabant verbum istud, et erat velatum ante eos, ut non sentirent illud, et timebant interrogare eum de hoc verbo. ⁴⁶Intravit autem cogitatio in eos, quis eorum maior esset. ⁴⁷At Iesus sciens cogitationem cordis illorum, apprehendens puerum statuit eum secus se ⁴⁸et ait illis: «Quicumque susceperit puerum istum in nomine meo, me recipit; et, quicumque me receperit, recipit eum, qui me misit; nam qui minor est inter omnes vos, hic maior est». ⁴⁹Respondens autem Ioannes dixit: «Praeceptor, vidimus quendam in nomine tuo eicientem daemonia, et prohibuimus eum, quia non sequitur nobiscum». ⁵⁰Et ait ad illum Iesus: «Nolite prohibere; qui enim non est adversus vos, pro vobis est». ⁵¹Factum est autem dum complerentur dies assumptionis eius, et ipse faciem suam firmavit, ut iret Ierusalem, ⁵²et misit nuntios ante conspectum suum. Et euntes intraverunt in castellum Samaritanorum, ut pararent illi. ⁵³Et non receperunt eum, quia facies eius erat euntis Ierusalem. ⁵⁴Cum vidissent autem discipuli Iacobus et Ioannes dixerunt: «Domine, vis dicamus, ut *ignis descendat de caelo et consumat illos?*». ⁵⁵Et conversus increpavit illos. ⁵⁶Et ierunt in aliud castellum. ⁵⁷Et euntibus illis in via, dixit quidam ad illum: «Sequar te, quocumque ieris». ⁵⁸Et ait illi Iesus: «Vulpes foveas habent et volucres caeli nidos, Filius autem hominis non habet, ubi caput reclinet». ⁵⁹Ait autem ad alterum: «Sequere me». Ille autem dixit: «Domine, permitte mihi primum ire et sepelire patrem meum». ⁶⁰Dixitque ei Iesus: «Sine, ut mortui sepeliant mortuos suos; tu autem vade, annuntia regnum Dei». ⁶¹Et ait alter: «Sequar te, Domine, sed primum permitte mihi renuntiare his, qui domi sunt». ⁶²Ait ad illum Iesus: «Nemo mittens manum suam in aratrum et aspiciens retro, aptus est regno Dei». **[10]** ¹Post haec autem designavit Dominus alios septuaginta duos et misit illos binos ante faciem suam in omnem civitatem et locum, quo erat ipse venturus. ²Et dicebat illis: «Messis quidem multa, operarii autem pauci; rogate ergo Dominum messis, ut mittat operarios in messem suam. ³Ite; ecce ego mitto vos sicut agnos inter lupos. ⁴Nolite portare sacculum, neque peram neque calceamenta, et neminem per viam salutaveritis. ⁵In quamcumque domum intraveritis, primum dicite: "Pax huic domui". ⁶Et si ibi fuerit filius pacis, requiescet super illam pax vestra; sin autem ad vos revertetur. ⁷In eadem autem domo manete edentes et bibentes, quae apud illos sunt: dignus enim est operarius mercede sua. Nolite transire de domo in domum. ⁸Et in quamcumque civitatem intraveritis, et susceperint vos, manducate, quae apponuntur vobis, ⁹et curate infirmos, qui in illa sunt, et dicite illis: "Appropinquavit in vos regnum Dei". ¹⁰In quamcumque civitatem intraveritis, et non receperint vos, exeuntes in plateas eius dicite: ¹¹"Etiam pulverem, qui adhaesit nobis ad pedes de civitate vestra, extergimus in vos; tamen hoc scitote quia appropinquavit regnum Dei". ¹²Dico vobis quia Sodomis in die illa remissius erit quam illi civitati. ¹³Vae tibi, Chorazin! Vae tibi, Bethsaida! Quia si in Tyro et Sidone factae fuissent virtutes, quae in vobis factae sunt, olim in cilicio et cinere sedentes paeniterent. ¹⁴Verumtamen Tyro et Sidoni remissius erit in iudicio quam vobis. [15]Et tu, Capharnaum, numquid *usque in caelum exaltaberis? Usque ad infernum demergeris!* [16]Qui vos audit, me audit; et qui vos spernit, me spernit; qui autem me spernit, spernit eum, qui me misit». [17]Reversi sunt autem septuaginta duo cum gaudio dicentes: «Domine, etiam daemonia subiciuntur nobis in nomine tuo!». [18]Et ait illis: «Videbam Satanam sicut fulgur de caelo cadentem. [19]Ecce dedi vobis potestatem calcandi supra serpentes et scorpiones et supra omnem virtutem inimici; et nihil vobis nocebit. [20]Verumtamen in hoc nolite gaudere quia spiritus vobis subiciuntur; gaudete autem quod nomina vestra scripta sunt in caelis». [21]In ipsa hora exsultavit Spiritu Sancto et dixit: «Confiteor tibi, Pater, Domine caeli et terrae, quod abscondisti haec a sapientibus et prudentibus et revelasti ea parvulis; etiam, Pater, quia sic placuit ante te. [22]Omnia mihi tradita sunt a Patre meo; et nemo scit qui sit Filius nisi Pater, et qui sit Pater nisi Filius et cui voluerit Filius revelare». [23]Et conversus ad discipulos seorsum dixit: «Beati oculi, qui vident, quae videtis. [24]Dico enim vobis: Multi prophetae et reges voluerunt videre, quae vos videtis, et non viderunt, et audire, quae auditis, et non audierunt». [25]Et ecce quidam legis peritus surrexit tentans illum dicens: «Magister, quid faciendo vitam aeternam possidebo?». [26]At ille dixit ad eum: «In Lege quid scriptum est? Quomodo legis?». [27]Ille autem respondens dixit: «*Diliges Dominum Deum tuum ex toto corde tuo et ex tota anima tua et ex omnibus viribus tuis* et ex omni mente tua et *proximum tuum sicut teipsum*». [28]Dixitque illi: «Recte respondisti; hoc fac et vives». [29]Ille autem, volens iustificare seipsum, dixit ad Iesum: «Et quis est meus proximus?». [30]Suscipiens autem Iesus dixit: «Homo quidam descendebat ab Ierusalem in Iericho et incidit in latrones, qui etiam despoliaverunt eum et, plagis impositis, abierunt, semivivo relicto. [31]Accidit autem, ut sacerdos quidam descenderet eadem via et, viso illo, praeterivit; [32]similiter et Levita, cum esset secus locum et videret eum, pertransiit. [33]Samaritanus autem quidam iter faciens, venit secus eum et videns eum misericordia motus est, [34]et appropians alligavit vulnera eius infundens oleum et vinum; et imponens illum in iumentum suum duxit in stabulum et curam eius egit. [35]Et altera die protulit duos denarios et dedit stabulario et ait: "Curam illius habe, et, quodcumque supererogaveris, ego, cum rediero, reddam tibi". [36]Quis horum trium videtur tibi proximus fuisse illi, qui incidit in latrones?». [37]At ille dixit: «Qui fecit misericordiam in illum». Et ait illi Iesus: «Vade et tu fac similiter». [38]Cum autem irent, ipse intravit in quoddam castellum, et mulier quaedam Martha nomine excepit illum. [39]Et huic erat soror nomine Maria, quae etiam sedens secus pedes Domini audiebat verbum illius. [40]Martha autem satagebat circa frequens ministerium; quae stetit et ait: «Domine, non est tibi curae quod soror mea reliquit me solam ministrare? Dic ergo illi, ut me adiuvet». [41]Et respondens dixit illi Dominus: «Martha, Martha, sollicita es et turbaris erga plurima, [42]porro unum est necessarium; Maria enim optimam partem elegit, quae non auferetur ab ea». [11] [1]Et factum est cum esset in loco quodam orans, ut cessavit, dixit unus ex discipulis eius ad eum: «Domine, doce nos orare, sicut et Ioannes docuit discipulos suos». [2]Et ait illis: «Cum oratis, dicite: Pater, sanctificetur nomen tuum, / adveniat regnum tuum; / [3]panem nostrum cotidianum da nobis cotidie, / [4]et dimitte nobis peccata nostra, / siquidem et ipsi dimittimus omni debenti nobis, / et ne nos inducas in tentationem». [5]Et ait ad illos: «Quis vestrum habebit amicum et ibit ad illum media nocte et dicet illi: "Amice, commoda mihi tres panes, [6]quoniam amicus meus venit de via ad me, et non habeo, quod ponam ante illum"; [7]et ille de intus respondens dicat: "Noli mihi molestus esse; iam ostium clausum est, et pueri mei mecum sunt in cubili; non possum surgere et dare tibi". [8]Dico vobis: Et si non dabit illi surgens, eo quod amicus eius sit, propter improbitatem tamen eius surget et dabit illi, quotquot habet necessarios. [9]Et ego vobis dico: Petite, et dabitur vobis; quaerite, et invenietis; pulsate, et aperietur vobis. [10]Omnis enim qui petit, accipit; et, qui quaerit, invenit; et pulsanti aperietur. [11]Quem autem ex vobis patrem filius petierit piscem, numquid pro pisce serpentem dabit illi? [12]Aut si petierit ovum, numquid porriget illi scorpionem? [13]Si ergo vos, cum sitis mali, nostis dona bona dare filiis vestris, quanto magis Pater de caelo dabit Spiritum Sanctum petentibus se». [14]Et erat eiciens daemonium, et illud erat mutum; et factum est cum daemonium exisset, locutus est mutus. Et admiratae sunt turbae; [15]quidam autem ex eis dixerunt: «In Beelzebul principe daemoniorum eicit daemonia». [16]Et alii tentantes signum de caelo quaerebant ab eo. [17]Ipse autem sciens cogitationes eorum dixit eis: «Omne regnum in seipsum divisum desolatur, et domus supra domum cadit. [18]Si autem et Satanas in seipsum divisus est, quomodo stabit regnum ipsius? Quia dicitis in Beelzebul eicere me daemonia. [19]Si autem ego in Beelzebul eicio daemonia, filii vestri in quo eiciunt? Ideo ipsi iudices vestri erunt. [20]Porro si in digito Dei eicio daemonia, profecto pervenit in vos regnum Dei. [21]Cum fortis armatus custodit atrium suum, in pace sunt ea, quae possidet; [22]si autem fortior illo superveniens vicerit eum, universa arma eius auferet, in quibus confidebat, et spolia eius distribuet. [23]Qui non est mecum, adversum me est; et, qui non colligit mecum, dispergit. [24]Cum immundus spiritus exierit de homine, perambulat per loca inaquosa quaerens requiem et non inveniens dicit: 'Revertar in domum meam unde exivi'. [25]Et cum venerit, invenit scopis mundatam et exornatam. [26]Et tunc vadit et assumit septem alios spiritus nequiores se, et ingressi habitant ibi; et sunt novissima hominis illius peiora prioribus». ²⁷Factum est autem cum haec diceret, extollens vocem quaedam mulier de turba dixit illi: «Beatus venter, qui te portavit, et ubera, quae suxisti!». ²⁸At ille dixit: «Quinimmo beati, qui audiunt verbum Dei et custodiunt!». ²⁹Turbis autem concurrentibus, coepit dicere: «Generatio haec generatio nequam est; signum quaerit, et signum non dabitur illi nisi signum Ionae. ³⁰Nam sicut Ionas fuit signum Ninevitis, ita erit et Filius hominis generationi isti. ³¹Regina austri surget in iudicio cum viris generationis huius et condemnabit illos, quia venit a finibus terrae audire sapientiam Salomonis, et ecce plus Salomone hic. ³²Viri Ninevitae surgent in iudicio cum generatione hac et condemnabunt illam, quia paenitentiam egerunt ad praedicationem Ionae, et ecce plus Iona hic. ³³Nemo lucernam accendit et in abscondito ponit, neque sub modio, sed supra candelabrum, ut, qui ingrediuntur, lumen videant. ³⁴Lucerna corporis est oculus tuus. Si oculus tuus fuerit simplex, totum corpus tuum lucidum erit; si autem nequam fuerit, etiam corpus tuum tenebrosum erit. ³⁵Vide ergo, ne lumen, quod in te est, tenebrae sint. ³⁶Si ergo corpus tuum totum lucidum fuerit, non habens aliquam partem tenebrarum, erit lucidum totum, sicut quando lucerna in fulgore suo illuminat te». ³⁷Et cum loqueretur, rogavit illum quidam pharisaeus, ut pranderet apud se; et ingressus recubuit. ³⁸Pharisaeus autem videns miratus est quod non baptizatus esset ante prandium. ³⁹Et ait Dominus ad illum: «Nunc vos pharisaei, quod de foris est calicis et catini, mundatis, quod autem intus est vestrum, plenum est rapina et iniquitate. ⁴⁰Stulti! Nonne, qui fecit, quod de foris est, etiam id, quod de intus est, fecit? ⁴¹Verumtamen, quae insunt, date eleemosynam, et ecce omnia munda sunt vobis. ⁴²Sed vae vobis pharisaeis, quia decimatis mentam et rutam et omne holus et praeteritis iudicium et caritatem Dei! Haec autem oportuit facere et illa non omittere. ⁴³Vae vobis pharisaeis, quia diligitis primam cathedram in synagogis et salutationes in foro! ⁴⁴Vae vobis, quia estis ut monumenta, quae non parent, et homines ambulantes supra nesciunt!». ⁴⁵Respondens autem quidam ex legis peritis ait illi: «Magister, haec dicens etiam nobis contumeliam facis». ⁴⁶At ille ait: «Et vobis legis peritis: Vae, quia oneratis homines oneribus, quae portari non possunt, et ipsi uno digito vestro non tangitis sarcinas! ⁴⁷Vae vobis, quia aedificatis monumenta prophetarum, patres autem vestri occiderunt illos! ⁴⁸Profecto testificamini et consentitis operibus patrum vestrorum, quoniam ipsi quidem eos occiderunt, vos autem aedificatis. ⁴⁹Propterea et sapientia Dei dixit: Mittam ad illos prophetas et apostolos, et ex illis occident et persequentur, ⁵⁰ut requiratur sanguis omnium prophetarum, qui effusus est a constitutione mundi, a generatione ista, ⁵¹a sanguine Abel usque ad sanguinem Zachariae, qui periit inter altare et aedem. Ita dico vobis: Requiretur ab hac generatione. ⁵²Vae vobis legis peritis, quia tulistis clavem scientiae! Ipsi non introistis et eos, qui introibant, prohibuistis». ⁵³Cum autem inde exisset, coeperunt scribae et pharisaei graviter insistere et eum allicere in sermone de multis ⁵⁴insidiantes ei, ut caperent aliquid ex ore eius. [12] ¹Interea multis circumstantibus, ita ut se invicem conculcarent, coepit dicere ad discipulos suos primum: «Attendite a fermento pharisaeorum, quod est hypocrisis. ²Nihil autem opertum est, quod non reveletur, neque absconditum, quod non sciatur. ³Quoniam, quae in tenebris dixistis, in lumine audientur, et quod in aurem locuti estis in cubiculis, praedicabitur in tectis. ⁴Dico autem vobis amicis meis: Ne terreamini ab his, qui occidunt corpus, et post haec non habent amplius, quod faciant. ⁵Ostendam autem vobis quem timeatis: Timete eum, qui postquam occiderit, habet potestatem mittere in gehennam. Ita dico vobis: Hunc timete. ⁶Nonne quinque passeres veneunt dipundio? Et unus ex illis non est in oblivione coram Deo. ⁷Sed et capilli capitis vestri omnes numerati sunt. Nolite timere; multis passeribus pluris estis. ⁸Dico autem vobis: Omnis, quicumque confessus fuerit in me coram hominibus, et Filius hominis confitebitur in illo coram angelis Dei; ⁹qui autem negaverit me coram hominibus, denegabitur coram angelis Dei. ¹⁰Et omnis, qui dicet verbum in Filium hominis, remittetur illi; ei autem qui in Spiritum Sanctum blasphemaverit, non remittetur. ¹¹Cum autem inducent vos in synagogas et ad magistratus et potestates, nolite solliciti esse qualiter aut quid respondeatis aut quid dicatis: ¹²Spiritus enim Sanctus docebit vos in ipsa hora, quae oporteat dicere». ¹³Ait autem quidam ei de turba: «Magister, dic fratri meo, ut dividat mecum hereditatem». ¹⁴At ille dixit ei: «Homo, quis me constituit iudicem aut divisorem super vos?». ¹⁵Dixitque ad illos: «Videte et cavete ab omni avaritia, quia si cui res abundant, vita eius non est ex his, quae possidet». ¹⁶Dixit autem similitudinem ad illos dicens: «Hominis cuiusdam divitis uberes fructus ager attulit. ¹⁷Et cogitabat intra se dicens: "Quid faciam, quod non habeo, quo congregem fructus meos?". ¹⁸Et dixit: Hoc faciam: destruam horrea mea et maiora aedificabo, et illuc congregabo omne triticum et bona mea, ¹⁹et dicam animae meae: Anima, habes multa bona posita in annos plurimos; requiesce, comede, bibe, epulare". ²⁰Dixit autem illi Deus: "Stulte! Hac nocte animam tuam repetunt a te; quae autem parasti, cuius erunt?". ²¹Sic est qui sibi thesaurizat et non fit in Deum dives». ²²Dixitque ad discipulos suos: «Ideo dico vobis: nolite solliciti esse animae quid manducetis, neque corpori quid vestiamini. ²³Anima enim plus est quam esca, et corpus quam vestimentum. ²⁴Considerate corvos quia non seminant neque metunt, quibus non est cellarium neque horreum, et Deus pascit illos; quanto magis vos pluris estis volucribus. [25]Quis autem vestrum cogitando potest adicere ad aetatem suam cubitum? [26]Si ergo neque, quod minimum est, potestis, quid de ceteris solliciti estis? [27]Considerate lilia quomodo crescunt: non laborant, neque nent; dico autem vobis: Nec Salomon in omni gloria sua vestiebatur sicut unum ex istis. [28]Si autem fenum, quod hodie est agro est et cras in clibanum mittitur, Deus sic vestit, quanto magis vos, pusillae fidei. [29]Et vos nolite quaerere quid manducetis aut quid bibatis, et nolite solliciti esse. [30]Haec enim omnia gentes mundi quaerunt; Pater autem vester scit quoniam his indigetis. [31]Verumtamen quaerite regnum eius; et haec adicientur vobis. [32]Noli timere, pusillus grex, quia complacuit Patri vestro dare vobis regnum. [33]Vendite, quae possidetis, et date eleemosynam. Facite vobis sacculos, qui non veterescunt, thesaurum non deficientem in caelis, quo fur non appropiat, neque tinea corrumpit; [34]ubi enim thesaurus vester est, ibi et cor vestrum erit. [35]Sint lumbi vestri praecincti et lucernae ardentes, [36]et vos similes hominibus exspectantibus dominum suum, quando revertatur a nuptiis, ut, cum venerit et pulsaverit, confestim aperiant ei. [37]Beati servi illi, quos cum venerit dominus invenerit vigilantes. Amen dico vobis, quod praecinget se et faciet illos discumbere, et transiens ministrabit illis. [38]Et si venerit in secunda vigilia et si in tertia vigilia venerit et ita invenerit, beati sunt illi. [39]Hoc autem scitote quia, si sciret pater familias qua hora fur veniret, non sineret perfodi domum suam. [40]Et vos estote parati, quia, qua hora non putatis, Filius hominis venit». [41]Ait autem Petrus: «Domine, ad nos dicis hanc parabolam an et ad omnes?». [42]Et dixit Dominus: «Quis putas est fidelis dispensator et prudens, quem constituet dominus super familiam suam, ut det illis in tempore tritici mensuram? [43]Beatus ille servus, quem cum venerit dominus eius invenerit ita facientem. [44]Vere dico vobis: Supra omnia, quae possidet, constituet illum. [45]Quod si dixerit servus ille in corde suo: "Moram facit dominus meus venire", et coeperit percutere pueros et ancillas et edere et bibere et inebriari, [46]veniet dominus servi illius in die, qua non sperat, et hora, qua nescit, et dividet eum partemque eius cum infidelibus ponet. [47]Ille autem servus, qui cognovit voluntatem domini sui et non praeparavit vel non fecit secundum voluntatem eius, vapulabit multis; [48]qui autem non cognovit et fecit digna plagis, vapulabit paucis. Omni autem, cui multum datum est, multum quaeretur ab eo, et cui commendaverunt multum, plus petent ab eo. [49]Ignem veni mittere in terram et quid volo? Si iam accensus esset! [50]Baptisma autem habeo baptizari et quomodo coartor, usque dum perficiatur! [51]Putatis quia pacem veni dare in terram? Non, dico vobis, sed separationem. [52]Erunt enim ex hoc quinque in domo una divisi: tres in duo et duo in tres; [53]dividentur pater in filium et *filius in patrem*, mater in filiam et *filia in matrem*, socrus in nurum suam et *nurus in socrum*». [54]Dicebat autem et ad turbas: «Cum videritis nubem orientem ab occasu, statim dicitis: "Nimbus venit", et ita fit; [55]et cum austrum flantem, dicitis: "Aestus erit", et fit. [56]Hypocritae, faciem terrae et caeli nostis probare, hoc autem tempus quomodo nescitis probare? [57]Quid autem et a vobis ipsis non iudicatis, quod iustum est? [58]Cum autem vadis cum adversario tuo ad principem, in via da operam liberari ab illo, ne forte trahat te apud iudicem, et iudex tradat te exactori, et exactor mittat te in carcerem. [59]Dico tibi: Non exies inde, donec etiam novissimum minutum reddas». **[13]** [1]Aderant autem quidam ipso in tempore nuntiantes illi de Galilaeis, quorum sanguinem Pilatus miscuit cum sacrificiis eorum. [2]Et respondens dixit illis: «Putatis quod hi Galilaei prae omnibus Galilaeis peccatores fuerunt, quia talia passi sunt? [3]Non, dico vobis, sed nisi paenitentiam egeritis, omnes similiter peribitis. [4]Vel illi decem et octo, supra quos cecidit turris in Siloam et occidit eos, putatis quia et ipsi debitores fuerunt praeter omnes homines habitantes in Ierusalem? [5]Non, dico vobis, sed si non paenitentiam egeritis, omnes similiter peribitis». [6]Dicebat autem hanc similitudinem: «Arborem fici habebat quidam plantatam in vinea sua et venit quaerens fructum in illa et non invenit. [7]Dixit autem ad cultorem vineae: "Ecce anni tres sunt, ex quo venio quaerens fructum in ficulnea hac, et non invenio. Succide ergo illam. Ut quid etiam terram evacuat?". [8]At ille respondens dicit illi: "Domine, dimitte illam et hoc anno, usque dum fodiam circa illam et mittam stercora, [9]et siquidem fecerit fructum in futurum; sin autem succides eam"». [10]Erat autem docens in una synagogarum sabbatis. [11]Et ecce mulier, quae habebat spiritum infirmitatis annis decem et octo, et erat inclinata nec omnino poterat sursum respicere. [12]Quam cum vidisset Iesus vocavit et ait illi: «Mulier, dimissa es ab infirmitate tua», [13]et imposuit illi manus; et confestim erecta est et glorificabat Deum. [14]Respondens autem archisynagogus, indignans quia sabbato curasset Iesus, dicebat turbae: «Sex dies sunt, in quibus oportet operari; in his ergo venite et curamini et non in die sabbati». [15]Respondit autem ad illum Dominus et dixit: «Hypocritae, unusquisque vestrum sabbato non solvit bovem suum aut asinum a praesepio et ducit adaquare? [16]Hanc autem filiam Abrahae, quam alligavit Satanas ecce decem et octo annis, non oportuit solvi a vinculo isto die sabbati?». [17]Et cum haec diceret, erubescebant omnes adversarii eius, et omnis populus gaudebat in universis, quae gloriose fiebant ab eo. [18]Dicebat ergo: «Cui simile est regnum Dei, et cui simile existimabo illud? [19]Simile est grano sinapis, quod acceptum homo misit in hortum suum, et crevit et factum est in arborem, et volucres caeli requieverunt in ramis eius». ²⁰Et iterum dixit: «Cui simile aestimabo regnum Dei? ²¹Simile est fermento, quod acceptum mulier abscondit in farinae sata tria, donec fermentaretur totum». ²²Et ibat per civitates et castella docens et iter faciens in Hierosolymam. ²³Ait autem illi quidam: «Domine, pauci sunt, qui salvantur?». Ipse autem dixit ad illos: ²⁴«Contendite intrare per angustam portam, quia multi, dico vobis, quaerent intrare et non poterunt. ²⁵Cum autem surrexerit pater familias et clauserit ostium, et incipietis foris stare et pulsare ostium dicentes: "Domine, aperi nobis"; et respondens dicet vobis: "Nescio vos unde sitis". ²⁶Tunc incipietis dicere: "Manducavimus coram te et bibimus, et in plateis nostris docuisti"; ²⁷et dicet loquens vobis: "Nescio vos unde sitis; discedite a me, omnes operarii iniquitatis". ²⁸Ibi erit fletus et stridor dentium, cum videritis Abraham et Isaac et Iacob et omnes prophetas in regno Dei, vos autem expelli foras. ²⁹Et venient ab oriente et occidente et aquilone et austro et accumbent in regno Dei. ³⁰Et ecce sunt novissimi, qui erunt primi, et sunt primi, qui erunt novissimi». ³¹In ipsa hora accesserunt quidam pharisaeorum dicentes illi: «Exi et vade hinc, quia Herodes vult te occidere». ³²Et ait illis: «Ite, dicite vulpi illi: "Ecce eicio daemonia et sanitates perficio hodie et cras et tertia consummor. ³³Verumtamen oportet me hodie et cras et sequenti ambulare, quia non capit prophetam perire extra Ierusalem". ³⁴Ierusalem, Ierusalem, quae occidis prophetas et lapidas eos, qui missi sunt ad te, quotiens volui congregare filios tuos, quemadmodum avis nidum suum sub pinnis, et noluistis. ³⁵Ecce *relinquitur vobis domus vestra*. Dico autem vobis: Non videbitis me, donec veniat cum dicetis: *"Benedictus, qui venit in nomine Domini"*». **[14]** ¹Et factum est, cum intraret in domum cuiusdam principis pharisaeorum sabbato manducare panem, et ipsi observabant eum. ²Et ecce homo quidam hydropicus erat ante illum. ³Et respondens Iesus dixit ad legis peritos et pharisaeos dicens: «Licet sabbato curare an non?». ⁴At illi tacuerunt. Ipse vero apprehensum sanavit eum ac dimisit. ⁵Et ad illos dixit: «Cuius vestrum filius aut bos in puteum cadet, et non continuo extrahet illum die sabbati?». ⁶Et non poterant ad haec respondere illi. ⁷Dicebat autem ad invitatos parabolam, intendens quomodo primos accubitus eligerent, dicens ad illos: ⁸«Cum invitatus fueris ab aliquo ad nuptias, non discumbas in primo loco, ne forte honoratior te sit invitatus ab eo, ⁹et veniens is, qui te et illum vocavit, dicat tibi: "Da huic locum"; et tunc incipias cum rubore novissimum locum tenere. ¹⁰Sed cum vocatus fueris, vade, recumbe in novissimo loco, ut, cum venerit qui te invitavit, dicat tibi: "Amice, ascende superius"; tunc erit tibi gloria coram omnibus simul discumbentibus. ¹¹Quia omnis, qui se exaltat, humiliabitur; et, qui se humiliat, exaltabitur». ¹²Dicebat autem et ei, qui se invitaverat: «Cum facis prandium aut cenam, noli vocare amicos tuos neque fratres tuos neque cognatos neque vicinos divites, ne forte et ipsi te reinvitent et fiat tibi retributio. ¹³Sed cum facis convivium, voca pauperes, debiles, claudos, caecos; ¹⁴et beatus eris, quia non habent retribuere tibi. Retribuetur enim tibi in resurrectione iustorum». ¹⁵Haec cum audisset quidam de simul discumbentibus, dixit illi: «Beatus, qui manducabit panem in regno Dei». ¹⁶At ipse dixit ei: «Homo quidam fecit cenam magnam et vocavit multos; ¹⁷et misit servum suum hora cenae dicere invitatis: "Venite, quia iam paratum est". ¹⁸Et coeperunt simul omnes excusare. Primus dixit ei: "Villam emi et necesse habeo exire et videre illam; rogo te, habe me excusatum". ¹⁹Et alter dixit: "Iuga boum emi quinque et eo probare illa; rogo te, habe me excusatum". ²⁰Et alius dixit: "Uxorem duxi et ideo non possum venire". ²¹Et reversus servus nuntiavit haec domino suo. Tunc iratus pater familias dixit servo suo: "Exi cito in plateas et vicos civitatis et pauperes ac debiles et caecos et claudos introduc huc". ²²Et ait servus: "Domine, factum est ut imperasti, et adhuc locus est". ²³Et ait dominus servo: "Exi in vias et saepes, et compelle intrare, ut impleatur domus mea. ²⁴Dico autem vobis quod nemo virorum illorum, qui vocati sunt, gustabit cenam meam"». ²⁵Ibant autem turbae multae cum eo, et conversus dixit ad illos: ²⁶«Si quis venit ad me et non odit patrem suum et matrem et uxorem et filios et fratres et sorores, adhuc et animam suam, non potest esse meus discipulus. ²⁷Et, qui non baiulat crucem suam et venit post me, non potest esse meus discipulus. ²⁸Quis enim ex vobis volens turrem aedificare, non prius sedens computat sumptus, si habet ad perficiendum? ²⁹Ne, posteaquam posuerit fundamentum et non potuerit perficere, omnes, qui vident, incipiant illudere ei ³⁰dicentes: "Hic homo coepit aedificare et non potuit consummare". ³¹Aut quis rex, iturus committere bellum adversus alium regem, non sedens prius cogitat si possit cum decem milibus occurrere ei, qui cum viginti milibus venit ad se? ³²Alioquin, adhuc illo longe agente, legationem mittens rogat ea, quae pacis sunt. ³³Sic ergo omnis ex vobis, qui non renuntiat omnibus, quae possidet, non potest meus esse discipulus. ³⁴Bonum est sal; si autem sal quoque evanuerit, in quo condietur? ³⁵Neque in terram neque in sterquilinium utile est, sed foras proiciunt illud. Qui habet aures audiendi, audiat». **[15]** ¹Erant autem appropinquantes ei omnes publicani et peccatores, ut audirent illum. ²Et murmurabant pharisaei et scribae dicentes: «Hic peccatores recipit et manducat cum illis». ³Et ait ad illos parabolam istam dicens: ⁴«Quis ex vobis homo, qui habet centum oves, et si perdiderit unam ex illis, nonne dimittit nonaginta novem in deserto et vadit ad illam, quae perierat, donec inveniat illam? [5]Et cum invenerit eam, imponit in umeros suos gaudens [6]et veniens domum convocat amicos et vicinos dicens illis: "Congratulamini mihi, quia inveni ovem meam, quae perierat". [7]Dico vobis: Ita gaudium erit in caelo super uno peccatore paenitentiam agente quam super nonaginta novem iustis, qui non indigent paenitentia. [8]Aut quae mulier habens drachmas decem, si perdiderit drachmam unam, nonne accendit lucernam et everrit domum et quaerit diligenter, donec inveniat? [9]Et cum invenerit, convocat amicas et vicinas dicens: "Congratulamini mihi, quia inveni drachmam, quam perdideram". [10]Ita dico vobis: Gaudium fit coram angelis Dei super uno peccatore paenitentiam agente». [11]Ait autem: «Homo quidam habebat duos filios. [12]Et dixit adulescentior ex illis patri: "Pater, da mihi portionem substantiae, quae me contingit". Et divisit illis substantiam. [13]Et non post multos dies, congregatis omnibus, adulescentior filius peregre profectus est in regionem longinquam et ibi dissipavit substantiam suam vivendo luxuriose. [14]Et postquam omnia consummasset, facta est fames valida in regione illa, et ipse coepit egere. [15]Et abiit et adhaesit uni civium regionis illius, et misit illum in villam suam, ut pasceret porcos; [16]et cupiebat saturari de siliquis, quas porci manducabant, et nemo illi dabat. [17]In se autem reversus dixit: "Quanti mercennarii patris mei abundant panibus, ego autem hic fame pereo. [18]Surgam et ibo ad patrem meum et dicam illi: Pater, peccavi in caelum et coram te [19]et iam non sum dignus vocari filius tuus; fac me sicut unum de mercennariis tuis". [20]Et surgens venit ad patrem suum. Cum autem adhuc longe esset, vidit illum pater ipsius et misericordia motus est et accurrens cecidit supra collum eius et osculatus est illum. [21]Dixitque ei filius: "Pater, peccavi in caelum et coram te; iam non sum dignus vocari filius tuus". [22]Dixit autem pater ad servos suos: "Cito proferte stolam primam et induite illum et date anulum in manum eius et calceamenta in pedes [23]et adducite vitulum saginatum, occidite et manducemus et epulemur, [24]quia hic filius meus mortuus erat et revixit, perierat et inventus est". Et coeperunt epulari. [25]Erat autem filius eius senior in agro et, cum veniret et appropinquaret domui, audivit symphoniam et choros, [26]et vocavit unum de servis et interrogavit quae haec essent. [27]Isque dixit illi: "Frater tuus venit, et occidit pater tuus vitulum saginatum, quia salvum illum recepit". [28]Indignatus est autem et nolebat introire. Pater ergo illius egressus coepit rogare illum. [29]At ille respondens dixit patri suo: "Ecce tot annis servio tibi et numquam mandatum tuum praeterii, et numquam dedisti mihi haedum, ut cum amicis meis epularer, [30]sed postquam filius tuus hic, qui devoravit substantiam tuam cum meretricibus, venit, occidisti illi vitulum saginatum". [31]At ipse dixit illi: "Fili, tu semper mecum es, et omnia mea tua sunt; [32]epulari autem et gaudere oportebat, quia frater tuus hic mortuus erat et revixit, perierat et inventus est"». [16] [1]Dicebat autem et ad discipulos: «Homo quidam erat dives, qui habebat vilicum, et hic diffamatus est apud illum quasi dissipasset bona ipsius. [2]Et vocavit illum et ait illi: "Quid hoc audio de te? Redde rationem vilicationis tuae; iam enim non poteris vilicare". [3]Ait autem vilicus intra se: "Quid faciam, quia dominus meus aufert a me vilicationem? Fodere non valeo, mendicare erubesco. [4]Scio quid faciam, ut, cum amotus fuero a vilicatione, recipiant me in domos suas". [5]Convocatis itaque singulis debitoribus domini sui, dicebat primo: "Quantum debes domino meo?". [6]At ille dixit: "Centum cados olei". Dixitque illi: "Accipe cautionem tuam et sede cito, scribe quinquaginta". [7]Deinde alii dixit: "Tu vero quantum debes?". Qui ait: "Centum coros tritici". Ait illi: "Accipe litteras tuas et scribe octoginta". [8]Et laudavit dominus vilicum iniquitatis, quia prudenter fecisset, quia filii huius saeculi prudentiores filiis lucis in generatione sua sunt. [9]Et ego vobis dico: Facite vobis amicos de mammona iniquitatis, ut, cum defecerit, recipiant vos in aeterna tabernacula. [10]Qui fidelis est in minimo, et in maiori fidelis est; et qui in modico iniquus est, et in maiori iniquus est. [11]Si ergo in iniquo mammona fideles non fuistis, quod verum est, quis credet vobis? [12]Et si in alieno fideles non fuistis, quod vestrum est, quis dabit vobis? [13]Nemo servus potest duobus dominis servire: aut enim unum odiet et alterum diliget, aut uni adhaerebit et alterum contemnet. Non potestis Deo servire et mammonae». [14]Audiebant autem omnia haec pharisaei, qui erant avari, et deridebant illum. [15]Et ait illis: «Vos estis qui iustificatis vos coram hominibus; Deus autem novit corda vestra, quia, quod hominibus altum est, abominatio est ante Deum. [16]Lex et Prophetae usque ad Ioannem; ex tunc regnum Dei evangelizatur, et omnis in illud vim facit. [17]Facilius est autem caelum et terram praeterire, quam de Lege unum apicem cadere. [18]Omnis, qui dimittit uxorem suam et ducit alteram, moechatur; et qui dimissam a viro ducit, moechatur. [19]Homo quidam erat dives et induebatur purpura et bysso et epulabatur cotidie splendide. [20]Quidam autem pauper nomine Lazarus iacebat ad ianuam eius ulceribus plenus [21]et cupiens saturari de his, quae cadebant de mensa divitis; sed et canes veniebant et lingebant ulcera eius. [22]Factum est autem ut moreretur pauper et portaretur ab angelis in sinum Abrahae; mortuus est autem et dives et sepultus est. [23]Et in inferno elevans oculos suos cum esset in tormentis, videbat Abraham a longe et Lazarum in sinu eius. [24]Et ipse clamans dixit: "Pater Abraham, miserere mei et mitte Lazarum, ut intingat extremum digiti sui in aquam, ut refrigeret linguam meam, quia crucior in hac flamma". [25]At dixit Abraham: "Fili, recordare quia recepisti bona tua in vita tua, et

Lazarus similiter mala; nunc autem hic consolatur, tu vero cruciaris. [26]Et in his omnibus inter nos et vos chaos magnum firmatum est, ut hi, qui volunt hinc transire ad vos, non possint, neque inde ad nos transmeare". [27]Et ait: "Rogo ergo te, Pater, ut mittas eum in domum patris mei [28] —habeo enim quinque fratres— ut testetur illis, ne et ipsi veniant in locum hunc tormentorum". [29]Ait autem Abraham: "Habent Moysen et Prophetas; audiant illos". [30]At ille dixit: "Non, pater Abraham, sed si quis ex mortuis ierit ad eos, paenitentiam agent". [31]Ait autem illi: "Si Moysen et Prophetas non audiunt, neque si quis ex mortuis resurrexerit, credent"».   [17] [1]Et ad discipulos suos ait: «Impossibile est ut non veniant scandala; vae autem illi, per quem veniunt! [2]Utilius est illi si lapis molaris imponatur circa collum eius et proiciatur in mare, quam ut scandalizet unum de pusillis istis. [3]Attendite vobis! Si peccaverit frater tuus, increpa illum, et si paenitentiam egerit, dimitte illi; [4]et si septies in die peccaverit in te et septies conversus fuerit ad te dicens: "Paenitet me", dimittes illi». [5]Et dixerunt apostoli Domino: «Adauge nobis fidem!». [6]Dixit autem Dominus: «Si haberetis fidem sicut granum sinapis, diceretis huic arbori moro: "Eradicare et transplantare in mare", et oboediret vobis. [7]Quis autem vestrum habens servum arantem aut pascentem, qui regresso de agro dicet illi: "Statim transi, recumbe", [8]et non dicet ei: "Para, quod cenem, et praecinge te et ministra mihi, donec manducem et bibam, et post haec tu manducabis et bibes"? [9]Numquid gratiam habet servo illi, quia fecit, quae praecepta sunt? [10]Sic et vos, cum feceritis omnia, quae praecepta sunt vobis, dicite: "Servi inutiles sumus; quod debuimus facere, fecimus"». [11]Et factum est dum iret in Ierusalem, et ipse transibat per mediam Samariam et Galilaeam. [12]Et cum ingrederetur quoddam castellum, occurrerunt ei decem viri leprosi, qui steterunt a longe, [13]et levaverunt vocem dicentes: «Iesu praeceptor, miserere nostri!». [14]Quos ut vidit, dixit: «Ite, ostendite vos sacerdotibus». Et factum est dum irent, mundati sunt. [15]Unus autem ex illis, ut vidit quia sanatus est, regressus est cum magna voce magnificans Deum [16]et cecidit in faciem ante pedes eius gratias agens ei; et hic erat Samaritanus. [17]Respondens autem Iesus dixit: «Nonne decem mundati sunt? Et novem ubi sunt? [18]Non sunt inventi qui redirent, ut darent gloriam Deo, nisi hic alienigena?». [19]Et ait illi: «Surge, vade; fides tua te salvum fecit». [20]Interrogatus autem a pharisaeis: «Quando venit regnum Dei?», respondit eis et dixit: «Non venit regnum Dei cum observatione, [21]neque dicent: "Ecce hic" aut: "Illic"; ecce enim regnum Dei intra vos est». [22]Et ait ad discipulos: «Venient dies, quando desideretis videre unum diem Filii hominis et non videbitis. [23]Et dicent vobis: "Ecce hic", "Ecce illic"; nolite ire neque sectemini. [24]Nam sicut fulgur coruscans de sub caelo in ea, quae sub caelo sunt, fulget, ita erit Filius hominis in die sua. [25]Primum autem oportet illum multa pati et reprobari a generatione hac. [26]Et sicut factum est in diebus Noe, ita erit et in diebus Filii hominis: [27]edebant, bibebant, uxores ducebant, dabantur ad nuptias, usque in diem, qua intravit Noe in arcam, et venit diluvium et perdidit omnes. [28]Similiter sicut factum est in diebus Lot: edebant, bibebant, emebant, vendebant, plantabant, aedificabant; [29]qua die autem exiit Lot a Sodomis, pluit ignem et sulphur de caelo et omnes perdidit. [30]Secundum haec erit, qua die Filius hominis revelabitur. [31]In illa die, qui fuerit in tecto et vasa eius in domo, ne descendat tollere illa, et qui in agro, similiter non redeat retro. [32]Memores estote uxoris Lot. [33]Quicumque quaesierit animam suam salvam facere, perdet illam; et, quicumque perdiderit illam, vivificabit eam. [34]Dico vobis: Illa nocte erunt duo in lecto uno: unus assumetur, et alter relinquetur; [35]duae erunt molentes in unum: una assumetur, et altera relinquetur». [37]Respondentes dicunt illi: «Ubi, Domine?». Qui dixit eis: «Ubicumque fuerit corpus, illuc congregabuntur et aquilae».   [18] [1]Dicebat autem parabolam ad illos quoniam oportet semper orare et non deficere, [2]dicens: «Iudex quidam erat in quadam civitate, qui Deum non timebat et hominem non reverebatur. [3]Vidua autem erat in civitate illa et veniebat ad eum dicens: "Vindica me de adversario meo". [4]Et nolebat per multum tempus; post haec autem dixit intra se: "Etsi Deum non timeo nec hominem revereor, [5]tamen quia molesta est mihi haec vidua, vindicabo illam, ne in novissimo veniens suggillet me"». [6]Ait autem Dominus: «Audite quid iudex iniquitatis dicit; [7]Deus autem non faciet vindictam electorum suorum clamantium ad se die ac nocte, et patientiam habebit in illis? [8]Dico vobis: Cito faciet vindictam illorum. Verumtamen Filius hominis veniens, putas, inveniet fidem in terra?». [9]Dixit autem et ad quosdam, qui in se confidebant tamquam iusti et aspernabantur ceteros, parabolam istam: [10]«Duo homines ascenderunt in templum, ut orarent: unus pharisaeus et alter publicanus. [11]Pharisaeus stans haec apud se orabat: "Deus, gratias ago tibi quia non sum sicut ceteri hominum, raptores, iniusti, adulteri, velut etiam hic publicanus; [12]ieiuno bis in sabbato, decimas do omnium, quae possideo". [13]Et publicanus a longe stans nolebat nec oculos ad caelum levare, sed percutiebat pectus suum dicens: "Deus, propitius esto mihi peccatori". [14]Dico vobis: Descendit hic iustificatus in domum suam ab illo. Quia omnis, qui se exaltat, humiliabitur; et, qui se humiliat, exaltabitur». [15]Afferebant autem ad illum et infantes, ut eos tangeret; quod cum viderent, discipuli increpabant illos. [16]Iesus autem convocans illos dixit: «Sinite pueros venire ad me et nolite eos vetare; talium est enim regnum Dei. [17]Amen dico vobis: Quicumque non acceperit regnum Dei sicut puer, non intrabit in illud». [18]Et interrogavit eum quidam princeps dicens: «Magister bone, quid faciens vitam aeternam possidebo?». [19]Dixit autem ei Iesus: «Quid me dicis bonum? Nemo bonus nisi solus Deus. [20]Mandata nosti: *non moechaberis, non occides, non furtum facies, non falsum testimonium dices, honora patrem tuum et matrem*». [21]Qui ait: «Haec omnia custodivi a iuventute». [22]Quo audito Iesus ait ei: «Adhuc unum tibi deest: omnia, quaecumque habes, vende et da pauperibus et habebis thesaurum in caelo et veni, sequere me». [23]His ille auditis, contristatus est, quia dives erat valde. [24]Videns autem illum Iesus tristem factum dixit: «Quam difficile, qui pecunias habent, in regnum Dei intrant. [25]Facilius est enim camelum per foramen acus transire, quam divitem intrare in regnum Dei». [26]Et dixerunt, qui audiebant: «Et quis potest salvus fieri?». [27]Ait autem illis: «Quae impossibilia sunt apud homines, possibilia sunt apud Deum». [28]Ait autem Petrus: «Ecce nos dimisimus nostra et secuti sumus te». [29]Qui dixit eis: «Amen dico vobis: Nemo est, qui reliquit domum aut uxorem aut fratres aut parentes aut filios propter regnum Dei, [30]et non recipiat multo plura in hoc tempore et in saeculo venturo vitam aeternam». [31]Assumpsit autem Duodecim et ait illis: «Ecce ascendimus Ierusalem, et consummabuntur omnia, quae scripta sunt per Prophetas de Filio hominis: [32]tradetur enim gentibus et illudetur et contumeliis afficietur et conspuetur, [33]et, postquam flagellaverint, occident eum, et die tertia resurget». [34]Et ipsi nihil horum intellexerunt; et erat verbum istud absconditum ab eis, et non intellegebant, quae dicebantur. [35]Factum est autem cum appropinquaret Iericho, caecus quidam sedebat secus viam mendicans. [36]Et cum audiret turbam praetereuntem, interrogabat quid hoc esset. [37]Dixerunt autem ei: «Iesus Nazarenus transit». [38]Et clamavit dicens: «Iesu, fili David, miserere mei!». [39]Et qui praeibant, increpabant eum, ut taceret; ipse vero multo magis clamabat: «Fili David, miserere mei!». [40]Stans autem Iesus iussit illum adduci ad se. Et cum appropinquasset, interrogavit illum: [41]«Quid tibi vis faciam?». At ille dixit: «Domine, ut videam». [42]Et Iesus dixit illi: «Respice! Fides tua te salvum fecit». [43]Et confestim vidit et sequebatur illum magnificans Deum. Et omnis plebs, ut vidit, dedit laudem Deo.   [19] [1]Et ingressus perambulabat Iericho. [2]Et ecce vir nomine Zacchaeus, et hic erat princeps publicanorum et ipse dives. [3]Et quaerebat videre Iesum quis esset, et non poterat prae turba, quia statura pusillus erat. [4]Et praecurrens ascendit in arborem sycomorum, ut videret illum, quia inde erat transiturus. [5]Et cum venisset ad locum, suspiciens Iesus dixit ad eum: «Zacchaee, festinans descende, nam hodie in domo tua oportet me manere». [6]Et festinans descendit et excepit illum gaudens. [7]Et cum viderent, omnes murmurabant dicentes: «Ad hominem peccatorem divertit!». [8]Stans autem Zacchaeus dixit ad Dominum: «Ecce dimidium bonorum meorum, Domine, do pauperibus, et, si quid aliquem defraudavi, reddo quadruplum». [9]Ait autem Iesus ad eum: «Hodie salus domui huic facta est, eo quod et ipse filius sit Abrahae; [10]venit enim Filius hominis quaerere et salvum facere, quod perierat». [11]Haec autem illis audientibus, adiciens dixit parabolam, eo quod esset prope Ierusalem, et illi existimarent quod confestim regnum Dei manifestaretur. [12]Dixit ergo: «Homo quidam nobilis abiit in regionem longinquam accipere sibi regnum et reverti. [13]Vocatis autem decem servis suis, dedit illis decem minas, et ait ad illos: "Negotiamini, dum venio". [14]Cives autem eius oderant illum et miserunt legationem post illum dicentes: "Nolumus hunc regnare super nos!". [15]Et factum est ut rediret, accepto regno, et iussit ad se vocari servos illos, quibus dedit pecuniam, ut sciret quantum negotiati essent. [16]Venit autem primus dicens: "Domine, mina tua decem minas acquisivit". [17]Et ait illi: "Euge, bone serve; quia in modico fidelis fuisti, esto potestatem habens supra decem civitates". [18]Et alter venit dicens: "Mina tua, domine, fecit quinque minas". [19]Et huic ait: "Et tu esto supra quinque civitates". [20]Et alter venit dicens: "Domine, ecce mina tua, quam habui repositam in sudario; [21]timui enim te, quia homo austerus es: tollis, quod non posuisti, et metis, quod non seminasti". [22]Dicit ei: "De ore tuo te iudico, serve nequam! Sciebas quod ego austerus homo sum, tollens quod non posui et metens quod non seminavi? [23]Et quare non dedisti pecuniam meam ad mensam? Et ego veniens cum usuris utique exegissem illud". [24]Et adstantibus dixit: "Auferte ab illo minam et date illi, qui decem minas habet". [25]Et dixerunt ei: "Domine, habet decem minas!". [26]Dico vobis: "Omni habenti dabitur; ab eo autem, qui non habet, et, quod habet, auferetur". [27]Verumtamen inimicos meos illos, qui noluerunt me regnare super se, adducite huc et interficite ante me!». [28]Et his dictis, praecedebat ascendens Hierosolymam. [29]Et factum est cum appropinquasset ad Bethfage et Bethaniam, ad montem, qui vocatur Oliveti, misit duos discipulos [30]dicens: «Ite in castellum, quod contra est, in quod introeuntes invenietis pullum asinae alligatum, cui nemo umquam hominum sedit; solvite illum et adducite. [31]Et si quis vos interrogaverit: "Quare solvitis?", sic dicetis: "Dominus eum necessarium habet"». [32]Abierunt autem, qui missi erant, et invenerunt, sicut dixit illis. [33]Solventibus autem illis pullum, dixerunt domini eius ad illos: «Quid solvitis pullum?». [34]At illi dixerunt: «Dominus eum necessarium habet». [35]Et duxerunt illum ad Iesum; et iactantes vestimenta sua supra pullum imposuerunt Iesum. [36]Eunte autem illo, substernebant vestimenta sua in via. [37]Et cum appropinquaret iam ad descensum montis Oliveti, coeperunt omnis multitudo discipulorum gaudentes laudare Deum voce magna super omnibus, quas viderant, virtutibus [38]dicentes: «*Benedictus, qui venit rex in nomine Domini! / Pax in caelo et gloria in excelsis!*». [39]Et quidam pharisaeorum de turbis dixerunt ad illum: «Magister, increpa discipulos tuos!». [40]Et respondens dixit: «Dico vobis: Si hi tacuerint, lapides clamabunt!». [41]Et ut appropinquavit, videns civitatem flevit super illam [42]dicens: «Si cognovisses et tu in hac die, quae ad pacem tibi! Nunc autem abscondita sunt ab oculis tuis. [43]Quia venient dies in te, et circumdabunt te inimici tui vallo et obsidebunt te et coangustabunt te undique [44]et ad terram prosternent te et filios tuos, qui in te sunt, et non relinquent in te lapidem super lapidem, eo quod non cognoveris tempus visitationis tuae». [45]Et ingressus in templum, coepit eicere vendentes [46]dicens illis: «Scriptum est: "*Et erit domus mea domus orationis*". Vos autem fecistis illam *speluncam latronum*». [47]Et erat docens cotidie in templo. Principes autem sacerdotum et scribae et principes plebis quaerebant illum perdere [48]et non inveniebant quid facerent; omnis enim populus suspensus erat audiens illum.   [20] [1]Et factum est in una dierum, docente illo populum in templo et evangelizante, supervenerunt principes sacerdotum et scribae cum senioribus [2]et aiunt dicentes ad illum: «Dic nobis: In qua potestate haec facis aut quis est qui dedit tibi hanc potestatem?». [3]Respondens autem dixit ad illos: «Interrogabo vos et ego verbum; et dicite mihi: [4]Baptismum Ioannis de caelo erat an ex hominibus?». [5]At illi cogitabant inter se dicentes: «Si dixerimus: "De caelo", dicet: "Quare non credidistis illi?"; [6]si autem dixerimus: "Ex hominibus", plebs universa lapidabit nos; certi sunt enim Ioannem prophetam esse». [7]Et responderunt se nescire unde esset. [8]Et Iesus ait illis: «Neque ego dico vobis in qua potestate haec facio». [9]Coepit autem dicere ad plebem parabolam hanc: «Homo *plantavit vineam* et locavit eam colonis et ipse peregre fuit multis temporibus. [10]Et in tempore misit ad cultores servum, ut de fructu vineae darent illi; cultores autem caesum dimiserunt eum inanem. [11]Et addidit alterum servum mittere; illi autem hunc quoque caedentes et afficientes contumelia dimiserunt inanem. [12]Et addidit tertium mittere; qui et illum vulnerantes eiecerunt. [13]Dixit autem dominus vineae: "Quid faciam? Mittam filium meum dilectum; forsitan hunc verebuntur". [14]Quem cum vidissent coloni, cogitaverunt inter se dicentes: "Hic est heres. Occidamus illum, ut nostra fiat hereditas". [15]Et eiectum illum extra vineam occiderunt. Quid ergo faciet illis dominus vineae? [16]Veniet et perdet colonos istos et dabit vineam aliis». Quo audito, dixerunt: «Absit!». [17]Ille autem aspiciens eos ait: «Quid est ergo hoc, quod scriptum est: / "*Lapidem, quem reprobaverunt aedificantes, / hic factus est in caput anguli*"? [18]Omnis, qui ceciderit supra illum lapidem, conquassabitur; supra quem autem ceciderit, comminuet illum». [19]Et quaerebant scribae et principes sacerdotum mittere in illum manus in illa hora et timuerunt populum; cognoverunt enim quod ad ipsos dixerit similitudinem istam. [20]Et observantes miserunt insidiatores, qui se iustos simularent, ut caperent eum in sermone, et sic traderent illum principatui et potestati praesidis. [21]Et interrogaverunt illum dicentes: «Magister, scimus quia recte dicis et doces et non accipis personam, sed in veritate viam Dei doces. [22]Licet nobis dare tributum Caesari an non?». [23]Considerans autem dolum illorum dixit ad eos: [24]«Ostendite mihi denarium. Cuius habet imaginem et inscriptionem?». [25]At illi dixerunt: «Caesaris». Et ait illis: «Reddite ergo, quae Caesaris sunt, Caesari et, quae Dei sunt, Deo». [26]Et non potuerunt verbum eius reprehendere coram plebe et mirati in responso eius tacuerunt. [27]Accesserunt autem quidam sadducaeorum, qui negant esse resurrectionem, et interrogaverunt eum [28]dicentes: «Magister, Moyses scripsit nobis, si frater alicuius mortuus fuerit habens uxorem et hic sine filiis fuerit, ut accipiat eam frater eius uxorem et suscitet semen fratri suo. [29]Septem ergo fratres erant: et primus accepit uxorem et mortuus est sine filiis; [30]et sequens [31]et tertius accepit illam, similiter autem et septem non reliquerunt filios et mortui sunt. [32]Novissima mortua est et mulier. [33]Mulier ergo in resurrectione cuius eorum erit uxor? Siquidem septem habuerunt eam uxorem». [34]Et ait illis Iesus: «Filii saeculi huius nubunt et traduntur ad nuptias; [35]illi autem, qui digni habentur saeculo illo et resurrectione ex mortuis, neque nubunt, neque ducunt uxores. [36]Neque enim ultra mori possunt: aequales enim angelis sunt et filii sunt Dei, cum sint filii resurrectionis. [37]Quia vero resurgant mortui et Moyses ostendit secus rubum, sicut dicit: "*Dominum Deum Abraham et Deum Isaac et Deum Iacob*". [38]Deus autem non est mortuorum sed vivorum: omnes enim vivunt ei». [39]Respondentes autem quidam scribarum dixerunt: «Magister, bene dixisti». [40]Et amplius non audebant eum quidquam interrogare. [41]Dixit autem ad illos: «Quomodo dicunt Christum filium David esse? [42]Ipse enim David dicit in libro Psalmorum: "*Dixit Dominus Domino meo: Sede a dextris meis, / [43]donec ponam inimicos tuos scabellum pedum tuorum*". [44]David ergo Dominum illum vocat; et quomodo filius eius est?». [45]Audiente autem omni populo, dixit discipulis suis: [46]«Attendite a scribis, qui volunt ambulare in stolis et amant salutationes in foro et primas cathedras in synagogis et primos discubitus in conviviis, [47]qui devorant domos viduarum et simulant longam orationem. Hi accipient damnationem maiorem».   [21] [1]Respiciens autem vidit eos, qui mittebant munera sua in gazophylacium, divites. [2]Vidit autem quandam viduam pauperculam mittentem illuc minuta duo [3]et dixit: «Vere dico vobis: Vidua haec pauper plus quam omnes misit. [4]Nam omnes hi ex abundantia sua miserunt in munera; haec autem ex inopia sua omnem victum suum, quem habebat, misit». [5]Et quibusdam dicentibus de templo quod lapidibus bonis et donis ornatum esset dixit: [6]«Haec, quae videtis, venient dies in quibus non relinquetur lapis super lapidem, qui non destruatur». [7]Interrogaverunt autem illum dicentes: «Praeceptor, quando ergo haec erunt, et quod signum, cum fieri incipient?». [8]Qui dixit: «Videte, ne seducamini. Multi enim venient in nomine meo dicentes: "Ego sum" et: "Tempus appropinquavit". Nolite ergo ire post illos. [9]Cum autem audieritis proelia et seditiones, nolite terreri; oportet enim primum haec fieri, sed non statim finis». [10]Tunc dicebat illis: «Surget gens contra gentem et regnum adversus regnum; [11]et terrae motus magni et per loca fames et pestilentiae erunt, terroresque et de caelo signa magna erunt. [12]Sed ante haec omnia iniicient vobis manus suas et persequentur tradentes in synagogas et custodias, et trahemini ad reges et praesides propter nomen meum; [13]continget autem vobis in testimonium. [14]Ponite ergo in cordibus vestris non praemeditari quemadmodum respondeatis; [15]ego enim dabo vobis os et sapientiam, cui non poterunt resistere vel contradicere omnes adversarii vestri. [16]Trademini autem et a parentibus et fratribus et cognatis et amicis, et morte afficient ex vobis, [17]et eritis odio omnibus propter nomen meum. [18]Et capillus de capite vestro non peribit. [19]In patientia vestra possidebitis animas vestras. [20]Cum autem videritis circumdari ab exercitu Ierusalem, tunc scitote quia appropinquavit desolatio eius. [21]Tunc, qui in Iudaea sunt, fugiant in montes; et, qui in medio eius, discedant; et, qui in regionibus, non intrent in eam. [22]Quia dies ultionis hi sunt, ut impleantur omnia, quae scripta sunt. [23]Vae autem praegnantibus et nutrientibus in illis diebus! Erit enim pressura magna super terram et ira populo huic, [24]et cadent in ore gladii et captivi ducentur in omnes gentes, et Ierusalem calcabitur a gentibus, donec impleantur tempora nationum. [25]Et erunt signa in sole et luna et stellis, et super terram pressura gentium prae confusione sonitus maris et fluctuum, [26]arescentibus hominibus prae timore et exspectatione eorum, quae supervenient orbi, nam *virtutes caelorum* movebuntur. [27]Et tunc videbunt *Filium hominis venientem in nube* cum potestate et gloria magna. [28]His autem fieri incipientibus, respicite et levate capita vestra, quoniam appropinquat redemptio vestra». [29]Et dixit illis similitudinem: «Videte ficulneam et omnes arbores: [30]cum iam germinaverint, videntes vosmetipsi scitis quia iam prope est aestas. [31]Ita et vos, cum videritis haec fieri, scitote quoniam prope est regnum Dei. [32]Amen dico vobis: Non praeteribit generatio haec, donec omnia fiant. [33]Caelum et terra transibunt, verba autem mea non transibunt. [34]Attendite autem vobis, ne forte graventur corda vestra in crapula et ebrietate et curis huius vitae, et superveniat in vos repentina dies illa; [35]tamquam laqueus enim superveniet in omnes, qui sedent super faciem omnis terrae. [36]Vigilate itaque omni tempore orantes, ut possitis fugere ista omnia, quae futura sunt, et stare ante Filium hominis». [37]Erat autem diebus docens in templo, noctibus vero exiens morabatur in monte, qui vocatur Oliveti. [38]Et omnis populus manicabat ad eum in templo audire eum. [22] [1]Appropinquabat autem dies festus Azymorum, qui dicitur Pascha. [2]Et quaerebant principes sacerdotum et scribae quomodo eum interficerent; timebant vero plebem. [3]Intravit autem Satanas in Iudam, qui cognominabatur Iscarioth, unum de Duodecim; [4]et abiit et locutus est cum principibus sacerdotum et magistratibus quemadmodum illum traderet eis. [5]Et gavisi sunt et pacti sunt pecuniam illi dare. [6]Et spopondit et quaerebat opportunitatem, ut eis traderet illum sine turba. [7]Venit autem dies Azymorum, in qua necesse erat occidi Pascha. [8]Et misit Petrum et Ioannem dicens: «Euntes parate nobis Pascha, ut manducemus». [9]At illi dixerunt ei: «Ubi vis paremus?». [10]Et dixit ad eos: «Ecce introeuntibus vobis in civitatem occurret vobis homo amphoram aquae portans; sequimini eum in domum, in quam intrat. [11]Et dicetis patri familias domus: "Dicit tibi Magister: Ubi est deversorium ubi Pascha cum discipulis meis manducem?". [12]Ipse vobis ostendet cenaculum magnum stratum; ibi parate». [13]Euntes autem invenerunt, sicut dixit illis, et paraverunt Pascha. [14]Et cum facta esset hora, discubuit, et apostoli cum eo. [15]Et ait illis: «Desiderio desideravi hoc Pascha manducare vobiscum, antequam patiar. [16]Dico enim vobis: Non manducabo illud, donec impleatur in regno Dei». [17]Et accepto calice, gratias egit et dixit: «Accipite hoc et dividite inter vos. [18]Dico enim vobis: Non bibam amodo de generatione vitis, donec regnum Dei veniat». [19]Et accepto pane, gratias egit et fregit et dedit eis dicens: «Hoc est corpus meum, quod pro vobis datur. Hoc facite in meam commemorationem». [20]Similiter et calicem, postquam cenavit, dicens: «Hic calix novum testamentum est in sanguine meo, qui pro vobis funditur. [21]Verumtamen ecce manus tradentis me mecum est in mensa; [22]et quidem Filius hominis, secundum quod definitum est, vadit; verumtamen vae illi homini, per quem traditur!». [23]Et ipsi coeperunt quaerere inter se quis esset ex eis, qui hoc facturus esset. [24]Facta est autem et contentio inter eos, quis eorum videretur esse maior. [25]Dixit autem eis: «Reges gentium dominantur eorum et, qui potestatem habent super eos, benefici vocantur. [26]Vos autem non sic, sed qui maior est in vobis, fiat sicut iunior; et, qui praecessor est, sicut ministrator. [27]Nam quis maior est: qui recumbit, an qui ministrat? Nonne qui recumbit? Ego autem in medio vestrum sum sicut qui ministrat. [28]Vos autem estis qui permansistis mecum in tentationibus meis; [29]et ego dispono vobis, sicut disposuit mihi Pater meus regnum, [30]ut edatis et bibatis super mensam meam in regno meo, et sedeatis super thronos iudicantes duodecim tribus Israel. [31]Simon, Simon, ecce Satanas expetivit vos, ut cribraret sicut triticum; [32]ego autem rogavi pro te, ut non deficiat fides tua. Et tu, aliquando conversus, confirma fratres tuos». [33]Qui dixit ei: «Domine, tecum paratus sum et in carcerem et in mortem ire». [34]Et ille dixit: «Dico tibi, Petre, non cantabit hodie gallus donec ter abneges nosse me». [35]Et dixit eis: «Quando misi vos sine sacculo et pera et calceamentis, numquid aliquid defuit vobis?». At illi dixerunt: «Nihil». [36]Dixit ergo eis: «Sed nunc, qui habet sacculum, tollat, similiter et peram; et, qui non habet, vendat tunicam suam et emat gladium. [37]Dico enim vobis: Hoc, quod scriptum est, oportet impleri in me, illud: *"Cum iniustis deputatus est"*. Etenim ea, quae sunt de me, adimpletionem habent». [38]At illi dixerunt: «Domine, ecce gladii duo hic». At ille dixit eis: «Satis est». [39]Et egressus ibat secundum consuetudinem in montem Olivarum; secuti sunt autem illum et discipuli. [40]Et cum pervenisset ad locum, dixit illis: «Orate, ne intretis in tentationem». [41]Et ipse avulsus est ab eis, quantum iactus est lapidis, et, positis genibus, orabat [42]dicens: «Pater, si vis, transfer calicem istum a me; verumtamen non mea voluntas sed tua fiat». [43]Apparuit autem illi angelus de caelo confortans eum. Et factus in agonia prolixius orabat. [44]Et factus est sudor eius sicut guttae sanguinis decurrentis in terram. [45]Et cum surrexisset ab oratione et venisset ad discipulos, invenit eos dormientes prae tristitia [46]et ait illis: «Quid dormitis? Surgite; orate, ne intretis in tentationem». [47]Adhuc eo loquente, ecce turba, et qui vocabatur Iudas, unus de Duodecim, antecedebat eos, et appropinquavit Iesu, ut oscularetur eum. [48]Iesus autem dixit ei: «Iuda, osculo Filium hominis tradis?». [49]Videntes autem hi, qui circa ipsum erant, quod futurum erat, dixerunt: «Domine, si percutimus in gladio?». [50]Et percussit unus ex illis servum principis sacerdotum et amputavit auriculam eius dextram. [51]Respondens autem Iesus ait: «Sinite usque huc!». Et cum tetigisset auriculam eius, sanavit eum. [52]Dixit autem Iesus ad eos, qui venerant ad se principes sacerdotum et magistratus templi et seniores: «Quasi ad latronem existis cum gladiis et fustibus? [53]Cum cotidie vobiscum fuerim in templo, non extendistis manus in me; sed haec est hora vestra et potestas tenebrarum». [54]Comprehendentes autem eum, duxerunt et introduxerunt in domum principis sacerdotum. Petrus vero sequebatur a longe. [55]Accenso autem igni in medio atrio et circumsedentibus illis, sedebat Petrus in medio eorum. [56]Quem cum vidisset ancilla quaedam sedentem ad lumen et eum fuisset intuita, dixit: [57]«Et hic cum illo erat!». At ille negavit eum dicens: [58]«Mulier, non novi illum!». Et post pusillum alius videns eum dixit: «Et tu de illis es!». Petrus vero ait: «O homo, non sum!». [59]Et intervallo facto quasi horae unius, alius quidam affirmabat dicens: «Vere et hic cum illo erat, nam et Galilaeus est!». [60]Et ait Petrus: «Homo, nescio quid dicis!». Et continuo adhuc illo loquente cantavit gallus. [61]Et conversus Dominus respexit Petrum; et recordatus est Petrus verbi Domini, sicut dixit ei: «Priusquam gallus cantet hodie, ter me negabis». [62]Et egressus foras flevit amare. [63]Et viri, qui tenebant illum, illudebant ei caedentes, [64]et velaverunt eum et interrogabant eum dicentes: «Prophetiza: Quis est, qui te percussit?». [65]Et alia multa blasphemantes dicebant in eum. [66]Et ut factus est dies, convenerunt seniores plebis et principes sacerdotum et scribae et duxerunt illum in concilium suum [67]dicentes: «Si tu es Christus, dic nobis». Et ait illis: «Si vobis dixero, non credetis; [68]si autem interrogavero, non respondebitis mihi. [69]Ex hoc autem erit *Filius hominis sedens a dextris virtutis Dei»*. [70]Dixerunt autem omnes: «Tu ergo es Filius Dei?». Qui ait ad illos: «Vos dicitis quia ego sum». [71]At illi dixerunt: «Quid adhuc desideramus testimonium? Ipsi enim audivimus de ore eius!».   **[23]** [1]Et surgens omnis multitudo eorum, duxerunt illum ad Pilatum. [2]Coeperunt autem accusare illum dicentes: «Hunc invenimus subvertentem gentem nostram et prohibentem tributa dare Caesari et dicentem se Christum regem esse». [3]Pilatus autem interrogavit eum dicens: «Tu es rex Iudaeorum?». At ille respondens ait: «Tu dicis». [4]Ait autem Pilatus ad principes sacerdotum et turbas: «Nihil invenio causae in hoc homine». [5]At illi invalescebant dicentes: «Commovet populum docens per universam Iudaeam et incipiens a Galilaea usque huc!». [6]Pilatus autem audiens interrogavit si homo Galilaeus esset [7]et ut cognovit quod de Herodis potestate esset, remisit eum ad Herodem, qui et ipse Hierosolymis erat illis diebus. [8]Herodes autem, viso Iesu, gavisus est valde: erat enim cupiens ex multo tempore videre eum, eo quod audiret de illo et sperabat signum aliquod videre ab eo fieri. [9]Interrogabat autem illum multis sermonibus; at ipse nihil illi respondebat. [10]Stabant etiam principes sacerdotum et scribae constanter accusantes eum. [11]Sprevit autem illum Herodes cum exercitu suo et illusit indutum veste alba et remisit ad Pilatum. [12]Facti sunt autem amici inter se Herodes et Pilatus in ipsa die, nam antea inimici erant ad invicem. [13]Pilatus autem, convocatis principibus sacerdotum et magistratibus et plebe, [14]dixit ad illos: «Obtulistis mihi hunc hominem quasi avertentem populum, et ecce ego coram vobis interrogans nullam causam inveni in homine isto ex his, in quibus eum accusatis, [15]sed neque Herodes: remisit enim illum ad nos. Et ecce nihil dignum morte actum est ei. [16]Emendatum ergo illum dimittam». [18]Exclamavit autem universa turba dicens: «Tolle hunc et dimitte nobis Barabbam!», [19]qui erat propter seditionem quandam factam in civitate et homicidium missus in carcerem. [20]Iterum autem Pilatus locutus est ad illos volens dimittere Iesum, [21]at illi succlamabant dicentes: «Crucifige, crucifige illum!». [22]Ille autem tertio dixit ad illos: «Quid enim mali fecit iste? Nullam causam mortis invenio in eo; corripiam ergo illum et dimittam». [23]At illi instabant vocibus magnis postulantes, ut crucifigeretur, et invalescebant voces eorum. [24]Et Pilatus adiudicavit fieri petitionem eorum: [25]dimisit autem eum, qui propter seditionem et homicidium missus fuerat in carcerem, quem petebant, Iesum vero tradidit voluntati eorum. [26]Et cum abducerent eum, apprehenderunt Simonem quendam Cyrenensem venientem de villa et imposuerunt illi crucem portare post Iesum. [27]Sequebatur autem illum multa turba populi et mulierum, quae plangebant et lamentabant eum. [28]Conversus autem ad illas Iesus dixit: «Filiae Ierusalem, nolite flere super me, sed super vos ipsas flete et super filios vestros, [29]quoniam ecce venient dies, in quibus dicent: "Beatae steriles et ventres, qui non genuerunt, et ubera, quae non lactaverunt!". [30]Tunc incipient *dicere montibus:* "Cadite super nos!", *et collibus:* "Operite nos!", [31]quia si in viridi ligno haec faciunt, in arido quid fiet?». [32]Ducebantur autem et alii duo nequam cum eo, ut interficerentur. [33]Et postquam venerunt in locum, qui vocatur Calvariae, ibi crucifixerunt eum et latrones, unum a dextris et alterum a sinistris. [34]Iesus autem dicebat: «Pater, dimitte illis, non enim sciunt quid faciunt». *Dividentes* vero *vestimenta eius miserunt sortes.* [35]Et stabat populus *exspectans.* Et *deridebant* illum et principes dicentes: «Alios salvos fecit; se salvum faciat, si hic est Christus Dei electus!». [36]Illudebant autem ei et milites accedentes, *acetum* offerentes illi [37]et dicentes: «Si tu es rex Iudaeorum, salvum te fac!». [38]Erat autem et superscriptio super illum: «Hic est rex Iudaeorum». [39]Unus autem de his, qui pendebant, latronibus blasphemabat eum dicens: «Nonne tu es Christus? Salvum fac temetipsum et nos!». [40]Respondens autem alter increpabat illum dicens: «Neque tu times Deum, quod in eadem damnatione es? [41]Et nos quidem iuste, nam digna factis recipimus! Hic vero nihil mali gessit». [42]Et dicebat: «Iesu, memento mei cum veneris in regnum tuum». [43]Et dixit illi: «Amen dico tibi: Hodie mecum eris in paradiso». [44]Et erat iam fere hora sexta, et tenebrae factae sunt in universa terra usque in horam nonam, [45]et obscuratus est sol, et velum templi scissum est medium. [46]Et clamans voce magna Iesus ait: «Pater, *in manus tuas commendo spiritum meum*»; et haec dicens exspiravit. [47]Videns autem centurio, quod factum fuerat, glorificavit Deum dicens: «Vere hic homo iustus erat!». [48]Et omnis turba eorum, qui simul aderant ad spectaculum istud, et videbant, quae fiebant, percutientes pectora sua revertebantur. [49]Stabant autem omnes noti eius a longe, et mulieres, quae secutae erant eum a Galilaea, haec videntes. [50]Et ecce vir nomine Ioseph, qui erat decurio, vir bonus et iustus [51] —hic non consenserat consilio et actibus eorum— ab Arimathaea civitate Iudaeorum, qui exspectabat regnum Dei, [52]hic accessit ad Pilatum et petiit corpus Iesu, [53]et depositum involvit sindone et posuit eum in monumento exciso, in quo nondum quisquam positus fuerat. [54]Et dies erat Parasceves, et sabbatum illucescebat. [55]Subsecutae autem mulieres, quae cum ipso venerant de Galilaea, viderunt monumentum et quemadmodum positum erat corpus eius, [56]et revertentes paraverunt aromata et unguenta et sabbato quidem siluerunt secundum mandatum. [24] [1]Prima autem sabbatorum, valde diluculo venerunt ad monumentum portantes, quae paraverant, aromata. [2]Et invenerunt lapidem revolutum a monumento [3]et ingressae non invenerunt corpus Domini Iesu. [4]Et factum est, dum mente haesitarent de isto, ecce duo viri steterunt secus illas in veste fulgenti. [5]Cum timerent autem et declinarent vultum in terram, dixerunt ad illas: «Quid quaeritis viventem cum mortuis? [6]Non est hic, sed surrexit. Recordamini qualiter locutus est vobis, cum adhuc in Galilaea esset, [7]dicens: "Oportet Filium hominis tradi in manus hominum peccatorum et crucifigi et die tertia resurgere"». [8]Et recordatae sunt verborum eius [9]et regressae a monumento nuntiaverunt haec omnia illis Undecim et ceteris omnibus. [10]Erat autem Maria Magdalene et Ioanna et Maria Iacobi; et ceterae cum eis dicebant ad apostolos haec. [11]Et visa sunt ante illos sicut deliramentum verba ista, et non credebant illis. [12]Petrus autem surgens cucurrit ad monumentum et procumbens videt linteamina sola; et rediit ad sua mirans, quod factum fuerat. [13]Et ecce duo ex illis ibant ipsa die in castellum, quod erat in spatio stadiorum sexaginta ab Ierusalem nomine Emmaus, [14]et ipsi loquebantur ad invicem de his omnibus, quae acciderant. [15]Et factum est, dum fabularentur et secum quaererent, et ipse Iesus appropinquans ibat cum illis; [16]oculi autem illorum tenebantur, ne eum agnoscerent. [17]Et ait ad illos: «Qui sunt hi sermones, quos confertis ad invicem ambulantes?». Et steterunt tristes. [18]Et respondens unus, cui nomen Cleopas, dixit ei: «Tu solus peregrinus es in Ierusalem et non cognovisti, quae facta sunt in illa his diebus?». [19]Quibus ille dixit: «Quae?». Et illi dixerunt ei: «De Iesu Nazareno, qui fuit vir propheta, potens in opere et sermone coram Deo et omni populo, [20]et quomodo eum tradiderunt summi sacerdotes et principes nostri in damnationem mortis, et crucifixerunt eum. [21]Nos autem sperabamus quia ipse esset redempturus Israel; at nunc super haec omnia tertia dies hodie quod haec facta sunt. [22]Sed et mulieres quaedam ex nostris terruerunt nos, quae ante lucem fuerunt ad monumentum [23]et, non invento corpore eius, venerunt dicentes se etiam visionem angelorum vidisse, qui dicunt eum vivere.

[24]Et abierunt quidam ex nostris ad monumentum et ita invenerunt, sicut mulieres dixerunt, ipsum vero non viderunt». [25]Et ipse dixit ad eos: «O stulti et tardi corde ad credendum in omnibus, quae locuti sunt Prophetae! [26]Nonne haec oportuit pati Christum et intrare in gloriam suam?». [27]Et incipiens a Moyse et omnibus Prophetis interpretabatur illis in omnibus Scripturis, quae de ipso erant. [28]Et appropinquaverunt castello, quo ibant, et ipse se finxit longius ire. [29]Et coegerunt illum dicentes: «Mane nobiscum, quoniam advesperascit et inclinata est iam dies». Et intravit, ut maneret cum illis. [30]Et factum est, dum recumberet cum illis, accepit panem et benedixit ac fregit et porrigebat illis. [31]Et aperti sunt oculi eorum et cognoverunt eum; et ipse evanuit ab eis. [32]Et dixerunt ad invicem: «Nonne cor nostrum ardens erat in nobis, dum loqueretur nobis in via et aperiret nobis Scripturas?». [33]Et surgentes eadem hora regressi sunt in Ierusalem et invenerunt congregatos Undecim et eos, qui cum ipsis erant, [34]dicentes: «Surrexit Dominus vere et apparuit Simoni». [35]Et ipsi narrabant, quae gesta erant in via, et quomodo cognoverunt eum in fractione panis. [36]Dum haec autem loquuntur, ipse stetit in medio eorum et dicit eis: «Pax vobis!». [37]Conturbati vero et conterriti existimabant se spiritum videre. [38]Et dixit eis: «Quid turbati estis, et quare cogitationes ascendunt in corda vestra? [39]Videte manus meas et pedes meos, quia ipse ego sum! Palpate me et videte, quia spiritus carnem et ossa non habet, sicut me videtis habere». [40]Et cum hoc dixisset, ostendit eis manus et pedes. [41]Adhuc autem illis non credentibus prae gaudio et mirantibus, dixit eis: «Habetis hic aliquid, quod manducetur?». [42]At illi obtulerunt ei partem piscis assi. [43]Et sumens coram eis manducavit. [44]Et dixit ad eos: «Haec sunt verba, quae locutus sum ad vos, cum adhuc essem vobiscum, quoniam necesse est impleri omnia, quae scripta sunt in Lege Moysis et Prophetis et Psalmis de me». [45]Tunc aperuit illis sensum, ut intellegerent Scripturas. [46]Et dixit eis: «Sic scriptum est, Christum pati et resurgere a mortuis die tertia, [47]et praedicari in nomine eius paenitentiam in remissionem peccatorum in omnes gentes, incipientibus ab Ierusalem. [48]Vos estis testes horum. [49]Et ecce ego mitto promissum Patris mei in vos; vos autem sedete in civitate, quoadusque induamini virtutem ex alto». [50]Eduxit autem eos foras usque in Bethaniam et, elevatis manibus suis, benedixit eis. [51]Et factum est dum benediceret illis, recessit ab eis et ferebatur in caelum. [52]Et ipsi adoraverunt eum et regressi sunt in Ierusalem cum gaudio magno [53]et erant semper in templo benedicentes Deum.

Explanatory Notes

Asterisks in the text of the New Testament refer to these "Explanatory Notes" in the RSVCE.

THE GOSPEL ACCORDING TO LUKE

1:3, *Theophilus* is again referred to in Acts 1:1, but nothing is known of him.

1:5—2:52: The "Infancy Gospel;" as it is called, is written in a markedly Semitic style which differs from that of the rest of the Gospel. It appears to be based on the reminiscences of Mary.

1:30: The words of the angel are drawn from Messianic passages in the Old Testament.

1:46–55; The *Magnificat* is based on the Song of Hannah (1 Sam 2:1–10), and other Old Testament passages which describes God's favour towards Israel and especially towards the poor and lowly.

1:69, *a horn of salvation*: i.e., a mighty saviour.

2:7, *first-born*: The term connotes possession of certain rights, privileges and obligations; cf. Ex 13:1–2, 11–16. The word is used even in modern times without necessarily implying subsequent births.

2:34, *for the fall*: i.e., in the sense that by rejecting his claims many would sin grievously.

2:49: Jesus stresses the priority of his duty to his Father, which involves a high degree of independence of earthly ties.

3:2: See note on Jn 18:13.

3:7, *brood of vipers*: This epithet seems to have been directed mainly at the Pharisees; cf. Mt 3:7.

3:23: This genealogy, more universalist than that of Matthew, goes back to Adam, the ancestor of all men, and then to God, his Maker. Like Matthew, however, it gives the genealogy of Joseph, though Mary may well have been of the family of David.

4:16–30: This account of the visit to the synagogue seems to be composed of the details of more than one visit. Luke is trying here to underline the contrast between Christ's offer of salvation and the people's refusal of it.

6:20–49: Luke's discourse is shorter than that of Matthew because it does not contain Matthew's additional material collected from other occasions, or his details which would interest only Jews.

7:28: John, by virtue of his office, belonged to the old dispensation, the time of preparation for the kingdom. In terms of spiritual status, even the humbler members of the kingdom were superior to him.

7:47: The preceding parable suggests that she loved much because she had been forgiven much. Jesus now implies that her love is a sign rather than a cause of forgiveness, thus confirming the point of the parable.

8:19, *brethren*: See note on Mt 12:46.

8:39: There was no reason for secrecy (to avoid popular disturbance) in a non-Jewish area.

9:51: Here begins the "travel narrative" of Luke, which continues up to the Passion.
received up: i.e., into heaven; cf. 2 Kings 2:9–11; Acts 1:2, 11. The term here includes his passion, death, resurrection and ascension.

9:53: The Samaritans worshiped on Mount Gerizim, while orthodox Jews, of course, went to Jerusalem, and to Jerusalem only for sacrifice.

10:18: Jesus refers to the fall of the angels (cf. Rev 12:9), while he speaks of his conquest of the forces of evil.

14:26: Christ's disciples must be prepared to part from anyone who prevents them from serving him.

16:8: The master commended his foresight without approving what he actually did.

17:20: At that time, many people were expecting to see the kingdom inaugurated with striking manifestations; cf. 19:11.

19:41–44: These moving words spoken over the city are full of scriptural allusions. Moreover, the details given could apply as well to the siege of 587 BC as to that of AD 70. It is not safe, therefore, to argue from this passage that the fall of the city had already taken place when Luke wrote his Gospel.

20:37: As elsewhere (1 Cor 15:13–19), survival after death is linked with the resurrection of the body.

Explanatory Notes

21:24, *the times of the Gentiles*: i.e., those during which the Gentiles will take the place of the unbelieving people of Israel. Evidently, therefore, the end of the world does not coincide with the fall of Jerusalem. St Paul says that the Jews will be converted before the end (Rom 11:26).

22:52: Matthew and Mark describe the arrest first, before Christ's words. Luke and John both put his address to the soldiers and officials before the arrest, doubtless to stress his command over events.

23:2: They purposely produce political charges, as these alone would interest Pilate.

23:14: Luke, writing for Gentiles, makes it clear that Pilate wanted to release Jesus.

23:31: One does not burn green wood. The meaning is that, if an innocent man is thus punished, what must the guilty (dry wood) expect.

24:38: Luke stresses this episode for the benefit of his Greek readers, for whom the resurrection of the body was both impossible and absurd; cf. Acts 17:32.

Changes in the RSV for the Catholic Edition

	TEXT		FOOTNOTES	
	RSV	RSVCE	RSV	RSVCE
Lk 1:28	O favoured one	full of grace^{b2}		^{b2} Or *O favoured one*
Lk 8:19,20,21	brothers	brethren		
Lk 8:43		^{b}+ and had spent all her living upon physicians		^{b}Other ancient authorities omit *and had spent . . . physicians*
Lk 10:35			^{i}Delete existing note and substitute:	^{i}The denarius was a day's wage for a labourer
Lk 15:8			^{t}Delete existing note and substitute:	^{t}The dracma, rendered here by *silver coin*, was about a day's wage for a labourer
Lk 19:13			^{e}Delete existing note and substitute:	^{e}The mina, rendered here by *pound*, was about three months' wages for a labourer
Lk 22:19–20		^{j}+ which is given for you. Do this in remembrance of me." ^{20}And likewise the cup after supper, saying, "This cup which is poured out for you is the new covenant in my blood."		^{j}Some ancient authorities omit *which is given . . . blood*
Lk 24:5		^{u}+ He is not here, but has risen.		^{u}Other ancient authorities omit *He is . . . has risen*

⟶

228

	TEXT			FOOTNOTES	
	RSV	RSVCE	RSV		RSVCE
Lk 24:12		v+12 But Peter rose and ran to the tomb; stooping and looking in, he saw the linen cloths by themselves; and he went home wondering at what had happened.			vOther ancient authorities omit verse 12
Lk 24:36		x + and said to them, "Peace to you!"			xOther ancient authorities omit *and said ... to you*
Lk 24:40		y+40And when he had said this, he showed them his hands and feet.			yOther ancient authorities omit verse 40
Lk 24:51		a+ and was carried up into heaven.			aOther ancient authorities omit *and was ... heaven*
Lk 24:52		b + worshipped him, and			bOther ancient authorities omit *worshipped him, and*

Headings added to the Biblical Text

Prologue 1:1

1. THE INFANCY OF JOHN THE BAPTIST AND OF JESUS
The birth of John the Baptist foretold 1:5
The annunciation and incarnation of the Son of God 1:26
The Visitation 1:39
The Magnificat 1:46
Birth and circumcision of John the Baptist 1:57
Canticle of Zechariah 1:67
The birth of Jesus 2:1
The adoration of the shepherds 2:8
The circumcision of Jesus 2:21
The purification of Mary and the presentation of Jesus in the temple 2:22

Simeon's prophecy 2:25
Anna the prophetess 2:36
The childhood of Jesus 2:39
The finding in the temple 2:41
The hidden life of Jesus at Nazareth 2:51

2. PRELUDE TO THE PUBLIC MINISTRY OF JESUS
John the Baptist preaching in the wilderness 3:1
John the Baptist imprisoned 3:19
Jesus is baptized 3:21
The ancestry of Jesus 3:23
Jesus fasts and is tempted in the wilderness 4:1

Part One: Jesus' ministry in Galilee

3. THE START OF HIS MINISTRY IN GALILEE
Preaching in Nazareth 4:16
In the synagogue in Capernaum 4:31
Curing of Peter's mother-in-law 4:38
Other cures 4:40
Jesus preaches in other cities in Judea 4:42
The miraculous catch of fish and the calling of the first disciples 5:1
Curing of a leper 5:12
Curing of a paralyzed man 5:17
The calling of Matthew 5:27
A discussion on fasting 5:33
The law of the sabbath 6:1
Curing of man with a withered hand 6:6

4. JESUS' MIRACLES AND PREACHING IN GALILEE
Jesus chooses twelve apostles 6:12
Preaching on the plain 6:17
The Beatitudes and the Woes 6:20
Love of enemies 6:27
Integrity 6:39
The centurion's faith 7:1
The son of the widow of Nain restored to life 7:11
Messengers from John the Baptist 7:18

Jesus reproaches his contemporaries 7:31
Forgiveness for a sinful woman 7:36
The holy women 8:1
Parable of the sower. The meaning of parables 8:4
Parable of the lamp 8:16
The true kinsmen of Jesus 8:19
The calming of the storm 8:22
The Gerasene demoniac 8:26
Jairus' daughter is restored to life. Curing of a woman with a haemorrhage 8:40

5. JESUS TRAVELS WITH HIS APOSTLES
The mission of the apostles 9:1
Herod's opinion about Jesus 9:7
Return of the apostles. First miracle of the loaves and fish 9:10
Peter's profession of faith 9:18
First announcement of the Passion 9:21
The need for self-denial 9:23
The Transfiguration 9:28
Curing of an epileptic boy 9:37
Second announcement of the Passion 9:43
Humility and tolerance 9:46

Part Two: Jesus' ministry on the way to Jerusalem

6. THE JOURNEY BEGINS
Samaritans refuse to receive Jesus 9:51
Requirements for following Jesus 9:57
The mission of the seventy disciples 10:1
Jesus reproaches cities for their unbelief 10:13
The seventy return from their mission 10:17
Jesus gives thanks 10:21

7. FURTHER PREACHING
Parable of the good Samaritan 10:25
Martha and Mary welcome our Lord 10:38
The Our Father 11:1
Effective prayer 11:5
The Kingdom of God and the kingdom of Satan 11:14
Responding to the word of God 11:27
The sign of Jonah 11:29
The lamp of the body, the light of the soul 11:33
Jesus reproaches scribes and Pharisees 11:37

Headings added to the Biblical Text

Part Three: The Jerusalem ministry

Sources quoted in the Navarre Bible New Testament Commentary

1. DOCUMENTS OF THE CHURCH AND OF POPES

Benedict XII
Const. *Benedictus Deus*, 29 January 1336
Benedict XV
Enc. *Humani generis redemptionem*, 15 June 1917
Enc. *Spiritus Paraclitus*, 1 September 1920
Clement of Rome, St
Letter to the Corinthians
Constantinople, First Council of
Nicene-Constantinopolitan Creed
Constantinople, Third Council of
Definitio de duabus
  in Christo voluntatibus et operationibus
Florence, Council of
Decree *Pro Jacobitis*
Laetentur coeli
Decree *Pro Armeniis*
John Paul II
Addresses and homilies
Apos. Exhort. *Catechesi tradendae*, 16 October 1979
Apos. Exhort. *Familiaris consortio*, 22 November 1981
Apos. Exhort. *Reconciliatio et paenitentia*, 2 December 1984
Apos. Letter. *Salvifici doloris*, 11 February 1984
Bull, *Aperite portas*, 6 January 1983
Enc. *Redemptor hominis*, 4 March 1979
Enc. *Dives in misericordia*, 30 November 1980
Enc. *Dominum et Vivificantem*, 30 May 1986
Enc. *Laborem exercens*, 14 September 1981
Letter to all priests, 8 April 1979
Letter to all bishops, 24 February 1980
Gelasius I
Ne forte
Gregory the Great, St
Epistula ad Theodorum medicum contra Fabianum
Exposition on the Seven Penitential
Ne forte
In Evangelia homiliae
In Ezechielem homiliae
Moralia in Job

Regulae pastoralis liber
Innocent III
Letter *Eius exemplo*, 18 December 1208
John XXIII
Pacem in terris, 11 April 1963
Enc. *Ad Petri cathedram*, 29 June 1959
Lateran Council (649)
Canons
Leo the Great, St
Homilies and sermons
Licet per nostros
Promisisse memememi
Leo IX
Creed
Leo XIII
Enc. *Aeterni Patris*, 4 August 1879
Enc. *Immortale Dei*, 1 November 1885
Enc. *Libertas praestantissimum*, 20 June 1888
Enc. *Sapientiae christianae*, 18 January 1890
Enc. *Rerum novarum*, 15 May 1891
Enc. *Providentissimus Deus*, 18 November 1893
Enc. *Divinum illud munus*, 9 May 1897
Lateran, Fourth Council of (1215)
De fide catholica
Lyons, Second Council of (1274)
Doctrina de gratia
Profession of faith of Michael Palaeologue
Orange, Second Council of (529)
De gratia
Paul IV
Const. *Cum quorumdam*, 7 August 1555
Paul VI
Enc. *Ecclesiam suam*, 6 August 1964
Enc. *Mysterium fidei*, 9 September 1965
Apos. Exhort. *Marialis cultus*, 2 February 1967
Apos. Letter *Petrum et Paulum*, 27 February 1967
Enc. *Populorum progressio*, 26 March 1967
Enc. *Sacerdotalis coelibatus*, 24 June 1967
Creed of the People of God: Solemn Profession of Faith, 30 June 1968
Apos. Letter *Octagesima adveniens*, 14 June 1971

Sources quoted in the Commentary

Apos. Exhort. *Gaudete in Domino*, 9 May 1975
Apos. Exhort. *Evangelii nuntiandi*, 8 Dec. 1975
Homilies and addresses
Pius V, St
Catechism of the Council of Trent for Parish Priests or *Pius V Catechism*
Pius IX, Bl.
Bull *Ineffabilis Deus*, 8 December 1854
Syllabus of Errors
Pius X, St
Enc. *E supreme apostolatus*, 4 October 1903
Enc. *Ad Diem illum*, 2 February 1904
Enc. *Acerbo nimis*, 15 April 1905
Catechism of Christian Doctrine, 15 July 1905
Decree *Lamentabili*, 3 July 1907
Enc. *Haerent animo*, 4 August 1908
Pius XI
Enc. *Quas primas*, 11 December 1925
Enc. *Divini illius magistri*, 31 December 1929
Enc. *Mens nostra*, 20 December 1929
Enc. *Casti connubii*, 31 December 1930
Enc. *Quadragesimo anno*, 15 May 1931
Enc. *Ad catholici sacerdotii*, 20 December 1935
Pius XII
Enc. *Mystici Corporis*, 29 June 1943
Enc. *Mediator Dei*, 20 November 1947
Enc. *Divino afflante Spiritu*, 30 September 1943
Enc. *Humani generis*, 12 August 1950
Apost. Const. *Menti nostrae*, 23 September 1950
Enc. *Sacra virginitas*, 25 March 1954
Enc. *Ad caeli Reginam*, 11 October 1954
Homilies and addresses
Quierzy, Council of (833)
Doctrina de libero arbitrio hominis et de praedestinatione
Trent, Council of (1545–1563)
De sacris imaginibus

De Purgatorio
De reformatione
De sacramento ordinis
De libris sacris
De peccato originale
De SS. Eucharistia
De iustificatione
De SS. Missae sacrificio
De sacramento matrimonio
Doctrina de peccato originali
Doctrina de sacramento extremae unctionis
Doctrina de sacramento paenitentiae
Toledo, Ninth Council of (655)
De Redemptione
Toledo, Eleventh Council of (675)
De Trinitate Creed
Valence, Third Council of (855)
De praedestinatione
Vatican, First Council of the (1869–1870)
Dogm. Const. *Dei Filius*
Dogm. Const. *Pastor aeternus*
Vatican, Second Council of the (1963–1965)
Const. *Sacrosanctum Concilium*
Decree *Christus Dominus*
Decl. *Dignitatis humanae*
Decl. *Gravissimum educationis*
Decl. *Nostrae aetate*
Decree *Optatam totius*
Decree *Ad gentes*
Decree *Apostolicam actuositatem*
Decree *Perfectae caritatis*
Decree *Presbyterorum ordinis*
Decree *Unitatis redintegratio*
Dogm. Const. *Dei Verbum*
Dogm. Const. *Lumen gentium*
Past. Const. *Gaudium et spes*

Liturgical Texts

Roman Missal: Missale Romanum, editio typica altera (Vatican City, 1975)
The Divine Office (London, Sydney, Dublin, 1974)

Other Church Documents

Code of Canon Law
Codex Iuris Canonici (Vatican City, 1983)
Congregation for the Doctrine of the Faith
Declaration concerning Sexual Ethics, December 1975
Instruction on Infant Baptism, 20 October 1980
Inter insigniores, 15 October 1976
Letter on certain questions concerning Eschatology, 17 May 1979

Libertatis conscientia, 22 March 1986
Sacerdotium ministeriale, 6 August 1983
Libertatis nuntius, 6 August 1984
Mysterium Filii Dei, 21 February 1972
Pontifical Biblical Commission
Replies
New Vulgate
Nova Vulgata Bibliorum Sacrorum editio typica altera (Vatican City, 1986)

234

Sources quoted in the Commentary

2. THE FATHERS, ECCLESIASTICAL WRITERS AND OTHER AUTHORS

Alphonsus Mary Liguori, St
Christmas Novena
*The Love of Our Lord Jesus Christ reduced to
    practice*
Meditations for Advent
Thoughts on the Passion
Shorter Sermons
Sunday Sermons
Treasury of Teaching Material
Ambrose, St
De sacramentis
De mysteriis
De officiis ministrorum
Exameron
Expositio Evangelii secundum Lucam
Expositio in Ps 118
Treatise on the Mysteries
Anastasius of Sinai, St
Sermon on the Holy Synaxis
Anon.
Apostolic Constitutions
Didache, or *Teaching of the Twelve Apostles*
Letter to Diognetus
Shepherd of Hermas
Anselm, St
Prayers and Meditations
Aphraates
Demonstratio
Athanasius, St
Adversus Antigonum
De decretis nicaenae synodi
De Incarnatio contra arianos
Historia arianorum
Oratio I contra arianos
Oratio II contra arianos
Oratio contra gentes
Augustine, St
The City of God
Confessions
Contra Adimantum Manichaei discipulum
De Actis cum Felice Manicheo
De agone christiano
De bono matrimonii
De bono viduitatis
De catechizandis rudibus
De civitate Dei
De coniugiis adulterinis
De consensu Evangelistarum
De correptione et gratia
De doctrina christiana
De dono perseverantiae
De fide et operibus

De fide et symbolo
De Genesi ad litteram
De gratia et libero arbitrio
De natura et gratia
De praedestinatione sanctorum
De sermo Domini in monte
De spiritu et littera
De Trinitate
De verbis Domini sermones
Enarrationes in Psalmos
Enchiridion
Expositio epistulae ad Galatas
In I Epist. Ioann. ad Parthos
In Ioannis Evangelium tractatus
Letters
Quaestiones in Heptateuchum
Sermo ad Cassariensis Ecclesiae plebem
Sermo de Nativitate Domini
Sermons
Basil, St
De Spiritu Sancto
Homilia in Julittam martyrem
In Psalmos homiliae
Bede, St
Explanatio Apocalypsis
In Ioannis Evangelium expositio
In Lucae Evangelium expositio
In Marci Evangelium expositio
In primam Epistolam Petri
In primam Epistolam S. Ioanis
Sermo super Qui audientes gavisi sunt
Super Acta Apostolorum expositio
Super divi Iacobi Epistolam
Bernal, Salvador
Monsignor Josemaría Escrivá de Balaguer,
    Dublin, 1977
Bernard, St
Book of Consideration
De Beata Virgine
De fallacia et brevitate vitae
De laudibus novae militiae
Divine amoris
*Meditationes piissimae de cognitionis humanae
    conditionis*
Sermons on Psalm 90
Sermon on Song of Songs
Sermons
Bonaventure, St
In IV Libri sententiarum
Speculum Beatae Virgine
Borromeo, St Charles
Homilies

235

Sources quoted in the Commentary

Catherine of Siena, St
Dialogue
Cano, Melchor
De locis
Cassian, John
Collationes
De institutis coenobiorum
Clement of Alexandria
Catechesis III, De Baptismo
Commentary on Luke
Quis dives salvetur?
Stromata
Cyprian, St
De bono patientiae
De dominica oratione
De mortalitate
De opere et eleemosynis
De unitate Ecclesiae
De zelo et livore
Epist. ad Fortunatum
Quod idola dii non sint
Cyril of Alexandria, St
Commentarium in Lucam
Explanation of Hebrews
Homilia XXVIII in Mattheum
Cyril of Jerusalem, St
Catecheses
Mystagogical Catechesis
Diadochus of Photike
Chapters on Spiritual Perfection
Ephrem, St
Armenian Commentary on Acts
Commentarium in Epistolam ad Haebreos
Eusebius of Caesarea
Ecclesiastical History
Francis de Sales, St
Introduction to the Devout Life
Treatise on the Love of God
Francis of Assisi, St
Little Flowers
Reflections on Christ's Wounds
Fulgentius of Ruspe
Contra Fabianum libri decem
De fide ad Petrum
Gregory Nazianzen, St
Orationes theologicae
Sermons
Gregory of Nyssa, St
De instituto christiano
De perfecta christiana forma
On the Life of Moses
Oratio catechetica magna
Oratio I in beatitudinibus
Oratio I in Christi resurrectionem

Hippolytus, St
De consummatione saeculi
Ignatius of Antioch, St
Letter to Polycarp
Letters to various churches
Ignatius, Loyola, St
Spiritual Exercises
Irenaeus, St
Against Heresies
Proof of Apostolic Preaching
Jerome, St
Ad Nepotianum
Adversus Helvidium
Comm. in Ionam
Commentary on Galatians
Commentary on St Mark's Gospel
Contra Luciferianos
Dialogus contra pelagianos
Expositio in Evangelium secundum Lucam
Homilies to neophytes on Psalm 41
Letters
On Famous Men
John of Avila, St
Audi, filia
Lecciones sobre Gálatas
Sermons
John Chrysostom, St
Ante exilium homilia
Adversus Iudaeos
Baptismal Catechesis
De coemeterio et de cruce
De incomprehensibile Dei natura
De sacerdotio
De virginitate
Fifth homily on Anna
Hom. De Cruce et latrone
Homilies on St Matthew's Gospel, St John's
    Gospel, Acts of the Apostles, Romans,
    Ephesians, 1 and 2 Corinthians, Colossians,
    1 and 2 Timothy, 1 and 2 Thessalonians,
    Philippians, Philemon, Hebrews
II Hom. De proditione Iudae
Paraeneses ad Theodorum lapsum
Second homily in praise of St Paul
Sermon recorded by Metaphrastus
John of the Cross, St
A Prayer of the Soul enkindled by Love
Ascent of Mount Carmel
Dark Night of the Soul
Spiritual Canticle
John Damascene, St
De fide orthodoxa
John Mary Vianney, St
Sermons

Sources quoted in the Commentary

Josemaría Escrivá, St
Christ Is Passing By
Conversations
The Forge
Friends of God
Furrow
Holy Rosary
In Love with the Church
The Way
The Way of the Cross
Josephus, Flavius
Against Apion
Jewish Antiquities
The Jewish War
Justin Martyr, St
Dialogue with Tryphon
First and Second Apologies
à Kempis, Thomas
The Imitation of Christ
Luis de Granada, Fray
Book of Prayer and Meditation
Guide for Sinners
Introduccíon al símbolo de la fe
Life of Jesus Christ
Sermon on Public Sins
Suma de la vida cristiana
Luis de León, Fray
Exposición del Libro de Job
Minucius Felix
Octavius
Newman, J.H.
Biglietto Speech
Discourses to Mixed Congregations
Historical Sketches
Origen
Contra Celsum
Homilies on Genesis
Homilies on St John
In Exodum homiliae
Homiliae in Iesu nave
In Leviticum homiliae
In Matth. comm.
In Rom. comm.
Philo of Alexandria
De sacrificio Abel
Photius
Ad Amphilochium
Polycarp, St
Letter to the Philippians
del Portillo, A.
On Priesthood, Chicago, 1974
Primasius
Commentariorum super Apocalypsim B. Ioannis libri quinque
Prosper of Aquitaine, St
De vita contemplativa

Pseudo-Dionysius
De divinis nominibus
Pseudo-Macarius
Homilies
Severian of Gabala
Commentary on 1 Thessalonians
Teresa of Avila, St
Book of Foundations
Exclamations of the Soul to God
Interior Castle
Life
Poems
Way of Perfection
Tertullian
Against Marcion
Apologeticum
De baptismo
De oratione
Theodore the Studite, St
Oratio in adorationis crucis
Theodoret of Cyrrhus
Interpretatio Ep. ad Haebreos
Theophylact
Enarratio in Evangelium Marci
Thérèse de Lisieux, St
The Autobiography of a Saint
Thomas Aquinas, St
Adoro te devote
Commentary on St John = Super Evangelium S. Ioannis lectura
Commentaries on St Matthew's Gospel, Romans, 1 and 2 Corinthians, Galatians, Ephesians, Colossians, Philippians, 1 and 2 Timothy, 1 and 2 Thessalonians, Titus, Hebrews
De veritate
Expositio quorumdam propositionum ex Epistola ad Romanos
On the Lord's Prayer
On the two commandments of Love and the ten commandments of the Law
Summa contra gentiles
Summa theologiae
Super Symbolum Apostolorum
Thomas More, St
De tristitia Christi
Victorinus of Pettau
Commentary on the Apocalypse
Vincent Ferrer, St
Treatise on the Spiritual Life
Vincent of Lerins, St
Commonitorium
Zosimus, St
Epist. Enc. "Tractoria" ad Ecclesias Orientales

237